DECONSTRUCTING AND RECONSTRUCTING THE COLD WAR

Deconstructing and Reconstructing the Cold War

Editor
ALAN P. DOBSON

Assistant Editors
SHAHIN P. MALIK
GRAHAM EVANS

University of Wales, Swansea

Routledge
Taylor & Francis Group
LONDON AND NEW YORK

First published 1999 by Ashgate Publishing

Reissued 2018 by Routledge
2 Park Square, Milton Park, Abingdon, Oxon, OX14 4RN
711 Third Avenue, New York, NY I 0017, USA

Routledge is an imprint of the Taylor & Francis Group, an informa business

A Library of Congress record exists under LC control number: 98044664

ISBN 13: 978-1-138-61421-5 (hbk)
ISBN 13: 978-1-138-61423-9 (pbk)
ISBN 13: 978-0-429-46381-5 (ebk)

Contents

List of Contributors *vii*
Preface *x*

Introduction
Alan P. Dobson and Graham Evans 1

SECTION 1: THEORY 23

1 Reconstructing the Cold War: The Evolution of a Consuming Paradigm
Alastair Murray 25

2 Explaining the Cold War
Charles Reynolds 44

SECTION 2: STRETCHING OUT THE PARADIGMS 67

3 Anglo-American Relations and the Cold War
Alan P. Dobson 69

4 The Limits of US Cold War Hegemony: Lessons from the Anglo-Iranian Oil Crisis
Steve Marsh 89

5 Explaining Outside Interests in the Persian Gulf
Shahin P. Malik 110

6 The Great Simplifier: The Cold War and South Africa, 1948-1994
Graham Evans 136

7 The United States and India: The Challenge of Neutralism to Bipolarity
Jacqueline Dix 152

SECTION 3: BEYOND THE PARADIGMS 179

8 The Cross and the Bear: The Vatican's Cold War Diplomacy in East Central Europe
David Ryall 181

9 Learning from the Cold War Nuclear Confrontation
Paul Rogers 202

10 Soviet and Russian Perspectives on the Cold War
Robert Bideleux 226

CONCLUSION 251

11 The Cold War in the Context of World History
Clive Ponting 253

Bibliography 270

Index 288

Contributors

Robert Bideleux is a senior lecturer in the Department of Political Theory and Government, and Director of the Centre of Russian and East European Studies, University of Wales Swansea. His publications include *Communism and Development* (1985) and *A History of Eastern Europe* (1998, with Ian Jeffries). He is currently working on the oil economy, crisis and change in Eastern Europe and on civil society democracy and the state.

Jacqueline Dix is a PhD student and tutorial assistant in the Department of Political Theory and Government, University of Wales Swansea. She has presented papers at several national conferences, including the BISA International History Group Conference at the University of Exeter in 1996. In 1997 she carried out an extensive research programme in the USA, funded by the Harry S. Truman Institute, on US Cold War foreign policy and neutralism with special reference to India.

Alan P. Dobson is a Reader in the Department of Political Theory and Government, University of Wales Swansea. He has written extensively on Anglo-American relations and the international airline system. His most recent books are: *Flying in the Face of Competition* (1995); and *Anglo-American Relations in the Twentieth Century* (1995). He was a senior research fellow at the Norwegian Nobel Institute in 1997 and he is a Fellow of the Royal Historical Society and a member of the Royal Aeronautical Society. He is presently working on *US Economic Statecraft: Aspects of Economic Warfare and Strategic Embargo Policies 1933-90* (Routledge, forthcoming 2000), and a short history of postwar US foreign policy.

Graham Evans is a senior lecturer in the Department of Political Theory and Government, University of Wales Swansea. He is author of *The Dictionary of World Politics* (with J.D. Newnham) and *The Penguin Dictionary of International Relations* (1998). He has published widely in scholarly journals and is a member of the Southern Africa Study Group at the Royal Institute for International Affairs and the UK Association of Electoral Administrators.

Shahin P. Malik is a Lecturer in International Relations at the University of Wales Swansea. He is also completing a Doctoral Thesis at the University of Birmingham and has research interests in Foreign Policy Analysis and International Security. His publications include *Peacekeeping and the United Nations* (Dartmouth, 1996); a chapter in Dorman, A. & Otte, T. (eds), *Military intervention: from gunboat diplomacy to humanitarian intervention,* (Dartmouth, 1995); and an article in *Strategic Studies*, (Institute of Strategic Studies, Islamabad, vol.xvi, no.4, September 1994). He is also the editor of *Multilateralism and its Relevancy in Post-Cold War Crises*, (Ashgate, forthcoming 1999).

Steve Marsh is a Jean Monnet Lecturer at the University of Wales, Cardiff. He worked previously at the University of Wales Swansea and has research interests in postwar Anglo-American relations and the European Union. He is currently engaged in preparing an analysis of the Special Relationship in the context of the Anglo-Iranian oil crisis and is also co-author of US *Foreign Policy Since 1945*, commissioned by Routledge and forthcoming 1999.

Alastair Murray is a Lecturer in International Theory at the Department of Political Theory and Government, University of Wales Swansea. His most recent work is a study of realist thought entitled: *Reconstructing Realism - Between Power Politics and Cosmopolitan Ethics*, published by Keele University Press, (1997).

Clive Ponting is Senior Lecturer in the Department of Political Theory and Government, University of Wales Swansea. His main interests are environmental politics and world history. His most recent publications are: *A Green History of the World* (1991); *Churchill* (1994); *Armageddon: the Second World War* (1995); and *Progress and Barbarism: the World in the Twentieth Century* (1998).

Charles Reynolds is a Senior Lecturer in the Department of Politics, University of Durham. He has written several books on theory and explanation in international relations and his most recent work is: *The World of States: An Introduction to Explanation and Theory* (1992).

Paul Rogers holds a personal chair at the Department of Peace Studies at the University of Bradford. He has published widely in the field and some of his more recent works include: Rogers, P. and Dando, M., *A Violent Peace: Global Security after the Cold War*, Brassey's. London, 1992; 'Reviewing Britain's Security, *International Affairs*, 1997.

Dr David Ryall teaches International Relations in the Department of Political Theory and Government at the University of Wales Swansea, and formerly taught in the School of European Studies at Cardiff University. Educated at University College Dublin and University of Wales Swansea, he has published articles in *Studdii Europene*; *Third World Quarterly*; and *International Relations*; and he has contributed chapters to C. Popeti (ed.) *Paradigma Europeana*; and S. Malik (ed.), *Multilateralism and its Relevancy to Post-Cold War Crises* (forthcoming 1999).

Preface

Much of the thought, reading and planning for *Deconstructing and Reconstructing the Cold War* took place at the Norwegian Nobel Institute where I was a senior research fellow in the early part of 1997. The opportunity to carry this and other projects forward was invaluable and I am deeply grateful to the Institute for the research time that it gave me. I also need to thank Shahin Malik and Graham Evans for assisting with the editing of the book and Fiona Wells for her painstaking proof reading. The contributors are all colleagues or postgraduates from the Swansea Department, with the notable exceptions of Charles Reynolds from the University of Durham and Paul Rogers from the University of Bradford. They have all been helpful throughout and constructively responsive to drafts of the introduction. The introduction was written by me with help from Graham Evans who authored the section on international relations studies and the Cold War. He and I therefore take responsibility for our respective parts of the introduction and absolve all other contributors of responsibility for any errors or quirks of interpretation to be found there.

Alan P. Dobson
Swansea, July 1998

Introduction

ALAN P. DOBSON and GRAHAM EVANS

From Stettin in the Baltic to Trieste in the Adriatic, an iron curtain has descended across the continent ... , far from the Russian frontiers and throughout the world, Communist fifth columns are established and work in complete unity and absolute obedience to the directions they receive from the Communist centre.

Winston Churchill, 5 March 1946

Hitler began his work of unleashing war ... declaring that only German-speaking people constituted a superior nation. Mr. Churchill sets out to unleash war with a race theory, asserting that only the English-speaking nations are superior nations, who are called upon to decide the destinies of the entire world.

Joseph Stalin, 13 March 1946

The seeds of totalitarian regimes are nurtured by misery and want. They spread and grow in the evil soil of poverty and strife. They reach their full growth when the hope of people for a better life has died. We must keep that hope alive. The free peoples of the world look to us for support in maintaining their freedoms. If we falter in our leadership, we may endanger the peace of the world - and we shall surely endanger the welfare of our own nation.

Harry S. Truman, 12 March 1947

this [the Marshall] Plan is an attempt to split Europe into two camps ..., to complete the formation of a bloc of several European countries hostile to the interests of the democratic countries of Eastern Europe and most particularly to the interests of the Soviet Union.

Andrei Vyshinsky, 18 September 1947

For the young such words do not resonate in the way that they did in the past. To those who lived through much, if not all, of the Cold War, it is something of a shock to encounter students who have no direct recollection of it and it is difficult to advise them on how to negotiate a way through the vast array of often contentious Cold War literature. It is now nearly ten years since the Cold War ended, but debate goes on about its origins, character, the impact it had on the international system, its place in world history, and the nature and causes of its demise. The scholarly positions adopted, be they orthodox or revisionist, realist or idealist, neo-realist or neo-liberal, are often so polarised that it sometimes appears more important to score points than explain events. As approaches and theories have proliferated and complicated the scholarly terrain, they have also each tended to oversimplify in order to structure a vast array of historical evidence, or to retain consistency within particular assumptions, or to limit the number of variables for the sake of producing parsimonious theories to explain, predict and help policy-makers control the international environment. In this book Murray and Reynolds specifically address these issues; Dobson, Marsh, Malik, Evans and Dix celebrate an eclecticism that, at the very least, stretches out conventional wisdoms and paradigms; Ryall, Rogers and Bideleux go beyond the paradigms; and in the conclusion Ponting addresses the wider context.

These essays are not deconstructive in the postmodern sense. None of the authors have that depth of scepticism about knowledge claims, but they are all concerned that the schools of both historiographical thought and international relations (IR) theory have tended to: oversimplify by inappropriately bounding the terms of reference of Cold War enquiry; over concentrate on superpower relations and leadership; inappropriately over emphasise some variables at the cost of others; establish unwarranted claims about stability; and occidentalise world history. There is then, amidst diversity, some common ground upon which the authors stand, but that common ground does not provide easy answers to Cold War questions. On the contrary, the essays in this collection show that there is no magical key to understanding and that there are no simple explanations. The chapters (in reverse order of sequence in the book), historically contextualise the Cold War, challenge some of the parameters of Cold War studies and question axiomatically received wisdoms such as stability and the time frame, provide new perspectives on misconstrued relationships that fall within (or at least partially within) the conventional paradigms, and offer theoretical analyses which create a more nuanced understanding of the problems of explaining the Cold War. That understanding avoids the pitfalls of oversimplification which both led the superpowers to make serious errors of judgement while the Cold War was ongoing and caused puzzlement when it suddenly ended.

The rest of this introduction falls into four sections. The first two respectively give overviews of the origins and the broad contours of the development of the Cold War for that generation of students who have little or no knowledge of it. The third gives guidance on the historiography of the Cold War and on the way it was conceived of by IR studies. The last says something about the main aims and themes of the chapters that follow.

Providing overviews seems to embrace the kind of weakness that this book attempts to remedy. By their very nature overviews must be great simplifiers. But what follows in the next two sections is not explanation, it is a chronology and an identification of events that require explanation. Obviously selection of events, outlines of contending economic and political doctrines, and dispositional characterisation of statesmen and policy-makers are all informed by contestible assumptions about international relations and appropriate levels of analysis (system, unit, and individual actor), domestic politics, and human agency. However, the overviews provide some context for the specialised essays that follow and give a flexible frame of reference for those unfamiliar with the Cold War. There is no intention to prescribe an ontology or specify a methodology. The overviews do not try to solve the problem of how agency, structure and process interacted to produce the events of the Cold War, they simply try to map out the field to provide the broad focus that anyone would need in order to embark upon Cold War studies. At the margin, the boundary lines will always remain vague: some of the chapters try to demonstrate just how contestible and moveable they are and therefore that the ontology of the Cold War is not and cannot be exactly defined.

The Origins and the Onset of the Cold War 1945-49[1]

Where and when the Cold War started is just as hotly disputed as how and why it ended. For some, including Bideleux in chapter ten, the Bolshevik Revolution is the starting point, others follow the nineteenth century view of Alexis de Tocqueville that the USA and Russia would inevitably become the two great contenders for world hegemony because of their size, resources and power. Whatever view one takes, it is clear that competition between the two powers was partially suspended from 1941 until 1945 because of the common enterprise of defeating the Axis Powers. From 1945 onwards there was a renewal of tensions which developed into what is commonly referred to in the West as the Cold War. In order to grasp its nature, it is helpful to think of its origins in terms of history, economics, ideology, and geopolitics.

American-Soviet relations before 1945 were mixed, but, on the whole, tended to antagonism. The USA intervened with other capitalist powers on the side of the White Russians in the Civil War and refused to recognise the Soviet Union until 1933. After recognition, relations improved only to deteriorate badly because of Stalin's purges, his show trials, the Nazi-Soviet Pact of 1939 and the partitioning of parts of Europe that followed in its wake. From 1941, when Hitler turned on his erstwhile ally Stalin, until 1945, there was a US-Soviet alliance of convenience against Nazi Germany. Americans acknowledged the huge cost that the Soviets paid in defeating Germany and the Soviets were grateful for Lend-Lease supplies. Nevertheless, relations were still punctuated with disputes and suspicions. The Soviets feared that the British and Americans might make a separate peace with Hitler that would allow him to continue the war on the eastern front (a sort of Nazi-Soviet Pact in reverse). When that did not happen they suspected that the West deliberately delayed invading Europe so that the Red Army would bear the brunt of the fighting against the *Wehrmacht*. For their part the Americans were suspicious about the Katyn massacre of much of the Polish officer class (which was indeed perpetrated by the Soviets) and about the pause of the Red Army on the outskirts of Warsaw while the pro-Western Polish Home Army was slaughtered by the Germans. There were also mutual suspicions about postwar intentions.

Three clusters of economic facts were of great significance: the devastation of the USSR and Soviet hopes for Western help; the colossus of the US economy and American ambitions to father a new economic world order; and European recovery and the role of Germany. Soviet hopes for aid were dashed when the USA abruptly stopped Lend-Lease after victory in Europe. This was a legal requirement, but the Soviets saw it as an unfriendly act and as a preliminary to demands from the USA for political concessions in return for economic help: a tactic that the USA did indeed pursue. For its part the USA emerged as the world's dominant economy with about 50 percent of total world manufacturing capacity. How to sustain that was of deep concern to US planners. They wanted to make the face of international capitalism acceptable and its performance more stable and accountable through US management exercised by the International Monetary Fund and the General Agreement on Tariffs and Trade. Unfortunately this economic vision was not compatible with the command economy of the Soviets and their desperate need for reconstruction, and by 1946 Stalin had rejected participation in the US grand capitalist design and disputes soon arose about reparations and aid. Thirdly, Europe needed economic reconstruction and greater self-sufficiency, otherwise the USA would have to pour in endless resources to feed, house and clothe people. As Germany was still the potential economic powerhouse of Europe, logic dictated that its economy had to be revived. As most of it was in Western hands, its revival would unavoidably antagonise and threaten the Soviets, but for the USA the alternative was an unacceptable financial drain and possibly a re-run of the interwar tragedy if economic distress delivered Europe once again into the hands of extremists.

The ideological divide between US liberal capitalism and Soviet communism soon began to have more effect on affairs after the war's end. The incompatibilities of their two ideologies, derived from different economic systems and clashing views on individual and collective rights, regained prominence once the overriding priority of defeating Hitler had been achieved and the wartime agreements made at the Yalta and Potsdam conferences began to unravel. Parts of this ideological war and its domestic and international implications are explored by Ryall and Bideleux in chapters eight and ten. Ideological differences surfaced not only over economic issues but also over Poland and the treatment of the rest of Soviet liberated Eastern Europe. Controversy arose about democracy and freedom. The West found it difficult to accept Soviet sway over Poland when France and Britain had, at least nominally, gone to war to safeguard it from Nazi totalitarianism. The Soviets, however, stipulated that the Polish Government had to be "friendly". This was understandable given that the USSR had been invaded three times in thirty years via Poland and had lost over 20 million people in the most recent attack. But this security demand involved Soviet style democracy for Poland which was hard for the West to accept.

Geopolitical concerns were not the monopoly of Stalin, they also troubled President Roosevelt for much of the war. He believed that it was imperative to co-opt the Soviets into postwar security arrangements. Those arrangements were an artful mixture of idealistic collective security and realist power politics. The UN looked like a collective security organisation where all would be responsible for each other's security, but effective policing depended upon great power unanimity and enforcement. Derived from this realist view of power was the provision of the right of veto for the five permanent members of the Security Council. In addition both Roosevelt and Truman expected that each great power would take primary responsibility within its own area. In the USA, internationalism might have triumphed over isolationism, but there was little desire to remain politically and militarily in the heart of Europe.

The great problem with all this was how to maintain great power solidarity. Immediately after the war, with France temporarily out of the power equation, China in the throes of civil war, and Britain weakened by her efforts against the Axis, the key factors were Soviet and US actual and German potential power. Once the Soviets and the Americans began to fear each other's intentions then neither side could allow Germany to move fully into the other's camp. The potential power shift would have been profoundly destabilising. This was the main reason why the German problem was so difficult to resolve, why it was such a sensitive issue, and why partition became semi-permanent. However, mutual suspicion and fear spread wider than Germany. The Soviets had no atom bomb and that caused insecurity. They also feared US economic prowess and the spread of capitalism. Most of all, they wanted security and felt that the West was set to deny them that by interfering in Eastern Europe and by denying them any say in the occupation of Japan. The USA for its part had learnt the lesson that isolationism was unviable. As economic and political unrest spread through Western Europe, and as the rhetoric of the Soviets became harsh and they made bids for strategic and economic gains in Turkey and Iran which the West saw as provocative and illegitimate, American worries were exacerbated. Most of all, they feared a Kremlin inspired wave of internal commotion in Western Europe that would make it succumb to communism.

By 1946 US-Soviet relations were fraught with problems and dangers. The UN, with its Security Council governed by the veto power and riven between France, Britain, China and the USA on one side and the Soviets on the other, could not act decisively. The USA would have to look after its own affairs. The US *chargé d'affaires* in Moscow, George Kennan, wrote his famous long telegram in February warning of the need to respond to Soviet pressure for expansion with economic and political counterpressures at shifting points along a containment line. That same month, Churchill warned in apocalyptic terms of the threat of a new dark age if Anglo-American solidarity were not upheld in order to defend the West. A year later the USA felt that economic and social unrest in Europe could become critical. In March the president announced the Truman Doctrine specifically providing aid for Greece and Turkey, but also pledging help to all those challenged by internal subversion or outside threat. A few months later the more ambitious Marshall Plan to help European reconstruction was set in motion. With it came the final economic division of Europe and, most important of all, of East from West Germany with the introduction of the Deutschmark. This was highly provocative to the Soviets with the danger of capitalist infection spreading via the Deutschmark into Eastern Europe. They responded with the Berlin Blockade, June 1948 to May 1949, and a clamp down in Eastern Europe which removed, most notably in Prague, the last vestiges of pro-Western elements from government. In 1949, after considerable pressure from the West Europeans, the USA agreed to a peacetime security commitment to Europe: towards the end of the year NATO was signed. The Soviets responded with the Warsaw Pact. The perceived threat and response syndrome was established, a pattern was set and lines were drawn in Europe. But containment held an ambiguity within: was its purpose to contain Soviet power or communism in general? Was its rationale primarily power-political or ideological? Containment evolved not just in Europe but globally over the following forty years and carried with it this underlying ambiguity which helped to spread US commitments.

Who was responsible for this renewal of US-Soviet tensions? What motives governed their actions and which of them impacted most forcefully to propel the two sides forward into the Cold War? The Soviets had taken actions, seemingly out of security concerns, which had offended the West: the absorption of Estonia, Latvia, and Lithuania into the Soviet Union, the imposition of client governments in Poland, East Germany, Bulgaria and Romania, the exertion of pressure on Iran for oil concessions and for the creation of a puppet state in Iranian Azerbaijan, and demands on Turkey for access to the Mediterranean. They had also responded negatively to a number of Western initiatives. Most significantly they rejected the Baruch Plan to control nuclear weapons, which they saw as a means of perpetuating a US monopoly. In contrast to these actions, the Soviets had initially allowed relatively free elections in Czechoslovakia and Hungary, co-operated both in founding the UN and in setting the future of Austria and Finland, and limited help to communists in other countries. This kind of balance of account, one that could be repeated for the Western side, has made explaining responsibility for the Cold War difficult.

The Unfolding of the Cold War 1949-89

By 1949 the containment line in Europe was well established. Yugoslavia had asserted its independence from Moscow in 1948 and hovered between the two camps, but was not a destabilising factor in Cold War relations. Only Berlin remained as a flash point and a source of vulnerability to the West, but interestingly the Soviets did not exploit that when West Germany was integrated into NATO and re-armed in the mid 1950s. It was largely in the nuclear arms race and in relations outside Europe that there were uneasy and destabilising developments after 1949.

The explosion of the Soviet atom bomb, the fall of China in 1949 and the onset of the Korean War in 1950 changed the character of the Cold War. The US response to the events of 1949 was a strategic review, NSC-68, which proposed to change Kennan's original idea from primarily economic and political, as in the Marshall Plan, to globalised military containment in the expectation that there could be a war with the communists some time in the following five years. At first the costs looked prohibitive, but the Korean War made the expense politically justifiable, while McCarthy-inspired anti-communist hysteria helped to sustain the momentum for strong Cold War policies. John L. Gaddis has described this strategy as symmetrical: the West would respond in kind to anything that the Communists might do. By 1953/54, with the end of the Korean War and the communists held successfully on the 38th parallel, the USA downgraded the likelihood of a major war and instead looked to a long-haul confrontation with communism with containment as the panacea for Western problems everywhere, even though it had produced serious difficulties and questions about relations within the alliance and about

Indian neutralism. Some of those problems are explored by Dobson, Marsh and Dix in chapters three, four and seven respectively.

Despite some problems with containment, its overall success helped accelerate an already changing US perspective on Asia, which had now become vital for the West. There was no longer to be any differentiation between core and peripheral strategic areas: all were core. Policy on Japan changed to allow its rapid economic development and with that came a concern to protect its Asian markets and sources of supply. As a result American involvement in Vietnam, begun in 1949, was expanded during the Korean War. Finally Korea also changed US policy toward the Nationalist Chinese on Taiwan from one of disengagement to full economic, political and defence support. This policy created dangers and difficulties throughout and beyond the Cold War.

The Eisenhower Administration and the successive regimes of Malenkov and Krushchev were confronted with this new militarised and globalised zero-sum Cold War game that spread from Europe to Asia and then to the Middle East, the Western Hemisphere and finally to Africa. Both sides adopted somewhat different policies from their predecessors. The Soviets embarked upon new policies after the death of Stalin in March 1953 and began a trade offensive that was to take them deep into the affairs of Third World states. They also rapidly developed their nuclear capability and delivery systems and achieved a major triumph in 1957 with the launch of Sputnik. Krushchev talked of peaceful co-existence, but, despite Sputnik, there developed a serious nuclear capability gap between the USSR and the USA by the early 1960s which tempted him into adventurism and the placing of nuclear missiles on Cuba. Nuclear relations between 1949 and 1962 contributed to, rather than diminished, volatility in superpower relations, but, ironically, the Cuban Missile Crisis ushered in an era of at least apparent stability. This was helped by the emergence of serious differences between the Soviets and communist Chinese.

Eisenhower and Secretary of State Dulles were concerned that containment implicitly handed the initiative to the Soviets and their allies. They decided on a New Look that would seize the initiative back for the West and reduce defence costs. Eisenhower believed that the great danger for the West would be to undermine its strongest attribute - the ability of a free market economy to satisfy the needs of a mass population - by defence spending itself into bankruptcy. The New Look involved greater reliance on nuclear weapons and a reduction of expensive US conventional capabilities, the threat of using an asymmetrical strategy of massive retaliation if the communists broke through the containment line, an expansion of conventional capabilities by allies, more psychological economic and covert warfare, and an elaborate system of Western alliances.

The shortcomings of the New Look were exposed by the fragility of some of the alliances, by the failure of allies to meet conventional force targets, and by the West's inability to resort to massive retaliation in response to the Soviet invasion of Hungary in 1956. In 1961 the Kennedy Administration reverted to a symmetrical strategy which they called 'flexible response'. US actions would be carefully calibrated to match any communist challenge. Defence expenditure was increased, nuclear capabilities were diversified, and conventional and unconventional forces were expanded. By 1962 the USA had a massive military lead over the Soviets in nuclear, naval and air power. Those facts troubled Krushchev and led to the climax of Cold War superpower confrontation.

Between 1958 and 1962 the Cold War heated up. There had been a mild thawing of relations with the Geneva Summit in 1955 - the first since the end of the war. However, the Soviet invasion of Hungary and the Anglo-French invasion of Egypt during the Suez Crisis of 1956, the launching of Sputnik, the renewal of tensions over Berlin, and the spread of wars of national liberation in the Third World with Krushchev's blessing and support had caused renewed tensions. One of the most provocative of developments for the USA had been the success of the Castro regime on Cuba and it was here that Krushchev made his move both to support Third World communism (by trying to deter the USA from a second invasion attempt of Cuba after the abortive Bay of Pigs fiasco in 1961) and to narrow the margin of US nuclear superiority by placing nuclear missiles on the island. The resolution of the crisis produced a new pattern of superpower relationships that sought stability. However, the extent to which they were able to manage that stability is revealed by Rogers in chapter nine.

The Cuban Missile Crisis was a turning point in the Cold War in two important senses. The first was that the Soviets realised that their conventional as well as their nuclear military inferiority had led them to humiliation in the Cuban Missile Crisis. The Soviets resolved that this should never happen again and thus continued to plough ever more resources into their defence programme - a policy that contributed to the sclerosis in the Soviet economy in the 1980s and thus to the eventual end of the Cold War (Bideleux, chapter ten). The second was that both superpowers realised that neither direct relationships between them, such as in Berlin, nor third party issues such as Cuba, or later Vietnam, should be allowed to draw them into a potentially conflictual situation. The USA and the USSR developed better communications, tensions over Berlin subsided once the Wall helped to stabilise things, and the two superpowers and Britain moved ahead to the 1963 Nuclear Partial Test Ban Treaty. Bilateral and multilateral East-West talks developed through various stages, assisted by Chancellor Willy Brandt's Ostpolitik and later by *détente* promoted by the USA, to SALT 1 and 2, the longstanding Conference on Security and Co-operation in Europe and the Helsinki Accords of 1975. There were still dangers, particularly during the 1973 Yom Kippur War when the USA supported Israel and it looked as if the Soviets might intervene to prevent the defeat of Egypt, and in the early 1980s when Reagan raised the temperature of the Cold War, but after 1962 the aim of the USA and the USSR was to establish a stable deterrent nuclear relationship based on mutual assured destruction in the event of a nuclear exchange. The main focus of East-West conflict, already shifting to the Third World in the 1950s, now became fixed there, but wars by proxy between client groups or states did not normally affect the stability of superpower relations: *détente* and the height of the Vietnam War, for example, coincided. The nature of these conflicts varied immensely. There were not just wars by proxy, but a jostling for position throughout the Third World which put a Cold War gloss on affairs that disguised the real nature of regional problems and relationships. Just how distorting Cold War assumptions could be in these regions is amply explained by Malik in chapter five and Evans in chapter six.

The later stages of the Cold War can be divided into four clear phases: divisions within the Western and Eastern camps; *détente*; the second Cold War; and the end game. From 1962 to 1969 moves towards a more stable superpower nuclear relationship were accompanied by the escalation of the war in Vietnam, growing divergences within both the Western and the Communist camps and increasing East-West tension in the Third World. In the West de Gaulle took France out of the military structure of NATO, the development of the EEC created friction over trade with the USA, and more independent European policies generally came to the fore. The most significant of these in the late 1960s was Brandt's Ostpolitik which sought to stabilise postwar boundaries and improve relations between East and West Germany. In the communist bloc the rift between China and the Soviets broke out into the open and in Europe Czechoslovakia led the way for a more independent and liberal mode of development until the invasion by Warsaw Pact troops in 1968. The pronouncement of the Brezhnev Doctrine, asserting the Soviet right to intervene in the affairs of fellow socialist regimes, was a formal reassertion of the Kremlin's hegemony over the socialist world and it deeply worried not only the more liberal inclined East European states, but the Chinese as well.

The second phase of development was the rise and collapse of *détente* from 1969-79. Despite the hot war between East and West in Vietnam, which was not resolved until 1973-75, *détente* between the USA and the Soviets and the opening of relations with the People's Republic of China moved ahead apace. *Détente* opened up East-West trade and moderated the arms race. It seemed beneficial for both the USA and the USSR, which were feeling the strain of their respective hegemonic roles, and opening relations with China created a better balance of power for the USA and China in their relations with the Soviets. But *détente* was part and parcel of Nixon and Kissinger's linkage policy: connecting concessions and gains in different policy areas in order to further US and Western interests. In short, it was a tactic to wage the Cold War in changed circumstances. Nixon explained on Guam in July 1969, that the USA could not shoulder all the responsibility for Western defence and continue as it had done in the past. *Détente* was part of this new strategy and was to be assessed accordingly. When it did not prevent a serious crisis in Soviet-US relations in the 1973 Yom Kippur War and did not change the nature of the Soviet regime, questions about its efficacy began to arise. Problems over Jewish immigrants and dissidents in the Soviet Union, fears that the Soviets had gone beyond nuclear parity, communist advances in the Third World and, most importantly, instability in the Middle East in 1979 with the fall of Iran to Islamic fundamentalists and the Soviet invasion of Afghanistan, all undermined *détente*. Americans felt that they had lost direction and that the Soviets had used *détente* to steal a lead on the West.

The third phase - the Second Cold War, 1979-85 - thus began. In 1979 President Carter expanded the US defence programme and imposed sanctions on the Soviets in moral condemnation of their invasion of Afghanistan. These were strong actions but the USA remained demoralised and uncertain of itself until President Reagan entered the White House in 1981. Things then changed. There was a resurgence of self-confidence and purpose and Reagan delivered the most intense anti-communist rhetoric since McCarthyism. Meanwhile the Soviet Union was troubled by instability as elderly and infirm leaders succeeded one another. They were incapable of dealing with the challenge of what was now a massive US rearmament programme, or with the sclerosis of the Soviet economy, or with problems in their East European empire. Aspects of these last two issues are considered in chapters eight and ten by Ryall and Bideleux.

The year 1983 exemplified the new sense of crisis and the adversarial style of foreign policy championed by Reagan in his first term. In March there was the announcement of the Strategic Defense Initiative (SDI) or Star Wars programme and Reagan's condemnation of the USSR as an "evil empire". In late 1983 the Soviets shot down a civilian Korean jumbo jet, Lek Walensa the Polish trade union reform leader won the Nobel Peace prize, and there was a Middle East alert after a car bomb outrage in Beirut killed 241 US marines. In October the US invaded Grenada to remove a pro-Moscow regime and in November NATO's Able Archer exercise was initially mistaken by the

Soviets for the real thing. The US deployed Cruise and Pershing 2 missiles in Europe to counter previous Soviet deployments and the Soviets quit intermediate and long-range missile talks in protest. Relations were getting worse. They peaked symbolically in 1985 with the Reagan Doctrine calling for assistance for groups fighting regimes aligned with the Soviets, but then things changed rapidly as Reagan perceived a window of opportunity that he could exploit with the young new Soviet leader Mikhail Gorbachev.

Between 1985 and 1991 a combination of US-Soviet talks and an uncontrollable tide of events in the USSR and Eastern Europe drove the Cold War to its death. This was the end game. It began with Gorbachev coming to power and realising that the deep-seated economic and social problems of his country could not be dealt with by traditional means. He introduced *glasnost* (openness) and *perestroika* (restructuring). Those changes in turn convinced Reagan that there were opportunities for fruitful talks with the Soviets, particularly about nuclear armaments - a subject on which Rogers has much to say in chapter nine. The time for brandishing nuclear weapons and lurid condemnation of the Soviets was over. Reagan believed he could win the Cold War by negotiation from a position of strategic strength.

At Reykjavik in October 1986 Reagan scared the hell out of both his hardline realist advisers and his close friend British Prime Minister Margaret Thatcher when he agreed in principle with Gorbachev to eliminate all nuclear weapons. It was only when Gorbachev insisted that this should include the abandonment of SDI that Reagan retracted his offer. By November 1987, on the eve of the December Washington Summit, it was clear that an arms limitation agreement was imminent. At the meeting an Intermediate Range Nuclear Force Treaty was signed. The following May in Moscow the foundations for a Strategic Arms Reduction Treaty were laid. When Reagan left office and was succeeded by George Bush there was a temporary pause in what had become a headlong rush to dismantle Cold War hardware and strategies. Gorbachev was not pleased with the pause and in any case developments in the Soviet Bloc were beginning to run out of control of the Kremlin. By the time Bush and Gorbachev had their summit in Malta in December 1989 the Soviet empire in Eastern Europe had gone. On 9 November the Berlin Wall was opened. Nineteen days later West German Chancellor Kohl put forward a ten point plan for reunification (it was consummated by October 1990) and in December the Brezhnev Doctrine was renounced. Bush had not had to do anything. The vortex of events set in motion by Reagan, Gorbachev and the internal conditions of the USSR and the East European satellites had taken charge. To the surprise of so many who believed in bipolarity and the neo-realist paradigm, the Cold War had ended.

Suggestions about what we should make of this and how we might put it into context are made by Ponting in chapter eleven.

Historiography and International Relations Studies

Cold War literature is vast and a few words here cannot hope to do justice to the variety and sophistication of many of the arguments and interpretations that have been forthcoming over the years. Furthermore, the division between history and IR with respect to much that has been writtten about the Cold War is patently artificial. Historical work has often provided the raw data for the development and nuancing of IR theories, and IR theories have often informed the perspectives and analyses of historians. Thus Cold War paradigms have not been the sole preserve of IR theory. They have also been used and adapted by historians for purposes of focus and for ordering and prioritising evidence. It is important to bear that in mind as we examine historical interpretations before turning to IR theory.

The main schools of historical interpretation are the orthodox or traditionalist, the revisionist and the postrevisionist. Traditionalists such as Herbert Feis (Feis, 1957, 1960), see the USA as the defender of liberty and as a benign force in the world. For them the Cold War was caused by Stalin's paranoia and the Soviet Union's totalitarian aggressiveness and expansionist ambitions fuelled by ideology and traditional security concerns. To all this the USA responded responsibly. It provided leadership, but not hegemonic dominance of the West, and economic help, but not economic imperialism. Having just defeated one totalitarian regime it could not give free rein to another. Isolationism was not an option and thus the USA felt somewhat reluctantly obliged to deploy its power to balance, and ultimately contain the threat from the Soviets. In much of this we can detect the influence of realist concerns with the anarchy of the international system and the overriding need for states to pursue their own security through the use of power.

The revisionist project, fathered by William Appleman Williams (Williams, 1962), aimed to dispel the intellectual hubris of the traditionalists whose interpretation seemingly invited disaster because it failed to acknowledge US responsibility for the Cold War, overlooked America's arrogance of power, and did not perceive that economic expansionism was at the heart of US policy. When disaster struck in Vietnam, the revisionists looked vindicated.

For revisionists the key factor is economics (Kolko, 1968; Horowitz, 1965). The dynamic of US capitalism, empowered by the open-door doctrine and its offspring, drove American interests abroad. Trade, investment opportunities and raw materials were needed to secure the future of corporate

America and so the USA designed a postwar economic order based upon free trade, stable exchange rates, and the open-door. This liberal multilateral economic system necessarily collided with the command economy of the Soviets. Put more simply, the USA wished to internationalise capitalism, the Soviets felt compelled to resist. Add to this America's monopoly of the atom bomb (Alperowitz, 1965), Soviet wartime devastation and fears for its territorial security, and a different picture emerges from that painted by the traditionalists. Now the USA becomes the expansionist power and the Soviet Union the threatened one which takes cautious and well measured defensive steps.

In the 1980s attempts were made to synthesise traditionalist and revisionist interpretations, but with little success. The postrevisionist thesis was articulated by John L. Gaddis (Gaddis, 1983). He argued that new documentary evidence demonstrated that the traditionalists had failed to give due emphasis to economic factors and had underestimated how US actions could have reasonably been construed as aggressive by the Soviets. Nevertheless, Gaddis believes that after Pearl Harbor - the defining event for US postwar foreign policy - the USA had legitimate security concerns regarding the Soviet Union and that there was little else that it could do except try to contain the obnoxious regime of Stalin and its geo-political threat. So, on balance, the traditionalists got it right, but some credence needs to be given to the legitimate security fears of the Soviets, and more weight needs to be given to economic factors.

Neither traditionalists nor revisionists have been reconciled to the postrevisionist synthesis. Revisionism remains alive and well in the work of Bruce Cummings (Cummings, 1981, 1990) and William McCormick (McCormick, 1989) with their ideas of US hegemonic leadership of a capitalist world system, the theoretical genealogy of which stretches back to the world systems theory of Immanuel Wallerstein and Fernand Braudel. For their part, the traditionalists disagree over the role of Stalin, the precise emphasis to be given to economic factors and so on. The problem with these conflicting interpretations lies not so much with the weight or lightness of evidence (which Gaddis sees as the key to successful synthesis), but with the preconceived notions of significance that they bring with them. On the one hand there is a preoccupation with power and security and a conviction of the morality of US policies and on the other economic dynamics and scepticism, if not outright condemnation, of the morality of US policy. These assumptions determine both what counts as evidence and how to interpret it. They cannot be reconciled.

These brief comments on the main historical approaches to the Cold War beg many questions and leave much out of account, but at least they provide a crude template for recognising what types of interpretation are at play.

IR scholars have had rather different priorities to historians and although there are areas of overlap, for example the emergence of a post-revisionist synthesis, there are major differences of emphasis, concern and intellectual approach. Apart from chronological/analytical accounts of events and developments during the period covered by the Cold War (which is itself a bone of contention, since commentators tend to agree on when it ended, but not when it began), academic analyses in the dominant Anglo-American IR tradition revolve round three fundamental questions: why did it arise, what was it, and why did it end? Methodologically these questions have been considered by theorists predominantly at the systemic level of analysis which is conceived of in terms of the competition inducing logic of anarchy, variated by the distribution of power, and, on neoliberal accounts, by the level of international institutionalisation as well. In such accounts, the state is treated as a rational actor whose interests are exogenously given and whose personalities or domestic regime have little impact on the character of its foreign policy.

The systemic level is thus generally conceived of in terms of distributions of power and processes of interaction and has been dominant in postwar IR theory, but there are two other levels of analysis that have had purchase in the on-going methodological debates: the units of the system, i.e. the state, and individual agents. The state is seen either as a rational actor where rationality is dictated by a realist power analysis composed of the overriding priorities set by the security dilemma in an anarchical world order (the neo-realist analysis), or as an actor where international law and institutions and the domestic regime count and have impact on the international system; as a result, its zero-sum character can be, but may not always be, transcended (the neo-liberal analysis). A further liberal variant of the latter is the claim that democratic states do not go to war with each other even when in an anarchical world order with an omnipresent security threat. Finally, individual agency is treated in terms of roles, or rational action/decision-making explanations cast in generalisations about human behaviour. It is within this broad type of theoretical framework that IR scholarship has addressed the crucial questions about the Cold War. It has always been a search for explanation through generalisations. Not surprisingly therefore both individual human and unit agency, even though themselves dealt with by generalising theories, have tended to be squeezed out in the search for ever more parsimonious and exalted levels of general theory. The main questions therefore are how accurate systemic explanations of the Cold War have been and how effective they have been in supplying means to predict and thus help control events.

Regarding cause, early commentaries tended to assign responsibility to the USSR, international communism's long term commitment to world revolution and/or chronic paranoia in Soviet leadership circles. Thus within the orthodox action-reaction dynamic generated by conventional readings of the anarchy problematique, Soviet policy objectives occasioned the Western response of containment (Kennan, 1947). Up to the early 1960s, this was the intellectual frame of reference within which most Western academics and policy-makers located the conflict. It was viewed as a particular twentieth century bipolar manifestation of the 'security dilemma' - no different in essence from that described by the great-grandfather of political realism regarding the cause of the Pelopponesian War in the fifth century BC: 'what made war inevitable was the growth in Athenian power and the fear that this caused Sparta' (Thucydides, 1959, p.161). Reacting to this archetypal realist/neorealist view, revisionist accounts began to appear in the 1960s and early 1970s, which, while generally accepting the broad ideational framework of the earlier readings, particularly regarding the anarchic/bipolar nature of the international system, assigned blame not to the Soviets, but to Western imperialism and the capitalist quest for global domination. Western leaderships, especially, but not exclusively in the USA, were thus perceived to be witting or unwitting agents of this historic project (Williams, 1959; Kolko and Kolko, 1972). In the 1980s a 'postrevisionist' school completed the analytical triad allotting blame to both camps, often citing 'misperceptions' as the proximate cause, but nonetheless staying within the parameters of the anarchy paradigm shared by the other two (Jarvis, 1976; Lebow and Stein, 1994). This dovetailing of the neo-realist/neo-liberal schools (apart that is from the allocation of blame) led later international theorists to dub this 'the neo-neo synthesis' (Weaver, 1996). Of course these categories have been simplified and cannot fit all scholars in the field. Gaddis for example, often regarded as the father of the post-revisionist school, still clearly apportions the greatest weight of blame to the Soviets (Gaddis, 1997, pp.292-8).

Regarding the nature of the conflict, since a bipolar security dilemma and a balance of power (or 'terror') was assumed as foundational in the Anglo-American version of things, it is hardly surprising that most accounts viewed the Cold War as a struggle for power, dominance and influence in a highly decentralised environment. Thus, although the conflict might be presented as a 'crusade' of one kind or another (ideological, political or economic) it was at root a particular historical representation of a chronic age-old phenomenon, the rivalry of dominant state actors within a political system characterised above all else by self-help and self-interest (Morgenthau, 1960). So, whether the struggle between mutually exclusive economic interests or a straightforward power-political affair, the Cold War was essentially about establishing hierarchy within anarchy. Its essence was about who ruled, or, more brutally, who prevailed.

Regarding the end of the Cold War, there is no doubt as to who prevailed. On any reading of the 'two-minus-one' argument, the demise of the Soviet Union in 1991 meant that bipolarity, at least temporarily, had given rise to the 'unipolar moment'. Whether or not unipolarity gave way to tripolarity or multipolarity is beyond the scope of this study, but there is a consensus in the texts that the single most important factor in the ending of the Cold War was Michail Gorbachev's 'new thinking' and his pursuit of *glasnost* and *perestroika* in the USSR from 1985 onwards. The wide ranging concessions that these initiatives engendered - accelerated and complemented first by Reagan's doctrine of initiating a 'second Cold War' after the 'decade of neglect' of the *détente*-happy seventies and then by his willingness to negotiate - effectively brought the Cold War to an end. That this involved the disintegration of the Soviet Union itself is generally viewed as an unintended, unforeseen consequence (Nye, 1997). In addition, in acknowledging the pivotal role played by Gorbachev, many of the more ideological accounts have also concluded that the end of the Cold War in fact represented the 'triumph' of the West and its conceptions of politics, economics, society and ethics. For example, Francis Fukuyama in a celebrated essay wrote that 'what we are witnessing is not just the end of the Cold War, or the passing of a particular period of post-war history, but the end of history as such: that is, the endpoint of man's ideological evolution and the universalization of Western liberal democracy as the final form of human government.'(Fukuyama, 1992, p.4). Although the unabashed triumphalism of Fukuyama may have abated somewhat, the Kantian/Wilsonian thesis that liberal democracy is the solution to domestic and international conflict has now become the orthodoxy in the discipline (Doyle, 1983).

Universally welcomed as it was, the end of the Cold War occasioned something of a crisis in IR theory. Neither of the two main paradigms that had hitherto dominated accounts of the conflict, Neorealism and Neoliberalism, had predicted systemic change of this order of magnitude. The individual agency of Gorbachev and to a lesser extent that of Reagan in the unfolding of such momentous change posed problems for those who relied on the high level generalisations of systemic theories of explanation.That none of the major theoretical approaches had in any way anticipated the end of the Cold War led one prominent specialist to conclude that this was damning evidence against IR scholarship and that consequently the field had proved itself to be 'bankrupt' (Gaddis, 1992, p.44). This is an extreme view, and one not without irony since Gaddis's own conceptualisation of the Cold War as the 'long peace' (Gaddis, 1987) is not immune from the same kind of criticism that he has levelled against IR theory. However, few in the discipline now doubt that the events of 1989 constitute a 'complex failure' for the subject as a whole in that it failed to interpret properly the empirical information at hand. With hindsight it is relatively easy to see signs of systemic breakdown, stretching back to the Malenkov administration and the early years of his successor Nikita Krushchev. However, IR scholars and, perhaps to a lesser extent, their Soviet Studies' counterparts were collectively misled by their attachment to untested deterministic assumptions about Great Power behaviour and the role of structure, ideas, belief systems and leadership in effecting outcomes. As a consequence, as critical and postmodern theorists gleefully suggest (George, 1996), the research agenda of mainstream IR was obsessed with questions relating to maintaining superpower stability (the long peace) rather than with change or transformation (a notable exception to this was Gilpin, 1981). Accordingly, the post-Cold War period has witnessed not just a return to normative theory (Brown, 1992), but also a renewed interest in co-operation under conditions of anarchy and the exploration of different modes of explanation and alternative political, social and economic orders (Lebow and Risse-Kappen, 1995).

Another major consequence of consensual and uncritical attachment to the narrow analytical boundaries of the neo-neo accounts of the Cold War was the empirical and theoretical marginalisation of the Third World. For over forty years IR scholarship focused almost exclusively on the dynamics of East-West confrontation. Little sustained attention was given to the Third World and, when it was considered, it was invariably located within the dominant narrative. The period from the late 1940s to the 1980s was marked by a large number of conflicts in the Third World, yet, in the dominant Anglo-American rendering, this period was best characterised as the 'long peace', indicating the essential permissability of regional or 'off-piste' conflict so long as it did not affect, or was controlled by, the bipolar world order. As Waltz bluntly put it: 'In a bipolar world there are no peripheries. With only two powers capable of acting on a world scale anything that happens elsewhere is potentially of concern to both of them.' (Waltz, 1979, p.171). Since the superpowers were preoccupied with the necessity for 'balance', states of the Third World were conceptualised not as *sui generis*, but in terms of strategies of alignment or strategies of denial. These 'peripheral' countries gained importance only by virtue of their position *vis-á-vis* the 'core'. Although the phenomenon of non-alignment was meant to be an explicit rejection of this, its conspicuous lack of success in generating a 'third way' in international politics is testimony to the all-inclusive nature of the Cold War script. So complete was the fit between the Cold War and the discipline of IR that the role of the Third World and the distinctive nature of its problems were relatively unexplored for nearly half a century (Neuman, 1998). Pre-occupation with systemic great power polarity/stability issues meant that all conflicts were analysed from a Cold War-centred perspective.

Even the 'dependency/*dependencia* paradigm, which is now acknowledged to be a specific Third World/Southern contribution to international theory, was widely read as a neo-Marxist off-shoot of the central East-West conflict. In this way economic underdevelopment in the 'periphery' was linked to injustices perpetrated by the exploitative and capitalist 'core'. This preoccupation with systemic great power polarity/stability issues meant that Third World affairs were either subsumed within the 'core-core' confrontation, or else marginalised as largely irrelevant to the Manichean struggle between the competing systems (Neuman, 1998).

In sum, just as the failure to predict the end of the Cold War is a serious indictment of IR studies, so too are the 'silences' or 'closures' it encouraged. Now that the Cold War is over there is clearly a sense in which the discipline itself has been liberated. IR is slowly freeing itself from the straitjacket of the Westphalian/Eurocentric obsession that reached its apogee during these dismal years.

The Chapters

The chapters are marshalled under the headings of: theory; stretching out the paradigms; beyond the paradigms; and historically contextualising the Cold War.

The two theory chapters by Murray and Reynolds approach the problem of explanation in different ways. Murray focuses on the genealogy of the dominant realist/neo-realist Cold War paradigm. He argues that traditional realism, as articulated by Hans J. Morgenthau, was not stipulatively constrictive in the way that neo-realism became later. Murray claims that the main reason for the change of character in theorising between realism and neo-realism was the pursuit of a more positivist, or hard scientific, methodology. Reynolds' approach is somewhat broader. He is concerned with identifying the logical requirements for explanation and he finds deficiencies in the theories and paradigms that have been constructed to explain the Cold War. For him, it is important first to draw a clear distinction between meaning and understanding on the one hand and explanation on the other, and second to establish that different kinds of enquiry need different kinds of explanation. Scientific necessary and sufficient causal explanation is one kind, reason giving historical explanation is another and so on. But what often passes for explanation in Cold War literature fails to meet the threshhold of criteria for them to be truly explanatory: they have no criteria independent of that which is to be explained by which claims can be assessed or tested for accuracy.

In stretching out Cold War paradigms Dobson, Marsh, Malik, Evans and Dix look successively at US relations with Britain; relations between Britain, the USA, Iran and the oil majors; the Gulf States and the Cold War; South Africa and the Cold War; and Indian neutralism and the Cold War. Dobson and Marsh challenge ideas of US hegemony within the Western Alliance and Marsh takes the analysis further by showing how the USA had problems with its own mulitinational oil companies. Malik convincingly demonstrates the importance of indigenous sources of conflict within the Middle East and Evans the existence of similar factors in South Africa. The latter demonstrates how Cold War rhetoric was manipulated by the South Africans, that their problems preceded Cold War origins, and that far from being creatures of the Cold War the parties to the indigenous conflict used it for their own ends. It is a case of the domestic tail wagging the international neo-realist dog. Dix brings out how neutralism, denied by Cold War bipolarity and the principles of collective security, eventually had to be acknowledged by the USA and played a significant role in Cold War international relations. The work of all five authors, in their respective ways, challenges the efficacy of neo-realist analysis and explanation and critiques the way that assumptions derived from that position have been used in historical explanation.

In the section entitled beyond the paradigms, Ryall explains the importance of the spiritual battle fought by Roman Catholicism buttressed by the supranationalism of the Vatican and its diplomacy. He emphasises the role of the Catholic Church in the development of affairs in Eastern Europe and how totalitarian communism could neither eradicate nor absorb the Catholic Church and its spiritual life. Rogers challenges the axiom that nuclear deterrence created stability and alerts us to the dangers of following proliferation, which some neo-realists have advocated, as a means of creating stability in a multipolar world order. Bideleux presents a Soviet perspective to correct the excessive Western focus and emphasis of so much of Cold War literature and argues that the Cold War of 1945-91 was no more than a continuation of conflicts with capitalism that began in 1918. He also argues that the Soviets were often more willing to practise peaceful co-existence than they have usually been given credit for. One might describe the work of these three authors as the Horatio critique: 'There are more things in heaven and earth Horatio, Than are dreamt of in your philosophy.'

In the conclusion, Ponting places the Cold War in the context of world history. His chapter provides a corrective to Eurocentrism and Occidentalism. It calls to account Cold War scholarship which has overemphasised the superpower confrontation at the expense of studies of more significant things such as the environment, the world economy, the re-emergence of China as a great power, and the shift of power from Europe to the USA. In short, Cold War studies have distorted our perception of what was really important in international developments since 1945. Ponting challenges many conventional views and provides a perspective which shows how fatuous the claims of all-embracing paradigms are.

Note

1 The following two sections are based on material drawn from numerous secondary sources. Some of the standard works are: Leffler and Painter (1994); Gaddis (1982, 1987, 1997); Maier (1996); McCormick (1989); Zubok and Pleshakov (1996); Reynolds (1995).

Section 1: Theory

1 Reconstructing the Cold War: The Evolution of a Consuming Paradigm

ALASTAIR MURRAY

Traditionally, the "discipline" of international relations has tended to approach the post war period through the lens of what we might term a "Cold War paradigm", explaining the majority of what occurred by reference to the ebbs and flows of superpower tension, and forcing to the margins of debate that which cannot be so explained. At the theoretical level, for instance, we find that the dominant neorealist orthodoxy has tended to assume that the bipolar structure of the post war system explains the character of international relations within it.[1] At the strategic level, we find that security specialists have habitually assumed that the strategy, and, in particular, the nuclear strategy, of the two superpowers explains the level of stability prevailing in different periods of the post war era.[2] And, at the empirical level, we find that diplomatic historians have frequently assumed that the superpower conflict represents the essential fact of post war international politics, and thus the appropriate point from which to begin any explanation of their course.[3]

The impact of this tendency almost to equate "post war" with "Cold War" is two-fold. First, it has seriously distorted our understanding of the events of the post war years. As the chapters in this volume by Dix and Evans demonstrate, by approaching post war international politics in these terms, we have been prevented from understanding the way that events developed independently of the conflict between the superpowers in the large areas of the world which remained outside the alliance structures, such as Southern Africa and the Indian Subcontinent. Indeed, as the chapters by Dobson and Marsh show, this type of approach to post war international politics cannot even offer an adequate explanation of the relations *within* the alliance structures, because it prevents us from understanding the role that non leading alliance members often played independently of, and even in defiance of, the bloc leader and the Cold War priorities it promulgated.

Second, and perhaps, in the long run, more importantly, the exclusionary focus of the Cold War "paradigm" forced potentially significant qualitative developments in the structure of the international system to the margins of debate.[4] The focus on the potential for military conflict in the system obscured a profound growth in economic interdependence.[5] The focus on hostility between the superpowers obscured a profound growth in co-operation between other states.[6] The focus on east-west relations obscured the growing significance of north-south tensions for the international system.[7] The focus on the potential threat from a nuclear exchange obscured the growing danger of a crisis in the global ecosystem.[8] Only in recent years have such issues received anything like serious consideration in the mainstream of international relations.

The "discipline" of international relations has effectively employed as a heuristic framework with which to approach post war international politics a "paradigm" which, far from clarifying matters, has involved both the premature closure of its terms of reference and the distortion of its analysis within these parameters. It is this paradox which this chapter seeks to address. The conventional wisdom amongst those critical of this rather curious situation is that it can be explained solely in terms of the influence of realist thought on the study of international politics. Imposing upon the "discipline" as a whole its own very narrow power political approach, the theory is held to have delineated "legitimate" research areas, marginalising other perspectives and the diverse facets of international relations with which they were concerned.[9] Against this, I argue that the "paradigm" was not a static, once and for all, creation of realism, but rather evolved dynamically over time. Whilst realism contained its seeds, it was only in the behavioural revolution that these seeds germinated, and only in neorealism that they flowered. Consequently, I suggest that the misconceptualisation of the post war period should be explained less in terms of realist assumptions than in terms of the methodological shift to positivism which was later imposed upon them.

In order to demonstrate this, I attempt in this chapter to reconstruct the evolution of the Cold War "paradigm," identifying the assumptions which originally informed it, and tracing the way that these assumptions were developed over time. I begin, in section I, by examining the realist theory in which critics have traditionally found the rise of the Cold War "paradigm," arguing that, if the seeds of the "paradigm" clearly lie within it, they are as yet undeveloped. In section II, I then go on to look at the behaviouralist and neorealist modifications of the realist framework by examining, respectively, the theories of Kaplan and Waltz, in order to demonstrate the way in which, by progressively narrowing its content, they fostered the constrictive agenda we associate with the Cold War "paradigm." Given that the dynamic view of the "paradigm" which emerges from this analysis refutes traditional understandings of its causes, I proceed, in section III, to examine the factors which underlay its development, arguing that it is the attempt to render the realist framework scientific which led the seeds of the "paradigm" contained within it to germinate, rather than any inherent quality. Finally, in section IV, I go on to consider some of the factors which motivated this attempt, in order both to determine the ultimate causes of the "paradigm" and to set its development in context.

The Origins of the Cold War Paradigm

The tendency to read post war international politics as little more than an expression of the Cold War obviously finds its initial stirrings in the approach to the subject developed by realist thinkers. Whereas the idealist thought of the interwar period focused largely on international law and organisation as the key to understanding the international system,[10] realist thought treated such institutions simply as a reflection of the interests and the values of the major powers, and adopted the position that concentrating on the struggle for power between such states offered the best way to approach international politics.[11] Indeed, its conviction that the struggle between *status quo* and 'imperial' or 'revisionist' powers for control of such institutions represented the principal threat to such stability as could be said to exist in the international system led it inevitably to regard such a focus as not only empirically valid but, moreover, morally essential (Murray, 1997, Chs. 2-3). Hence, in the face of the frustration of interwar ideals, Carr sought to explain the problems of the League of Nations in terms of a revisionist challenge from Germany, advocating a policy of appeasement to reconcile it to the international order (Carr, 1939).[12] And, in the face of the frustration of wartime ideals, Kennan sought to explain the collapse of allied unity in terms of a brewing revisionist challenge from the Soviet Union, advocating a policy of containment to reconcile it to the international order (Kennan, 1946, pp.701-3; 1947, pp.575-6, pp.580-1).

It is thus very tempting to locate the source of the problems that the "discipline" has had in approaching the post war period in realist doctrine. It is obviously but a short step from the position that international politics is best understood through an analysis of the struggle between the major powers to the position that this struggle is a sufficient explanation of international politics in general and the post war period in particular. It is then a relatively straightforward matter to establish a link between these assumptions and the problems involved in the Cold War "paradigm," given the crucial role that realist doctrine played in shaping the development of the "discipline" of international relations.[13] If it was displaced as the theoretical orthodoxy by the 1960s, 'the behavioural revolt did not change the "paradigm" of the field but provided a conception of scientific methodology' (Vasquez, 1983, p.13). Indeed, by the 1980s, any doubts about the influence of such assumptions were removed with the establishment of neorealism as the new theoretical orthodoxy, and the reassertion of traditional realist tenets in explicit terms.[14] Thus Vasquez was able to suggest in the early 1980s that 'international relations theory in the last thirty years or so can be viewed as an attempt to articulate the realist "paradigm" in light of research, whilst at the same time learning and debating what constitutes scientific research' (Vasquez, 1983, p.22). Hence the complaints that realism is responsible for the premature closure of "disciplinary" enquiry might seem to have a certain plausibility. It seems to have advocated the appropriate type of ideas for accomplishing this, and to have possessed the right type of influence.

Yet, if it is but a short step from the type of assumptions put forward by realism to the assumptions which underlay the Cold War "paradigm", it is a step which realism does not seem to have actually taken. The emphasis on the struggle for power between the major states that we find in the theory is actually a very flexible approach, which can in no way be compared to the narrow, distorting focus involved in the Cold War "paradigm." It is clear, to begin with, that realism did not limit its understanding of the structure of the international system simply to matters of the number and arrangement of the major powers, but rather remained open to consideration of precisely the type of qualitative shifts that critics of the Cold War "paradigm" have sought to highlight. In *Politics Among Nations*, for instance, Morgenthau went to considerable trouble to discuss the challenge posed by nuclear weapons to the traditional, spatial division of political authority, and the consequent need to move towards more universal modes of governance in the international system (Morgenthau, 1960, Chs. 29-30). In much the same way, Kennan was to spend a considerable proportion of his career highlighting the global environmental threat, and the consequent need to undertake radical measures to prevent a catastrophe arising.[15] Similarly, Kissinger was able to recognise the significance of both increasing economic interdependence and growing north-south tensions, and the consequent need to build a more inclusive framework of international order (Kissinger, 1977, pp.152, 219-20, 240-72; 1981, pp.25-39, 49-67; 1985, pp.68-72, 127-138, 221-236). Ultimately, if realism attempted to bound its field of enquiry, this closure was not premature, but rather perfectly compatible with the type of research agenda emphasised by its critics today.

More specifically, however, it is also clear that, within this framework, realism did not so privilege structural explanation as to imply that an analysis of the struggle for power between the major actors could constitute a sufficient explanation of the character of international politics in any given period. In theoretical terms, if Morgenthau emphasised the importance of the tension between *status quo* and 'imperialist' powers to any explanation of international politics, this was treated as little more than a provisional starting point capable of providing a framework in which other factors might be considered (Morgenthau, 1960, p.37). In more practical terms, if Kennan sought to explain the difficulties which the United States faced in the post war environment largely in terms of a revisionist challenge from the Soviet Union, he consistently opposed attempts to reduce international politics to this struggle, emphasising that a large proportion of the earth's surface exceeded the terms of the conflict and had to be addressed on its own terms (Kennan, 1954, Ch.2; 1978, Chs.3-12). Ultimately, realism's concern with the power political structure of the system was not as disproportionate as critics have implied, but rather roughly commensurate with what even they would accept. There are few, for instance, who would contest that the centrality of the major powers in terms of their ability to construct, singularly or severally, the norms, regimes, and organisations which constitute the international order holding in any particular historical epoch makes comprehending their relations an essential guide to understanding what occurs in the system.[16] And there are few who would dispute that the centrality of the major powers in terms of the extent of their interests and the extent of their capability to defend these interests makes understanding the incidence of major power war in the system an essential indicator of the level of security that all states may enjoy.[17] Ultimately, if we find some of the seeds of the Cold War "paradigm" in realism's conviction that the explanation of international politics must begin by examining the struggle between the major powers, it is difficult to claim that this conviction involved either the level of distortion or the premature closure of enquiry that we tend to associate with the "paradigm" in its full form. If we are to understand the consuming obsession of the "discipline" with the Cold War, we need to look at the way that this initial framework was developed.

The Development of the Paradigm

It is only with the behaviouralist revolution of the late 1950s and early 1960s that we see the first signs of difficulty. If it is in political realism that we first find the conviction that international politics is best approached by studying the struggle between the major powers, it is in behaviouralism that we first find this rough heuristic device transformed into a constrictive framework. Under its auspices, the structure of the system was increasingly narrowly drawn in terms of the number and arrangement of such powers, and this structure was increasingly privileged in the explanation of international politics. If we examine, for instance, Kaplan's *System and Process in International Politics*[18] we find that, because of the turnover between, and change within, units, international politics is studied in terms of 'systems of action,' composed of 'the essential rules of the system,' 'the transformation rules,' 'the actor classificatory variables,' 'the capability variables,' and 'the information variables' (Kaplan, 1957, pp.4, 9-11). The structural component of these systems is 'the essential rules of the system' and 'the transformation rules' (Waltz, 1979, p.53). Given that the essential rules relate solely to the 'general relationships between the actors of the system,' that the range of actors is narrowly delimited, emphasising major or 'essential' states, and that the transformatory rules relate exclusively to the changes produced by these states' deviations from the essential rules, it should be apparent that the conception of system structure which Kaplan's theory presents is narrowly circumscribed, treating the number and arrangement of the major powers as the predominant variable, to the exclusion of qualitative variations such as the density of interactions, the depth of interdependence, and the richness of institutions (Kaplan, 1957, pp.9-11, 22-23).[19]

Furthermore, this much narrower conception of structure is then privileged in explanation, such that the struggle for power between the major actors becomes the predominant source of explanations of the character of international politics. There is, it should be stressed, no suggestion here that the structure of the system is determinist: the major actors can deviate from the essential rules under certain circumstances, sparking a transformation in the system (Kaplan, 1957, pp.10-11). But it is the structure of the system which is used to explain the character of international politics in any given period. Hence we find that enquiry into the international system of the eighteenth, nineteenth and early twentieth centuries is guided by the premise that the character of the system depends on the numbers, objectives and relative power of the 'essential national actors' (Kaplan, 1957, pp.22-35). And we find that enquiry into the post war system is guided by the premise that '[t]he functioning of the loose bipolar system depends upon the organisational characteristics of the supranational blocs' (Kaplan, 1957, pp.37-8). In Kaplan's behaviouralism, the seeds of the Cold War "paradigm" which were sown with realism begin to germinate. Imposing, for the first time, a narrow definition of the structure of the system and privileging explanation within this structure, it effectively advocated a position which held that the character of international politics should be explained not only primarily, but also predominantly, by the analysis of the struggle between the major powers, crucially nourishing the temptation to read the international politics of the post war period in terms of the Cold War between the superpowers.

It is in neorealism, however, that this tendency culminates. Whereas, in Kaplan's *System and Process in International Politics*, the analysis of the struggle for power between the major states became a predominant element in any explanation of international politics, in Waltz's *Theory of International Politics* it became a sufficient explanation in and of itself.[20] To begin with, the definition of the structure of the system that neorealism advances is extremely narrow, to the extent that the number of the major powers becomes its sole variable. In the theory, whilst the anarchic condition of the international system represents the constant which determines the power political structure of the game, the distribution of capabilities amongst the units of the system becomes the sole variable determining the relative stability of international relations, defined in terms of system preservation and war incidence (Waltz, 1979, pp.88-101).[21] Hence the persistent criticisms that neorealism's understanding of the system structure excludes other vital factors from consideration. Important long term shifts in the density of interactions between units, in the richness of information, norms, and institutions between them, in the structures organising their economic relations, are all simply marginalised to the unit level, and play no part at the systemic level.[22]

Having first drawn the structure so tightly, however, we then find, second, that neorealism arbitrarily privileges it in explanation to the extent that the theory is almost structurally determinist. As Waltz has been at pains to point out, this is certainly not his intention: structures 'shape and shove,' and can be successfully bucked (Waltz, 1986, pp.343-4). Yet it is surely right to point to a fundamental contradiction between the formal construction of his theory and its operational deployment. Compare, for instance, the abstract assertion that '[o]ne can believe that some causes of international outcomes are located at the level of interacting units... Causes at the level of units and systems interact ...', (Waltz, 1979, p.68) with the interpretation that '[s]o long as one leaves the structure unaffected it is not possible for changes in the intentions and the actions of particular actors to produce desirable outcomes or to avoid undesirable ones.' (Waltz, 1979, p.108). Given that Waltz presupposes that no systemic transformation has ever occurred, indeed, that it is hard to imagine such a transformation, the unit level appears utterly constrained (Waltz, 1986, p.328).[23] Thus, whilst Waltz allows unit level freedom in his theory's conception, when it comes to explaining how the structure actually operates on units in practice, he moves towards a much more determinist stance. This pull towards an ever more determinist position would not seem to be accidental. It is the inevitable result of Waltz's initial restriction of the definition of his structure to material factors, ignoring ideational inputs. As human practice plays no role in it, human agency has little ability to reform it (Ashley, 1988, pp.227-9, 238-241, 252-3; 1989, pp.287, 292-4, 297-8; Wendt, 1992, pp.391-396, 409-10; 1994, pp.387-8, 393-4). The units of the system almost cease to possess any capacity for action independent from the dictates of structure. Thus, having reduced the structure of the system solely to the number of the major powers, Waltz then privileges it over all other factors, such that system polarity becomes a sufficient explanation of international politics.

As a result of this double move, the story of post war international politics becomes explicable solely in terms of the bipolar conflict which informs the structure. Waltz, of course, would dispute such a claim (Waltz, 1979, pp.174-5). But to take just one example, the increasing integration of Western Europe in the post war years is explained in the neorealist account solely in terms of the shift from a multipolar distribution of power between several European states to a bipolar distribution of power between the superpowers, solely in terms of the development of the Cold War. The need to establish a balance of power against the threat posed by the Soviet Union encroaching deeper and deeper into the continent, and the presence of an American hegemon willing to organise a grand coalition against this encroachment, appear in conjunction as the efficient cause of Western Europe's transcendence of its past security competition and willingness to create transnational structures of authority. Consideration of matters such as sociological change within societies and ideological homogeneity between regimes can play no part in the explanation. Furthermore, the poverty of this understanding leads inevitably to the claim that, with the collapse of this threat and potential for departure of the hegemon, European co-operation will inevitably break down, as balance of power considerations force the major European states to be wary of, and coalesce against, each other as potential threats (Waltz, 1979, pp.70-1; 1993, p.71; Mearsheimer, 1990, pp.6-7, 46-8; 1994-5, pp.340-1; Layne, 1995, pp.164-176). Consideration of such matters as institutional embeddedness and economic interdependence cannot influence the prediction. The situation of Europe, in other words, is accounted for simply in terms of the traditional pattern of the formation of a grand coalition with the development of a revisionist power and its collapse in the aftermath of the defeat of that revisionist power. As Waltz puts it, 'organisations are created by their enemies. Alliances are organised against a perceived threat. We know from balance-of-power theory as well as from history that war-winning coalitions collapse on the morrow of victory, the more surely if it is a decisive one' (Waltz, 1993, p.71). Ultimately, neorealism leads to the assumption that what happened between the superpowers is all we need to know to understand post war international politics.

The Cold War "paradigm" should thus be seen, not as a one-off creation of realist assumptions, but rather as a dynamic construct which evolved gradually over time. In realism, the number and arrangement of the major powers was considered to be only one of several important components of the structure of the international system, and this structure was treated merely as an important background feature against which other factors operated, such that the struggle between the major powers appeared simply as a necessary element of any explanation of international politics. The Cold War between the superpowers could thus be seen as an important factor in the explanation of the post war international system, but not the definitive factor. Behaviouralist theory, however, defined the structure of the system much more narrowly, such that the number and arrangement of the major powers became by far and away the most important variable in it, and then privileged this structure over other factors to the extent that the struggle between the major powers became the single most important component of any explanation of international politics. The Cold War between the superpowers thus became the predominant factor in the explanation of the post war international system. Finally, neorealism defined the structure of the system so narrowly that the number of the major powers became the *only* variable in it, and then arbitrarily privileged this structure over other factors to the extent that the struggle between the major powers became a sufficient explanation of international politics. The Cold War between the superpowers thus reached its apogee, becoming an adequate explanation of the post war international system in and of itself.

Reconsidering the Causes of the "Paradigm's" Evolution

If the Cold War "paradigm" is a dynamic construct which evolved gradually through behavioural and neorealist modifications of realist assumptions, we can clearly no longer locate the causes of the distortion of the "discipline's" understanding of the post war period exclusively in realist theory, but must now look to other factors. The principal cause that emerges here is the attempt to render the study of international relations more scientific. Whilst realism was largely traditional in its orientation, attempting to produce a theory which might set forth a loose collection of inductively generated law-like propositions, behaviouralism hoped to be much more scientific, attempting to provide a theory which might promulgate a coherent set of deductively generated law-like propositions, and neorealism completed this move, attempting to create a theory which might not only promulgate a coherent set of law-like propositions but also explain why such law-like regularities existed in the first place. To achieve theories which might be capable, not only of promulgating law-like regularities, but also of explaining their operation, behaviouralists and neorealists had to bound the realm with which they dealt and simplify its content considerably. Hence their attempt to render realism's original framework scientific ultimately culminated in the reduction of its content.

Realism is, of course, frequently treated as positivist in orientation.[24] This is incorrect. Even if we restrict ourselves to what is held to be the best example of this tendency, the 'science' of international politics that Morgenthau developed in *Politics Among Nations*, we find that it is very limited in its claims and objectives in comparison with what came later. Morgenthau's intention was not to provide a theory capable of the precision of the natural sciences, but rather one which might set forth 'however imperfectly and one-sidedly' certain 'laws of politics' in order 'to bring order and meaning to a mass of phenomena which without it would remain disconnected and unintelligible' (Morgenthau, 1960, pp.3-8). Furthermore, even this limited "positivism" was combined with aspects of a much more interpretative approach. Realism was concerned to understand politics from within the realm of statesmen, on the basis of a reading of the intersubjective understandings generated by that community, as much as to explain politics from the outside, on the basis of a "positivist" theorising of a determining necessity (Ashley, 1981, pp.210-4, 215-21; George, 1988, pp.92-3; Walker, 1993, p.119). Hence Morgenthau could simultaneously identify his theory as a 'science,' based on 'objective laws that have their roots in human nature,' and as an interpretation designed to allow us 'to retrace and anticipate, as it were, the steps a statesman -past, present or future- has taken or will take on the political scene. We look over his shoulder when he writes his dispatches; we listen in on his conversation with other statesman, we read and anticipate his very thoughts' (Morgenthau, 1960, pp.4-5). Ultimately, realism was conceived in a strictly heuristic mould. Far from being statements of invariant associations, its "laws of politics" were probabilistic rules of thumb, designed to guide enquiry in a field of study too complex to be comprehensible to the naked eye, and to counsel practice in a field of policy too complex to be susceptible to idealist modes of action.[25] If its methodological eclecticism deprived its theory of the rigour contemporary international relations has come to expect, it did at least protect it from the side-effects associated with such rigour. It actively militated against any attempt to arbitrarily constrict the field of study by keeping the door open to new variables and factors.

It is only with behaviouralism that we find a move to the reduction of variables to a *systematisable* level, and only in neorealism that we find this move reach its logical culmination in the reduction of variables to one, because it is only in behaviouralism, and, particularly, in neorealism, that we find an effort to lay the foundations necessary for international relations to develop as a scientific "discipline" capable of generating cumulative research findings. The theory developed in *System and Process* aimed to 'direct research in such a way that the data of international politics could be handled comparatively and cumulatively' (Kaplan, 1964, *preface*).[26] The theory developed in *Theory of International Politics* sought to effect a transformation in international relations equivalent to the transformation effected in economic thought by the Physiocrats in the mid-eighteenth century (Waltz, 1995, pp.67-72). Both consequently sought to go beyond realism's multiplication of inductively generated laws and generate a "genuine" theory of international politics. Kaplan was more cautious, attempting to move beyond induction to create by deduction a theory which would provide, not merely a 'collection,' but 'a coherent body' of law-like propositions, in which their interrelations could be specified (Kaplan, 1957, p.3; 1964, *preface*).[27] Waltz was more ambitious, aiming to move beyond 'the necessarily barren hypothetico-deductive approach' to construct 'creatively,' by a flash of 'brilliant intuition,' a theory which would be, 'rather than mere collections of laws... statements which explain them... [and] show why those associations pertain' (Waltz, 1979, pp.5-11).[28] Nevertheless, each was confident that his approach represented a move towards a genuine science of international politics (Kaplan, 1964, preface; Waltz, 1979, pp.5-6).

Both consequently were required to reduce the variables employed in the explanation of international politics. If theory was to be able, not only to promulgate law-like regularities, but also to systematise them into a coherent set, it had to narrow the variables involved to a systematisable level. Hence the need for Kaplan to treat international politics in terms of 'systems of action,' in terms of a set of variables so related that significant 'describable behavioural regularities' characterise their relations, lest the frequency of change and turnover in units render impossible even the loosely scientific type of international politics that he wanted (Kaplan, 1957, p.4).[29] And if theory were not only to promulgate law-like regularities but perhaps even explain why these interconnections held, it would have to reduce the variables involved even further. Hence the need for Waltz to treat international politics as 'a bounded realm or domain of activity,' first taking a manageable number of factors on their own and treating other things as if they were equal, and then further simplifying the content of it so drastically by abstracting from them the necessary factors, aggregating these into easily manageable categories, and then transforming them into ideal type variables (Waltz, 1979, pp.7-10). In this way, the struggle for power between the major powers which realism had initially employed as a useful starting point from which to understand international politics was progressively transformed until it became, in the hands of neorealists, a technical quantity capable of explaining variations in the behaviour predicted by the master assumption of anarchy.

The Ultimate Causes of the Paradigm

The distortion of the study of post war international politics can thus be seen to derive from the methodological shift to positivism effected by behaviouralist and neorealist theorists. Yet, if such an approach is perhaps good scientific practice, it is, even against the standards such positivists set for themselves, bad international relations. The test of a theory's utility for both groups is its usefulness, its heuristic power, its ability to illuminate, its explanatory capability (Kaplan, 1957, p.xiii; Waltz, 1979, p.6). However, as we have seen, the theories of both Waltz and Kaplan are gravely deficient in this respect. By employing narrow understandings of the structure of the system, they obscure long term trends in its character. By awarding this structure a dominant position in explanation, they obscure a wide variety of factors which are necessary to obtain an accurate picture of what is actually going on in any given period. Ultimately, by the time we reach neorealism, we find that, as Stanley Hoffmann put it, Waltz's 'attempt at laying the groundwork for theory is conceptually so rigorous as to leave out much of the reality he wishes to account for' (Hoffmann, 1977, p.52). The positivist move in international relations may have improved the "discipline's" methodological rigour, but it clearly did so at the price of weakening our understanding of what actually goes on in international politics.

The final question which therefore confronts us is that of why the "discipline" should have gone down this road, why it should have accepted this cost. In order to answer this question, we need to probe beneath the methodological preferences which informed the post war study of international relations, into the matter of the purpose to which theory was dedicated. The development of international relations as a "social science" was heavily associated with the efforts of American scholars, and, as Hoffmann has suggested, these academics were informed by an enlightenment confidence in the ability of scientific method to solve even social problems, were surrounded by a group of policy makers struggling to deal with the consequences of America's rise to prominence in world affairs, and existed in an institutional system which allowed them to interact with this group to an unprecedented degree (Hoffmann, 1977, pp.45-50). These unusual conditions produced in the "discipline" of international relations a desire to produce theory that could assist policy makers to predict or even to control international politics, a desire which led directly to its scientific move and thus to its reduction of international politics to the struggle between the major powers.

In realism, this tendency was contained by the natural scepticism of its proponents. Morgenthau, Kennan, and Kissinger operated as advisor, planner, and policy maker, respectively, leading many to see in their theory little more than 'a diplomats' manual of statecraft' (Rosenberg, 1990, p.289).[30] Yet realism consistently avoided going down the route of turning international relations into a predictive social science which might serve policy making. First, its belief in the corrupting influence of power imbued it with a deep scepticism about involvement in politics which acted as a check on any temptation to serve it too completely. It recognised the obligations incumbent on the social scientist, Morgenthau observing that '[n]o study of politics, and certainly no study of international politics in the mid-twentieth century, can be disinterested in the sense that it is able to divorce knowledge from action and to pursue knowledge for its own sake...' (Morgenthau, 1960, p.22). But it was also acutely aware of the dangers involved in allowing the study of international relations to be coopted into the service of policy making. It was precisely this danger which Morgenthau railed against in *Truth and Power*. The intellectual may serve a useful function assisting government by 'expert advice,' but he must always remember that '[o]ne small step separates these independent positions from that in which the intellectual becomes an agent of the powers-that-be... becomes an ideologue.' It was this danger that led Morgenthau ultimately to prefer the position of 'prophetic-confrontation' to that of 'expert' (Morgenthau, 1970, pp.15-6, 27-8). Hence his conclusion of *Politics Among Nations*, not with any technical manual for the triumph of American foreign policy in its struggle with other communities, but with nine rules designed to reinvigorate diplomacy as a tool of mutual understanding and accommodation between communities (Morgenthau, 1960, pp.561-9). Perhaps more importantly, however, realism was marked by a profound scepticism of predictive claims. It was precisely the scientific ethos which imbued American academia that Morgenthau railed against in *Scientific Man VS Power Politics*. He argued that the analogy between the social and natural realm, and thus between the social and natural sciences, was false. The degree of logical coherence, the complexity of sequences, and the possibility of scientific certainty about causes and effects dramatically differ between the two. Consequently, 'the social sciences can, at best... present a series of hypothetical possibilities, each of which may occur under certain conditions - and which of them will actually occur is anybody's guess.' Ultimately, '[p]olitics is an art and not a science...' (Morgenthau, 1965, pp.2, 10, 95, 126-30, 136-8).[31]

In American scholars who contributed to the development of behaviouralism and neorealism, however, scepticism about politics and science was replaced by a characteristic American faith in the possibilities of the two in conjunction. With the weakening of the realist grip on the "discipline" and the behaviouralist revolution in the 1960s, international relations was drawn ever more closely into the provision of a predictive science for the improvement of policy (Hoffmann, 1977, p.49). Hence Kaplan aimed to devise a theory that might generate predictions about what rational, informed statesmen would do in particular types of circumstances, the conditions under which this characteristic behaviour might change, and the results such a transformation might produce. Such predictive statements might, he hoped, yield prescriptive statements about what constituted optimal modes of behaviour under different types of conditions (Kaplan, 1957, pp.xvii-xviii; 1964, preface).[32] With the weakening of the behaviouralist grip and the subsequent rise of neorealism in the 1980s, international relations moved a stage further, beyond prediction and towards control. Hence, as Waltz observes at the opening of *Theory of*

International Politics, '[t]he urge to explain is not born of idle curiosity alone. It is produced also by the desire to control... rather than merely to predict.' If prediction allows one to detect problems in advance, and perhaps 'get out of the way,' control allows one to prevent such problems arising in the first place (Waltz, 1979, p.6).

It is this shift in purpose which, more than anything else, underlies the methodological shift in international politics and thus ultimately bears responsibility for the constriction of the "disciplinary" research agenda. The traditional approach of realism might offer interesting observations but, because it could specify laws only 'imperfectly' and could not explain how they interacted in practice, it was too imprecise and unsystematic to allow hard predictive statements to be made. To predict, one had to be certain of the laws, and certain how they worked. Hence the behaviouralists' emphasis on the need for the study of international relations to become much more 'analytical' and much more 'systematic' (Kaplan, 1957, p.3).[33] Even the coherent sets of laws which behaviouralism offered could not, however, provide the type of control neorealism sought. As Waltz put it, '[b]ecause a law does not say *why* a particular association holds, it cannot tell us whether we can exercise control and how we might go about doing so. For the latter purposes we need a theory' (Waltz, 1979, p.6). We need, effectively, to know what underlies the laws and makes them work if we are to manipulate their operation. Hence the need for the "discipline" to abstract itself so far from reality. To fulfil its new pretensions, it required a scientific confidence traditional methods could not provide.

Thus, whereas realism was sceptical about the prospect of developing theory which might yield predictive insights, and frankly dubious about the prospect of developing one which might yield a degree of control over the international system, behaviouralism and neorealism embraced this project wholeheartedly. What occurred was, in other words, a fundamental shift in the idea of the purpose of theory, from being an intellectual exercise which might, in passing, assist government, to being a technical instrument concerned with the prediction of patterns specifically for its benefit (Ashley, 1981, pp.210-5; 1984, p.265). As Hoffmann himself conceded, '[b]orn and raised in America, the "discipline" of international relations is, so to speak, too close to the fire' (Hoffmann, 1977, p.59). It lost its critical distance, becoming simply a problem solving exercise at the behest of policy makers. And, as Booth has put it, 'problem-solving means attention to the agendas of policy-makers. As a result, those academics who seek the ears of princes necessarily have their horizons foreshortened' (Booth, 1991, p.538).[34] This cooption of the study of international relations into the service of policy must, of course, be seen in context. The Cold War which the realists faced was an emerging struggle between two, formerly allied, great powers to determine who would shape the post war international order. The Cold War which the positivists faced was, by way of contrast, a battle between the "free world" and an "evil empire" for the heart and soul of mankind. If one can perhaps stand aloof from a traditional struggle for pre-eminence between major powers, it is difficult to remain detached from a Manichean battle between light and darkness. Just as neutrality became discredited in the realm of practice, it was perhaps inevitable that it would dissolve in the realm of theory. In the final analysis, the primary cause of the development of the Cold War paradigm was the ideological nature of the Cold War itself. Yet, it is nevertheless ironically true that a "discipline" which took so much from Morgenthau forgot what is perhaps his most prophetic lesson - that its function is to speak truth to power, to advise, chastise, but never to conspire (Morgenthau, 1970, pp.15-6).

Reconsidering the Cold War

What this analysis suggests is that we need to understand the Cold War "paradigm" as a much more complex phenomenon than has previously been thought. Multicausal rather than monocausal in its genesis, dynamic rather than static in its development, and multidimensional rather than unidimensional in its operation, it exceeds conventional understandings of both its nature and form. Rather than being simply the product of an emphasis on the importance of examining the struggle between the major powers if one were to understand the context of international politics, it developed out of the conjunction of a narrowing of understandings of the system structure and a privileging of this structure in explanation. Rather than coming into being with the inception of a single theory, it grew slowly as the broader positivist project which informed the majority of post war international relations theory developed, gaining strength only gradually, in each new step towards science. Rather than operating by straightforwardly privileging the reading of the post war period through the Cold War, it subtly constricted both the breadth and depth of the "discipline's" focus by progressively eliminating the background noise of events beyond the reach of the balance of power, all the time justifying this tunnel vision in the name of parsimonious explanation. Above all, however, what this analysis implies is that the myth of progress according to which the "discipline" has advanced in the post war period towards a superior, scientific understanding of international politics is mistaken. The distorting influence of the Cold War "paradigm" is ultimately rooted in precisely this modernist agenda, rendering suspect not only its claims, but above all its ambitions.

Notes

1 Perhaps the best example of this is Kenneth Waltz's *Theory Of International Politics*, (1979, pp.88-101).

2 For a good critique of this tendency, see Barry Buzan's *People, States, and Fear*, (1991, pp.1-14).

3 For a good example of this tendency, see Richard Crockett's *The Fifty Years Wars*, (1995).

4 In this volume, this type of complaint is reflected in the chapters by Ponting and Rogers.

5 See, on this subject, Keohane and Nye (1989), Jones and Willets (1984), Rosenau and Tromp (1989).

6 See, on this subject, Krasner (1983), Rosenau and Czempiel (1992), Ruggie (1993), Rittberger (1995).

7 On this subject, see, for instance, Donaldson (1986), Krasner (1985).

8 On this subject, see Adamson (1990), Cairncross (1990), Kennedy (1994), Hurrell and Kingsley (1992), Porter and Brown (1991).

9 See, for instance, Booth (1991, p.530), Rosenberg (1990, p.298), Wendt, (1992, pp.391-5).

10 For an excellent overview of idealist thought see Wilson and Long (1996).

11 The best examples of this position are Morgenthau (1960, Pt.2), and Kissinger (1964, pp.1-3).

12 The reference to what amounted to appeasement was, of course, removed from the second edition (Smith, 1986, pp.83-7).

13 The role that realism has played in framing the "discipline's" approach to international politics has been well documented. See, for instance, Dougherty and Pfaltzgraff (1971, p.15), Gaddis (1992/3, p.7), Hoffmann (1977, p.44), Olson (1972, pp.19-20), Vasquez (1983).

14 Just how much neorealism reflects traditional realist concerns is, of course, a matter of intense debate. See especially, on this subject, Ashley (1981, 1984). However, it is not disputed that neorealism adopts from classical realism its emphasis on the structure of major power politics.

15 The classic examples of this element of his thought are *The Cloud of Danger*, (1978, pp.32-41), and *The Nuclear Delusion*, (1984, pp.72-4), but it is worth noting that this theme was present as early as the mid 1950s (Kennan, 1954, pp.110-4).

16 Even institutionalists, for instance, concede the importance of a hegemonic power to the construction of regimes: they only contest whether the collapse

of hegemony implies a collapse of regimes. See, for instance, Keohane (1984).

17 Even critical theorists concede this. They only contest whether this is all we should focus on. See, for instance, Booth (1991, p.530).

18 I examine Morton Kaplan's theory here because it is the single most influential attempt to construct a theory of international politics from a behaviouralist perspective - Finnegan's 1972 survey of international relations scholars finding that his *System and Process in International Politics* was cited as the leading scholarly work in the field by respondents after only *Politics Among Nations* (Finnegan, 1972, cited in Vasquez, 1983, pp.26, 42-6). For a wider perspective on behaviouralist thought, see, for instance, the essays contained in Singer's *Human Behaviour and International Politics* (1965) and *Quantitative International Politics* (1968).

19 Criticism of the narrowness of Kaplan's theory was made most notably by Hedley Bull (1969, pp.31-3). Also see, on this point, Kaplan's defence of his position against Bull's wider critique (1969).

20 Whilst there are, of course, a wide variety of "neorealist" positions, I focus here very specifically on Waltz because of his dominant position within the school. For a wider perspective on neorealism see, for instance, the essays contained in Brown *et al* (1995), Baldwin (1992), and Kegley (1995).

21 It is worth noting that Waltz removes the arrangement of the units from the conception of structure (1979, pp.58, 98, 168-9).

22 This criticism was voiced most explicitly by Ruggie (1986, pp.148, 151-2). However, it has also been made by a wide variety of other authors, most noticeably Booth (1991 p.537), Buzan *et al* (1993, pp.25-8 and Ch.4 passim), Cox (1986, pp.218-20), Keohane (1986, pp.190-7), Kratochwil (1993, p.64), Rosenberg (1990, p.295).

23 See also on this point, Buzan *et al* (1993, pp.23-4, 42), Linklater (1995, p.253).

24 See, for instance, Griffiths (1995, pp.35-77), Rosenberg, (1990, pp.289-92).

25 For a more detailed exposition of this conception of realist theory, see Murray (1996, pp.93-6) and (1997, pp.73-9).

26 Similar concerns are reflected in behaviouralism more generally. See, for instance, Singer (1965, pp.1-4; 1968, pp.1-3).

27 Again, similar concerns were reflected across the field, see for instance, Singer (1965, pp.4-5; 1968, p.6). Given that what is at stake here is the impact of the attempt to generate a science of international relations, I do not propose to evaluate either the merits of such claims nor whether Kaplan fulfils them here. For criticism of Kaplan's success in living up to these standards see Hoffmann (1959, p.357) and Bull (1969, pp.32-3). For a more general critique of Kaplan's understanding of science see Levy (1969, pp.88-106). It should be noted in this context that Kaplan did not claim to have achieved such a fully deductive theory; it was merely that this was his objective (1964, preface; 1969, pp.46-7 n.9).

28 Again, given that what is at stake here is the impact of the attempt to generate a science of international relations, I do not propose to evaluate either the merits of such claims nor whether Waltz fulfils them here. For a good survey of the problems in Waltz's understanding of theory, however, the reader may refer to Charles Jones' section in *The Logic of Anarchy* (Buzan *et al*, 1993, Pt. 3, esp. pp.186-90).

29 More generally, on this problem, see Kaplan's comments in "Problems of theory building and theory confirmation," (1961). Again, a similar concern for the reduction of variables to systematisable proportions was reflected across the behaviouralist movement. See, for instance, Singer (1966, p.14; 1968, p.7).

30 Specifically, Rosenberg was referring to *Politics Among Nations* and, to a lesser extent, Carr's *Twenty Years Crisis* here.

31 These themes were to characterise Morgenthau's work throughout his life (1958, pp.17-8; 1970, pp.241-61).

32 It should be noted that Kaplan did not claim to be able to predict individual actions due to the presence of "too many free parameters." Similar predictive concerns informed those who followed Kaplan. See, for instance, Singer (1965, pp.1-2).

33 Again, similar concerns pervade the work of those who came after Kaplan. See, for instance, Singer (1968, p.6).

34 See also on this theme, Cox (1986, pp.207-8).

2 Explaining the Cold War

CHARLES REYNOLDS

There are two principal questions to be asked when explaining the Cold War. The primary one is what is explanation? It is primary because in answering it we can then proceed to the secondary question, "What was the Cold War?" Explanation is a means of creating knowledge. Although it is productive of understanding and intelligibility this is not its main purpose. A situation may be meaningful but not true. Meaning is not a sufficient condition for truth. By truth I do not mean some universal, absolute, or objective standard, against which all claims to knowledge can be measured, but some criterion of adequacy external to the putative explanation which provides a means of assessing it.[1]

A full account of explanation is not possible here but some basic points can be made. There are certain conditions which require satisfaction if a claim to knowledge is made. Firstly, the explanation must be logically independent of the subject of explanation. Secondly, if there is a generalising element in the putative explanation some justification is necessary. Is the argument causal? If so, then the application and extent of the necessary and sufficient conditions for that class of events and the principle of association must be specified. If the generalising is probabilistic then the frequency principle must be stated together with the associated conditions and so on. If the argument is teleological or colligatory, then again some justification of the criteria of selection of empirical data or facts is needed. Thirdly, the putative explanation should be testable according to some external criteria of reference so that it can be shown to be adequate. In doing this solipsism or circular argument can be avoided. If putative explanations do not or cannot fulfil these conditions, then, however intelligible or plausible, they cannot genuinely explain.

Descriptions are factual statements which are satisfying where we understand their coherence and where their factual content is true. However, they do not provide us with more than understanding. Although meaningful, they do not answer the question "why"? In the context of the Cold War they offer a record or chronicle but not an explanation.

If we challenge a description the challenge is usually either about the criterion of selection or its completeness. But a complete description is a chimaera. Explanations are challenged on the grounds of their adequacy (Lipton, ... p.22) and this depends on a criterion external to them. Descriptions are often associated with explanations, either with the tentative hypotheses which begin an enquiry, or with the results of an enquiry, but they are not substitutes for explanation. The answer to a question often constitutes a state of affairs which is shown to be the case. Showing it to be the case is what an explanation does.

From this necessarily brief account we can see that the question *what was the Cold War,* or indeed any empirical question, will pose further questions which ask why certain events occurred, actions and decisions were taken, and why there were specific consequences. The way in which these questions are answered and to some extent the way in which they are formulated will depend on whichever methodology is chosen. It must produce answers which are testable and the product of genuine explanation if we are to claim knowledge. It is my contention that while there are general conditions for explanation such as I have outlined above, there are different and varied modes of explanation which have their own additional criteria of logic and adequacy.

In the context of the Cold War there are a number of approaches which range from broad generalising conceptual frameworks such as neo-realism, the materialist framework of the neo-Marxists, to colligations organised around a specific concept, and particularist views which centre on historical narrative, historical individualism and reason-giving accounts. There are problems with all of them (Smith, 1987, Bhaskar, 1989). Before considering them let us examine the problem of the focus for an explanation of the Cold War.

This is intimately tied to the question of methodology.[2] If for example, the focus is on Soviet-US rivalry in terms of the personalities of the political leaders of these countries then the Cold War becomes a series of actions-reactions-interactions in terms of their reasoning and perceptions. The context of such reasoning is limited to their rivalries and their manifestation. Much is thus left out as either irrelevant or epiphenomenal, including domestic and international contexts. Other concerns which existed both contingent on, and parallel to, the Cold War, such as economic policy and national interests only tangential to the asserted Soviet or US challenge are ignored. Events such as Suez, the workings of the Bretton Woods system, the creation of the EEC, and Middle East politics, to take but a few examples, yet which form part of the warp and woof of international politics and the perceptions and agendas of political leaders, are marginalised. The contextual nature of the policy and of decision making is thus limited by a focus on the Cold War and by an emphasis on personality.

Equally, a focus on processes and structure is also limited in terms of selection of facts and events. A methodology based on interactive and determining processes ignores personalities and selects facts which are then treated as discrete events independent of a context of reasoning. The reasoning of the actors is considered to be either irrelevant or epiphenomenal to be explained in terms of structure. The same is true of putative explanations which refer to factors and variables such as ideologies or economic forces. The point being made here is that the subject matter of an explanation of the Cold War is not given but is determined by the nature of the explanatory approach. It follows from this that the facts selected will not be the same facts for different methodological approaches. The creation of NATO for example and the US commitment to Western Europe are certainly facts. But they can be seen as the consequence of security competition (neo-realism)[3] and therefore explicable in terms of structure and process. Or they can be seen as acts stemming from specific intentions and reasoning (historical individualism). The "facts" do not speak for themselves. Selection is inevitable accepting that the past is a "seamless web" and all things are ultimately interrelated. But selection should not produce a distortion of the enquiry because of unexamined assumptions about its focus. The account must not be solipsistic or circular.

Let us look at the sort of questions which might be asked about the Cold War. The first are concerned with the problem of origins. Why did the wartime alliance dissolve into two mutually hostile groups of states? Why was there no peace treaty dealing with Germany? Why did a system of mutually opposed alliances appear together with an arms race firstly in Europe and then extending to the globe? Why did this confrontation not result in actual belligerence, except marginally in areas remote from the main areas of contention? Was this a balance of power? Why did convergence in security policy and strategy begin in the 1960's? Why did this turn into co-operative security based on mutual defensive deterrence with a common rationale? Why did relations between the nominally contending states change? Why and when did the Cold War end?

These questions of course contain assumptions which are in themselves questionable. They also beg the fundamental question "what was the Cold War?" Nor do they constitute an exhaustive list. But answers to them may well produce an explanation of the Cold War. At the beginning of an enquiry such questions and their assumptions stand as conjectures or empirical hypotheses and do not determine conclusions in a closed loop. As the enquiry continues, depending on its methodology, questions change or are redefined.

Nor should it be assumed that they can be asked and answered in an empirical void. The innovative aspect of the post-war period was the emergency in world politics of two states which were formerly isolated - the United States and the USSR. Most of the initiatives which led to the confrontation known as the Cold War were taken by them. Their rivalry seemed to be the pivot around which all international politics revolved. However, the assumption of bi-polarity and of Cold War dominance is facile. There were trends and developments in the world of states which were independent of the relationship between the Soviet Union and the United States which were to produce a situation which neither of them could control or exploit unilaterally, albeit that it was to some extent largely of their own making. It was the unintended product of their own decisions and actions.

The two most important developments were firstly, the nuclear arms race (Freedman, 1981) which led to strategic impasse. The second was the emancipation of the major European empires and a huge increase in the number of nation-states. This in conjunction with the policy of free trade based on the Bretton Woods system and the dominance of the dollar, produced a great expansion in trade and economic exchange in the free world economy. It spelled the end of economic nationalism and the kind of economic autarchy and protectionism which preceded the Second World War. Although this process was initially dominated by the United States it evolved into a de-regulated interdependent multilateral economic system. Parallel with this development was the appearance of regional associations such as the EEC (EU). This was far from being a bi-polar world.

The movement towards de-colonisation, de-regulation and free trade was directly linked to the revolution in strategy produced by the unintended consequences of the nuclear arms race. National economies, particularly those of the states which were to form the G7 group, could be disconnected from security needs in a way not possible in the pre-war and early post war periods. Security was not compromised by an opening of national economies to world market forces once the major states had moved into mutual defensive deterrence, stabilised by arms control agreements. A radical shift had occurred by the early 1970s in the overall strategic relationship. The base strategies and the complex network of political relationships necessary to support them had ceased to be relevant.

In addition there were political relationships and conflicts which were largely outside the Cold War. These included the Arab-Israeli conflict, the Sino-Soviet split, the rise of the Far East and South-Eastern economies and of Japan, regional conflicts between India and China, India and Pakistan, and the Suez crisis, and Middle East politics generally, to name but a few.

The Cold War itself was not a static relationship.[4] We can discern a number of distinct phases in US-Soviet relations. The first was the containment and consolidation of the strategic, economic and diplomatic positions of the major powers over the period 1946-55. It is this period which most closely fits the bi-polar model. In 1955 the Austrian State treaty cleared up the remaining post-war anomaly (with the important exceptions of Germany and Korea) and two alliance systems faced each other in Europe. Effectively a balance of power system seemed to exist.

The US policy of containment extended beyond Europe although here serious divisions existed between the Allies and also between the Soviet Union and China. The phase of the global containment of communism effectively ended with the Vietnam War. At the same time as US policies became global, convergence in strategic policy began with the Cuban Missile Crisis of 1962. The period between 1962 and 1972 saw the development of ICBM/thermo-nuclear weapons systems as the main basis for security. The arms race in its qualitative phase was abandoned with the SALT 1 Treaty in which ABM systems were effectively banned. From that point the strategic rationale of mutual defensive deterrence was maintained and security co-operation rather than competition was the basis of the US-Soviet relationship. The final phase came with the abandonment of extended deterrence with the INF treaty of 1987 and the collapse of the Soviet Union and the re-unification of Germany. The so-called Second Cold War was essentially a conflict over extended deterrence stemming from the emplacement of Soviet SS 20 missiles in Eastern Europe exacerbated by the Soviet intervention in Afghanistan. It was not a renewal of the strategic arms race. Nor was the United States' Strategic Defence Initiative (Star Wars) more than a threat to begin a highly expensive arms race with the Soviet Union at a time when the Soviet economy was in great difficulties. The INF Treaty effectively resolved the conflict. The term "the Cold War" seems an ambiguous label to cover all these developments and radically oversimplifies the complex politics of the US-Soviet relationship.

However, leaving aside the questions of labelling and focus, we can make the nominal assumption that the Cold War was a number of different forms of military, economic and political competition between the United States and the Soviet Union, the former associated with a number of allies not wholly sharing its concerns, and the latter with a number of satellite states lacking independent foreign and defence policies. In seeking to explain this competition there are two broad methodological options (Neufeld, 1995) containing a number of variants. The first is theoretical in that generalising arguments and concepts are used to explain in structural and systemic terms the inter-relations of states. In this category there are the neo-realist and the neo-Marxist schools. The colligatory approach[5] is something of a hybrid between this and the second approach. This last treats states not as an entity with specific attributes and functions, but as governments engaged in reasoning, making decisions, and taking action. The focus here is placed upon individuals, policies and perception. In my view these are not complementary approaches nor can they be synthesised because they employ two completely different sets of references and two distinct criteria of adequacy. Colligations, as we shall see, have implications which relate to both.

Turning to neo-realism as an explanatory approach to the Cold War (Outhwaite, 1987, pp.51-54, 107-116), the central concept is that of structure. Structure is seen as an inherent set of constraining or inducing conditions which act as parameters for options and choice. In the context of inter-state relations the dominant "reality" is security competition arising out of the prevalent condition of anarchy. The state is the only guarantor of its liberty and freedoms and coexists with other states equally occupied with guaranteeing their existence. National security is preoccupied with translating the danger from other states into practical policies for survival. Given that the mode of inter-state politics is adversarial, following from the condition of anarchy, the state is engaged in creating and maintaining the means of survival, i.e. a capability for successful defence and for improving the chances of survival by extending this capability through successful war and the creation of a peace or form of order which makes it more secure. Negotiation and diplomacy are backed with threats, actual or potential, of inimical action. Alliances are only temporary truces between states, and allies become enemies, and vice versa, as the empirical conditions, military, political and technological, change. No war has ever finally settled the question of national security because one state's security is always another state's insecurity and the struggle goes on. States do not have the choice to opt out of this struggle because neutrality is not respected should their existence impinge on the struggles of the other powers.

There are a number of variables which affect this competition and attempts to control them have been unsuccessful. The key variable is weapons technology which, although static at times, is open to radical innovations which seriously affect military relativities and temporary periods of stability. The most recent of these is the thermo-nuclear weapon and the inter-continental ballistic missile. Other variables are political stability, population, technological sophistication, economic structure and strength, command over resources, spatial relations and geography, logistics and communication and so on. Each individual state has its own unique security problem depending on the relevance and weighting of these variables. They are contingent on the extant weapons technology and circumstances. In the present nuclear age, for example, the significance of man-power, spatial relations and overall resources are no longer relevant to security, although they may well be to the non-nuclear states.

The essence of the neo-realist approach is that states exist in a condition of anarchy. The only guarantor of security is the state. States are thus compelled to increase their capabilities to provide it. They are structured to do so. If we look at the Cold War in the light of this argument it is clear that from the point of view of security the Second World War solved nothing. There was a security dilemma for both the victors and the vanquished. Britain for example, pursuing its centuries old policy of frustrating great power domination over the continent of Europe, had merely replaced Germany with the Soviet Union. The United States, although possessing a monopoly of both atomic bombs and a delivery system, could not deploy these in a satisfactory defence without forward bases. Aware that this monopoly could not be maintained indefinitely, it could not withdraw into isolation. The Soviet Union feared both the United States and its monopoly but also feared a future German recovery. This last fear was shared by both France and Britain.

The consequence of security fears was the division of Europe[6] with the creation of the two Germanies, the formation of two opposed alliance systems, the Warsaw Pact and NATO, and a nuclear arms race joined in not only by the United States and the Soviet Union but also by France and Britain and, later, China. A traditional balance of power system appears to have come into being by 1955. Relative stability existed in Europe, marred by the equivocal status of Germany and Berlin; elsewhere, the two major powers sought to extend their power and influence. Why was the Cold War so stable? Why did war not occur?

The answer seems to lie in the nuclear arms race which, contrary to expectations, resulted neither in a war nor the superiority of one side over the other but in a stalemate which destroyed the conventional balance. Co-operative security, underpinned by tacit consent and formal arms control agreements, took its place. Avoiding war became the chief preoccupation of the contending states because the consequences of a nuclear war would be so radical that no state interest, including that of security, could be served by it. The contortions of extended deterrence and the attempt to protect non-nuclear allies, as well as the retention of control over territory, only masked the powerlessness of the nuclear states in their attempt to relate political power to military capability. The final folly of the Vietnam War (and perhaps that of the Soviet intervention in Afghanistan) indicated that increasing capability by extending control and influence over other states was irrelevant in the nuclear age unless specific interests were engaged as in the Gulf. Economic benefits could be realised by engagement in a free global interdependent and multilateral market. The Soviet Union and China came eventually to realise this.[7] Security was based on the possession of a viable nuclear deterrent and command economies were irrelevant to this. In the case of the Soviet Union control over subordinate states and territories and the fear of a revived and reunified Germany could be abandoned. The nature of national security had radically changed.

None of these changes are explained by the neo-realist thesis. In particular the interplay between the domestic dimension of the state and its outward face and the interplay between economics and politics are ignored or minimised. It is assumed that value systems, ideologies, policy making and political cultures, where they are deemed relevant, simply reinforce the outward drive of the state to power. The influences of co-operation between states, whether as part of a global market system, or through regional association, or both, and its réciprocating effects inside and outside the state are not analysed (Spero, 1990). Welfarism and the demand for material prosperity together with enhanced expectations within national societies are subordinated to the dynamics of inter-state competition.

If we look at the neo-realist argument more closely we can see that structure is its most important concept. All action is structured in the sense that it is based on expectations of proper action, i.e. it takes place in a social context. The contention of the neo-realists is that this constitutes a structure which is imposed on action. The state exists in an environment which is anarchic and therefore action is structured by it and linked directly to self-preservation and its conditions. This context-structure is in some sense independent of the state but is also constituted by the actions of the state. In other words structure is both a "given" and an artefact.

If structure has this Janus-like character is it independent of the actor so that it stands as a cause of action? Alternatively, is it a product of the actor's reasoning in that it stands as a set of assumptions and expectations about the world of states which itself can change and be revised? Do we, in short, look at structure from the point of view of the actor or from the point of view of the neo-realist? The methodological implications of this distinction are, firstly, if we cannot distinguish between action and structure, either causally, or as empirical phenomena, then our conclusions simply reify our assumptions. Secondly, if we cannot refer to an independent criterion of adequacy we have no means of attesting our claim to explanation. If structure does not constitute a cause of action what is its function in explanation? As a concept it may help us to understand that action is in some way systematised and often interactive but this does not advance beyond description. If it is treated as an aspect of reasoning then, if we can identify the assumptions made by the actor (which may well conform to the model of security competition) we can separate intention from action in a non-causal way and so explain it. The criterion of adequacy here is evidence of reasoning. Reasoning and action stand in a non-causal relation in that having intentions does not entail the action.[8] They are independent of each other and we can only know what the action (or inaction) was, *ex post facto*.

Inter-state relations are indeed structured and rule-guided as is any form of practical reasoning. Rationality in the pursuit of security is instrumental in the sense that means are formulated to fulfil ends in the light of what is taken to be capability. This can be illustrated by the Vietnam War in which the overall end, that of securing a friendly government, was not related to other ends, such as seeking accommodation with the Soviet Union over nuclear co-operation. The means were limited so as to guarantee either an expanding and different war or defeat. This process of reasoning is open to change and assumptions may be revised as circumstances change and other priorities emerge. But changes of this kind are not explained through an appeal to structure. If structure is constituted as an artefact then change can simply be explained in terms of the reasoning itself and not by an appeal to externalities of action. Although action may be rule-guided in the form of a bounded rationality this is derived from the perceptions of the actor as to the nature of the context of action. Misconceptions abound in the world of action; the case of the Vietnam War again illustrates this in the gulf existing between the perceptions of the North Vietnamese and those of the United States. But the process of reasoning is flexible enough to adapt to the proposition that circumstances alter cases. The contenders during the Cuban Missile Crisis of 1962 (Lechuga, 1995) certainly had no common ground at its beginning and there was considerable misapprehension as to each other's motives and intentions, but they had common ground at the end.

The same point can be made about power conceived of as capability. This again is not an external attribute but an assessment of relative strengths, weaknesses, and options, which may be confounded when put to the test. By common-sense standards the United States had the power to annihilate North Vietnam but in practice it was not able to exercise it. Neo-realism ignores choice in political judgement. Power is a concept which is inherently ambiguous when applied to political action. We can only know when power exists after it has been exercised and this makes it tautologous. To have succeeded, power must have been exercised, but what is power? It has a rough equivalence to certain attributes in practical reasoning. A David does not normally beat a Goliath. But instrumental rationality[9] is not based on rigid theoretical grounds and the question of capability and its constitution is a matter of political judgement made by actors based on assumptions open to change.

Neo-realism thus seems to collapse into idealism (Reynolds, 1992, p.80) if it simply constitutes a set of assumptions about the "real" world. These assumptions, if held by the actors themselves, can be part of an explanation. But their imposition on the world of states by neo-realists independent of this requires the satisfaction of the conditions relevant to valid explanations. If the subjective understanding of the actor is the basis of the alleged structure which he helps to create then explanation lies in establishing the level and degree of intersubjectivity between actors. There is no impersonal and objective structure for action operating as a determinant operating independently of the actors.

If it is asserted that the intersubjective domain exists independently of the actors and is the basis of explanation, then this should not be a circular argument with the actors' behaviour being asserted as evidence of this pre-existing intersubjective structure. Anarchy cannot at one and the same time be both a cause and an effect of human action. And, if it is an artefact, it is the reasoning which constitutes it which is the source of explanation and this is restricted *ex post facto* to time, place and the individuals. It is a product of consciousness. How this last can be incorporated into an explanatory form will be examined later in this chapter.

If we look at the reverse of the neo-realist approach[10] and examine the concept of structure in terms of the social dimension of the state we face similar objections. If structures are to be defined as a set of rules and assumptions constraining and inducing forms of action how can such influences be shown to operate? We cannot, as we have seen, demonstrate them through action itself without circularity. In the case of the Cold War there are a number of applications of the concept of social based structures which seek to explain it. First of all, the Cold War can be conceived of as an ideological struggle between two belief systems, both incompatible and both relating to action with a clear set of core values in specific nation-states each with their ideologically defined agendas. Indeed this view was made explicitly by Truman and Stalin and continued by their successors. The struggle was between revolutionary communism represented by the Soviet Union (and China) and by liberal democracy represented by the United States and her democratic allies. The defeat of fascism brought about another ideological confrontation. The argument here is that the outward aspect of a state is determined by its internal composition, its polity and its belief system. This is compatible with the core value of the defence of the integrity of the state as a state. More is being defended here than territory; a way of life is at stake. Certainly the Soviet Union was considered to be the revolutionary leader embodying Marxist values and integrity. The conflict with China was conducted in ideological terms as much as in military confrontation. Equally, the United States was represented as the leader of the Free World and guardian of its values. But did the Cold War originate over ideological differences as an extension of domestically based value systems with universal claims? Did domestic social structures determine the outward stance of the state in a world of states? (Ashley in Keohane, 1986, p.271). The neo-realist would consider this aspect as merely reinforcing the state in its struggle for security.

If social structure was seen to have the same role as global political structure in the neo-realist argument then the same objections considered earlier would apply. The point here in terms of explanation is that if it turns on perception and intention then we are asking the question "Were the policy makers of the Cold War ideologically motivated?"

The crude determinism of structurally directed action is not relevant here. Nor is any psychosocial or psychologistical theory of consciousness being proposed. The question is one of distinguishing between explanation and justification. This entails establishing whether reasons proferred by actors (which might indeed be ideological) were the actual reasons reflecting motive and intention or are arguments which seek to justify action as a means of engaging support or deflecting dissent. This is almost entirely a problem for assessing action within a democratic framework where persuasion and manipulation are the main methods of obtaining consent. Secrecy, of course, is useful. In non-democratic states the problem is different, secrecy makes investigation difficult and repression and non-accountability compound the difficulty. Certainly the language of justification abounds during the Cold War; so far as the United States and the Soviet Union are concerned this was mostly a dialogue of the deaf. The sterile debates of the United Nations are evidence of this. It must be assumed that political leaders were addressing their domestic clientele and using declaratory rhetoric for domestic purposes (Siracusa, 1978, pp.178-

186, 224-229). Was this more than rhetoric? If, for example, we look at the origins of the Cold War, both the Truman Doctrine speech of 1947 and Stalin's speech in Moscow in 1946 were ideological statements. They had profound significance as a declaration of position without being precise about policy. They were statements of principle while retaining a degree of pragmatism. We know far more about Truman's domestic situation than about Stalin's. Truman was in a weak position in spite of being leader of the world's most dominant economy and in military terms most powerful state.

He was an obscure politician who inherited the Presidency on Roosevelt's death in April 1945. He did not represent his party, two members of which, Henry Wallace, a former Vice-President and James Byrnes, who had been promised the Vice-Presidency, which Roosevelt offered to Truman, were much more powerful figures. Politics in the United States were moving away from the New Deal era and towards the right. The economy was booming and federal intervention was no longer necessary or indeed politic. Yet adjustment to peace-time conditions and the absorption of twelve million service people into the economy presented problems. The near bankruptcy of Britain and the devastation of the second most important world economy, Germany, threatened a return to the chaotic conditions, both economic and political, which preceded the Second World War. A new force had appeared, the Soviet Union, and Stalin's triumphalism, couched in ideological terms as a victory for Socialism, indicated that at the very least the Soviet Union would have a major say in postwar European, if not world, politics. Truman faced important decisions from a domestically weak position.[11] His policy had two dimensions; improving his domestic position, through cultivating a bi-partisan programme and engaging in rhetorical persuasion to awake the electorate to a new danger - communism - and engaging in largely secret diplomacy and graduated steps to establish a permanent commitment to Western European security. He was mindful of the failure of the Democrat President Wilson to obtain both Congressional and electoral support for the post-First World War settlement.

The Truman Doctrine speech was only one of many attempts to gain general support for a major change both in foreign and economic policy. Lend-lease had provided some basis for the opening out of the US economy and the Keynes mission loan to Britain, with its conditions, indicated that the direction of economic policy was towards a free world market economy (Hogan, 1987). The major problem for Truman was European economic recovery, in particular German economic revival. This would require large amounts of federal aid to a former enemy as well as to Britain, France and

Italy, a "co-belligerent". But national security also required foreign entanglements. The German problem could not be resolved by economic means alone, given the fears in Europe, including the Soviet Union, of German recovery. What would restrain a revitalised Germany from making yet another challenge to the post-war world order? A stable security system with the United States as its principal guarantor and a solution to the German problem were the answers. This would provide the basis for the development of an open system of economic exchange. NATO and Marshall Aid were the two pillars of this policy.

The period when ideological rhetoric was at its strongest was also the period in which the policies and decisions on both sides were implemented resulting in the division of Europe. The diplomatic and political stalemate known as the Cold War ended with the resumption of negotiations in 1955 and agreement on the Austrian State treaty.[12] After this, although relations were often acrimonious and although there appeared to be a permanent confrontation, the traditional search for relative advantage within a balanced framework of diplomacy replaced intransigence. The world outside Europe presented problems and its political instability, resulting from the collapse of imperial rule, offered opportunities for contention and conflict, but Europe itself had been stabilised. The absence of anything other than rhetorical denunciation of the Soviet interventions in Hungary in 1956 and in Czechoslovakia in 1968 on the part of the United States indicated this. Underlying this "normal" diplomacy was the nuclear arms race which was to have its own radical effects on US/USSR relations.

Ideological statements, while often used as justifications for policy, such as defence appropriation, or foreign interventions, for internal purposes, never prevented serious negotiation. Issues such as human rights or Jewish emigration from the Soviet Union were used selectively. "The evil Empire" image although first expressed by President Reagan in his first term of office reflected the image generally purveyed by past US Administrations. In this particular case, the arguments against arms control agreements with the Soviet Union became arguments for arms control, culminating in the INF Agreement of 1987. The problem for the Administration was that the demons conjured by them to support ventures such as intervention in Central and South America, the Vietnam War, etc. or expensive weapons programmes, aroused unfulfillable expectations and inhibited changes of policy. The propaganda battle fought at the height of the Cold War to obtain popular support locked future Administrations into a set of assumptions and expectations in American political culture which inhibited their freedom of action in foreign and defence policy.[13]

It was Nixon, a well known anti-communist, who was to release the United States from these inhibitions, although it took the divisions and defeats of the Vietnam War to provide the inducement (Kissinger, 1979). The point here is that attitudes linked to anti-communist rhetoric and to prevalent values in US society have only a constraining influence. They do not dictate policy. Action is expected but not directed. Both Kennedy and Johnson would have faced political difficulties if they had not satisfied expectations over intervention of some kind in Indo-China in the early 1960s. Yet at the same time, after the Cuban Missile Crisis of 1962, a convergence between the United States and the Soviet Union on security issues and the nuclear arms race was beginning to emerge, which undermined the assumptions of the policy of the global containment of communism. Vietnam represented the high point of the attempt to enforce global containment, and its failure reduced the importance of declaratory policy with its ideological connotations. Later use associated with the "Second Cold War" was manipulative but did not prevent serious negotiation. Indeed, serious negotiation with the Soviet Union continued over the Cold War period, beginning with the Austrian State Treaty of 1955, the Cuban Missile Crisis, the Kissinger-Nixon negotiations, and on arms control, including SALT I and II, numerous limitation agreements and the INF Agreement of 1987. Ideology seemed relevant only in a domestic context and that only as an aspect of political manipulation. In this context it should be noted that the United States had allies, equally democratic, whose justification of policy, while often appealing to commonly held values, did not adopt the strident anti-communism championed by their major ally. While adhering to a common line in Europe, albeit differing in terms of their contributions to NATO and in their separate security policies, there was a conspicuous absence of agreement on the global aspects of the containment of communism, especially in SE Asia and the Far East.[14]

Turning to materialist explanations of the Cold War, we find that there are two aspects to this, one corresponding to the quasi-determinist approach of the neo-realist, but substituting economic forces rather than the power-security dynamic. The other stresses the importance of economics in formulating policies and decisions. A concern for security is really a concern for the political stability necessary for the promotion of economic ends, notably, on the one side, the promotion of liberal exchange and the creation of a free world market economy dominated by the dollar, and on the other side the promotion of socialism and an economic system which ultimately destroyed the state itself. In a sense, both of these approaches are ideological in nature, based upon universalist principles and values. They have different methodologies however, and implications for explanation which depend on different criteria.

The first approach is theoretical and is based upon propositions and concepts which treat modes of production as the determinant of the epiphenomena of political, social and cultural life. It is Marxist in inspiration in that it has a materialist base.[15] Only a brief summary of the argument is possible here. It was not Marx who developed a theory of imperialism, but Lenin and his followers (Lenin, 1917). Marx conceived of the contradictions of capitalism arising out of class conflict and the labour theory of value in which capital is extracted from a finite labour supply, eventually ending in collapse as it is exhausted. But it was Lenin who moved the locus of capitalism from the nation-state *per se* to its international form as imperialism. Using Hilferding's (Hilferding, 1910) concept of finance-capitalism and Hobson's thesis, (Hobson, 1902) he argued that capital sought to exploit world labour in the form of competition for economic territory. This too was finite and, after catastrophic wars, capitalism would eventually collapse with world revolution. Later, neo-Marxist revisionists explained why world revolution was delayed and asserted a new form of capitalism which exploited both the advanced industrialised countries and the developing states. Formal empire had yielded to an expansion of capitalism in the form of new institutions, such as the multi-national corporation, (Lall and Streeten, 1977; Reynolds, 1981) which exploited both home and host countries. Originating in the most advanced capitalist state, the United States, the process of capitalist development began with the Bretton Woods system, dominated by the dollar and the commanding position of the US economy in the world, and became free of national control. The contemporary free world market economy was the result, unregulated, distorting both advanced and undeveloped economies alike.

On the other side of the equation socialist economies sought both to preserve the authenticity of the revolution and the building of communism and to extend it to the rest of the world. They had both an evangelical and a defensive role, resisting the expansion of capitalism. In the event, this effort failed. The "explanation" of the Cold War and indeed of international politics in general is thus seen as an inter-play between economics and politics. The economic dynamic of capitalist expansion dictates the competitive nature of inter-state relations. There is competition between the capitalist states and the socialist states and between the capitalist states and the underdeveloped states. The Cold War itself is only one manifestation of this competition. It is a mirror image of the neo-realist argument in that it replaces power politics with an economic drive. The former are simply the consequences of the latter. Marshall Aid's European Recovery Programme, the Bretton Woods system itself, the evolution of GATT, local protectionism such as the EU, the spread of capitalism to SE Asia, the Far East and Japanese economic growth and incorporation all manifest the dominance of this economic drive.

The problems with this argument are the same as those of neo-realism. They extend from the ambiguity of the central concepts, in this case - capitalism - to the circularity of the thesis. How can the existence of this economic drive be separated from the phenomena which "prove" it so that the conclusions do not reify the assumptions? The concept of capitalism as an impersonal economic phenomenon which determines economic and political outcomes is not proven by demonstrating that political leaders are often concerned by economic problems. Materialist considerations are not the sole form of motivation. What is called welfare and the relationship between the state and citizens are enmeshed as much with economics as with politics. Values are involved in policy making and these are not determined by economic drives yet have an impact on political actions and decisions. They do not necessarily reflect economic rationalisation.

In the context of the Cold War economic recovery and a viable economic order were uppermost in the minds of the victor powers. This was as true of Stalin as it was of the Western leaders. But so also was a concern for a stable post-war political order and for security. Stalin emphasised continually the primacy of Soviet security in his negotiations with his former allies. Protecting the Soviet state as a launching pad for revolution and as the cradle of socialism, certainly was an internal justification for policies as we saw earlier, but in external relations there was sufficient flexibility and desire for compromise to indicate that Soviet leaders were not driven by economic forces. The governments which chose to accept free market economics or command economic systems made political decisions. The Western states did not wish to return to the economic nationalism and protectionism which were factors leading to world war in the inter-war period. Nor did they wish Germany to become a major power in Europe. The solution was US engagement in Europe, the Marshall Plan and NATO. Equally, the Soviet Union feared German recovery. They tacitly acquiesced in the division of Europe and accepted a balance which lasted a long time. These were choices and not the consequence of some deterministic force which compelled them to make these specific choices. They had options and these were considered.

The tension in this analysis of attempts to explain the Cold War has been between arguments which seek to explain in terms of a conceptual framework which treats individuals as acting within a structure, economic or political, which constrains choice or which induces them to act in a particular way, and arguments which emphasise the reasoning of individuals and their conception of context and choice. They are different arguments which lead to different explanations not in terms of their content or empirical focus, but in terms of their methodology. The former are theoretical and generalising and some general proposition which is empirically testable, should emerge from them. The latter are particularist and depend upon direct evidence of reasoning and for a full explanation of action and decision on evidence of the actor's conception of context, which may include values and expectations. I turn now to an "explanatory" form which is something of a hybrid and this involves the use of colligations. A colligation is a narrative which organises events around a central concept. It could be, as in the case of neo-realism, the concept of structure in which certain constraining environmental factors - anarchy - exercise an influence on action such as the need to acquire capability. Indeed, shorn of its theoretical pretensions this is what neo-realism actually is - a colligation. We understand inter-state relations as a series of conflicts and competitions in which violence is always a possibility. Of course, explanation is not forthcoming, because this is a descriptive framework which we accept or reject on largely subjective grounds. We could on the same grounds accept the materialist thesis, or indeed any other assembly of facts and events which makes sense of the past. Colligations are most often found in historical interpretations. They employ concepts such as pattern, process, trend, development, rise and fall, sequence, progress, movement and so on. The point here is that a pattern is imposed on events and action by an interpreter who stands outside the context of action. The connection between events and their consequences are revealed to the reader so that sense is made of history. The complex is rendered intelligible. The interpreter has of course the advantages of hind-sight making his or her account from the vantage-point of the "future" so far as the actors are concerned. But what makes this explanatory? (McCullough, 1984; Lloyd, 1992). There is a presupposition that events are somehow connected. The assassination at Sarajevo somehow "led" to world war. The negotiations at Yalta "led" to Soviet domination of Eastern Europe and the division of Germany. If this is not a causal argument, in that some events caused others as effects, and this can be demonstrated, then what kind of argument is it? Why should we, and on what grounds, accept one colligation over another? Do they explain actions on the actors terms? Clearly not, because they adduce connections which are unknown to the actor. Certainly consequences follow actions and these might not be considered or even expected by those who initiate action and events (Nicholson, 1996). But these still form part of reasoning, in the form of reaction, revision, or some form of accommodation, and so on. Equally, there are continuities in reasoning which pass from actor to actor until new sets of assumptions and expectations are formulated. The traditional British concern for security in terms of major power dominance of the continent of Europe, for example, lasted a long time until changing technology and its implications changed policy. The point here is that colligations are rationalisations which depend upon the concepts and the constructs of the interpreter. They are insusceptible to any test, except perhaps that of coherence. And they are independent of the reasoning of the actors whose actions the colligator seeks to explain. Anachronism thus becomes a problem. The interpreter's values and priorities are superimposed upon those of the actor.

Rationalisation in effect substitutes the reasoning of the observer for that of the actor. The basic assumption is that it is a substitution for the actor's own intentionality and meaning. This leads to a common form of rationalisation which asserts the "logic of the situation" as a means of explaining action. The inference is that knowing what a "rational" actor would do in a given situation, once we have identified a similar situation, we can know what the actor actually did or intended. This is often accompanied by some optimalising principle which defines instrumental rationality.

Hence a judgement of rationality is being made in this sort of construct but it is one made by the observer and not the actor. It forms a basis for criticism and for discussions of opportunities missed and mistakes made. It is essentially counter-factual (Edgley, 1969; Elster, 1979; Benn and Mortimore, 1976).

If we are concerned with the rationality of ends in relation to means, then three distinct positions emerge. Firstly, to assert a rational end may imply a principle of rationality which is normative in character, the pursuit, for example, of happiness or the maximisation of satisfaction. This is clearly culturally derived and such principles are linked to value systems that are socially referred rather than universal. Empirical references will be varied and not supportive of a universal generalisation. This is true of both time and space.

Secondly, a rational end may be one that is attainable in terms of the satisfaction of specific empirical conditions. This implies a valid theory, causal in character, that allows us to determine effective action knowing means - ends relationships and their dynamics.

Thirdly, we can conceive of a rational end in terms of attainment but only on the basis of probability, and in the light of experience. This is the practical reasoning of everyday life and is non-theoretical. It is usually the reasoning of the actor, although the other two modes are not precluded; both value based and theoretical forms of reasoning co-exist in policy-making.

In practice, the use of concepts such as rationality in terms of action - the choice of both means and ends - is *ex post facto*, i.e. it takes the form of judgements of past action. Rationalisations made by the observer interpolate a dimension of anachronism in that the narrator judges past actions in the light of his context and understanding. The consequence is a narrative which displaces the centrality of the actor and his or her reasoning and replaces it with the reasoning of the narrator. On what grounds is this explanatory and productive of knowledge? What are the criteria of reference and adequacy to which we can refer competing narratives?

The Cold War seen as a linear progression of actions and events can be constructed as a narrative, or indeed narratives, which make sense according to the framework imposed on it by its interpreters. Intelligibility is certainly possible and sense can be made of the complexities of action. But only description emerges. And descriptions are never complete. Nor are they substitutes for explanation. The central question "Why did an actor decide on action (or inaction)?" is not answered.

If historical colligations and rationalisations are non-explanatory what of historical individualism? This places the focus on the actors reasoning and its criterion of adequacy lies in direct and collateral evidence of this reasoning. What is sought as knowledge is knowledge of what the action was and so no generalisation or causality is involved. On this basis it is the perceptions and understanding of actors which lie at the heart of explanations of the Cold War. In effect, that is what the Cold War was. And of course both actors and perceptions change over time. It was argued earlier that the Cold War, seen in nominal terms as a conflict or conflicts between the United States and the Soviet Union, had several phases depending on the interaction of the perceptions, assumptions, and expectations of the actors. Initially, the conflict was over a Peace treaty for Germany and over different conceptions of economic and security relations. It widened as the United States extended "containment" to the world and as the Soviet Union (and China) countered this move. From treaty building and the creation of spheres of influence the contenders engaged in marginal contests and crises. But underlying this ducking and feinting was an arms race which as it developed was to change radically both sides' assumptions and perceptions of each other's position. The Cuban Missile Crisis in 1962 marked the beginning of this change. Although the decade of the 1960s saw the Vietnam War and the attempt by the United States to maintain the global containment of communism, albeit unsupported by her allies, moves were made in the area of arms control and a general recognition that nuclear war served no rational purpose appeared. The culmination of this recognition came with SALT 1 and the Peace Treaty with Vietnam in 1972 and 1973 respectively. Its political consequences not only included recognition of the defeat in Vietnam, and withdrawal from South East Asia, but also recognition of the People's Republic of China and disengagement from Taiwan. Changes appeared in Europe, with the acceptance of Willy Brandt's *ostpolitik* and of the Potsdam protocols on Germany's eastern frontiers.

The period 1962 to 1972 saw growing co-operation between the major nuclear powers in the area of arms control. Significantly, it was in this period that Britain, against considerable opposition from the Kennedy Administration, obtained an independent nuclear deterrent through the Nassau agreement. And it was in this period that de Gaulle removed NATO Headquarters from Fontainebleau and French forces from NATO. Clearly, Cold War attitudes characteristic of the alliance building period had radically changed. Full acceptance of the implications of this change took some time to work out. The strategic need for alliances and for a defensive glacis in Eastern (and Western) Europe had ended, yet the political apparatus remained intact, (France still remained a member of NATO). The fear of a revived Germany no longer dominated East and West thinking - a nuclear deterrent removed it. The full consequences of these changes occurred when domestic pressures in the Soviet Union and a general realisation that the assumptions of the Cold War were no longer valid "ended" the Cold War. But in substance the Cold War had ended long ago.

From the early 1960s the "Cold War" was characterised by caution, inaction, and accommodation, accompanied by declaratory policy and rhetoric. The most characteristic agreements were negative in that the United States and the Soviet Union agreed to differ, to refrain from certain courses of action, to withdraw, to limit intervention, and to accept the *status quo*. They were positive in another sense, in that restraint and control were preferred to adventurism and confrontation. The existence of mutual defensive deterrence and the joint acceptance of its conditions were largely responsible for this. From confrontation the nominal enemies became tacit allies in maintaining a system of co-operative security which in turn became the basis for an armed peace.

The explanation for this development and its political consequences lies in the understanding, reasoning and perceptions of the actors and not in any pattern, theoretical or colligatory, superimposed on actions and events by "observers" or "narrators". Returning to the methodological points related to explanation made at the beginning of this chapter, such an account is referable to independent criteria in the form of evidence of reasoning, is not circular in that intention can be separated from action, and fulfils both the logical and empirical criteria for explanation. Its conclusions are neither final nor absolute and revision is always possible. New evidence may be discovered and old "evidence" discredited or superseded. Nor does it close off further questions or put enquiry into a closed and ultimately empty conceptual framework.

Notes

1 For a full account of this view of explanation see Reynolds, C., 1992, *The World of States*, Edward Elgar, Aldershot, Chap.1, pp.1-48. See also Hollis, M. and Smith, S., 1990, *Explaining and Understanding International Relations*, Clarendon Press, Oxford; and *International Relations Handbook of Current Theory*, Frances Pinter, London. For an alternative view of explanation but one which stresses the importance of referral and adequacy see Bohman, J., 1991, *New Philosophy of Social Science*, Polity Press, Oxford.

2 A survey of various methodological approaches can be found in Marsh, D. and Stoker, G. eds., 1995, *Theory and Methods in Political Science*, Macmillan, Basingstoke.

3 See Waltz, K.N., 1979, *Theory of International Relations*, Random House, New York; and Keohane, R.O. ed., 1986, *Neo-Realism and its Critics*, Columbian University Press, New York. For a general critical analysis see Outhwaite, W., 1987, *New Philosophies of Social Science*, St Martin's Press, New York.

4 The literature on the Cold War is immense. See in particular Gaddis, J.L., 1987, *The Long Peace*, Oxford University Press, and *We Now Know*, Clarendon Press, Oxford.

5 The term colligation was coined by William Whewell in the 19th century. See Walsh, W.H., 'Colligatory Concepts in History', in Gardiner, P. ed., 1959, *Theories of History*, Free Press, New York.

6 For a good analysis of this development see Loth, W., 1988, *The Division of the World 1941-1945*, St Martin's Press, New York; and Reynolds, D. ed., 1994, *The Origins of the Cold War in Europe: international perspectives*, Yale University Press, New Haven.

7 The USSR consistently refused to accept the concept of deterrence until 1986 (a year before the INF agreement) see 'Study on Deterrence Report of the Secretary-General of the UN 41 Session 7 General Assembly item 64(g)

A/41/432 23rd July 1946'; and Buzan, B., 1987, *The International Politics of Deterrence*, Frances Pinter, London.

8 For an analysis of this distinction see Davidson, D., 1980, 'Actions, Reasons and Causes' in *Essays on Actions and Events*, Oxford University Press, pp.3-20.

9 See Hindess, B., 1988, *Choice, Rationality, and Social Theory*, Urwin Hyman, London; Putnam, H., 1981, *Reason Truth and History*, Cambridge University Press, Cambridge, Chap.7; and for an alternative view Nicholson, 1992, *Rationality and the Analysis of International Conflict*, Cambridge University Press, Cambridge.

10 See Cox, R.W., 'Social Forces States and World Orders' in Keohane, R.O., *Neo-Realism and its Critics*, op. cit., pp.204-244. See also Scholtc, J.A., 'From Power Politics to Social Change' as an alternative form for international studies, in *Review of International Studies*, 1993, p.3-31.

11 For an analysis of the foreign policy of the Truman Period see Leffler, M.P., 1992, *A Preponderance of Power*, Stanford University Press, Stanford.

12 This treaty ended Allied occupation of Austria and Vienna. It restored Austrian independence on the condition of neutrality.

13 McCarthyism was its most pernicious manifestation.

14 The Geneva Accords were negotiated in 1954 and included the People's Republic of China. The United States refused to ratify them although they were supported by both Britain and France.

15 There is a huge literature on "Marxism" see Avineri, S., 1968, *Karl Marx on Colonialism and Modernisation*, Anchor Books and Doubleday, New York.

Section 2: Stretching Out the Paradigms

3 Anglo-American Relations and the Cold War

ALAN P. DOBSON

The Problem

During the last twenty five years, or so, there has been widespread criticism of the state-centric approach to the study of international relations. The reasons for this range from the growing permeability of the state and the consequent compromising of traditional sovereignty, to the growth in importance of non-state actors, particularly in the economic sphere. In short, the state just does not seem to be an adequate analytical starting point any longer - if it ever were.[1] It seems to me that there is a similar, though not quite so radical, problem with the Cold War and international studies.

Historians and international relations scholars alike have all too often approached the problem of explaining post-war international relations through an over-simplified Cold War paradigm. For many, the disposition of power between the two blocs and their collisions and interactions have dominated the entire post-war international scene producing a system within the system, which has a privileged status both in terms of focus and explanation. Assumptions are made about the cohesion of blocs, leadership and hierarchy and about the overriding imperative to pursue individual state security through the bloc system because it is the only means of delivering a plausible defence strategy. Typical of these assumptions are the following quotations taken from some of the classic texts of the late 1960s and early 1970s: 'Bipolarity left the NATO countries little choice, for the countries of Europe were militarily and economically completely dependent upon the United States' (Spanier, 1972, p.73). 'The essential constancy of the international environment evoked an essentially uniform response from the United States throughout the eight year period (1949-1956)' (Rosenau, 1971, p.166). 'In today's bipolar world which is split ideologically as well as geographically ... independence outside the superpowers themselves is greatly imperilled' (Herz, 1967, p.135). Even recently, there is still a strong tendency to see the Cold War as the defining event of the post-war period - the crucible from which all significant post-war international relations were cast. 'For fifty years relations between the United States and the Soviet Union were the deciding factor in international affairs' (Crockatt, 1994, p.3). It was the: 'global contest that dominated international relations', 'the central factor in world politics' (Painter, 1997, p.273, and Leffler and Painter, 1994, p.1).

Two inter-related problems arise from this type of position: the first concerns the assertion that the Cold War was the main feature of the post-war world; the second is the over-simplified paradigm that it spawned. Elevating the Cold War to the status of the defining event of the post-war world is a case of occidental privileging when many, even in the West, would argue that there were other equally, if not more, important post-war developments. But the issue here is not so much an argument about whether or not the Cold War was important - I do not want to deny that - but the extent to which this importance is taken in order to exclude contemporary perceptions of other significant events and developments. The claim is not that the Cold War was unimportant, but that it has been over-privileged at the cost of other factors. The result has been an over-simplified paradigm which offers an analysis based on a bipolar zero-sum security conflict between contending and irreconcilable socio-political economic systems led by two superpowers accompanied by their attendant acolytes. In the immense complexity of the contemporary interdependent and interpenetrated world of states this paradigm produced a means of seeing the trees as a wood. It enabled scholars to explain international events and developments by imposing a systemic relationship over the main international actors. For example, in the 1940s through to the 1960s, and in some cases beyond, bipolarity was conceived of in an extreme form. Not only was there the bilateral superpower nuclear confrontation, but also a socio-economic-political rift. In the East the universalist doctrine of Marxist Leninism buttressed the position of the Soviets and underpinned what was thought to be a unity that both transcended the nation state and which was pitted against the West. And in the West there developed a form of hegemonic leadership, or empire by invitation, or international capitalism with similar transcendent qualities, in which the lead role was taken by the USA and in which the needs of survival in the conflict with communism would always prevail over other considerations. The Cold War paradigm, in short, forcefully suggested that both camps had to respond to each other in uniform and similar ways.

In this scenario, where the fate of the world depended upon East and West not going to war with each other, the interests of the Third World became peripheral. Its main claim to significance was as a battle ground, either literally or metaphorically, for hearts and minds. Major developments in the Third World, no less than in the First and Second Worlds, were rendered intelligible - were explained - in terms of outcomes of, or reactions to, the Cold War: West European integration and reconstruction were products of US Cold War policies; Indian non-alignment was a response to the East-West conflict. Bipolar contagion produced variants on these types of explanation, but without the realist security assumptions. For example the New Left depicted the Cold War as the outcome of a global conflict between capitalism and Marxist-Leninist economic systems.[2] Again the details of international relations fell (or sometimes were compressed) into the pattern set by the paradigm (I am almost tempted to say 'Hempelian-like covering law paradigm', but Cold War scholarship only rarely became quite that theoretical and abstracted). World systems theory, most notably in the work of Wallerstein, McCormick and Cumings is of a similar kind (Wallerstein, 1984; McCormick, 1989; Cumings, 1992). Even the most industrious of historians often feel that they have to have some kind of organisational concept or colligation: Gaddis for instance in his most recent book on the Cold War recommends the concept of imperialism with hegemonic leadership as an implicit adjunct (Gaddis, 1997). The danger of all this is that accuracy is sacrificed on the altar of simplification which celebrates the facility the paradigm has to explain the broad contours of international relations, but overlooks the detail which determines both whether the contours were accurately drawn in the first place and how they change over time.

In the last twenty years or so some of the original contours have been re-drawn. The images of coherent, hegemon led, contending blocs have been eroded by international historians such as David Reynolds, John Kent, Anne Deighton and Marc Trachtenberg who have emphasised both the complexities in the Western alliance and inputs into the Cold War from Britain and other Western European countries (Reynolds, 1994; Kent, 1994; Deighton 1990; Trachtenberg 1996; Carroll, 1989). Similarly economic and diplomatic historians such as Michael Hogan, Alan Milward and Peter Burnham have emphasised the scope for independent economic action and policies in Western Europe (Hogan, 1987; Milward, 1984; Burnham 1992), and refreshingly independent minded scholars such as Clive Ponting and Paul Rogers have identified themes of development within as well as between the contending Eastern and Western blocs and also see other important themes in post-war international developments (Rogers, 1998; Ponting. 1998).[3] Nevertheless, the focus of attention that mainstream Cold War studies established still needs further revision. And by that I do not mean a further development of the traditionalist-revisionist-postrevisionist debate, though what I have to say here does have some impact on it. Evidence to support the claim that the conceptual baggage of Cold War studies needs further fine tuning can be found in the reaction to the end of the Cold War among its scholars. The surprise at its swift demise suggested to many that the analytical categories spawned by Cold War scholarship - the privileged factors of bipolarity, implacable East-West hostility, and overriding security priorities - had somehow failed to predict the end and were wanting in explaining how it happened. In short something had gone wrong (Cox, 1994; Gaddis, 1993).

Cold War studies have been preoccupied with war, security and nation states and have been over-influenced by both traditional realism and more perniciously, according to Murray in chapter one of this volume, by a restrictive neo-realism in search of a positivist methodology. As the main threat to humanity was seen as nuclear war and as the main international nuclear contenders were the USA and the Soviet Union attention homed in on this bipolar world of vital strategic and security implications and a disposition of power that could unleash a war of such immensity only imaginable in our worst nightmares. However, the overall picture has within it a paradox. The realist and neo-realist preoccupation with security has always seen the state as the main actor in the pursuit of security, but in the Cold War scenario we have two groupings of states where the individual security of a state can only be achieved through collective action and subjection to the leadership and policy priorities of the collective and its leader - the hegemonic superpower, either the USA or the USSR. Thus to sustain state security and independent sovereignty against a collective of opponent states, the state has to surrender much of its independence and sovereignty to a hegemonic superpower. To secure sovereignty the state has to sacrifice sovereignty. How that paradox worked itself out in the Cold War confrontation brings me to the central issues. To what extent did the Cold War override national interests? And, how accurate is it to portray the USA as the hegemonic leader of the West? Answers to these questions have a direct bearing on the way neo-realism restricted the variables of explanation in the Cold War paradigm and they raise serious doubts about the results that this produced.

In posing these questions I do not mean to suggest that the Cold War as a concept and as a means of analysing the post-war international system should be discarded as irrelevant. But, it is important to acknowledge that other things were happening that had little to do with the Cold War, that they sometimes cut across its priorities in individual state decision-making and that among those states intimately involved in the Cold War configuration of power there were competing views about the nature of the conflict. As one scholar has recently put it: 'The overarching Soviet-American bipolarity concealed how much scope there was for customised national policies and strategies to flourish.' (Maier 1994, p.170) In short, the world was not as bipolar as Cold War literature suggests and assumptions of undifferentiated relations among alliance members and between them and the alliance leader produce a very distorted picture. Cold War priorities did not carry all before them: they were not always privileged by political and bureaucratic leaders. The USA could not therefore always draw on agreed aims and priorities to persuade its allies and was not as hegemonic as it is sometimes portrayed. And finally, different Western countries had different views of the conflict with communism to the extent that, at times, it looks as if there were very different Cold Wars being fought.

In addressing my two questions: How hegemonic was the USA? and: To what extent did individual states override Cold War priorities? I shall examine three aspects of Anglo-American relations. The first looks at Britain's refusal to integrate and lead Western Europe from within as the Americans wanted. The second explores aspects of their atomic relationship to see the force of Britain's determination to maintain an independent defence capability. The third takes a broad overview of the different approaches of the two countries to economic warfare. These case studies raise questions about the adequacy of the conventional Cold War paradigm by explaining relationships between both collective Cold War and national defence priorities and between the USA and its allies.

European Integration

In the European Recovery Program, or Marshall Plan as it was better known, the USA wanted Britain to lead integration in Europe. It thought this would be the most efficient way to rebuild Europe, and with Britain firmly in the integration movement Germany would be better contained and France reassured. Above all, Western Europe would become strong, stable, and a bulwark against the spread of communism. As late as the autumn of 1949, the USA thought that the success of its policy for Europe depended on Britain. This was a Cold War priority of immense importance.[4]

There were two obstacles to the realisation of these aims: first, the US relationship of interdependence with Britain; second, the British refusal to integrate. They did not see the dictates of Cold War imperatives in the same light as the Americans. They had sound national reasons, notwithstanding their genuine commitment to prosecuting the Cold War vigorously, that persuaded them not to integrate with Europe. Unlike the continental Europeans in whom the Second World War aroused scepticism about the viability of the nation state and created a disposition receptive to ideas of integration promulgated from both within Europe and from Americans, the British had no such doubts or inclinations. When they looked at Europe they saw greater economic chaos there than in Britain and, having already paid a heavy cost for sustaining the population in their German zone of occupation, feared that if they took a leadership role in European integration this would only drain more of their meagre economic resources. In any case, to be locked into Europe was too parochial for Britain with her commonwealth and, ironically, her special relationship with the USA. Along with these national perspectives on her foreign policy priorities, the British Labour Government also had a domestic partisan fear that European integration would detract from Britain's economic sovereignty in a way that would damage its industrial nationalisation programme, and employment and welfare policies: socialist economic policies and the US version of liberal capitalism were not always easy bedfellows.[5] For reasons of state, therefore, the British were wary of integration, and in late October 1949 the Cabinet decided against a commitment to Europe that went beyond a point from which it could withdraw with ease.[6]

The dilemma posed by the British was discussed by US ambassadors in Paris in October 1949. The meeting took place against the backcloth of Britain's September devaluation of sterling from $4.03 to $2.80 and amidst fears both about the future of Europe and British decline and her possible retreat behind more economic controls. There was a general consensus that Britain could not be left in 'the back yard' if European integration were to go ahead. But as the ambassador to the Court of St. James, Lew Douglas, explained, the Labour Cabinet felt that integration would undermine socialist policies: this was a sensitive political issue and one Douglas thought that the USA should avoid.[7] Averell Harriman was less circumspect. After observing that 'the British prevailed in setting the pattern of (the OEEC) whose impotency was now becoming alarming', he said that the British should be 'bluntly told' that their stance was directly contrary to the US aim for European integration.[8] Ambassador Bruce emphasised that: 'No Frenchman ... can conceive of the construction of a viable Western Europe world from which the UK would be absent.'[9] The Americans were angry that British policy was undermining their conception of regional integration, threatening economic recovery in Europe, leaving France to work out a long-term solution to the German problem, and compromising the potential strength of the West in Europe. Anger was one thing, solving the dilemma was another matter. George W. Perkins, Assistant Secretary of State for European Affairs, observed that: 'There was a deep conviction (in Washington) that the U.S. needed Great Britain above everything else ... All these things must be taken into consideration when studying how far to press Britain in the matter of European integration.'[10] At this time Paul Hoffman, ERP Administrator, was so incensed by British recalcitrance that he wanted to blackmail them into integration by threatening to suspend Marshall Aid. It was left to Secretary of State Dean Acheson and his deputy James Webb to point out to Hoffman that Britain was too important to be antagonised in this way and that Truman would not endanger the ERP by alienating Britain.[11] By the end of October Acheson was urging that the French would have to go it alone on integration without the British. Even if the USA could have pushed Britain into Europe, the Americans reasoned that that would probably have slowed down the very process of integration that they wanted to speed up (Hogan, 1987, ch.6).

This was not the only time Britain foiled plans for integration. A few months later when the French came forth with the Pleven Plan for a European army the story was the same. The problem was how to rearm the Germans in order to boost the West's feeble manpower resources when compared to the Soviets', without panicking the French. The French proposal was for a fully integrated European army where there would be no strong German identity. After initial scepticism, the plan was backed by the Americans, but the British took a strong dislike to it. At his meeting with Truman in January 1952, Prime Minister Churchill explained to the President that his idea of a European army was very different to Pleven's. He envisaged a European army as 'a bunch of faggots bound together, stronger as a bunch than as individual sticks, but each retaining its individual characteristics in the bunch. Pleven's ... Army ... is a bucket of wood pulp'.[12] The British would not join Pleven's army and without them the French soon began to feel uneasy about it as a means for rearming Germany and as a result the proposal fell in the French Assembly. Once again British national policy overrode Cold War priorities as conceived of by the USA.

The irony of all this was that the reason that the USA had to give way to the British on these issues was that the USA needed to retain British co-operation for waging the Cold War more broadly construed. On successive occasions the Americans reiterated how important their relationship was with Britain. In early 1950 US ambassador Douglas spoke of the existence of a special relationship as being an inescapable fact.[13] The State Department Policy Planning Staff in November 1951 stated that 'We have in fact, at the present time, a special relationship with the U.K.'.[14] Briefing papers for the Churchill-Truman talks of 1952 described the British as the 'most resolute and effective of our allies and, through their Commonwealth ties and influence with other areas, represent an element of strength in the free world second in importance only to the U.S.'[15] This was America's dilemma: the need for help, primarily but not exclusively in the Cold War, meant that she had to tolerate British departures from Cold War priorities for the sake of general ongoing co-operation. Western countries had scope and the ability to pursue independent policies within the alliance. Whatever hegemonic pretensions the

USA had they did not stretch to being able to propel Britain into either economic or military integration in Europe. And the Cold War did not impose a uniform pattern of response on the USA and the West: differentiated national interests could and did override collective Cold War priorities. In this case, at least, the realist/neo-realist conception of agency is not convincing.

Atomic Considerations

Alliances bring together two or more countries with areas of shared interests, but they cannot overcome the fact that no two nations have identical interests. US and British atomic policies clearly illustrate that the collective priority of waging the Cold War successfully could not obviate the need for differentiated national defence policies. First of all, because it was conceivable that a conflict could arise with the Soviets where some members of the Western Alliance would not be willing to follow the NATO maxim of one for all and all for one; and secondly because a national nuclear deterrent might also be needed in non-Cold War circumstances. Even though it made the Western Alliance against the Cold War adversary less effective than it might have been, France and Britain insisted on having national nuclear deterrents which thus duplicated R&D and manufacturing costs, complicated command and targeting procedures, and raised the possibility that Germany might at some point claim the same right. Alliances necessarily subdue the individual voice of national interest for the sake of the collective good, but they can never eliminate that voice: even an alliance leader as powerful as the USA could not accomplish that. These factors are important because atomic policies were nationalistic at the expense of collective Cold War strategic priorities. They showed that national security could not be exhaustively defined in Cold War terms. And they also endangered broader economic and political priorities that the USA wished to promote.

The Soviet success with Sputnik in 1957 alarmed the USA and emphasised the importance of co-operation. The British were making progress with their own atomic programme and there were various opportunities for economies and fruitful co-operation in terms of sharing atomic test facilities and intelligence gathering. Out of this came the 1958 Agreement for Co-operation in the Uses of Atomic Energy for Mutual Defence Purposes which renewed Anglo-American wartime nuclear co-operation and created an atomic special relationship that the USA had with no other country.[16] This was later to raise serious difficulties.

The problem of collective Western interests and divergent national interests had not been lost on either the French or the British. The latter in particular had immediately taken up a national nuclear programme once the USA unilaterally abandoned wartime nuclear co-operation. After Suez and the rift between the USA on the one hand and France and Britain on the other the importance of a national defence capability was underlined, particularly for the French who now rapidly developed their independent nuclear *force de frappe*. In 1962 the Americans received their own lesson on the importance of national as opposed to alliance vital interests - the Cuban Missile Crisis. It was the very kind of security event which raised the nightmare of whether the West really would react in a one for all and all for one way. The Americans thought that there was a serious danger that this would not be so. On the first day of the crisis, presidential national security adviser McGeorge Bundy pointed out that the 'amount of noise we would get from our allies saying that they can live with Soviet MRBMs, why can't we, the divisions in the alliance; the certainty that the Germans would feel that we were jeopardising Berlin because of our concern over Cuba. The prospect of that pattern is not an appetizing one ...' (Trachtenberg, 1985, p.179). The Americans saw the issue as a challenge to their vital national interests: the Europeans might not see it as a challenge to theirs. Chances with US vital national interests could not be taken. Therefore, the US dealt with the problem unilaterally: the West European Allies were not involved in the decision-making process. It was this type of strategic logic that shortly afterwards caused such a crisis in Anglo-American relations over the Skybolt and Polaris missile systems.

The nuclear co-operation between Britain and the USA had wide ramifications and impacted on several of America's policy priorities, most of which were heavily influenced by Cold War considerations. The first of these ramifications was to do with the US desire to centralise control over the entire nuclear arsenal of the West, i.e. bring it under US command. This would make it operationally more effective and efficient, as Defense Secretary McNamara explained in a speech at Ann Arbor on 16 June 1962. It would also prevent the USA from being dragged into a nuclear exchange by her allies against her will: the kind of problem highlighted by Suez and the Cuban Missile Crisis. And it would help to deal with the German problem. That problem was to do with the dangers of instability in Germany as Chancellor Adenauer came to the end of his long reign - he was succeeded by Ludvig Erhard in October 1963 - and the possibility that Germany might insist on equal status with other major West European powers and claim its right to develop nuclear weapons. The Americans thought that they could pre-empt that by taking away independent control of Britain's and France's nuclear deterrents and placing them under a NATO Multilateral Nuclear Force in which all NATO members, including Germany, would participate. As President Johnson explained to Prime Minister Wilson in December 1964 this 'would keep the Germans with us and keep their hand off the trigger.'[17] Unfortunately for the Americans the logic of this was not lost on the French or the British: keeping the German finger off the trigger in this scenario also meant removing France's and Britain's.

The second ramification was also partly to do with the German problem, but more importantly with the overall development of the NATO area and with America's growing economic problems. President Kennedy was deeply disturbed by the declining economic performance of the USA (Zeiler, 1992; Borden, 1989). One of the corrective strategies conjured up by his administration was known as the 'grand design'. It involved the US Congress passing the 1962 Trade Expansion Act and the executive branch then using delegated authority to negotiate freer trade with the EEC in a process of moving towards the creation of a north atlantic free trade area. A supplementary strategy for the realisation of this 'grand design' was Britain's entry into Europe to help counterbalance and steady Germany and to make the EEC outward looking and more free-trade oriented especially in the field of agricultural imports. The Americans rightly feared that the Common Agricultural Policy would strangle their agricultural export market in Europe. The main obstacle to British entry was President Charles de Gaulle who resented the dominance of Anglo-Saxons in the Western world, did not want Britain to challenge his leadership of the EEC, and who thought, correctly, that Britain was too close to the USA to be a good European power.[18]

American policy was an amalgam of their conceptions of Cold War collective goods and more exclusive national interest. They wanted to realise their 'grand design', get Britain into the EEC, and gain control of all the West's nuclear capability, but the Anglo-American nuclear relationship severely undermined the chances of success of all these objectives.

In 1960 Prime Minister Macmillan and President Eisenhower agreed, as part of the new nuclear special relationship, that Britain could buy an aircraft-launched nuclear delivery missile, Skybolt, to replace the obsolete British Blue Streak. There was also a gentleman's agreement that Britain could have an option on the Polaris system if things went wrong with Skybolt. In addition, but not as a strict *quid pro quo*, the Americans were allowed to have a nuclear submarine base at Holy Loch in Scotland and a massive early warning station at Fylingdales in Yorkshire. Unfortunately, by the end of 1962 the Americans wanted to abandon Skybolt and were unhappy about perpetuating a British independent nuclear deterrent by selling them Polaris. The details of how the British got Polaris have been told elsewhere and do not concern us here (Clark, 1994). What do concern us are the reasons why the USA eventually sold the Polaris system to Britain, what this tells us of the

Anglo-American relationship, and what impact this had on the US 'grand design', Britain's application to the EEC, and the US attempt to control the West's nuclear arsenal.

Despite considerable advice to the contrary Kennedy agreed to sell Polaris to Britain at his summit with Macmillan at Nassau. Why did he do that? First of all, Macmillan reassured Kennedy that any decision on Polaris would not affect Britain's application to join the EEC. Secondly, he explained the precarious state of his government and that if he did not get a Polaris deal it could bring his administration down. This had impact on Kennedy who was a close friend of Macmillan. Also a State Department paper had warned the President of the dangers of a Labour Government coming to power which would be equivocal about the EEC and which might drift towards a Scandinavian type of neutralism that would weaken NATO.[19] Kennedy was also unhappy about the way the Skybolt crisis had unfolded and mindful of understandings reached between Macmillan and Eisenhower. He later commented to his aide Sorensen that 'it might well be concluded that ... we had an obligation to provide an alternative (to Skybolt)': the obligation was to a country with which the specialness of relations might have been in decline for some time, but there was still enough sense of interdependence and friendship to unsettle American Cold War policy ambitions (Sorensen, 1965, p. 566; Dobson, 1990). For these reasons the Polaris deal was struck. The impact was to perpetuate Britain's independent nuclear status, for national reasons rather than for Cold War collective interests. Cold War priorities suffered in other ways as well. The deal strengthened de Gaulle's conviction that Britain was too close to the USA to be allowed into Europe. A few days after the Nassau meeting he vetoed Britain's application to the EEC and in doing so he torpedoed the US 'grand design' to stabilise and strengthen and economically liberalise the EEC through Britain's entry. The Polaris deal also complicated the question of nuclear proliferation and the German problem. Fortunately, fears that German nuclear ambitions might develop did not materialise.

So, nuclear matters within the Western alliance in the early 1960s reveal a tangled web of ambitions and interests, many of which cut across Cold War priorities. The USA found itself unable to control or significantly change disagreeable policies of its allies. The 'grand design' for Europe, much influenced but not totally so by Cold War priorities, and the US's aim to control all the nuclear firepower of the West, both came to nought. The Multilateral Nuclear Force proposal never made headway with France or Britain. In 1966 France even went so far as to withdraw from the military structure of NATO. Bipolarity and the implacable zero-sum game of hostility with the Eastern Bloc is not an adequate analytical framework to explain what happened. Independent national defence policies in France and Britain overrode the exclusive priority of the collective Cold War response to the Soviets and the Chinese because they would not accept the idea that simple bipolarity exhausted the idea of the security threat. There were always dangers that the all for one and one for all principle might break down, there were the possibilities that non-Cold War threats might arise that required nuclear deterrence, and there was also the fact that Britain and others in Europe did not conceive of the Cold War itself in the same terms as the USA. To illuminate that we now need to turn to ideas of economic warfare and embargo.

Economic Warfare, Economic Embargo

The story of Western attempts to deny the Soviets both strategic materials and technology that would accelerate their economic growth is too long and complicated to relate here. Among other things it is not just a Western attempt in the singular: different countries had different ideas about how and what to embargo and what it actually meant. Was it an embargo, or did it go further than that and amount to economic warfare? What was a strategic good? Where did the relative advantage lie in questions of whether or not to trade? To what extent should the fungibility of items affect the decision to embargo or not to embargo? Was the main aim to inflict economic pain and restrict the strategic growth of the Soviets or were there other less obvious motives at work? The Miller Committee investigation of 1965 in the USA concluded that the embargo had neither significant military or economic effects on the Soviet Union and yet the embargo was not to be abandoned, largely for psychological and tactical bargaining reasons.[20] Clearly there were motives at play other than strategic denial and limiting economic growth.[21] What I want to extract from this highly complex issue area are several points about Anglo-American relations and views about the Cold War. In order to do that I am going to take some snapshot pictures of: the economic embargo policy in 1949 at the point that the Western multilateral co-ordinating committee, or COCOM, was established; the period 1953-4 after the death of Stalin and when the Korean War was drawing to a close; and the 1960s with the main focus on 1962-3 when the Americans began to review radically their embargo policy. The first picture illuminates the limits that interdependence placed on US power in the alliance; the second demonstrates Britain's ability to change policy contrary to US wishes; and the third emphasises the different attitude that the two countries had always had towards waging the Cold War by trade means, but which became very distinct and clear in the 1960s.

By March 1948, after much internal debate, the USA decided upon principles for implementing a strategic embargo policy against the Soviet Bloc.[22] For it to succeed the co-operation of its West European allies had to be engaged and that job was assigned to Averell Harriman. The guiding principles he had to sell were that the embargo would be selective; that it would be sensitive to the concept of relative gain - the West Europeans benefited from some trade more than the Soviets and that should not be curtailed; the embargo lists should be the same for both the USA and its allies or else there would be a form of *de facto* discrimination against US exporters; and finally the multilateral embargo had to be voluntary. The Americans already had a long 1a list of strategic goods for which they wanted a multilateral embargo, but they realised that there might have to be a trade off between allied co-operation and the length of their 1a list. Harriman was instructed to refer matters back to Washington if changes were necessary to secure 'substantial voluntary agreement by the European countries.'[23]

After several rounds of tortuous negotiations a multilateral agreement was eventually reached in November 1949 which covered most, but by no means all, items that the USA wanted to embargo. One reason for the outcome was that the USA exerted pressure indirectly and sometimes directly through its role as provider of aid. Later the Congress went to the extent of requiring aid recipients to observe embargo rules decided upon unilaterally by the USA. This was embedded in the Mutual Defense Assistance Control Act of 1951, the Battle Act, but there were provisions for Presidential waivers, a discretion that was exercised repeatedly. The act and US informal pressures caused much resentment, but one must remember that there was a lot of overlapping agreement between the USA and its allies. Britain did not need persuasion to institute an embargo. The debate was about how extensive and how damaging to overall trade with the Soviets it should be allowed to be. The British in fact took the lead in the negotiations in 1949 to bring the European allies together on an embargo agreement. The Americans kept out of it initially and comments sent to the Foreign Office by one of the British delegation throw light on the mood in London and the continental capitals: 'it would be most important that all the countries concerned should have definitely accepted the policy before the Americans come in since a large part of the discussions of the present stage is inevitably concerned with the extent to which American pressure can be resisted.'[24]

These negotiations set the pattern for the future. There was agreement on an embargo and on the setting up of a ministerial level Consultative Group and a working party, the COCOM, but it was a compromise. The Americans knew that they could not be coercive, that COCOM had to be a co-operative venture. The very same reasoning which had prevented the Americans from coercing the British into leading European integration from within also applied here. And so, the Americans found themselves always with a much more extensive national embargo list than the multilateral COCOM list and always with far less trade with the Soviet Bloc than its West European allies. For a short time during the Korean War the differential between the lists narrowed, but when the war wound down and Stalin died controversy about the extent of the embargo rekindled.

The death of Stalin on 6 March 1953 opened the curtain on what Churchill and others in Western Europe saw as a stage of opportunity to bring about a new post-war settlement. According to one recent account Churchill hoped to achieve 'the reunification of Germany and a German-Soviet non-aggression treaty guaranteed by Great Britain', through summit talks with the Malenkov regime (Larres, 1995, p.435). Just how clear Churchill was about this peace initiative remains contested, not least by Henry Kissinger. We shall never know what might have transpired because Churchill's desire for an East-West summit was opposed by the Foreign Office and torpedoed by the Americans for fear that the Soviets might exploit Western divisions, especially over the still unresolved problem of how to rearm Germany (Kissinger, 1994, pp.509-16; Dobson, 1995, p.110). However, this was an indicative episode. It highlighted the fact that substantially different attitudes were developing towards the Cold War and with respect to economic embargo policy these differences produced more substantial change than Churchill's abortive attempt to arrange a summit.

Eisenhower reacted very cautiously to the death of Stalin and appears to have been more concerned with taking advantage of the, at least temporarily, off-balance, but, nonetheless, active Soviets. One Soviet innovation certainly seemed to require a response: a Soviet drive for more trade with the West. Ironically, though Eisenhower was unwilling to lower the West's guard after Stalin's death, he was always somewhat of a heretic regarding the economic embargo. He favoured a mildly liberal policy, but was opposed by the overwhelming majority in his Cabinet and the NSC. Thus the Americans, notwithstanding the president's views, were highly conservative about relaxing the embargo and increasing trade. A similar line was taken by the British Foreign Office, but Churchill, the Board of Trade and the British Treasury had more radical views: 'The U.K. does not feel that the recent changes in trading patterns and tactics by the Russians are to be viewed primarily as a tactic in the Cold War, but are rather inclined to view them as primarily reflecting a Soviet desire for trade motivated by internal economic and political factors'.[25] The British wanted to slash the COCOM lists by half. The Americans were horrified, with the exception of Eisenhower, but even he agreed that the British position had to be opposed. Over the following months strenuous attempts were made to moderate the British line. But, Churchill was resolute. He supported and pushed the issue in Cabinet despite Foreign Office and Defence Department opposition and then tried to anticipate the outcome of talks with the Americans by announcing in the House of Commons on 25 February 1954 that 'a substantial relaxation would undoubtedly be beneficial in its proper setting'.[26]

The British did not get all they wanted but the lists were reduced by about a third. They were delighted and the British delegation who had negotiated the final arrangements reported to the Foreign Office: 'we have secured acceptance by all participating countries of a very substantial reduction in the International Lists. This must be regarded as a major achievement, bearing in mind all the difficulties we faced.'[27]

There has been considerable debate about who was responsible for the changes to the COCOM lists in 1954, and particularly about the role of Eisenhower. He was in favour of relaxing the lists but not as far as actually transpired. That was down to British pressure. The Americans could not prevent the British from engineering a massive change in the embargo policy which reflected their different interpretation of the Cold War and their different judgement about the importance of trade and its role in East-West relations. By the early 1960s the British had pushed through further liberalisation and had abandoned the so-called China Differential, which had restricted Chinese more than Soviet trade. It was now evident that there was a qualitatively different conception in Europe of at least certain aspects of the Cold War.

After Kennedy came to power he instigated an American review of the embargo. Little change came during his term of office because of differences within his administration and other matters which took higher priority, but there was significant development in the way Americans thought about the embargo. They moved away from justifying the embargo policy in terms of the damage it could inflict on the Soviet economy, the delay it could cause for development, and its ability to retard the Soviet military capability. Instead, they concentrated on its psychological impact and the bargaining chips it provided for negotiations. In short it was seen as a possible tool in the grander strategy of flexible response. This US thinking about the embargo was not indicative of a radically different conception of the Cold War so much as of a desire to gain further advantages in that conflict. Trade was to be a tool of flexible response to meet the Soviet challenges, particularly in the Third World. This was not how the British saw things.[28]

The episode that demonstrated most vividly the widening gulf between the British and the Americans concerned the export of wide diameter steel pipes which the Soviets needed to convey oil to distribution and refining points. This type of pipe was not on the COCOM list, so the Americans, after exerting considerable pressure on their allies, brought a proposal before the NATO Council on 21 November 1962. They sought a ban on the export of wide diameter steel pipes to the Soviets. There was unanimous approval with the exception of the British who dissociated themselves from the resolution and reserved their freedom of action.

There followed an unholy row which embroiled both Kennedy and Macmillan, but the British would not be persuaded despite personal appeals from the president. In fact the matter was one of principle. The only British company capable of supplying the right type of pipe was the South Durham Company and although negotiations took place, there were no sales because the price was too high. Nevertheless, before this became apparent, the Americans continued to bemoan British policy and make high level appeals to get them to line up with the NATO resolution.

On 12 February Thomas Finletter, US ambassador to NATO wrote to Secretary of State Rusk regarding the whole problem of Britain and East-West trade. 'Regret have to say this (the possibility of Britain bartering ships for Soviet oil) is latest in a series of HMG actions which imply UK seemingly give priority to its short range commercial interests over basic interests of the Atlantic Alliance. Others are large diameter pipe embargo, credits to Sov. Bloc, Viscount sales, economic counter measures, Cuban shipping. If Soviet oil deal consummated, UK will have achieved almost perfect score of opposition to us in NATO on all E/W trade issues.'[29] Eventually the controversy faded away as no contracts were signed for British pipes, but the message was clear: the Americans could not coerce the British and there now clearly existed a different view of the Cold War, of its intensity and immediacy, and of how to conduct it. The British were not prepared to use trade policy in any way that smacked of economic warfare. They would not export military equipment, but that was no different from their policy toward any other potentially dangerous state. The Cold War as a conflict was losing its uniqueness.

By the mid 1960s the British were prepared to trade in whatever commodities they could with the communists, provided they were not military goods strictly defined. For the British such trade was a deeply serious and important matter. Britain lived by trade; the USA did not. Trade was of such vital importance to Britain that it was prepared to disregard the highest level embargo appeals from the USA. In 1964 it extended 15 year credits to the Soviets breaking the consensus the Americans had previously crafted among the Western allies to limit credits to five years. Britain did not ignore the threat from the Soviets, but its leaders had always been more disposed to see differentiated relationships between East and West than the Americans.[30] By the 1960s this amounted to a qualitative down-grading of the Cold War as a threat. Other priorities, namely trade, were seen as being of more national advantage than a broadly construed embargo policy even though the collective Cold War Western leaders thought otherwise. The differences that had always existed in the Western alliance about the nature of the threat from the communist bloc were now widening into fissures. Soon the USA would have to deal with France leaving the military structure of NATO and German *Ostpolitik*. There was no longer a uniform conception of the Cold War upon which the USA could build its policy priorities and use the security threat from the Soviets to gain compliance. In other words, different Cold Wars meant different policies.

Conclusion

What does all this illustrate? Well, it shows that the USA was either a very strangely limited hegemon or not one at all and that individual state priorities frequently clashed and overrode Cold War considerations. By some direct argument and evidence and by implication it emerges that specific national concerns created more differentiated relationships within the Western Camp than is often assumed; that concentrating solely on East-West conflict impoverishes our understanding of what went on in the world in the post-war period between 1945 and 1989; and, arising from the previous point, that there continued to be important international priorities and developments that were not directly related to the Cold War. It has always struck me as rather arrogant to conceive of India as non-aligned solely in Cold War terms, as if India were incapable of projecting an image of itself without reference to what was going on in the First World. Does non-alignment cease to have any meaning now the Cold War is dead? More important for our present concerns, it has always struck me as implausible that in the pursuit of securing freedom from the ambitions of one hegemonic superpower suzerainty should be freely accepted from another - even though friendly. The main gist of the arguments in the case studies is that this did not in fact happen.

I set out to address the questions: To what extent have national priorities overridden Cold War ones, and: how hegemonic was the USA? The case studies show that time and again Britain took a policy line that cut across Cold War priorities on European economic integration, on European military integration, and on the Western nuclear deterrent. On questions of economic warfare she moved from the uneasy compromise that held from 1949 through the worst phase of the Korean War to embrace from 1953 onwards an ever diverging policy from the USA. By the 1960s it was clear that in the economic realm Britain had arrived at a very different understanding of the Cold War. The other side of the coin to this was whether or not the USA was hegemonic. That is of course a contested term, but even a minimalist definition of hegemony would have difficulty in effectively explaining US behaviour in the three case studies that I have developed here.[31]

International relations in the post-war period were far more differentiated than the bipolar, implacably hostile ideological collectives of the Cold War paradigm allow. National policies overrode Cold War priorities and the development of the interdependent world economy eroded their position. Non-Cold War issues still counted. The collectives were riven with differences and their so-called hegemonic leaders often, at least in the West, found themselves impotent to coerce, co-opt or persuade. If considerations like these had been given more prominence then perhaps the surprise at the collapse of the Soviet Union might have been milder, the attempts to explain it easier to get underway, and the continuation of the NATO Alliance and its expansion more readily understandable.

Notes

1 The literature on this is now legion, but for one of the most influential and consistent voices see: Susan Strange, (1970), and (1995). See also Guehenno, (1995); and for recent non-state developments in international relations studies, Brown, (1992); Rittberger, (1995); Booth and Smith, (1995); and Chan, (1996).

2 Kolko, (1968); Williams, (1962); Gardner, (1970); and various works by David Horowitz, Harry Magdoff, and Theresa Hayter. For a polemical attack on this school, see Maddox, (1973). Essentially the debate between the New Left and their critics is irresolvable because each side has a different conceptual scheme of significance. Both the choice of evidence and the interpretation of it are done by different means. For enlightenment on such problems see Reynolds, (1981) and his contribution to the present work. For guidance on the historiography of the Cold War see Leffler, (1994). For attempts to create a post-revisionist consensus see Gaddis, (1983), which in fact only sparked off further debate and a reassertion of the New Left position, most notably by Cumings, (1992) and (1994).

3 Rogers and Ponting in this volume. For the broad issue of hegemony and the USA, see Dobson, (1998).

4 The two classic texts on the ERP are Hogan, (1987); and Milward, (1984).

5 For more detailed discussion of this see Dobson, (1995).

6 Public Record Office (PRO), CAB 128, 3(47)2, 28 Jan. 1947; CAB 128, 62(49)6, 27 Oct. 1949 considering CAB 129, CP(49)203, 25 Oct. 1949, Bevin and Cripps, 'Proposals for the Economic Unification of Europe'.

7 Harry S. Truman Library (HST Lib.), PSF box 163, subject file conferences,

Sept. 1947 - Dec. 1950, folder: subject file conferences, Paris Conference, Oct. - Nov. 1949, US ambassadors meeting, 21 Oct. 1949.

8 *Ibid.*

9 *Ibid.*

10 *Ibid.*

11 *Ibid.*, Acheson Papers box 64, folder: memos. of conversation, minutes by Webb of luncheon meeting, 25 Oct. (Dated 3 Nov.) 1949; Foreign Relations of the United States (FRUS), 1949 vol. 4, p. 345, Acheson to US Embassy, London.

12 Acheson Papers box 67, memo. of conversation 1952, folder: Jan., Pearson to Acheson, 15 Jan. 1952.

13 Library of Congress, Harriman Papers box 271, folder: Marshall Plan country file, UK 20, Douglas to Acheson et al, 7 May 1950.

14 FRUS, 1951, vol. 4, pp. 980-85, PPS memo., 'Outline for Discussion at JCS Meeting', 21 Nov. 1951.

15 HST Lib., PSF box 116, folder: Central File Churchill - Truman Meetings, papers prepared for US-UK relations, 'Nature of US - UK relationship'. For a detailed analysis of US - UK relations at the Jan. 1952 Truman - Churchill talks see Dobson, (1997).

16 For the broad context of this see Dobson, (1995). For the defence side see Bayliss, (1984). For an excellent and detailed study of the atomic relationship see Clark, (1994). The only major reservation I have about Clark's book, a reservation shared by Milward as well, is his claim that Kennedy had decided *before* going to the Nassau meeting in December 1962 to sell Polaris to Britain.

17 Lyndon B. Johnson Library (LBJ Lib.), NSF boxes 18 & 19, memo. Meeting with Prime Minister Wilson, 7 Dec. 1964.

18 For the grand design and some of the problems spawned by its failure see Costigliola, (1984); (1994). For Britain and European integration see Kaiser, (1996).

19 John F. Kennedy Library (JFK Lib.), NSF box 235-8, folder: presidential trips, Nassau, Macmillan talks 12/62, briefing book.

20 LBJ Lib., NSF Committee File, box 25, folder: Miller Committee Report to the President, Miller Committee members to Johnson, 29 April 1965.

21 I deal with these matters at length in the opening chapters of Dobson, (forthcoming).

22 The initial research in this area was published by Adler-Karlsson, (1968). A theme in Dobson, (1988), and Dobson, (1988a), opened up some complexities of allied policy in COCOM which Adler-Karlsson had overlooked. See also Mastanduno, (1992); Fungiello, (1988); Young, (1996); V. Sorensen, (1989); Spaulding, (1993); Forland, (1991) which is largely drawn from his (1991a); and Jackson, (1997).

23 FRUS, 1948, vol. 4, pp. 564-68, Marshall and Hoffman to Harriman, 27 Aug. 1948.

24 PRO, FO 371/77799, UK delegation OEEC to FO, 24 June 1949. See also CAB 129/24, CP(48)72, 'The Threat to Western Civilisation', 3 March 1948.

25 FRUS, 1952-54, vol. 1, p. 1043, Lincoln Gordon to State Department, 10 Nov. 1953, reporting on British response to US proposals.

26 Hansard, 25 Feb. 1954, 524, pp. 582-91; for the 1954 controversy see Dobson, (1988), pp. 155-61, Young, (1996), Spaulding, (1993), and Forland, (1991).

27 PRO, FO 371/111214, UK delegation Paris to Mutual Aid Department FO, 24 July 1954.

28 For probably the most comprehensive picture of the way US thinking developed see paper by Walt Rostow, 'US Policy on Trade with the European Soviet Bloc', Policy Planning Council 26 July 1963 at JFK Lib., NSC box 320, folder: Trade East-West. For a more detailed account of the wide diameter pipe crisis see Dobson, (1988a).

29 JFK Lib., NSF box 171-3, folder: UK General 2/12/63 - 3/5/63, Finletter to Rusk, 12 Feb. 1963.

30 LBJ Lib., NSF Committee File box 16, File: Miller Committee Meetings, 4-5, 18-19, 25-26 March 1965. State Department papers, 'The Role of Western Europe and Japan', and ' Our Allies (NATO plus Japan)'.

31 For a more detailed consideration of hegemony see Dobson, (1998).

4 The Limits of US Cold War Hegemony: Lessons from the Anglo-Iranian Oil Crisis[1]

STEVE MARSH

The idea of American hegemony after the Second World War has been a popular one, for both theorists and those seeking to explain international relations. It has generated new academic discussion about what constitutes hegemony and spawned competing versions of hegemony theory. In some Cold War literature the USA is portrayed as the hegemonic leader of the West organising and directing the Cold War alliance against the Soviet bloc. Recent analyses however have begun to question the degree to which the US controlled the Western alliance. This chapter will carry these analyses forward. The character of post-war US power will be examined by taking one of the central problems of hegemony theory - the extent to which a hegemon can be pressed to compromise before it ceases to be hegemonic - and subjecting it to empirical analysis. The chapter does not address hegemony theory *per se*; instead it takes issue with over-simplistic applications of it in a post-war international relations model of tight bipolarity which leaves little scope for third party action. In reality, US dominance and its leadership role were substantially less than some have claimed. There was a far more differentiated and interdependent pattern of relationships within the western alliance than theories of hegemonic leadership allow.

The limits of US power and influence were demonstrated in the Anglo-Iranian oil crisis of 1950-54. This began as a commercial dispute between the Iranian Government and the Anglo-Iranian Oil Company about the amount that the company should pay for its oil concession, but it became a major international crisis once the Iranian Government nationalised the AIOC's assets in Iran. In May 1951, the British Government considered military action to get them back and the US tried to mediate a settlement. This was no longer a commercial dispute between company and government: it was a first order international political crisis.

This case study was chosen for several good reasons. First, it spans a period to which pro-hegemonists point as a high water mark of postwar American power. Second, the Middle East was traditionally an area of limited US influence and thus it provides an acid test for claims of postwar hegemony. And third, the oil crisis itself demonstrates the degree to which the US could, or could not, control three 'types' of international actor: Britain as a major power; Iran as an underdeveloped Third World country, and the US oil majors which are examples of powerful non-government organisations (NGOs).

The chapter falls neatly into four sections. The first deals with why the US was involved in what were ostensibly commercial negotiations between a foreign government and a foreign NGO. The other three deal with American relations respectively with Britain, Iran and the US oil majors. Each party shared American concern that Iran should not fall under the influence of communism. Nevertheless, the Americans experienced incredible difficulty in forcing the oil settlement they wanted for Cold War purposes onto the parties involved. Ultimately the oil crisis case study refutes claims that US hegemony within the bipolar Cold War system tightly circumscribed third party action. In fact, it fatally weakens the notion of US hegemony by revealing that a lack of power forced the USA into a series of concessions which cast it in the role of a reluctant, and not always dominant, collaborator rather than of a hegemon in the Middle East between 1950 and 1954.

Why American Involvement in the AIOC Dispute?

Why the US became embroiled in the Anglo-Iranian oil dispute has a simple answer - the Cold War. By 1950 US containment policy[2] as a response to a perceived threat from the Soviet Union was well established.[3] However, explosion of the first Soviet atom bomb and the fall of China in 1949 prompted a major review of US Cold War strategy. The outcome was National Security Council Resolution 68 (NSC-68). It was approved by the National Security Council (NSC) in April 1950 and it marked a turning point in containment policy. America and its allies were to establish a global perimeter fence to better contain the communist threat, a decision confirmed by the outbreak of the Korean war in the summer of 1950.

Thus NSC-68 militarised containment policy and transformed it from a Eurocentric to a global policy (Yergin, 1977, p.397). Inevitably the significance of the Middle East and Iran grew in the eyes of US policy makers. Until this point the US had been interested in the stability of the Middle East, its trade potential and its raw materials, especially oil.[4] Such factors had not warranted the US assuming greater political or military responsibilities in the area.[5] The region's strategic position had traditionally been of little significance to American security. US economic interests other than oil production were deemed 'not particularly outstanding'[6] and the onset of the Cold War had brought more pressing problems - especially in Europe. Practical American commitment to the Middle East was minimal, a conclusion demonstrated by the fact that, except for Turkey, the region received only small packets of US economic assistance during 1949, such as relief aid for Palestinian refugees.

However, the deepening Cold War revolutionised traditional US assessments of the Middle East. NSC-68 committed the US to actively 'foster a fundamental change in the Soviet system' and establish a global perimeter fence against further communist incursions (NSC-68 cited in Leffler, 1972, p.356). Acceptance of a global containment policy, coupled with the establishment of a *status quo* in Europe following the Berlin crisis and the establishment of the DDR and the Federal German Republic, changed traditional US strategic interests and switched US attention to more vulnerable areas such as South East Asia and the Middle East. The latter's geographic location recommended it to US military planners, not least because Middle Eastern countries were well placed to provide offensive and reserve defence bases in any conflict with the Soviets.[7] Its oil reserves were crucial for Western rearmament programmes, economic regeneration and military capabilities. Furthermore, the region lent itself to the worst case scenario of the domino effect. It was composed of numerous small states which were incapable of defending themselves against a Soviet military action. They were also unstable and thus vulnerable to communist subversion. And they were considered to be politically naive, a weakness compounded by their distraction from the dangers of the Cold War by internecine conflicts and disputes. In short, something had to be done to stabilise the region because its political, economic and military weaknesses invited communist opportunism (Nitze cited in Brands, 1989, p.444). As Secretary of State Dean Acheson recalled: 'we began to think that the Russian menace was a little more acute than we thought it was. The North Atlantic began to evolve, and we said "Well, we've got to have something comparable to that in the Middle East."'[8]

Iran was a classic example of a Middle Eastern state that found itself the object of American Cold War 'reclassification' following NSC-68. In 1946 it had been the scene of one of the first East-West disputes. The US had had to champion Iranian independence in the face of Stalin's refusal to withdraw Soviet troops from Northern Iran, something he was obliged to do under wartime agreements.[9] Ultimately the issue was raised in the United

Nations and the Soviet troops withdrew, but not before US attitudes towards the Soviets had hardened. Thereafter though, Iran fell low on the ever growing list of US Cold War priorities. The Americans prioritised Turkey and Greece over Iran,[10] especially as the potential of Iran's armed forces was considered very limited. As late as July 1949 the NSC exhibited a 'disinterested optimism' about Iran and its political stability, arguing that the Soviets would not risk overt aggression and that the communist Tudeh Party was incapable of overthrowing the Iranian Government.[11] Ironically in light of subsequent events, the State Department accused its own Ambassador to Iran, John Wiley, of periodic "cries of wolf"[12] when he warned of a real communist threat to Iran.[13]

NSC-68 and the events that led to its acceptance changed all of this. Iran's geo-strategic importance to the US rose. A Near East and Asian Department (NEA) paper assessing the Iranian situation in 1950 noted that access to the Persian Gulf was a historic Soviet objective and if it were accomplished through a communist take-over in Iran the USSR would acquire advance bases for military and subversive activities, hundreds of miles nearer probable US-UK lines of defence in the Middle East. The Soviets would also control part of the Middle Eastern oil reservoir and be able to threaten the remainder. Western communication and supply lines would also be jeopardised, not least continental air routes across Iran and adjacent areas as well as shipping in the Persian Gulf. Furthermore the will of Middle Eastern countries to resist Soviet aggression would be gravely damaged.[14]

Increased US concern for Iran was also demonstrated by the fact that the State Department now took Ambassador Wiley seriously. He continued his warnings that the US should 'decide either to let Iran go down the drain by default or else attempt something effective'.[15] Suddenly the State Department concurred. By March 1950 the Americans considered the situation in Iran 'dangerous and explosive'. General J. Lawton Collins feared a 'second China'[16] and others argued that the dangers were so great in Iran that the US could not afford to take any chances.[17] Between November 1949 and mid 1950 the Shah sank in US estimations from 'a dominant, unifying force'[18] to a leader whose indecision was monumental, his moral courage debatable and his attitude 'a little too westernised for an oriental country.'[19] Despite little advance by the communists since the NSC report of July 1949,[20] the State Department in March 1950 considered the Tudeh Party to be the only effective political organisation in Iran and one potentially capable of staging a communist *coup d'état*.[21] Even a return to neutralism, a traditional Iranian policy, would now have been considered by the US as a major Soviet success.

The run up to, and acceptance of, NSC-68 is thus pivotal in explaining American intervention in Iran. It marks a Cold War paradigm shift with two enormously important consequences for Iran. First, acceptance of global containment dramatically elevated the importance of Iran to US policy planners. Second, it caused US officials to perceive the threat to Iran differently. This is clearly demonstrated by the way US reports about Iran at this time become infused with urgent adjectives and a conviction that the country was in grave danger.[22] It did not matter that there had been little real change in Iran since the State Department had dismissed Ambassador Wiley's reports as alarmist. What mattered was that Iran was perceived to be in jeopardy and could not be lost to communism. The Anglo-Iranian oil dispute therefore had to be quickly resolved to provide Iran with the increased oil revenues necessary to foster economic and political stability. And this demanded that the US exert its power of "hegemonic" leadership of the Western Cold War alliance because British hardline policies - such as an oil embargo and economic sanctions - promised not to solve the oil dispute but instead to either push Iran behind the Iron Curtain or to so destabilise it that Iran would succumb to communist subversion from within. In short, American Cold War re-evaluation of the significance of the Middle East and Iran compelled them to try to mediate a solution to the oil crisis.

Anglo-American Relations

When Britain and America assessed the Iranian situation they shared many of the same concerns. Both desired to see Iran stable and tied into the Western camp. Both saw economic development as the key for locking the door against communism. And both recognised that a satisfactory settlement of the oil dispute was essential to the wellbeing of the Iranian economy and to Western prestige, not only in Iran but throughout the Middle East. Where Britain and America differed was over the priority each accorded to these objectives. For the Americans, Cold War considerations took precedence and from that basis they were prepared to deal with even the most difficult Iranian leaders. Provided a settlement did not undermine the sanctity of contract which could have damaging international repercussions for the US, they were prepared to endorse virtually any concessions to meet Iranian demands.

The British position was more complex. The concessions that the US so enthusiastically urged were at British, not American expense. In fact, the implications for Britain were very grave if His Majesty's Government (HMG) were to accept a bad oil settlement for the sake of Cold War expediency.[23] AIOC operations in Iran were the single largest British overseas investment and as such carried enormous economic, political and strategic weight. Four major considerations were uppermost in British minds throughout the dispute. First, oil revenues were vital for Britain at a time when it was experiencing severe balance of payments difficulties.[24] Second, Britain's dependence on overseas trade, investment and commercial activity made it especially vulnerable to, and sensitive about, challenges to the sanctity of contract.[25] Third, strategic considerations prior to World War One had persuaded HMG to purchase a controlling interest in the AIOC which thereafter acted as an agent to protect British interests in Iran. Fourth, the Iranian act of nationalisation struck at the heart of British hopes to retain a Great Power status between the two world superpowers by developing its traditional dominance in the Middle East as the new stronghold of the empire.[26] If Iran succeeded in its impudent challenge to British power, the consequences would be dire for British prestige and international interests across the Middle East and beyond.

These considerations prompted HMG to prioritise its immediate economic concerns in the Iranian crisis over its fears of communism. Throughout the dispute HMG pursued a hardline strategy against Iran and adhered to four basic principles: fair compensation; security for the effective payment of compensation; no movement beyond standard concessionary arrangements; and no negotiations on the basis of discrimination against British nationals.[27] In addition, Britain jealously guarded its monopoly on Iranian oil and was loathe to deal with Mosadeq, the Iranian Prime Minister and instigator of the nationalisation.[28]

The product of these different priorities was serious Anglo-American differences and tension. The Americans could not accept Britain putting its economic interests ahead of securing Iran from communism. Nor would they accept that hardline British tactics - an oil embargo, economic sanctions and action against Iran under international law - would produce an oil settlement. They thought it more likely that these tactics would accelerate both the economic collapse of Iran and the anticipated communist takeover. Furthermore, British reluctance to deal with Mosadeq threatened his position and ran against US attempts to use him as a bulwark against communism. As for the British, they were understandably angry that the US should adopt such a one-sided approach to the oil dispute and consistently demand British economic sacrifices to appease Iran for the sake of Cold War priorities which they did not accept as overriding. They resented too that their hardline tactics were fatally compromised by American panics about the Tudeh threat which led them to offer Mosadeq financial help and political support to prevent a communist takeover. The British even suspected the Americans of manipulating the crisis to advance their economic interests at their expense.[29]

These differences became so difficult that the US concluded that 'the British were so obstructive and determined on a rule-or-ruin policy in Iran that we must strike out on an independent policy or run the gravest risk of having Iran disappear behind the Iron Curtain and the whole military and political situation in the Middle East change adversely to us.' (Acheson, 1970, p.682).[30] However, when they tried to do this they found their options severely limited by their incontrovertible need for British co-operation in the prosecution of the global containment policy. Britain was America's only indispensable ally. Its economic and military power and political stability remained unequalled by any other ally and would continue to be so for the foreseeable future.[31] In 1949 Britain devoted a greater proportion of its national income to defence expenditure than even America and by 1950 British production was two and a half times more than France and 50 percent more than West Germany. Britain also retained an influential economic position at the centre of the Commonwealth and the Sterling Area. Its strategic position too remained important, as did its political power in Western Europe, the Near East and South East Asia. In fact, Britain was uniquely placed to fulfil many US Cold War objectives which the Americans either lacked the power, influence or willingness to tackle themselves. American policy planners envisaged Britain playing several roles: leadership in Western Europe; acting as a principal partner in strategic and economic planning; holding the Commonwealth together; guaranteeing political and economic stability in the Near and Middle East; and supplying strategic staging posts and military bases (especially nuclear ones in Britain itself).[32] These roles placed Britain 'in a special or preferred position - the facts of the world situation require it.'[33]

US adoption of a global containment policy therefore infused Anglo-American relations with sufficient sense of mutual dependency to nurture partnership rather than the asymmetric dependency characteristic of hegemony. This is not to say that the relationship was not asymmetric, but that in many areas it is better characterised by partnership rather than hegemony.[34] And nowhere was this partnership more equal than the Middle East. Political re-evaluations of the Middle East did not mean that the Americans were necessarily well placed to do anything decisive about their new-found security interest. They had no tradition of political involvement in the Middle East and thus lacked diplomatic power. In fact, Truman's sponsorship of the state of Israel in 1948 made the Americans particularly unpopular with Arab states. Their economic influence too was restricted by both its limited scope and the powerful British presence, notably through the Sterling Area. Even more importantly, the Americans were unwilling and unable to project military power into the region during 1950-54. Indeed, it is particularly interesting that at the very time that the Middle East was upgraded politically and the US concluded limited economic and technical agreements with a number of states in the region,[35] the American military moved in the opposite direction. In early 1950 George McGhee, Assistant Secretary for Near Eastern, South Asian and African Affairs, was informed that 'the military strategic interests in the N.E.A. area were now viewed as being almost negligible in light of interests in other areas.'[36] The primary security interests of the US outside of the Western hemisphere remained in the North Atlantic area (until the outbreak of the Korean war) and after the NATO Treaty the American Chiefs of Staff looked to develop an operational axis stretching from Morocco through Spain and into France. Implicit in this was the fact that naval operations in the Mediterranean would be geared to support a land campaign in Southern Europe and that consequently there would be an inevitable diversion of resources away from the Middle East.[37] The US military therefore neither wanted nor felt able to undertake any additional responsibilities in the Middle East. Instead, the Americans deferred to British military responsibility in the region.[38] After all, it had a long established presence in the Middle East that allowed it to wield influence beyond even that afforded directly by its substantial military presence centred on the huge Suez base.[39] In fact, the US military clung to hopes of British military prowess for the defence of the Middle East despite doubts as to their ability to fulfil the role. As George McGhee noted: 'it was a matter of deliberate policy that our Joint Chiefs of Staff very carefully thought out to do nothing in the Middle East so that if a vacuum occurred the British would have to attempt to fill it.'[40]

This global, and particularly Middle Eastern, dependency on British co-operation fundamentally questions ideas of US hegemony. The Americans were unable to take decisive unilateral action in Iran or compel Britain to accept the sacrifice of its national interest to the 'greater good' of the Cold War. The US recognised that an Anglo-American rift over the Middle East 'might well result in [the] frustration [of the] policies [of] both countries [in] that area and its eventual loss to international Communism.'[41] They acknowledged too that their lack of power in the region locked them into mutual dependency with Britain, to which in the military field they deferred 'in lieu of a better idea' (Devereux, 1990, p.250). They also admitted that they could not afford to break with Britain over Iran in the oil crisis. Time and again the Americans lost patience with British obstinacy and shoved them to the negotiating table but their dependence on Britain in the Cold War limited the pressure they could exert to force Britain to accept unpalatable Iranian demands. The Americans were forced to concede that there was 'general agreement that broad strategic considerations limit the extent to which we may force the U.K.'s terms for the purpose of achieving a compromise on the oil question'. As one person put it, 'there is no plan (for resolving the oil question) which we can afford to put forward which the British would not accept.'[42]

US-Iranian Relations

The problems that the US had with Iran during the oil dispute were different from those experienced with Britain but were no less difficult. At the root of American problems with Britain lay a US need for Anglo-American co-operation to pursue its policy of global containment. And although analysts[43] of the so-called 'Special Relationship' have rightly pointed to a number of factors making it a truly unusual phenomenon in international relations, the basis for this need for co-operation was calculations of power, particularly where US power was insufficient to maintain the integrity of the containment perimeter fence. US relations with Iran were very different. Iran was a small, economically backward state with few democratic pretensions. Its military capability was minimal, its leadership was habitually ineffective and its politics were notoriously corrupt. Most Americans would have struggled to place it on a map and those familiar with it found little to commend when set against the moral elements of US foreign policy.

Nevertheless, containment gave Iran importance beyond what might seem to be its intrinsic worth because it possessed oil, was adjacent to the Soviet Union and it was non-communist but vulnerable through its inherent political and economic instability. Iran's geo-strategic position thus became vital in Cold War terms because it could become a Soviet base in the Persian Gulf from which they could work to undermine neighbouring states. In January 1952 the Americans recognised this: 'It is not as though we were dealing with a country remote from the Soviet Union. It is in a bad spot.'[44] Moreover, Iran was central to preliminary US ideas for developing a North Eastern tier of countries, namely Iran, Greece and Turkey, to help deter Soviet aggression in the Middle East. Quite simply, America could not allow Iran to go communist. It would have broken the containment perimeter at a strategically important point and would also have been symbolically damaging if it were to come so soon after Mao-tse-Tung's embarrassing triumph in China.

This gave Iran a card with which to trump the Americans, and through them the British, in the game of diplomacy. This trump card took the form of invoking the dangers of communism. American determination to save Iran from communism made them vulnerable to Iranian demands. In turn,

American indications that they would act to stave off communism emboldened the Iranians to make ever greater demands. The net product was that Britain was subject to intense American pressure to sacrifice its economic interests to meet ever increasing Iranian demands.

Mosadeq in particular skilfully exploited US concerns. Four reasons explain his hold upon the Americans. First, his indisputable nationalist credentials endeared him, at least initially, to a Truman Administration keen to ally itself with the forces of Third World nationalism. By doing so it naively hoped to disassociate itself from the legacies of western imperialism and to harness nationalism against communism. Second, Mosadeq's ideological neutralism gave added weight to his threats to co-operate with the Soviets and, if not take Iran into the Eastern, certainly move it out of the Western camp. Third, for the bulk of the dispute there seemed to be no better alternative leader with whom to deal. Fourth, a combination of Mosadeq's dependence on radical nationalists and his inability to cope with events convinced the Americans that even if he did not intend to lead Iran to communism, he might just do so by default unless he had US help.

Throughout his time in office Mosadeq repeatedly used his communist card against the Americans to play for better terms in the oil dispute and secure US aid. The bargaining took a number of forms. He warned America about the growing popularity of Russia among his people.[45] He threatened to sell oil to the Soviet bloc knowing that this would alarm the US Administration and cause it great difficulty with Congress because the Mutual Defence Assistance Control (Battle Act) of 1951 required the US to terminate aid to any country selling 'strategic' goods to Iron Curtain countries.[46] He also threatened to, and did, interrupt Anglo-Iranian relations as a means of increasing pressure by making America the West's last contact with Iran. Furthermore, Mosadeq persistently warned that Iran was reaching a crisis point which, without US aid, would lead to a communist takeover. In March 1953 Mosadeq waved his communist card blatantly. He spoke to the American Ambassador to Iran, Loy Henderson, and demanded that the US buy Iranian oil to stave off economic crisis in Iran. Henderson told him that American opinion would not tolerate payments to Iran for oil from British sources which had been seized without proper compensation. In reply Mosadeq said: 'You could tell them that you were saving Iran from Communism'.[47]

Throughout the crisis HMG castigated the Americans for failing to understand that 'our only hope of dealing with Mosadeq is to show conclusively that neither the British nor the United States Governments are going to accept his blackmail ...'[48] However, this misses a crucial point. It was not that the Americans were unaware of what Mosadeq was doing. They knew that he was using the spectre of communism to extort economic aid from the West and play Britain off against the US in order to extract greater concessions from the AIOC. Rather, the crucial point is that the Americans came to realise that their intervention had created a vicious circle which they were unable to break. Their mediation made it more difficult to achieve an agreement acceptable to Britain because they undermined British hardline tactics and urged concessions to save Iran from communism. However, this encouraged Iran to demand more concessions and further play America off against Britain. Moreover, this had the additional advantage of damaging Anglo-American relations, thus preventing a lasting joint Anglo-American position which might have forced Iran to accept British terms.

In short, the US intervened for Cold War reasons in the oil dispute but because it had insufficient power to exercise decisive influence it created a vicious circle which exacerbated the crisis. American inability to break this circle exposed the capability-expectation gap within global containment and made the US vulnerable to the demands of weaker allies. Iran exploited this situation very well. Its communist card persistently secured *de facto* US patronage and allowed Iran to play America off against Britain and extract a much improved oil deal compared to the Supplemental Agreement that the British had originally offered in 1949. In a wider context the communist card also secured American support for Iranian leaders. This was most clearly demonstrated by the establishment of an American client state under the Shah. And as for the US, the oil dispute was a painful demonstration of both its lack of power in the Middle East and the consequences of this. Its desire to contain communism opened it up to manipulation by its allies - even small, backward states like Iran - and forced it either to compromise with, or simply to accept, their actions.

The US and the Oil Majors

The third indicator that claims about US hegemony are often exaggerated lies in the relationship between the US Government and the American oil majors. The oil companies were indispensable allies in US global strategy, particularly as Government planners conceived of national security in terms of hemispheric oil self sufficiency.[49] They provided secure, stable and constant supplies of oil that were essential to America and its allies, particularly in Western Europe, for both economic and strategic reasons.[50] The oil majors acted as *de facto* representatives of US and Western capitalism in the Third World.[51] They were a means through which US Administrations could circumvent Congress and supply indirect aid free from charges of blatant 'economic imperialism'.[52] And in some cases they were even better placed to secure US foreign policy objectives than US Administrations. This was particularly the case in the Middle East where official American power, both political and more especially military, had only a limited foothold.[53] For example, following the alienation of the Arab world by Truman's policy towards Israel, the NEA Department concluded it probable that 'the oil companies are in a position to recover lost ground...sooner than the U.S. Government.'[54] In fact, the NSC admitted that 'American oil operations are, for all practical purposes, instruments of our foreign policy toward these countries.'[55]

But the oil companies were not passive tools. The power of the oil lobby in Washington was formidable and bolstered by a frequent interchange of personnel between the industry and government. Over the years petroleum firm executives held important positions in the Departments of State, Defense, Commerce and Interior. Max Thornburg and R.K. Davies actually continued to receive salaries from their former employers whilst holding their government appointments.[56] Furthermore, the oil majors had shown that they were more than willing to use their influence against American administrations if necessary. For example, plans to establish an Anglo-American oil agreement during World War Two were abandoned because the State Department conceded that 'no agreement could be negotiated or would be workable which did not have the support of the ... industry.'[57] That support was not forthcoming. In fact, so powerful were the oil majors that Democratic Senator, Estes Kefauver, of Tennessee, once claimed that 'When the big oil companies take snuff, the State Department sneezes' (Chester, 1983, p.323).

The product of this disposition of power was that the oil majors and the US Government were locked in what Richard Barnet has rightly called 'a symbiosis based on mutual dependency' (Barnet, 1972, p.199). The American Government depended on the oil majors to supply oil and regulate its flow in the world markets.[58] It depended on the operations of oil companies to counter communism in Third World countries by fostering economic growth and stability. It used them to supply indirect aid. And the fulfilment of national security objectives was dependent on the co-operation of the oil majors, especially in areas like the Middle East where the American Government lacked official power.

The Anglo-Iranian oil crisis among other things was a further demonstration of US dependence on the co-operation of the oil companies. A prime example of this was when the State Department devised a plan in Autumn 1952 to solve the Iranian crisis. The actual details of the scheme are not important, other than that it envisaged the participation of one or more of the oil majors in lifting and distributing Iranian oil.[59] Success required that two conditions be met. First, that the oil majors be granted exemption from prosecution under the Sherman anti-trust legislation because they would be forming a cartel to market Iranian oil. Second, the oil majors had to be willing to co-operate.

The need to grant anti-trust immunity raised interesting issues of principle and practice. On 7 November 1952 Acheson secured Truman's agreement to use sections 708a and 708b of the 1950 Defense Production Act to allow one or more of the American oil companies to participate in a voluntary arrangement to lift Iranian oil. However, at the same time the US Justice Department was prosecuting the oil majors under anti-trust legislation. The State and Justice Departments were thus pitted against one another. In principle, it was accepted that 'U.S. policy objectives are tied into the stability of oil concessions',[60] meaning that some arrangement was required whereby oil production was controlled. Without an international regulatory body for petroleum, there had to be an informal voluntary arrangement and this was effectively supplied by the so-called Seven Sisters: Shell, AIOC, Standard (New Jersey), Socony Vacuum, Gulf Corporation, Texas, and Standard of California.[61] However, although the Seven Sisters helped US foreign policy, their quasi cartel arrangement was abhorrent to independent oil producers and contrary to the strict application of anti-trust legislation. Consequently, the Justice Department felt the need to prosecute the Seven Sisters while the State Department had an explicit interest in preserving the 'oil cartel'.

The Iranian dispute demonstrated the importance attached to the oil companies in US foreign policy. The State Department forced the Department of Justice into submission. On 6 January 1953, with the support of the Defence Department, it argued that an indictment of the oil majors by a Grand Jury on the instigation of the US Government would be immensely damaging to American interests.[62] Three days later the NSC considered the arguments put forward by State, Defence and Justice. The Justice Department argued that the international oil cartel was a threat to national security. State and Defence Departments refuted that by contending that to prosecute the oil majors would be more damaging to national security. They won. On 11 January the Truman Administration announced its decision to drop criminal proceedings against the oil majors.

The Truman Administration therefore appeased the oil majors and overrode the objections of the Justice Department on the basis of a relative judgement about threats to national security.[63] This cleared the way for the oil industry to co-operate in the government's plan to lift Iranian oil. This co-operation was not forthcoming.[64] The commercial appraisal of the situation by the oil majors dovetailed far more comfortably with the attitude of the

British Treasury than with the Cold War concerns of the State Department. Like the British they preferred that the US Government did not act to rescue Mosadeq from his own folly. Instead they wanted to demonstrate to the world the unacceptability of abrogating contracts and the undesirable consequences for any country that did so.[65] Nor did they see much gain for themselves in the scheme. They had no need of Iranian oil.[66] They still feared anti-trust prosecution, especially as the Defense Production Act was due to expire in June 1953. And they thought that any settlement which could be interpreted as better than the widely used 50:50 principle for oil concessions would open a Pandora's box which would undermine the entire world oil industry.

Most important of all though, the oil majors would not co-operate without British approval because they were deeply conscious of the need for solidarity within the oil industry and well aware that their affiliates required the co-operation of the British Government in their operations.[67] They had willingly collaborated with the AIOC in its embargo on Iranian oil and continued to do so even after the US government withdrew its formal support for the embargo in December 1952. They disliked the imagery of their hovering like vultures over the carcass of the AIOC and they realised that solidarity was essential to preserve the stability of oil concessions. In the end they refused to participate in the plan to lift Iranian oil without British approval and that fatally compromised the American initiative. Although they were NGOs their power was palpable and the US government again, when confronted by another recalcitrant international actor, was forced to acknowledge the limitations on its power even in the pursuit of what it perceived as vital Cold War priorities.

Conclusion

American policy during the Anglo-Iranian oil crisis of 1950-54 casts grave doubts on the notion of postwar US hegemony. Acceptance of global containment forced the US to adopt a position as mediator between Britain and Iran to avert a crisis that could offer opportunities for communist advances. Yet, once in that situation, it lacked the necessary power to take decisive action. The product was that US intervention deepened the crisis as the Americans became impotently trapped between the rival claims of their foremost, ex-imperial but still major colonial, Cold War ally and those of a nationalist led, but recalcitrant, Iran.

J.F. Goode's castigation of the US approach to the Middle East as 'a policy of neglect' therefore misses an essential point (Goode, 1989, p.23). The Americans recognised the increased Cold War significance of the region but lacked the will and more importantly the power to do anything decisive about it between 1950-54. For three years the Americans failed dismally to mediate an oil settlement in Iran. The reason was threefold. First, there were irreconcilable differences between American Cold War priorities and the prime concerns of Britain and Iran. Neither Britain nor Iran would accept that their national interests should be subordinated to the American obsession with containment. Second, the Americans did not have the power necessary to force either Britain or Iran to sacrifice their national interest and accept an oil settlement with which they did not agree. In fact, the Americans could not even force the oil majors to sacrifice their commercial interests for the sake of containment. Third, by intervening without sufficient power the Americans created a vicious circle which revealed their own impotence and worsened the dispute by encouraging Iran to play its communist card.

It might seem rather crude to reduce a situation as complex as the Anglo-Iranian oil dispute to a simple equation of power. Nevertheless, empirical analysis of the crisis leads to one clear conclusion about American hegemonic Cold War leadership in the Middle East at this time. The oil crisis exposed a credibility gap between the expectations created by global containment and American capabilities to maintain the integrity of the perimeter fence against communist incursion. This exposed the US to manipulation by its allies, regardless of their size and even their nature, given that the oil majors were NGOs.

The extent of US weakness in the Middle East during the crisis is well demonstrated by the fact that their ideas for an oil settlement were fatally compromised successively by Britain, Iran and the multinational oil companies. Dependence on Britain as its only indispensable Cold War ally restricted US manoeuvrability. This limitation was most forcefully felt in the Middle East because of America's lack of power there and Britain's entrenched position and historical legacy of influence, its client states and actual economic and military presence. The Americans at one point conceded that the US 'in the absence of any overall plan of approach to Iran or the Middle East as a whole, has been placed in the position of following the British line.'[68]

Despite this, though, the US could not accept British priorities in the oil crisis. Saving Iran from communism had to be the number one priority. Unfortunately though, the American position was also too weak to control other parties in the oil dispute. Their concern to protect Iran laid the Americans open to manipulation by the Iranians who persistently used the communist card to extort US aid and better terms for an oil settlement. Moreover, the weakness of official US power in the Middle East strengthened the position of the oil majors and their actions demonstrated that multinational companies as well as states could modify and even destroy US policies in the Middle East. For example, the importance of the oil majors persuaded the Truman Administration to abandon its criminal anti-trust proceedings against them. It also enabled them to scuttle Truman's original plan to settle the Iranian oil dispute by steadfastly refusing to participate in a deal without British approval.

The product of this situation was that the US was forced into a series of compromises, policy fluctuations and embarrassing climb-downs. The Americans admitted in July 1952 that their attempts to 'follow the middle-of-the-road' between colonial and Third World states had rendered basic US policies ineffective in combating neutralism and communism.[69] A good example of this came in 1953 when, under considerable British pressure, the US abandoned its long-held policy of supporting Mosadeq against communism and collaborated in a coup to oust him. This marked American acceptance of the British position. It involved an embarrassingly public sacrifice of their declared principle of non-involvement in the internal affairs of third countries and it did substantial damage to their efforts to harness Third World nationalism against communism because the US was seen actively to ally itself with the forces of imperialism. Moreover, the coup failed either to lead to the imposition of an oil settlement or remove the communist card from Iranian hands. Instead, America became dependent upon the Shah and had to wait another year before there was a sufficient coincidence of interest between Britain, Iran and the oil majors to allow an oil agreement.

In short, the paradigm shift created by NSC-68 radically changed US perspectives of Iran and caused it to over-reach itself badly. Eagerness to combat communism coupled with insufficient power to make a decisive intervention paralysed US policy. Even worse, American impotence was starkly revealed and in the oil dispute all parties played upon it. Britain used its position as America's prime Cold War ally to resist US attempts to make it subordinate its national interests to containment. Iran used its communist card with alacrity to secure American patronage and advance its national interests. And the oil majors used their importance to US foreign policy and influence in Washington to safeguard and advance their commercial interests. The US thus became a prisoner of its own ambitions, of its prime Cold War ally and of the interests of both lesser state and non-state international actors. Far from being an assertive hegemonic leader in the Middle East the US was forced to collaborate reluctantly, and not necessarily on its terms, with a range of actors because it could not project sufficient unilateral power to achieve its Cold War objectives.

Notes

1 I am indebted to the Harry S. Truman Library for their generous research grant and assistance.

2 Based on Kennan's 'Long Telegram' sent while on attachment to U.S. Embassy Moscow, 22 Feb 1946. Text in Kennan (1968) pp.547-59.

3 For details see especially Leffler (1972); also Gaddis (1982, Chap. 4). For an interesting introduction to, and a number of interpretations of, NSC-68, see May (1993). For an example of the on-going debate about NSC-68, see Heuser (1991) and Cox (1992).

4 Foreign Relations of the United States (FRUS) 1947, Vol. v, State Dept. memo, undated, p 513; DeNovo (1976), pp.913-36.

5 For further details see FRUS 1949, Vol. vi, Statement by US and UK Groups, 14 Nov 1949, p 63; Ibid., memo by G.P. Merriam, 13 Jun 1949, p.40; Hudson (1977, p.55).

6 FRUS 1947, Vol. v, State Dept. memo, 'specific current questions', undated, p.556.

7 Ibid., memo by Chief of Division of South Asian Affairs (Hare), 5 Nov 1947, p. 578.

8 Harry S. Truman Library (HST Lib.), Acheson Papers, Box 76, Folder 1, Princeton Seminar, 15-16 May 1954, Reel 5, Track 2, p.16.

9 For further details see Keddie (1992, p.95); Yergin (1977, p.179); Truman (1955, pp.460-61); Lytle (1987); Hess (1974, pp.117-46); Pfau (1977, pp.359-72); Ambrose (1971, p.131); McFarland (1980, p.351). For the text of the Clifford Memorandum see Krock (1968, Appendix A).

10 FRUS 1949, Vol. vi, memo by G.P. Merriam of the Policy Planning Staff, 13 Clifford Memorandum see Krock (1968, Appendix A).Jun 1949, pp.42-3; Hudson (1977, p.58).

11 FRUS 1949, Vol. vi, NSC-54, 27 Jan 1949, pp.545-52; Ibid., US Security Interests Resumé, undated annex, p.4.

12 FRUS 1950, Vol. v, daily meeting with Secretary, p.482; McGhee (1983, p.73).

13 FRUS 1950, Vol. v, Wiley to Acheson, 29 Mar 1949, p.496.

14 Ibid., NEA paper 'Political and economic factors involved in military assistance to Iran in FY 1951', p.466.

15 Ibid., Wiley to Sec. State, 27 Feb 1950, p.481; Ibid., Wiley to Sec. State, 30 Jan 1950, p.459; Ibid., Wiley to Sec. State, 15 Feb 1950, p.471.

16 Ibid., Collins to Gray, 10 Apr 1950, p.507.

17 Ibid., McGhee to Acheson, 'Iranian crisis', 25 Apr 1950, p.524.

18 HST, PSF, Intelligence File, Box 257, Central Intelligence Reports, ORE 1949, No. 90-100, 'current situation in Iran', 9 Nov 1949, p.3.

19 FRUS 1950, Vol. v, State Dept. Paper, 'Present crisis in Iran', undated, pp.509-18. Ibid., Wiley to Sec. State, 30 Jan 1950, p.463.

20 FRUS 1949, Vol. vi, NSC-54, 21 Jul 1949, pp.545-52.

21 FRUS 1950, Vol. v, Rountree to Jernegan, 23 Mar 1950, p.491.

22 Ibid., State Dept. Paper, 'Present crisis in Iran', undated, pp.509-18; Ibid., Rountree to Jernegan, 23 Mar 1950, p.491.

23 Public Record Office (PRO), POWE 33 1933, minute by Butler, 15 Feb 1952; PRO, FO 371 98695, Fergusson to Strang, 27 Aug 1952.

24 PRO, FO 371 82377, minute by P.E. Ramsbotham, 22 Nov 1950. AIOC contributions to the Treasury had soared as oil production in Iran increased dramatically from 16.8 million tons in 1945 to 31.75 million by 1950.

25 An indication of British reliance on Middle Eastern oil can be gained from oil import figures for 1949/50. £22.1 million from Bahrain and Kuwait, £25.4 million from Saudi Arabia, Iraq and Iran, and just £8.4 million from the rest of the world. Figures from Darby (1973, p.25).

26 For similar conclusions see Ponting (1994, p.772) and Reynolds (1986, p.6).

27 PRO, CAB 129, C (52) 276, memo by Foreign Secretary 'Persia', 5 Aug 1952.

28 PRO, FO 371 98691, FO to Washington Embassy containing personal message for Acheson, 9 Aug 1952; PRO, FO 371 98694, Fergusson to Makins, 7 Aug 1952; PRO, CAB 129, C (52) 275, note by Foreign Secretary 'Persia' containing circular of Chargé d'Affaires Teheran to J. Bowker, 5 Aug 1952.

29 PRO, CAB 129, C (52) 276, memo by Foreign Secretary 'Persia', 5 Aug 1952; PRO, FO 371 98692, Draft paper for submission by Sec. State to the Cabinet, 'Persia', with covering letter by Makins, 2 Aug 1952; PRO, CAB 129, C (52) 286, Note by Secretary of the Cabinet circulating texts of telegrams exchanged between the Prime Minister and the President, 19 Aug 1952; PRO, FO 371 98696, minute by R.J. Bowker, 27 Aug 1952; PRO, FO 371 98696, minute by ADM Ross, 27 Aug 1952.

30 For examples of US anger at Britain's hardline attitude and requests that the US meekly follow its lead see: PRO, FO 371 98700, Washington Embassy to FO, 3 Oct 1952; PRO, FO 371 98701, Washington Embassy to FO, 11 Oct 1952; PRO, FO 371 98701, Washington Embassy to FO, 12 Oct 1952; PRO, FO 371 98701, Washington Embassy to FO, 13 Oct 1952.

31 HST, PSF, Intelligence Files, Box 257, CIA Report 'The possibility of Britain's abandonment of overseas commitments', 23 Dec 1949, p.1.

32 Bell (1964, p.8) attributes particular significance to the latter point. See also Manderson-Jones (1972, p.75); Campbell (1984).

33 United States National Archives Washington (NA), RG 59, Box 2768, H.R. Labouisse Jr. to Perkins, 27 Feb 1950, p.4.

34 This conclusion is supported by Watt (1984: 118) who argues that the military implications of NSC-68 'reinforced the necessity of Britain to America...'

35 Technical cooperation agreements were concluded with Saudi Arabia (17 Jan 1950), Jordan (3 Mar 1950), Iraq (19 Apr 1950), and Lebanon (29 May 1950). In August 1950 a treaty of friendship, commerce and navigation was signed with Israel and later the US began a programme of assistance to the newly independent constitutional monarchy in Libya. It also secured a mutual defence treaty with Saudi Arabia and access to the Dhahran airfield. HST Lib., McGhee

Papers, Box 1, File Dept. State, 'South Asian Regional Conference of U.S. Diplomats and Consular Offices', 26 Feb - 3 Mar 1951, p.6; FRUS 1950, Vol. v, Secretary of State to Embassy Iran, 15 Jul 1950, p.173; Ibid., memo by McGhee to President, 28 Aug 1950, p.179.

36 Ibid., memo by Chief of Programme Staff MDAP (Bray) to Deputy Director MDA (Ohly), 25 Jan 1950, p.122.

37 This analysis draws heavily on Kent (1993, p.204); FRUS 1950, Vol. v, memo by Ohly to Bray, 6 Feb 1950, (footnote 6), p.123.

38 FRUS 1950, Vol. v, State Dept. paper, 11 May 1950, p.157; Ibid., memo by Ambassador at Large (Jessup) to Sec. State, 25 Jul 1950, p 189; Hahn (1987: 23-40); Acheson Papers, Box 167, 'Commonwealth capabilities and intentions in the Middle East', 31 Dec 1951; FRUS 1952-54, Vol. ix, Negotiating Paper prepared by State Department 'Middle East Command', 4 Jan 1952, pp.168-70; Acheson Papers, Box 167, 'circular airgram to certain missions in the Near East', 15 Aug 1952; Ibid., State Dept. to London Embassy, 6 Sep 1952; PRO, CAB 129, C (52) 159, memo by Defence Ministry 'Command in the Mediterranean', 12 May 1952; Devereux (1990, p.247).

39 Acheson Papers, Box 167, 'Commonwealth capabilities and intentions in the Middle East', 31 Dec 1951.

40 Acheson Papers, Box 76, Princeton Seminar May 15-16 1954, reel 6, p.7.

41 FRUS 1952-54, Vol. ix, Henderson to State Dept., 5 Jan 1952, p.304.

42 DDE, Ann Whitman file, NSC Series, Box 4, 136th meeting NSC, memoranda of 136th meeting NSC on Wednesday 11 Mar 1953, 12 Mar 1953.

43 Much has been written on the so-called Special Relationship. See, for example, Allen (1954); Bartlett (1992); Baylis (1984); Danchev (1998); Dobson (1995); Reynolds (1988). For a more sceptical interpretation of the Special Relationship see Beloff (1959); Beloff (1986). For a bibliography of UK-US relations see Lincove and Treadway (1988).

44 FRUS 1952-54, Vol. x, memo of Foreign Ministers' meeting, 9 Jan 1952, p.319.

45 Ibid., Henderson to State Dept., 5 Oct 1951, p.204.

46 Ibid., Ambassador in Iran (Henderson) to State Dept., 14 Feb 1953, p.665.

47 PRO, FO 371 104614, FO to Washington, 7 Mar 1953.

48 PRO, FO 371 98699, FO to Washington Embassy, 30 Sep 1952.

49 For details see Stoff (1980, p.212).

50 HST Lib., R.K. Davies papers, memo for the petroleum coordinator, 15 Oct 1941; Stoff (1980, p.212).

51 In 1952 the Texas Oil Company contended that American oil companies operating abroad 'constituted a private Point 4 program...' as cited in Stocking (1971, p.122).

52 This was done through the manipulation of tax credits. See Anderson (1988, p.143); Anderson (1981).

53 FRUS 1951, Vol. v, Istanbul Conference of Middle Eastern Chiefs of Mission,

14-21 Feb 1951, pp.67-71.

54 FRUS 1948, Vol. v, Hare to Lovett, 25 Aug 1948, pp.139-40; Lilenthal (1957: 59-60) contends that Truman's Palestine policy was responsible for the extremism of Arab nationalism.

55 HST, PSF, NSC 138/1, 6 Jan 1953, p.5.

56 For a discussion of the power of the oil lobby see Engler (1961).

57 J.A. Loftus, as cited by Anderson (1981, p.126). For further details of opposition from oil concerns see Davies Papers, folder 3, Draft interpretation of the Anglo-American Petroleum Agreement by R.E. Hardwicke (special consultant to P.A.W.), 1 May 1946.

58 For example, at the request of the Petroleum Administration for Defense (PAD) nineteen American oil companies operating abroad entered into Plan of Action No. 1. Authorised under the Defense Production Act, this was a voluntary arrangement designed to alleviate oil shortages created by the Iranian crisis. It enabled the supply of 19,429,000 barrels of crude oil and 26,558,000 barrels of refined products to areas in need in the 'free world'. The plan also allowed for an intensification of normal commercial activities and more effective utilisation of tanker capacity through voluntary re-routings. So successful were the actions of the oil companies that by 2 July 1952 P.A.D. was able to terminate the Plan Of Action. Two months later the Secretary of Defense wrote that the plan had been an outstanding example of advantages to be received through close government - industry co-operation. The benefits were advantageous to this country and all friendly foreign nations, and were in the interest of the national defense effort.' HST, PSF, Report to the NSC by the Sec. Interior and Petroleum Administrator for Defense, 8 Dec 1952, p.10.

59 For greater detail see FRUS Iran 1952-54, Vol. x, Sec. State to Iran Embassy, 10 Oct 1952, pp.488-90.

60 FRUS 1950, Vol. v, Background paper prepared by Funkhouser, Sep 1950, p.89.

61 They developed mutual understandings and a system of self regulation which effectively mitigated against a recurrence of the anarchic conditions of production and marketing that the industry had suffered in the past. Together with their subsidiaries they controlled, in 1952, 80 percent of oil production outside of the US.

62 HST, PSF, Box 219, NSC Meetings 124-28, Folder NSC Meeting 128, 9 Jan 1953, report to the NSC on 'National Security problems concerning free world petroleum demands and potential supplies.', 6 Jan 1953, p.9; FRUS, 1952-54, Vol. ix, Memorandum of Conversation by the Assistant Secretary of State for Near Eastern, South Asian and African Affairs (Byroade), 8 Aug 1952, pp.262-66.

63 Acheson Papers, Princeton Seminar, 15 May 1954, Reel 4, Track 2, p.6.

64 On 11 November Nitze met Holman of Standard Oil (New York). Similar approaches were made on 21 November to Standard Oil (California), Socony

Vacuum and the Texas Oil Company. Eight days later, Gulf Oil was also contacted. Acheson (1970, p.684).

65 NA, LM 73, Reel 39, B.B. Jennings to McGhee, 17 May 1951; Ibid., Standard Oil to McGhee, 18 May 1951; FRUS 1951, Vol. v, memo of conv. by Funkhouser, 14 May 1951, p 311. Fesharaki has argued that the fear of further nationalisation was the most important motive for solidarity of the US companies with AIOC. Fesharaki (1976, p.45).

66 On 4 December the American Government concluded that there had been no overall shortage of crude petroleum or petroleum products as a result of the loss of Iranian oil. NA, LM 73, Reel 40, memo by Eakins to Linder, 4 Dec 1952.

67 NA, LM 73, Reel 34, memo of conversation between Nitze and Texas Oil Company representatives (Rogers, Long, Lilly), 21 Nov 1952; Ibid., memo of meeting with oil company representatives, 4 Dec 1952.

68 HST, Student research B file, Iran oil 1951-53, Box 1, File 9, report by Psychological Strategy Board, 21 Sep 1951, p.2.

69 FRUS 1952-54, Vol. ix, Memorandum by the Acting Regional Planning Advisor, Bureau of Near Eastern, South Asian and African Affairs (Hoskins) to Assistant Secretary of State for Near Eastern, South Asian and African Affairs (Byroade), 'reappraisal of US Policies in the NEA Area', 25 Jul 1952, pp.256-62.

5 Explaining Outside Interests in the Persian Gulf

SHAHIN P. MALIK

Introduction

Since the onset of the Cold War in 1946, global political events have been explained in terms of a particular set of assumptions, commonly referred to as the Cold War paradigm. The central tenet of these assumptions is that of the emergence of a bipolar framework in the international system based upon the ideological rift and the nuclear confrontation between the two Superpowers. This has meant that the conflict between the United States and the Soviet Union has been seen as a prime motivating factor behind most regional disputes.

Closely associated with this bipolar frame of reference was Kenneth Waltz's neo-realist labelling of the international system as some form of structured entity which asserted the logic of power politics. Neo-realist theory offered a lucid account of Cold War security, focusing on the distribution of power in an international system structured along anarchic lines which in turn determined the actions of states. This preoccupation with the distribution of power, primarily between the two Superpowers, makes it relatively easy to understand why structural bipolarity has been used as the dominant explanatory tool for the Cold War era. This perspective is now being challenged, however, and my intention in this chapter is to analyse how adequate it is for explaining relationships involving the Persian Gulf.

The Persian Gulf is geostrategically crucial to the West in terms of oil, markets and as a financial store. In the light of this, therefore, it should come as no surprise that the West has continually sought to maintain stability in the region by whatever means necessary. This desire to preserve the *status quo* has traditionally been explained with reference to fear of Soviet expansion, thereby invoking the Cold War paradigm. But, in a region as complex as the Persian Gulf, can the Cold War paradigm provide an adequate explanation of events or are there other factors which must be considered? This chapter will attempt to address this question by proceeding along the following lines. Firstly, the Cold War paradigm's interpretation of events in the region will be examined. Secondly, a series of other possible influential factors will be evaluated. These will include the Gulf states' new found self assertion with regards to oil production and pricing and Western economic competition in the Persian Gulf marketplace, centring on the question whether economic factors influenced Western states' behaviour more than their perceptions that the Soviets intended to encircle the region. In addition, the effect on Western interests of the aftermath of the Iranian Revolution and the conflict between Iran and Iraq between 1980 and 1988 will be considered. This will raise the question of whether indigenous factors played a significant role in the formation of Western policy. In the light of these factors, the relevance of the Cold War paradigm will be questioned further.

The Cold War Paradigm

The West's concern with maintaining stability in the region stemmed from the existence of vital economic interests. In a region as turbulent as the Persian Gulf this led to the emergence of threat perceptions which were traditionally explained in terms of the Cold War paradigm, an interpretation which should not be overlooked. For the sake of clarity Cold War explanations can be subdivided into two interlinked categories. The first concerns the perceived weakness of the West in the face of an advancing and strengthened Soviet Union, and the second relates to the Soviet Union's own emergent shortcomings in terms of accessible oil and the need to obtain new and secure supplies. In order to fully understand the significance of these factors they need to be analysed in the context of the Soviet invasion of Afghanistan and the Iranian Revolution, both of which occurred in 1979, and both of which highlight a number of wider security issues that need to be addressed.

A Weak West

The Cold War paradigm argues that Soviet actions had significant policy implications for Western governments in the sense that, as Saivetz states, 'The record of Soviet involvement in the Third World suggest[ed] that Moscow's activities [were] guided by geopolitical considerations (i.e.

concern for ports and strategic access) and by the desire to counter Western ... influence positions' (Saivetz, 1989, p.20). He goes on to claim that both motivations were crucial in the Middle East, where the Soviet Union continually wished to establish a naval presence.[1] As events in 1979 demonstrated, the failure of the US to maintain a direct presence in the region increased the potential for Soviet expansion. Indeed, by the late 1970s the West did not appear to have sufficient power to contain the threat made apparent by the Soviet gains in Afghanistan.[2]

In this context it must be remembered that, according to the Cold War paradigm, assessment of Soviet motives was the key factor in the formation of US policy towards the Gulf. During the final years of the 1970s, concern about the Soviet Union had grown in the United States,[3] and the perception now was that the Soviet Union had changed from being a continental to a global power.[4] Whereas during the 1960s it had been concerned predominantly with 'immediately adjacent areas and with what came to be known as the *Socialist Commonwealth*' (Jacobsen, 1979, pp.132-33), it was now dealing with obligations and commitments in more distant parts of the world. This new Soviet assertiveness came at a time when there had been a worldwide slippage of the US position. Dimitri cites Kissinger's views, which indicate that the US was decreasing in terms of global power and influence in the face of a Soviet advance: 'there is a historical inevitability that if present trends in the military balance are not arrested and reversed, the United States will have to take new strategic realities into account in some future international crisis and either retreat or risk confrontation from a position of perceived weakness' (Dimitri, 1979-80, p.28).

Apart from the peace treaty between Israel and Egypt at Camp David in 1978, prospects for US foreign policy successes in the Middle East remained bleak. As Newell states 'from the Golan Heights to South-West China ... the ruins of US policy lay strewn across the path of potential Soviet advance' (Newell, 1981, p.175). Even the Camp David Treaty itself was not a total success, since it was to result in the creation of a split in the Arab world between Egypt and other Arab states who were firmly opposed to peace with Israel, and who disliked the US for what it had done at Camp David. Although not viewed as being favourable in the Soviet Union, the Arab split did provide the USSR with opportunities to increase influence in states such as Syria and Libya (part of the no-compromise front) which were against the peace deal.

The greatest problem confronting the USA, however, was that at the end of the 1970s the Persian Gulf had become the central focus for the Soviet Union. As Fred Halliday wrote at the time, the 'Persian Gulf is where the West [was] now said to have its major strategic interests ... and it [was] here that the full blast of the Soviet threat [was] stated to be most evident ... Almost as certainly as did Europe in the 1940s, the Gulf provide[d] *the* critical source of conflict between the United States and the Soviet Union' (Halliday, 1981, p.9). In addition, Iran had 'been perceived by several generations of US political leaders as the most likely site outside the European theatre where an armed clash with the Soviet Union might escalate into a global conflict' (Sick in Maull and Pick, 1989, p.122). Since the 1950s the US had been actively involved in restricting Soviet expansion in the Middle East, as indicated by its support of Gulf Arab states and other members of the Baghdad Pact (later referred to as the Central Treaty Organisation - CENTO), in particular Iran which, once it joined in 1955, left the West in no doubt of its pro-Western, anti-Communist stance.[5]

The 1979 revolution in Iran, therefore, was a serious setback for Western interests in the Middle East, but as such was welcomed by the Soviet Union, as it was likely to make Iran more susceptible to Soviet overtures and as any weakening of the US position was perceived as a gain for them.[6] US and British relations with the Shah had been developing to the extent that by the 1970s 'Iran became important not only as a dependable source of oil and as a stabilising power in the Persian Gulf, but as a force for moderation in a wider Asian setting' and in this 'she had been encouraged by the United States, whose longstanding involvement had grown in proportion to her stake in the region' (Chubin in Treverton, 1981, p.107). However, despite this high degree of involvement in Iran, the revolution caught the West off guard: 'The Iranian Revolution was a major concern ... we had been taken by surprise ... we failed in our dealings with the Shah, we lost contact with the country, we had got it so badly wrong ... It was a seismic shock'.[7]

It was also increasingly believed in the West that the central tenet of Soviet foreign policy was expansion, and the invasion of Afghanistan confirmed this view : '... the Russians' need for oil and their increased scope for exerting political and military pressure in the Middle East following the occupation of Afghanistan could lead them into further adventures in that area, with serious implications for the West'.[8] Various events during the 1970s had tripped the alarm about the growth of Soviet power.[9] Fear of Soviet adventures had been increasing since their support for Vietnam's occupation of Cambodia, the Soviet-Cuban intervention in Angola, and influence in Ethiopia and Somalia, which all pointed towards Soviet expansionism. In addition, 'The scope for Soviet intervention in the Third World [had] increased by the development of an increased threat in South Africa, Pakistan and Iran, in all of which important Western interests [were] at stake'.[10]

The US response to the possibility of Soviet expansion highlights the relevance of the Cold War paradigm. In particular the Carter Doctrine of 23 January 1980 indicated a US resolve to transcend the effects of the "Vietnam Syndrome" and begin operating from a strengthened position. In his State of the Union Address President Carter stated that 'an attempt by any outside force to gain control of the Persian Gulf will be regarded as an assault on the vital interests of the United States of America. It will be repelled by any means necessary, including military force'.[11] However, despite the credence which this lends to the Cold War paradigm, other factors must also be considered.

Soviet Needs

Consistent Soviet interest in the Middle East traditionally centred around two factors, the proximity of the Middle East and the Suez Canal to the USSR and the region's extensive resources.[12] The prevalent view amongst some Western countries (particularly the US and Britain) at the time of the invasion of Afghanistan, therefore, was that this represented a decisive Soviet move towards a warm water port, and also an attempt to control Persian Gulf wealth and the Western oil and trade sea lanes.

Western fears were also heightened by the fact that the future oil-export market would increasingly be dominated by fewer and fewer nations primarily centred in the Persian Gulf.[13] Although the Soviet Union had been a net exporter of oil and self sufficient in meeting its own energy requirements, there was a 'growing disjunction between the location of fuel reserves and major areas of consumption' (Cobb, 1979, p.357). The fact that the 'availability of easily extracted resources located in the Western part of the USSR was rapidly diminishing' combined with the fact that most of the Soviet Union's resources were increasingly 'concentrated in inhospitable areas of Siberia and Central Asia' meant that the Soviet Union stood at the edge of becoming a net importer of energy.[14] These prospects were full of serious implications since, as Cobb states, 'the entrance of the Soviet Union into competition for the world's increasingly scarce energy resources was likely to significantly alter Soviet strategic policies, particularly with respect to the oil-rich Persian Gulf' (Cobb, 1979, p.379), thus raising the possibility of direct confrontation with the West.

Soviet overtures to Iran following the revolution and the invasion of Afghanistan convinced the West that there was a 'persistent and systematic Soviet effort to spread her influence southward' (Khalilzad, 1980, p.156). The belief that the Soviets were attempting to encircle the Persian Gulf was further confirmed by their support for the Peoples Democratic Republic of

Yemen (PDRY), which meant that they were well placed to strengthen revolutionary forces in the Middle East.[15]

The preceding analysis has highlighted some of the central arguments put forward by the Cold War paradigm, which isolates the effects of the bilateral relationship between the West and the Soviet Union as the primary influential factors in the Persian Gulf. These conclusions must not be dismissed, but by concentrating purely on Cold War factors, a host of other issues are in danger of being overlooked. Analysts have all too often addressed the question of Western interests in the Persian Gulf solely in terms of Cold War factors and have, therefore, reached oversimplified conclusions. In fact, the Cold War paradigm has in the past dominated thinking to such an extent that the bipolar explanation has been allowed to eclipse other underlying factors of importance. A prime example of this was the common perception that the Soviets were trying to gain a foothold in Iran following the revolution, a development which was in fact not possible given that the new Islamic regime was as anti-Soviet as it was anti-Western. Another closely related example is the fact that the Iranian revolution also gave the Soviet Union cause for concern because of the large number of Muslims living within Soviet borders. The Soviets, therefore, recognised the very real danger of the revolution spreading to within their own territory, but in light of its dissociation from the Cold War paradigm, this is one of many factors which have been largely overlooked.

In the complex and turbulent atmosphere of the Persian Gulf, therefore, there were a range of other non-Cold War related factors which further discredit the oversimplified bipolar framework. Foremost amongst these was the economic importance of the region in terms of export markets, which was influential not only because of the Western economic interest in the market place, but also because, as their awareness of the importance of the power of oil grew, the Gulf states became more assertive. Another important factor indigenous to the region, also unrelated to the Cold War paradigm, was the threat to the economically vital Arab Gulf of the spread of Islamic fundamentalism, as perceived in the Iranian revolution. Although Iraq's invasion of Iran in 1980 may have countered this to some extent, this conflict itself later became a further source of instability in the area.

Beyond the Cold War paradigm

Since the Cold War paradigm fails to reflect adequately the complexity of the situation in the Persian Gulf between 1979 and 1985, we must now consider certain factors indigenous to the region itself. These can be broadly classified under four headings: (a) *self assertion* on the part of the Gulf states with regards to oil pricing and production levels; (b) *Western economic interest* in the Gulf marketplace; (c) *political changes* within the Gulf states; and finally, *(d) conflict* in the region.

a) Self assertion and Western security

To understand fully the importance of Persian Gulf oil the contemporary limitations of *oil* as a mere commodity must be transcended and it must be placed in a wider political frame of reference. The importance of oil is such that Haglund has gone so far as to label it a *national interest.* He highlights the connection between the concepts of "strategic minerals" (in this case Persian Gulf oil) and "interdependence", arguing that 'states have legitimate interests in access to oil (and other minerals), ... because they regard themselves as vulnerable to supply disruptions of minerals in which they have some degree of import dependence' (Haglund in Marantz, 1985, p.176).

This important point was highlighted by the 1973 Oil Crisis which, in addition to destroying the prevailing belief that oil supplies were abundant, propelled the Persian Gulf into being one of the most important theatres in the global politico-strategic struggle for secure energy supplies. Cunningham, writing in 1988, stated that the preoccupation with the Gulf came about due to the realisation that 'to date the world's discovered reserves of oil have totalled 1,180 billion barrels of which 700 billion remain to be produced. Over 56 percent of these reserves are in the Gulf' (Cunningham, 1988, p.9). He went on to claim that if established production patterns were to continue there would come a time when the 'only conventional reserves of oil' were in the 'hands of the governments of Saudi Arabia, Kuwait, Abu Dhabi, Syria and Iraq' (Cunningham, 1988, p.11).

Despite attempts to reduce dependency on oil through energy diversification and a search for alternative oil reserves, Western European and other states remained dependent on the Gulf and, in particular, 'the world remained enormously dependent on the production policies of one key OPEC (Organisation of Petroleum Exporting Countries) country - Saudi Arabia' (Levy, 1981, p.1084). Vital economic sectors remained heavily reliant on oil and therefore any disruption to supply would have damaged Western economies. While states such as the US and Britain may have had other interests in the Persian Gulf, one of the primary objectives was to secure access to the oil reserves of the Gulf states. It is therefore clear that the relationship with the Gulf states was pivotal to Western security. Table 1 illustrates that any loss of Gulf oil would have resulted in massive global economic and political instability.[16]

Table 1: World Petroleum Supplies in 1980: The "Top Ten" before the Iran-Iraq War

Oil Production			Oil Exports		Oil Reserves	
Rank	Country	MBD*	Country	MBD*	Country	Billions of Barrels
1	USSR	11.7	SA*	9.4	SA	168.0
2	SA	9.9	USSR	3.0	Kuwait	67.9
3	US	8.6	Iraq	2.3	USSR	63.0
4	Iraq	2.6	Nigeria	1.9	Iran	57.5
5	Venez'la	2.2	Venez'la	1.8	Mexico	44.0
6	China	2.1	Libya	1.7	Iraq	30.0
7	Nigeria	2.1	Abu D'i*	1.6	Abu D'i*	29.0
8	Mexico	1.9	Kuwait[17]	1.5	US	26.4
9	Libya	1.8	Indonesia	1.2	Libya	23.0
10	Kuwait	1.7	Iran	1.1	China	20.5

(* Saudi Arabia, * MBD - Million Barrels per Day, *Abu D'i - Abu Dhabi
Source: Cordesman, 1984, p.4.

The table shows that five Gulf states (Saudi Arabia, Kuwait, Iran, Iraq, and Abu Dhabi) were in the top ten league of oil producers, thus making this region strategically, politically and economically crucial to Western Europe, Japan and the United States. It is also important to realise that Saudi Arabia alone accounted not only for nearly 25 percent of the world's proven oil reserves but also for 30 percent of the sustained oil production capacity of OPEC.[18]

The other Gulf states, however, were also crucial in terms of their oil reserves and production capacity. Though not as wealthy or influential as Saudi Arabia, collectively they did have roughly 50 percent of the former's production capacity and approximately 16 percent of the world's proven oil reserves. Furthermore, estimation of proven oil reserves in Kuwait was to go up in 1981 from 67.9 billion barrels to over 167 billion barrels, thus significantly increasing the importance of the region and that particular Gulf state.

Before 1973 global energy issues were not a high priority in the West. This was essentially because at this time prices were largely determined by the efforts made by the oil companies in exploration, investment and production. Between 1945 and 1973 the oil companies set prices well below the costs of alternative fuels, thus ensuring that the international community had access to cheap and what seemed at the time an almost unlimited supply of oil.[19] This sense of false security brought about by adequate oil supplies not only contributed much to rapid economic expansion but caused what Haig terms an 'age of dependency for the industrial democracies' (Haig, 1980, p.755).

The 1973 oil crisis shattered these false illusions, however, and had the effect of immediately propelling the energy issue to the top of the Western security agenda. Concern increased as the crisis also demonstrated that nation states (in this case OPEC governments) had successfully seized control of their oil back from the oil companies and had become capable of setting prices unilaterally. In addition, OPEC's newly acquired power coincided with the fact that, despite the West's declared aims of reducing oil imports, imports actually increased and were likely to go on increasing.[20] Indeed, as figures for the US indicate, in 1947 it imported approximately 7.2 percent of its 2.1 billion barrel requirement. In 1970 this had increased to 23 percent of a 5.5 billion barrel requirement and by 1977 there had been a further increase to a staggering 47 percent of 6.8 billion barrels.[21]

Fiona Venn highlights a number of other factors for concern. She supports the view that the price escalation had a severe impact upon Western economies which were already experiencing the onset of recession. However, she stresses the fact that 'though it was the Western nations whose problems were the more immediately apparent, the impact was global in its implications' (Venn, 1986, p.152). These global effects were of particular significance since the West feared that other underdeveloped raw material producers would follow the precedent set by the oil rich states.

The effects of the crisis were compounded further as Western demand for oil continued to rise. This was in spite of the fact that many advocated conservation and the search for alternative fuels. The *self assertion* sweeping through OPEC capitals placed increasing pressure upon price constraint and high production levels and is further proof of the need to shift the focus of analysis from the Soviet-centric to the Gulf-centric viewpoint. It became apparent that it was simply not in the interests of the Gulf states to maintain high production levels as this would result in reduced prices. Indeed, during the 1970s, they came increasingly to the conclusion that revenues could be raised by restricting oil production.

This raised questions over continued access to secure oil supplies which, since oil began to be mentioned as a key factor in strengthening allied security, gave rise to the conviction that there was a strong relationship between oil and national security itself.[22] Denis Healey (Chancellor of the Exchequer of the British government until May 1979) stated at the time that oil producing countries had begun to think about restricting production in order to increase prices. He went on to state that 'oil [was] so important in so many ways that sudden changes in its price or supply [could] inflict great damage on the whole world economy. When change [was] sudden, the industrial consuming countries [could not] hope to meet it by conservation alone' (Healey, 1979/80, p.226). This situation proves that the concept of security in relation to the Persian Gulf region must be broadened to include indigenous threats to oil supplies, as these in fact constituted a more serious possibility of disruption than the Western perceived threat from Soviet encirclement.

(b) The economic importance of the region

Oil is not the only factor which prompted Western (especially US and British) action in the Persian Gulf. Apart from oil the importance of the Gulf region lay in providing a lucrative market place for Western exports, the sale of which provided much needed profits and employment in West European and US industrial sectors. As a nation importing goods Saudi Arabia, for instance, ranked behind only West European nations and the US. Although approaches to the market varied amongst West European states, reflecting in part historical ties, many had a stake in Gulf markets, exporting both defence and civilian products, and the market was vast. Oman alone was spending around 40 percent of its annual budget on defence and Saudi Arabia accounted for 8 percent of total global military spending. Amongst the West European states with a significant stake in Gulf markets, Britain, for instance, had a 'disproportionately large influence among the smaller Gulf states such as Oman, Bahrain, Qatar and the United Arab Emirates (UAE)' (Cunningham, 1988, pp.23-4) and, as Britain increasingly sought overseas defence markets, this interest was to widen significantly to include Saudi Arabia.

Another key factor was that since 1973 the West had spent vast amounts of money on the purchase of oil from the Persian Gulf, with the result that one of the primary objectives of states such as Britain and the US was to *recycle* these sums back into Western financial markets. Western states therefore attached great importance to establishing bilateral economic links with the Gulf states and providing programmes for infrastructural development in the Gulf countries. Arms sales and other general imports into the region became important methods by which money spent on purchasing oil could be channelled back into Western economies. As Table 2 shows, the oil revenues of all the Arab oil exporting countries were to increase substantially between 1973 and 1981, thereby ensuring that the importance of the bilateral links transcended any threats posed by the Soviet Union since any disruption of the existing economic order would have been equally damaging to Western interests.

Table 2: Oil Revenues of Key Arab Oil Exporters: US $ billions

	1964-73	73	75	77	79	81
Kuwait	11.8	2.8	5.9	8.9	16.7	14.9
SA	16.7	9.0	29.5	43.3	62.9	116.2
Qatar	1.8	0.6	1.8	2.0	3.6	5.4
UAE	2.2	1.9	6.8	9.1	12.9	18.8
Iraq	7.3	1.9	7.5	9.6	21.3	10.4
Oman	-	0.18	1.1	1.4	2.2	4.2
Bahr'n	-	0.05	0.29	0.4	0.53	3.0

Source: Taken from Eheteshami, 1992, p.161.

This lucrative situation naturally meant that the West sought to secure the market for its own products. Saudi Arabia in particular, with its sizeable defence budget, caught the attention of various Western governments, especially as its dominant strategic location on the Red Sea and its position as the leading member of OPEC meant that it became increasingly concerned about its own security. The Cold War paradigm would explain these concerns as stemming exclusively from the Soviet encirclement of the Gulf region. According to this argument Saudi Arabia saw Soviet gains in Ethiopia, South Yemen and Afghanistan as 'part of an overall Kremlin design to encircle the Arabian peninsula, topple its shaky conservative regimes, and gain control over the West's oil lifeline'.[23]

However, this viewpoint neglects other more pertinent issues which are not related to the Cold War paradigm. Two such factors, both of which gave more immediate cause for concern than the possibility of Soviet expansion, were the threat of Islamic fundamentalism as manifested in the Iranian Revolution, and the possibility of widening conflict emanating from the Iran-Iraq war. The fall of the Shah in 1979 began a chain of events which, by 1985, culminated in Britain securing its largest ever defence contract, the Al-Yamamah deal. The effects of the Iranian Revolution, therefore, were threefold: it firstly heightened security fears in the West as well as within the Persian Gulf itself; secondly, it highlighted the extent of the Gulf defence markets as states such as Saudi Arabia, fearful of Iranian fundamentalism, sought to acquire ever greater consignments of Western defence equipment; and thirdly, it led to intense intra-Western competition as various Western states vied for the opportunity to fulfil the increasing demand. The most profitable of the Gulf states for trade was Saudi Arabia whose market alone was worth over $20 billion a year, a massive slice of which centred around construction projects and the purchase of defence equipment.

By the mid-1970s the United States was by far the largest military supplier to Saudi Arabia; indeed between 1975 and 1978 US military sales to the Saudis amounted to over $15 billion. The US Army Corps of Engineers (USACE) on its own accounted for almost $1 billion worth of contracts between 1976 and 1979, as shown in Table 3, which highlights both civilian construction and the military angle of the contracts.

Table 3: Saudi Arabia: Major construction contracts awarded by the US Army Corps of Engineers: 1976-1979

Year	Nature of Contract	Amount (in $ millions)
1976	SANG HQ	208
	SNEP HQ	23
1977	Desalinisation Plant	20
	Airborne and Physical Training School	83.5
	RSAF HQ	77.2
	KKMC Support Services	88
	VIP Complex	22.8
1978	Jeddah Onshore Facilities	167.7
	2 Sewage Treatment Plants	28.6
	3 Schools	15.2
	Port Facilities	42
	5000 Man Mobilisation Camp	43.4
1979	Hospital	25.2
	Support Service	28.9
	Desalinisation Plant	25.3

Source: Shirreff, 1979, pp.4-5.

From the late 1970s to the early 80s the USACE was securing up to $1.5 billion worth of contracts in Saudi Arabia each year, a programme which had begun in the 1950s with the construction of Dharan airfield and which by 1981 was worth over $18 billion.[24] Escalating demand meant that by 1980 Saudi Arabia was America's biggest arms customer 'buying well over half of everything sold under the Foreign Military Sales (FMS) programme'.[25]

However, despite this strong trade connection, the relationship between the two countries became somewhat strained as a result of the pro-Israeli lobbies within the US Congress. This became particularly apparent when Saudi Arabia sought a commitment from the US for modifications that would give its McDonnell Douglas F-15 aircraft far greater range and striking power. Initially, in light of the Iranian Revolution and the outbreak of conflict between Iran and Iraq, the US State Department believed that there was considerable justification for allowing Saudi Arabia a more offensive, long-range version of the F-15. This was confirmed when a message received by the CIA from Saudi authorities specified that Iran had warned publicly that it would retaliate against any country aiding Iraq, since there were strong indications that many of the Gulf Arab monarchies, including Saudi Arabia, were in fact doing so. [26]

Strong support from the Pentagon and the White House resulted in the provision of 4 AWACs (Airborne Warning and Air Control Systems) which were seen as an ideal first step towards reassuring the Saudis of US support. The White House also went so far as to seriously consider the request for an upgrade to its US built and supplied F-15s, despite a promise made to Israel that such equipment would not be provided to the Saudis.[27] The potential danger of the situation in the Persian Gulf was such that in 1981 James Buckley (the then Undersecretary of State for Security Assistance) pointed to the Iranian Revolution, the Iran-Iraq War and the Soviet invasion of Afghanistan as being 'indicative of the growing threat to US and Western interests', thereby highlighting non-Cold War factors in addition to the Cold War paradigm.[28] He also stressed the Administration's determination 'to reverse this dangerous trend', which led to a commitment to supply equipment worth $8.5 billion including 5 additional AWACS, aerial refuelling aircraft, 1,177 AIM-9L Sidewinder missiles, and conformal fuel tanks to extend the range of the F-15s.[29]

However, although the Reagan Administration secured approval for the supply of this equipment, pro-Israeli lobbies within Congress ensured that the deal would not proceed without severe restrictions.[30] Such restrictions reinforced Saudi determination to diversify its arms procurement, as demonstrated in its massive deal with France for the development of its navy in mid-1981, thereby leading to intense West European competition for a share of the Saudi market.[31] These restrictions were also largely responsible for the Saudi decision to award Britain a contract to supply Tornado aircraft, rather than the US F-15s. This deal, signed on 17 February 1986, involved the sale of 132 military aircraft as well as support services, without restrictions, and was the biggest deal of its type that Britain had ever concluded. It was particularly significant for the UK as it had been won against strong competition from the French supplied Mirage 2000.[32] Such deals had crucial implications for Western economies, and their importance is reflected in the personal involvement of leaders such as Margaret Thatcher and Ronald Reagan: 'big defence sales benefited the economy and provided influence - major defence deals often lead to other trade. Mrs Thatcher realised this, and was prepared to make a personal effort'.[33]

The above analysis has proved that economic interests are of paramount importance when considering influential factors in the Persian Gulf region, despite not being connected to the Cold War paradigm. It has also demonstrated how highly the West prized the security of the region and that the provision of arms to states such as Saudi Arabia was one way of ensuring that they could protect themselves, thereby indirectly protecting the West's interests. As highlighted above, although the Soviet invasion of Afghanistan was a relevant security concern, more significant threats were Islamic fundamentalism (the 1979 Iranian Revolution) and conflict in the region (the Iran-Iraq war), to which we must now turn our attention.

c) The Iranian Revolution

In view of the crucial economic interests outlined above, a key Western objective was to safeguard them by maintaining a stable order in the Persian Gulf. Britain's announcement on 17 January 1968 that it was preparing to withdraw all its forces from 'east of Suez', ending its military and political presence in the Gulf, resulted in the emergence of a power vacuum in the region which was quickly filled by the US.[34] From 1973 onwards US policy centred on encouraging both Saudi Arabia and Iran to act as surrogates and police the Gulf on behalf of the West's economic interests, receiving American assistance in return for local military self-reliance. The Shah of Iran accepted the invitation to serve as guarantor of Gulf security, Western oil supplies and access through the straits of Hormuz, demanding in return considerable amounts of advanced weapons systems which, according to Whettan, amounted to approximately $18 billion worth.[35]

This framework for security continued until the Iranian Revolution in 1979, which was a destabilising political change in the region since the two-pillar policy adopted by the US after 1973 of 'employing' Iran and Saudi Arabia to 'manage' Western interests in the region was effectively destroyed. The 1979 demonstrations by countless Iranians in opposition to the Shah and his despotic rule were understood, in the West, to be attributable to 'fanaticism of the Iranian people' (Rouleau, 1980, p.1). In Western eyes this was clearly manifest in the emergence of a virulently anti-Western regime in Teheran headed by Ayatollah Khomeini. Khomeini and his followers, on the other hand, claimed that they stood against foreign domination, the Shah's despotism and injustice: 'precisely the evils', as Rouleau argues, 'suffered by the Iranian people under the reign of Mohammed Reza Shah'.[36] Khomeini's own broadcasts highlighted the anti-Western nature of the new regime by clearly indicating that Iran's problems largely lay in US interference in Iranian politics.[37]

The instability in Iran during 1978 began a process which culminated in increasing price anarchy in the oil market. The oil crisis began when, in winter 1978, strikes led to a total cutoff of Iranian oil exports, and when Iran did begin re-exporting, it was at a much reduced level. The fact that Iran had been Western Europe's second biggest oil supplier meant that the halt in oil caused serious disruptions, particularly in Sweden and in the United Kingdom, despite the fact that North Sea oil facilities were expanding.[38] Disruption to European oil supplies was also indicated when British Petroleum and Royal Dutch/Shell had to begin cutting deliveries to third party customers.[39]

The revolutionary movement in Iran proved that politics was to feature strongly in any future decision to export its oil, and in fact states such as Israel and South Africa were shut out completely.[40] The result of the Iranian blockage was a significant increase in the price of oil from $12.70 per barrel (pb) in December 1978 to $24 pb in December 1979 (representing a 93 percent increase), with some prices rising even higher to as much as $40 pb in early 1980.[41]

Saudi Arabia's importance for the West was once again demonstrated at the time of the Iranian disruption. By increasing their own oil production levels the Saudis were able to cushion the effects of the significant decrease in oil supply. The increase in European and US oil consumption levels, however, meant that the Saudi action did not provide lasting assistance. In addition, as Yergin and Stobaugh claim, the Saudis themselves were increasingly unable to influence the price and as a result were soon reluctant 'to go out on a limb against the other OPEC countries' - especially in light of the US's 'inability to control demand and reduce imports' (Stobaugh and Yergin, 1980, p.573).

It was against this background of revolution in Iran that yet another dilemma confronted the US. Radical Iranian students, undoubtedly influenced by Khomeini's religious fervour, seized the American embassy in Teheran on 4 November 1978 and thus prompted a crisis which was to last for over fourteen months. Relations deteriorated further following the Shah's admission into the US, particularly as Khomeini had been urging Iranian students to 'expand [their] attacks against America and Israel with full force, and to compel the US into extraditing this criminal deposed Shah'.[42] The hostage crisis, therefore, not only contributed to the deterioration in relations between Iran and the West but also hinted at the intractable nature of instability in the Persian Gulf and the problems yet to come.

The crisis also forced the West to acknowledge the existence of another serious threat. One US response to the seizure of the embassy was to freeze Iranian monetary assets held in Western banks. The US Treasury Department had to finally admit that states which had accumulated billions of dollars in surplus oil posed two threats in that they could weaken the dollar by moving their deposits and also create large losses for Western private banks by repudiating their debts.[43]

The US action provided Khomeini with a means of utilising the increasingly widespread anti-US feeling to mobilise Iran's population under his banner of Shi'ite Islam. This was reinforced by the bungled US attempt to rescue the hostages on 25 April 1979, providing Khomeini with the evidence he needed to convince the population that the main danger threatening Iran was foreign intervention.

The challenges posed by Iran's revolution were to last well into the 1980s, with the result that outside interests in the Persian Gulf were to be seriously affected. Many analysts agree that the fundamentalist regime of revolutionary Iran endangered the regional *status quo*.[44] Essentially, two different world views came into conflict with each other after the revolution, and there was a genuine fear in pro-Western Gulf states such as Saudi Arabia and Bahrain that their traditional monarchies had come under serious threat from the revolutionaries in Iran. It is widely accepted that Khomeini wanted to overthrow other forms of authority not only in Iran but elsewhere in the Middle East, and to replace them with theocratic systems of government.[45]

However, the real danger for Western interests lay in the fact that in the Middle Eastern (and global) Muslim populations the Shi'ites have traditionally been ruled as a disadvantaged class by the other major Islamic sect - the Sunnis. Even in Iraq where the Shi'ites were the majority sect (52 percent of the population), they did not have political control since Sunnis occupied 80 percent of top government posts.[46] Iran, being the only Middle Eastern country to have an absolute Shi'ite majority (90 percent of the total population), therefore had the potential of providing a powerful attraction to the Shi'ites elsewhere in the Gulf.

Paranoia and fear of Iranian fundamentalism among the Arab states was such that, in the case of Iraq, action was taken against *al-Dawaa*, an Iraqi Shi'ite group accused of attempting to assassinate Tariq Aziz (Iraq's Deputy Premier) in April 1980. In response to this attempted assassination up to 200,000 Iraqi Shi'ites, labelled as 'illegal Persian immigrants', were expelled from Iraq.[47]

Further evidence of the threats posed by the change in the political structure of Iran is provided by Iranian territorial claims in the Gulf region. Most notable were its claims to the *Shatt al-Arab* and Bahrain. The *Shatt al-Arab* is a stretch of water which runs from the confluence of the Tigris and Euphrates rivers to the Gulf, and which has raised issues of sovereignty since the period of the Persian (and Ottoman) Empire. Prior to 1969 Iraq had controlled the entire river, but after this the balance of forces shifted in Iran's favour and as a result it was able to begin navigating ships under its own flag. This also led to the Shah renewing claims to a line drawn down the channel in the centre of the river (*Thalweg* - or line of deepest water).

The problems between Iran and Iraq were further exacerbated by Iranian support for the Kurdish separatist movement in Iraq. The rebellion by the Kurds during the early 1970s had seriously weakened Iraq, and Iranian support for the Kurds was almost to lead to war in 1974. The Algiers Agreement, signed between Iran and Iraq on 6 March 1975, brought about a reduction in Iranian aid to Iraqi Kurds in exchange for a relocation of the frontier along the *Shatt,* a settlement which in effect meant that a major Iranian ambition had been achieved.[48]

The other Gulf states were themselves well aware of the potential threats posed by revolutionary Iran. Claims to Bahrain for instance have to be considered in light of the unsuccessful coup in Bahrain in December 1981. It was widely accepted that Iran was behind the attempt, and the fact that Ayatollah Rouhani (a leading member of the Iranian clergy) referred to Bahrain as Iranian in September 1979 must not be dismissed lightly.[49]

The Iranian Revolution was therefore perceived as a serious threat not only by the West, but also by the various Arab Gulf monarchies in which the West had important economic interests. Ayatollah Khomeini's success demonstrated that Islamic revolution was possible and this was 'a powerful sectarian example to the shi'ites in Bahrain, Lebanon, Saudi Arabia, Syria and the Yemens' (Cordesman, 1987, p.1). We have here therefore a prime example of an influential political factor which is indigenous to the Persian Gulf region, does not emanate from the Soviet Union and can hardly be linked to the Cold War paradigm.

d) Conflict within the Persian Gulf

A further significant non-Cold War factor in the region was the Iran-Iraq war, which had the potential of polarising Islamic populations in the Middle East between Sunni and Shi'ite, and which could have further divided the Arab world between secular states and those advocating some form of fundamental religious hegemony. Although Saddam Hussein's real motives may never be known, Iraq's invasion of Iran reflected to some extent the fear of Islamic fundamentalism felt by the other Gulf states and the West. However, although this might suggest that there would be tacit support for Iraq's actions, as the conflict progressed there was a danger that it would spread to other Gulf states, thereby itself further endangering the stability of the region.

The problems between Teheran and Baghdad did not begin with Ayatollah Khomeini's Islamic Revolution, however, but were rather the culmination of the conflict between two incompatible nations. Dilip Hiro saw the hostility between Iraq and Iran as a 'symptom of deeper conflicts between the two states on domestic social systems and international alignments' (Hiro, 1985, p.165). The new Iranian regime saw Iraq as being more pro-Shah, and since it was determined to reverse the basics of the Shah's foreign policy 'it was obvious that sooner or later Iraq's Ba'athist regime would be placed on Khomeini's enemy list' (Zabih, 1988, p.166). In order to understand the nature of the conflict and the threat it posed to the region, therefore, it must be understood that there were two aspects to Saddam Hussein's personality.

Firstly, 'the most common explanation views the invasion of Iran as evidence of Hussein's aggressive personality and his unbridled regional ambitions' (Karsh and Rautsi, 1991, p.135). This is reflected in the belief that Ayatollah Khomeini's new regime was an easy target, and that Saddam Hussein would speedily secure a victory.[50] This would have provided him with the status and prestige he sought from the Arab world, as the pro-Western Gulf Monarchies greatly feared a fundamentalist Iran intent on exporting its revolution, and would have seen him as something of a saviour. In McKnight's words, he was therefore 'laying claim to the status which President Nasser of Egypt once enjoyed in Arab politics' (McKnight, 1992, p.25). His desire for international prestige also explains his use of Egypt's new relationship with Israel to manoeuvre himself to take over Egypt's position at the centre of Arab politics. The first ever Arab summit in Iraq after the Camp David accords prepared the way for Baghdad to 'become the centre of inter-Arab politics, and Saddam a politician of regional stature and a champion of the Arab cause' (Karsh and Rautsi, 1991, p.104).

In domestic politics Saddam Hussein's absolutism is aptly explained by al-Khalil who indicates how personalised and complete Saddam's authority became over Ba'athist Iraq. He states 'Portraits of leaders signify power in the Middle East. But these are rarely as big and varied as in Ba'athist Iraq. A large painted cutout figure of Saddam Hussein towers over the entrance of every Iraqi village ... a thirty foot high version can be seen near Baghdad city centre. Photographs adorn every shop, school, police station, army barracks, and in public buildings ...' and he goes on to explain that not even the most popular Third World leaders commanded such a 'death-grip on this image and status as leaders' (Al-Khalil, 1989, p.117).

Saddam Hussein's territorial ambitions were also a factor of importance in the conflict, particularly the long-standing dispute over the *Shatt al-Arab*, a strategically crucial river. Although the 1975 Algiers Agreement had resolved this issue, Iraq felt that the agreement had been imposed upon them by the more powerful Iranian regime. Chubin and Tripp state 'In winning a war against the Kurds, the Iraqi government had apparently lost an unfought war against Iran ... The memory of the opportunity lost through military weakness, and the humiliation forced upon the Iraqi regime through the Shah's superior coercive power, clearly rankled, in particular with Saddam Hussein who had been ... personally responsible for the 1975 agreement' (Chubin and Tripp, 1988, p.23).

This humiliation felt by Saddam Hussein was compounded by the geopolitical implications of the agreement. Since the 65 mile stretch of the river closest to the Persian Gulf was Iraq's only access route, the agreement further restricted Iraq's ability to approach this vitally important area. As Schofield states the '*Shatt al-Arab* remains exceptional in constituting the only navigable estuarine international boundary in the Middle East' (Schofield, 1986, p.17), and it was obvious that Saddam Hussein would not accept this bitter reality for long. The relationship between Iran and Iraq following the 1975 agreement, therefore, may not have been one of war, but conflict to reverse the results of 1975 was inevitable.

A further example of Saddam Hussein's territorial ambitions is the revival of Iraq's historical claim to the Iranian region of Khuzistan. Annexation of this region, which had an Arab population of over 3 million, would have further supported Saddam's claims to be the champion of Arab rights. In addition, the large amount of oil present within the area could have enabled Iraq to assert its status as the pre-eminent Arab and Gulf state, as well as providing Saddam with grounds for becoming the most influential Arab leader.

Interlinked with his desire for power was 'most certainly Saddam Hussein's insecurity, a gnawing fearfulness bred by the precariousness he perceived in his own regime and by Iraq's glaring vulnerability vis-à-vis Iran. To the contemporary state of Iraq, Iran represented the major geo-political challenge' (Karsh and Rautsi, 1991, p.136). This therefore is the second aspect of his personality which must be considered, and which is typical of the general fear felt by the Gulf Arab monarchies.

Saddam Hussein had only recently secured his hold on Iraq and was naturally worried that his Shi'ite population might respond to Khomeini's fundamentalism. The fact that the Iranian revolution appealed not only to the sectarian and fundamentalist forces in Iraq, but also had the potential of disrupting the internal politics of other Gulf states such as Saudi Arabia and Bahrain, heightened Iraqi insecurity and forced it to moderate its behaviour in exchange for Gulf Arab funds and support. This meant that, although officially neutral, the Gulf states had a large stake in Iraq's political survival, and their fear of Iranian fundamentalism underlaid their continuing willingness to fund Iraq during the course of the war.[51] Iraqi diplomacy during 1980, therefore, succeeded in creating an 'Arab entente that brought together Saudi Arabia, Jordan and the smaller Gulf states in support of Iraq taking military action against Iran' (Wright, 1980/81, p.285).

This conflict between Iran and Iraq was not only the most recent development in the long-standing dispute between the Arabs and the Persians, however, but also had other serious implications. Of paramount importance to the West was the danger of the conflict spreading throughout the Gulf region, thereby endangering access to oil and the marketplace. Of particular concern to the West and the Arab Gulf states was the escalation in the "tanker war" in mid-1984 which consisted of both belligerents beginning missile attacks on neutral shipping passing through the Straits of Hormuz. As Cordesman highlights, the war did escalate to include the southern Gulf region in early June 1984 and there was increasing concern that the war could escalate further.[52] We have here a further example of indigenous factors, which are unrelated to the Cold War paradigm, playing a decisive role in Western policy options.

The West's Response

The above analysis has shown that both Cold War and indigenous factors featured in Western policy-making vis-à-vis the Persian Gulf. Since both of these categories contributed to the destabilisation of the region, the primary aim of any Western response had to be the maintenance of stability in the Gulf. In the late 1970s the US had begun to recognise that it could not rely on its twin-pillar policy indefinitely, a fact which was later confirmed in 1979 when, following the revolution, Iran could no longer participate in the US's security structures. This increased the role played by Saudi Arabia in subsequent US plans for developing new security options, as it was the only other significantly pro-Western regional power.

The onset of the Iranian revolution and the Soviet invasion of Afghanistan both meant that the US had to operate from a position of weakness. US policy at this time was heavily criticised for not anticipating the emerging problems in Iran at the outbreak of war. As Tahir-Kheli states, part of the difficulty was that the 'Carter Administration never did seem to understand how dependent its policy in Southwest Asia was on a single man' (Tahir-Kheli, 1980, p.343). As a result of this, the failure of the US to fully grasp the implications of the Shah's demise and its subsequent inability to handle the deteriorating situation in the Gulf distressed other countries in the region which had close ties to the US.

This was particularly true of Saudi Arabia, which was facing a potential threat from the Soviet Union and was having to deal with increasing Soviet influence in radical Arab states such as the Peoples Democratic Republic of Yemen (PDRY). This meant that Saudi Arabia and the other Gulf monarchies might have benefited from a US role in security arrangements for the Persian Gulf, and therefore reinforces the strength of Cold War explanations. The problem, however, was that a greater US involvement in the region might have invited anti-Western public opinion within the kingdom, and since certain other Arab states such as Iraq and Syria did not wish to see the US permanently based in the Persian Gulf, the Saudis settled on a limited US presence and a low profile in the provision of desired assistance. This shows that, despite the existence of Cold War related threats, indigenous factors played a more prominent role in preventing the establishment of actual US bases in Saudi Arabia, even though an 'over-the-horizon' presence was accepted.

Despite Saudi concerns over Arab opinion, the US response to the steadily deteriorating situation in the Gulf revolved around possible military solutions, commencing with Presidential Directive 18, signed by Carter on 24 August 1977. This called for the establishment of what would become the Rapid Deployment Force, defined as 'a deployment force of light divisions with strategic mobility for global contingencies, particularly in the Persian Gulf region and Korea' (Palmer, 1992, p.101). In order to facilitate this procedure the US Joint Chiefs of Staff (JCS) recommended that bases be expanded at Diego Garcia in the Indian Ocean and Saudi Arabia.[53] This expansion did indeed take place and the convergence of Saudi Arabian and US interests provided a base from which the Saudis were eventually willing to accept the over-the-horizon US military presence.

What does the US response then tell us about the adequacy of Cold War paradigm? The Carter Doctrine proved that the Soviet invasion of

Afghanistan should not be discounted, but also indicated President Carter's resolve to provide military assistance to Saudi Arabia (and other Gulf states) to protect oil shipping routes against the dangerous effects of a possible widening of the Iran-Iraq war. The West's presence also acted as a valuable deterrent to the Iranian regime, which might otherwise have been intent on exporting its revolution to the Arab members of the Gulf.

Conclusion

What then does the above analysis highlight? In this chapter I set out to question the adequacy of the Cold War paradigm as a tool for explaining events in the Persian Gulf during the last years of the Cold War. This paradigm, which is based upon neo-realist structural bipolarity, identifies the threats to Western interests in the Persian Gulf as emanating purely from the Soviet Union, and highlights important factors which must not be discounted. Its central argument is that by the end of the 1970s the Persian Gulf had become the central external focus for the Soviet Union, and analysts have cited its invasion of Afghanistan, its encirclement of the Persian Gulf, and its attempts to gain influence in Iran following the Islamic revolution, as prime examples of this.

However, Cold War factors, though useful, are in danger of providing oversimplified conclusions which have, in the past, been allowed to dominate, thereby eclipsing other more immediately pertinent issues. Furthermore, as has been seen, the traditional explanations themselves have certain shortcomings, for example, the Cold War argument that the West feared the possibility of Soviet gains in post-revolution Iran lacks credence in view of the fact that the new Iranian regime was as anti-Soviet as it was anti-Western. Similarly, despite Western predictions of a Soviet shortfall in oil by 1985, this did not actually occur, a fact which invalidates the argument for Soviet interest in forcibly acquiring Persian Gulf oil.

I have not entirely discounted Cold War factors, however, as exemplified by the importance attached to the US response to the Soviet invasion of Afghanistan. This military response not only contained the threat of further Soviet expansion, but also prevented the conflict between Iran and Iraq spreading into the remainder of the Gulf, as shown by British and US protection of neutral shipping through the Straits of Hormuz. The Western presence also served as a warning to the Iranian regime of the serious consequences of any attempt to spread its form of Islamic revolution to the other Gulf states.

This chapter has, therefore, gone beyond the Cold War paradigm by arguing that, although Cold War related explanations should not be overlooked, it is also crucial to focus on the events from additional angles, thus considering factors emanating from within the Gulf region itself which have also affected Western policy options and threat perceptions. It has demonstrated how the self assertion of the Gulf states, which took oil pricing and production practices out of the hands of the West, resulted in major price changes which were beneficial to the Gulf states but detrimental to Western economies. It has also highlighted how the economic importance of the region resulted in strong intra-Western competition for a share of the Gulf marketplace, and how the political and structural changes within the major Gulf states and conflict in the region also shaped Western policy options by threatening the stability of the region, another factor which was crucial to Western economies.

Concentrating purely on these four non-Cold War factors does not imply that I deny the existence of additional issues, indeed it is important to realise that the factors highlighted here, though of central importance, do not exhaust the wide range of issues that can be identified as having an impact on the region's events. Unfortunately further analysis is beyond the remit of this chapter, but any search for explanations has to take into account the far more fragmented nature of the international relations of the Persian Gulf than the Cold War paradigm, with its emphasis on bipolarity, allows. Ultimately by using both perspectives in conjunction a clearer overall picture undoubtedly emerges.

Notes

1 Saivetz, (1989, p.20).

2 Churba, (1980, p.353). Churba insists that even the Soviet invasion of Afghanistan and the potential threat it posed to the West's oil and trade routes changed US policy only on the surface, claiming that the US became very vocal but took little action.

3 Simes, (1979-80, p.28).

4 During the late 1960s and early 1970s there was evidence of rapid expansion in Soviet force projection capabilities. For example as MacFarlane mentions, 'between 1965 and 1977, the total lift of Soviet military air transport had grown by 132 percent ... The progressive increase in Soviet airlift capacity was graphically evident in a sequence of operations, beginning with the resupply of Syria and Egypt in 1967 and 1973, the ferrying of troops and equipment to Angola in 1975-1976, and the airlift to Ethiopia in 1977-1978 ... this was matched by a considerable expansion in Soviet long range amphibious transport capabilities' MacFarlane, in (Marantz and Steinberg,

1985, p.15). In addition, during the 1960s, the USSR achieved both nuclear parity with the United States and a *blue water navy,* confirming that it had indeed shifted from continental to global capabilities.

5 Calvocoressi, (1989, p.279).

6 The Soviet wish to allow the Revolution in Iran to continue uninterrupted was reinforced by Brezhnev, as quoted in Pravda on 19 November 1978 warning the West not to interfere in Iran: 'The Soviet Union ... emphatically declares that it is against outside interference in Iran's internal affairs by anyone, in any form and under any pretext. What is happening in Iran is a purely internal affair and the issues must be solved by the Iranians themselves ... It should be clear that any, particularly military interference in the affairs of Iran, a state directly bordering on the Soviet Union, would be regarded by the Soviet Union as affecting the interests of its security', quoted in ibid., p.69.

7 Author's interview with Stephen Day, British Ambassador to Qatar between 1981 and 1984.

8 Foreign Affairs Committee, Minutes of Evidence, 20 February 1980, 'Consequences of Soviet Expansion for British Foreign Policy', Memorandum by the Foreign and Commonwealth Office (FCO), (23/79-80/FM), p.123.

9 See Khalilzad, 1980. Khalilzad mentions changing power patterns in the Persian Gulf, crisis in Turkish-US relations, the disintegration of CENTO, the withdrawal of Britain from east of Suez and the relative buildup of Soviet military capabilities vis à vis the US, which all favoured Soviet power projection capacity.

10 FCO Memorandum, (23/79-80/FM), pp.123-4.

11 Extract from President Carter's State of the Union Speech quoted in 'Carter's crises; Iran, Afghanistan and presidential politics', *The World Today*, vol.36, no.5, 5 May 1980, p.167.

12 Dawisha, (1979, p.92).

13 Cobb, (1979, pp.353-4).

14 Idem. Other useful references are Stern, (1980) and Klinghoffen, (1981).

15 Yodfat, (1983, pp.34-49).

16 Cordesman, (1984, p.3).

17 Later in 1981 ARAMCO established that proven oil reserves in Kuwait had increased to 167.85 billion barrels, thus significantly raising the strategic significance of the sheikhdom.

18 Cordesman, (1984, p.1).

19 Madian, (1979, p.171).

20 Yergin, (1979, p.81).

21 Madian, (1979, p.174).

22 Bissell, (1980, p.830).

23 'Saudi Arabia: how true a friend', *US News and World Report*, 2 April 1979.

24 'US Army Corps - a closed fraternity from Mount Weather', *Middle East Economic Digest*, 6 March 1981, p.14.

25 'Saudis now biggest US arms customer', *Armed Forces Journal*, October 1979.

26 For more information see Gwertzman in *The International Herald Tribune*, 13 October 1980.

27 'US will upgrade Saudi fighter planes', *The International Herald Tribune*, 1-3 March 1981.

28 James Buckley quoted in Dybvik, Russell E., 'Backgrounder: the Reagan Administration's decision to sell air defense equipment to Saudi Arabia', in *International Communicational Agency*, Embassy of the United States, 25 August 1981.

29 Idem.

30 For instance, the US refused to allow the F-15s to be placed at Tabuk airfield, from which it was feared that the Saudis could launch an attack on Israel.

31 'Saudi defence chief meets Nott', *Financial Times*, 12 June 1981.

32 Bloom and Johns in *Financial Times*, 19 February 1986.

33 Author's interview with Sir Colin Chandler, Head of Defence Sales between 1985-1989, who played a leading role in negotiating and securing the Tornado deal with Saudi Arabia.

34 Cordesman, (1984, p.55).

35 Whetten, (1979, p.394).

36 Rouleau, (Fall 1980, p.3). As justification for his arguments Rouleau goes on to argue that the Shah's much vaunted agrarian reforms, for instance, 'benefitted only a minority of the peasants, who, in any case, were soon taken over by big companies engaged in large scale industrialised agriculture. The massive importing of agricultural goods, especially wheat from the United States - coupled with the absence or inadequacy of protective tariffs - contributed to the ruin of countless small farmers, aggravated rural unemployment and swelled migration to the cities'.

37 Mottahedeh refers to Khomeini's broadcasts in *Foreign Policy*, no.38, Spring 1980, p.30.

38 Maull, (1980, p.811).

39 Kemezis, (1980, p.769).

40 The cutoff to Israel demonstrated Iranian support for the Palestinian cause. This is a feasible reason because, despite the Arab-Persian rivalry and conflict, revolutionary Iran was equally if not more anti-Zionist in its orientation and as such was to repeatedly call for the destruction of Israel. Cutting off supplies to South Africa indicated its opposition to white dominance in that country.

41 Kemezis, (1980, p.766).

42 Extract from speech given by Khomeini quoted in Hiro, (1985, p.134).

43 Lissakers, (1981, p.107).

44 Bulloch and Morris, (1991, p.76).

45 The rise in this form of fundamentalism was a response to the crisis facing the Islamic world resulting from the impact of Western imperialism, extremely

rapid modernisation, and the challenge posed by Israel to the Arabs and Islam in general.

46 Freedman and Karsh, (1993, p.8).

47 McKnight in Pimlott and Badsey (ed.), (1992, p.25). McKnight quotes Samir al-Kabir, *Republic of fear*. Other writers are more conservative in their estimates with figures of around 15,000. See Hiro, (1985, p.18).

48 King, (1987, p.7).

49 Schofield in Schofield (ed.), (1994, p.41).

50 Mylroie and Miller, (1990, p.109).

51 King, (1987), p.19. For additional information see Dawisha, (1980-81). As this article outlines there were even growing rumours that the US National Security Advisor, Zbigniew Brzezinski, had met secretly with Saddam Hussein. Though this was denied Adeed claims that there were many signs that senior US officials were seeking ways to improve US-Iraqi relations.

52 Cordesman, (1987, p.67).

53 On 7 September 1978, the JCS were to approve the 'Review of the US Strategy Related to the Middle East and the Persian Gulf'. As Palmer highlights, this document identified three major US interests; (a) to ensure continuous access to petroleum resources, (b) to prevent an inimical power or combination of powers from establishing hegemony and (c) to ensure the survival of Israel. See Palmer, (1992, pp.102-103).

6 The Great Simplifier: The Cold War and South Africa, 1948-1994

GRAHAM EVANS

Introduction

Now that the Cold War is over, we can see clearly that one of its most seductive features was that it offered a deceptively simple frame of analysis for international affairs. The crude binary framework it provided - east/west, capitalist/communist, black/white, us/them, red/dead and so on - became part of the stock-in-trade of at least two generations of policy makers and International Relations (IR) scholars. So pervasive was this global paradigm that it was employed virtually to the exclusion of any other model, to analyse and categorise all sorts of international events and developments that occurred between 1946 and the early 1990s. Indeed in the dominant Anglo-American tradition at least, the Cold War became synonymous with international politics itself.

For over 50 years it set foreign policy agendas and conditioned actions, reactions, interactions and outcomes. In terms of this model, issue-areas and role players were assessed primarily from the perspective of their strategic significance to the binary divide and/or their overall political-cum-ideological orientation to it. The Cold War was perceived to structure international politics in such a way that virtually everything was defined in terms of it; nothing was taken at face value.

So complete was its ability to manipulate and control the global agenda that there was little room for 'any other business' and attempts to by-pass these dichotomies - for example non-alignment - were doomed to fail. Even self-styled rejectionists were forced to define their overall diplomatic orientation in terms of the master narrative. Non-alignment was merely a sub-plot of the main story since in a defining sense, it was a child of the Cold War, albeit an illegitimate and unwanted one. So, given its all embracing character - or as the guru of neorealism, Kenneth Waltz puts it - given that 'bipolarity knows no peripheries'[1] - it is hardly surprising that the Cold War was used to analyse and explain developments in and around South Africa from the year the National Party came to power in 1948 until the inauguration of Nelson Mandela's Government of National Unity in May 1994.

In this chapter then, my concern is to examine the extent to which this hegemonic realist paradigm provided a satisfactory analytical framework for understanding South African affairs both internally and externally during the apartheid years, that is, from the National Party's first administration under D. F. Malan in 1948 when apartheid was first systematically put on the statute books, to its last under F. W. de Klerk in 1989[2] when it entered its final throes.

Specifically, I will address two separate but related questions: one of a general nature, the other more particular. First, how did the Cold War impact on South Africa? Second, to what extent is the chronological conjuncture of the end of the Cold War and the demise of the apartheid state significant? To what extent were these parallel endings cause and effect as structural realism would have us believe? Is this synchronicity merely historical accident or coincidence in the same way as, say, the death of Mother Theresa shortly after that of the Princess of Wales in August-September 1997? Or is there more to it than this simplistic analysis suggests?

In terms of international theory, the issues these questions raise concern the general validity of neo-realism as an explanatory tool for the analysis of regional, sub-systemic affairs during the Cold War period. Specifically, how convincing is the Waltzian argument that actor behaviour is in an important sense conditioned by the prevailing distribution of power - in this case the structural bipolarity that characterised international affairs between 1946 and 1989?

Clearly there are some remarkable chronological similarities between the two sets of issue-areas and events associated with them. For example, the Cold War ended where it began, in Germany on 9 November 1989 when the Berlin Wall came down. Statutory apartheid also ended where it began, in Cape Town parliament on 2 February 1990 when President de Klerk announced the unbanning of the ANC and the release of the world's longest serving political prisoner, Nelson Mandela. Less than three months separated the two events. Did one cause the other? Were the two issues linked in such a way that the end of one pernicious system automatically triggered the end of the other? Or as *Private Eye* might put it: *are they in any way related?*

The Cold War as Simplifier and Alibi

The argument presented in this chapter is that the Cold War did indeed impact on events in South Africa in very important ways. However, despite what the structural neo-realists might say, its impact was both misleading and secondary. The main impetus for developments in the apartheid/ decolonisation sagas in South and southern Africa was provided by the local players themselves. Although the Cold War proved to be 'the great simplifier'[3] of world politics and was used as a reference point, a haven and an alibi by all sides in the conflict, it was essentially a secondary player both relating to the manner in which the conflict unfolded and in its eventual resolution.

In many respects the Cold War paradigm quickly evolved into a self-fulfilling prophecy especially in terms of the mirror-images and security dilemmas it generated. Actor behaviour was often conditioned by the expectations that each side had of each other. These expectations produced a 'definition of the situation'[4] which then fed back into a pattern of behaviour that seemed to confirm the initial position. This was just as true for the local players in southern Africa as it was for their superpower patrons - neither of whom had any intrinsic or 'vital' interests in the region. Both the USA and the Soviet Union in fact played the game of denial, the objective being the negative one of denying certain goods to the other side. The dominant assumption of Cold War politics was that all conflicts were inherently zero-sum: that one side's gain was *ipso facto*, the other side's loss.

Besides this mutually reinforcing strategy of denial[5] adopted by the West and the Soviet Union, the Cold War gained an exaggerated importance in the region's affairs because of the way it was seized upon by successive South African governments anxious to latch on to anything that would prolong the active life of the white regime. Virtually from the onset of the Cold War in the late 1940s, the containment text became a convenient ruse skilfully and deliberately hi-jacked by Pretoria to deflect attention away from an indigenous region-wide problem that pre-dated the East/West rivalry by at least 300 years. None of the major conflicts in South Africa or southern Africa owed their origins to the Cold War. The dominant issues, apartheid and colonialism and their legacies, were deeply rooted in indigenous soil long before anyone had ever heard of the Bolshevik revolution, or of the Yalta or Potsdam agreements.

In this sense, the Cold War was incidental to the conflict. It was certainly not foundational. Superpower rivalry provided an extra layer to it. It provided a dangerous gloss to the conflicts, and it almost certainly prolonged and distorted them. But essentially it was an extraneous matter, skilfully grafted on to Western threat-perception by an atavistic South African state that was to all intents and purposes fighting a rearguard action against history.

Furthermore, the fact that apartheid died alongside the Cold War in 1989-90 is of no great significance. President de Klerk, a consummate political strategist, chose this particular moment to throw in the towel because it suited his interests. The National Party had been looking for ways to get off the hook (or as de Klerk himself put it, 'to get the monkey off our backs') since Gorbachev had signalled the end of any lingering Soviet ambitions in Africa in 1985. But in 1985 the National Party was controlled by conservative (*verkrampte*) elements led by the *Groot Krokodil* himself, President P. W. Botha. For four years Botha, egged on by the military, refused to cross the Rubicon, preferring instead to lurk menancingly on its banks. Though President Botha had warned his colleagues of the need of 'adapt or die', in the end he refused to go the extra mile to reach a settlement with the ANC. Like Ceausescu in Romania, he was determined to hang on in there to the bitter end. His fortuitous heart-attack in 1989 gave the more enlightened Afrikaners their chance Thus, de Klerk was elected to office in 1989 with a brief that involved a negotiated political transition.

The liberal (*vertigte*) wing of the National Party believed that the ANC, suffering as it was from patron-bereavement, and unable to topple the state through military means, would be amenable to a power-sharing arrangement which would preserve important vestiges of influence and privileges for the whites. The strategy was that the blacks might gain government, but the whites were to retain power. The whites would thus retain a veto in any future administration. As Waldemeir puts it, the liberal wing of the NP represented by de Klerk were 'prepared to dilute power, share it, pass it around and circumscribe it - but not to give it away' (Waldemeir, 1997, p.110). By 1989 a combination of internal and external factors led the liberal faction of the NP and the business community it represented to believe that the moment was ripe for a favourable deal.

Gorbachev's disavowal of any Soviet ambitions in southern Africa at the 1986 Reykjavik summit signalled a significant weakening of the ANC's position. The liberal Afrikaners perceived this and resolved to act from a position of strength. That was why, on 2 February 1990, de Klerk unbanned the ANC, released Mandela and began the process of a negotiated solution to South Africa's problems. It was a deliberate calculation of strategic advantage. The timing was fortuitous. It could have been earlier. The connection with the Cold War's demise was a tactical matter. Strategically, it was all to do with the survivalist instincts of the beleaguered White Tribe of Africa. By the mid-1980s the South African conflict had reached what William Zartman calls a 'hurting stalemate'.[6] In effect neither side had anywhere else to go but to the negotiating forum. The demise of the Cold War was a convenient moment for a new political dispensation for both sides since the ANC for its part realised that although it could render South Africa ungovernable, it could not, without the support of a powerful patron, succeed in bringing the state down.

The neorealist argument that the structure of the international system - in this case Cold War bipolarity - inevitably factors straight into sub-systemic or local affairs and then conditions the way that they are managed - is unconvincing. The conflicts in South and southern Africa were essentially indigenous and their parameters had been set long before the impact of bipolarity. Of course the Cold War affected the dispute. It sharpened some issues and blunted others. But in the context of South Africa the overriding importance of the Cold War was that it presented the white regime with an opportunity to subsume the apartheid issue within the wider framework created by the political, military, economic and ideological divide that separated the two principle centres of power. The end of the Cold War and the perceived 'victory' of the West provided a window of opportunity to secure a power-sharing arrangement where the rights of minorities (i.e. the whites) were entrenched in any future constitutional settlement.

In effect, the Cold War served to provide the Afrikaner state with a means of legitimation and survival. In doing so, not only did it distort the nature of the conflict over apartheid - basically turning it from a human rights issue into a strategic one - it also reversed the logic of neorealism. In agent/structure[7] terms it was a case of the tail wagging the dog. South Africa used the Cold War, in particular Western vacillation over whether to follow its material interests or its normative ones, as a shield behind which it hoped to survive and prosper. In other words, there is a sense in which the West played a role of South Africa's choosing, not the other way around as the neorealist thesis predicts.

The Cold War and the Apartheid State

How did the Afrikaner regime succeed in connecting the issues of apartheid, internal colonialism and the survival of white supremacy on the southern tip of Africa with Cold War politics? The short answer is, surprisingly easily. From the outset in 1948, the overwhelming international objective of the apartheid state was to establish its pro-Western credentials in world politics.[8]

It did this by a judicious mix of selecting and manipulating a number of arguments calculated to appeal to a Western mind-set obsessed with the strategic imperatives of containment, the political/ideological imperatives of anti-communism and the economic imperatives of free market capitalism. Given the all embracing nature of the apartheid social engineering project, virtually all departments of state were involved in this outward projection of South Africa as an invaluable component of the Western camp. The departments which co-ordinated this effort were the Department of Foreign Affairs and the Department of Information which, significantly, were amalgamated in 1980. Separately and, after 1980, together these departments mounted a large-scale propaganda exercise to counter international hostility to apartheid, especially in the West.[9] Pretoria's policy planners had done their homework. They understood the geopolitical and philosophical universe inhabited by Western foreign policy establishments (especially in the USA and Britain) and deliberately selected arguments calculated to appeal to their interests and instincts (Geldenhuys, 1984). Three arguments were central to this process: a strategic one, an economic one and a political one.[10]

(a)Strategic: the Cape Route argument

South Africans were tireless in emphasising the importance of the Cape Route as one of the key 'choke-points' of world politics, and that in a geopolitical sense it was vital for the West to maintain control of the sea-lanes around the Cape of Good Hope.[11] The key strategic commodity here was oil. The Cape shipping lane is on the direct route from the Persian Gulf to the Western Hemisphere. Regarding the route to Europe, South Africans were quick to point out that the Suez Canal was a constant victim of the endemic volatility of Middle Eastern politics and therefore unreliable; in any case in the age of supertankers it was too narrow to be financially viable. Since the vast majority of oil from the Persian Gulf had to pass around the Cape, it was therefore self-evident that a friendly (i.e. a white) South Africa was a vital cog in the Western security machine. Cape Town, Simonstown and Silvermine together represented respectively the largest and most sophisticated deep-water harbour, docks and communications system in the southern hemisphere and the Cape was therefore a glittering strategic prize that the West dare not lose.

Put this way, an alliance with white South Africa, even an informal one, was an essential component of NATO's southern flank - notwithstanding any residual post-imperial guilt that western liberals might feel towards the blacks. Once the Soviets developed a blue-water naval capability - which they did by the late 1960s - then the Cape Route argument became South Africa's ace-in-the hole. The defence of South Africa was projected as a vital Western security interest, and the argument proved to be a very powerful one, especially in Republican and Conservative quarters in Washington and London.

Although South Africa failed to convince the West of a need for a SATO (a South Atlantic Treaty Organisation) to complement NATO, it is an open secret that even after the expiry of the Simonstown Naval Agreement with the UK in 1975 the Cape Route argument continued to find a receptive audience amongst Western defence planners (Berridge, 1985). US naval ships were forbidden to dock in South Africa after 1967 - primarily because of the shore treatment of black US sailors - but the defence of the Cape shipping lane continued to form part of NATO's overall Cold War defence posture. In 1980, for example, NATO's Secretary General, Dr. Joseph Luns said in Cape Town that notwithstanding the political differences between South Africa and the West 'we have made contingency plans to defend the Cape Route in time of war.'[12]

Thus, although the South Africans failed to persuade the West of the need for a formal NATO-like treaty linking Brazil, Argentina, the US, the UK and South Africa in defence of the South Atlantic, they were in no doubt that the Tropic of Cancer formed the southern boundary of NATO's area of operations in theory only. In practice, South Africa remained 'in' not 'out of' area to Western defence planners. Pretoria's propaganda machine ensured that this continued to be the case throughout the Cold War period.

(b) Economic: mineral resources

The second argument concerned mineral resources. It was employed in much the same way as the Cape Route argument, that is, that South Africa uniquely possessed key minerals that were critical to the economies of the Western industrial democracies. South Africa is an impressive world producer of many important precious and strategic minerals, amongst which are the following: gold, diamonds, antimony, vanadium, chromium, the platinum group metals, manganese, and crucially uranium (which is needed of course for nuclear fission).

Overall South Africa has, since the Second World War, consistently been the world's second or third largest producer and supplier of non-fuel minerals. Now apart from gold and diamonds, (which are irrational minerals in the sense that they have no intrinsic worth except those we put on them) the West was perceived to be critically dependent on South African supplies of these vital commodities (Bowman, 1985, pp.129-33). The fact that South Africa was only exceeded in the production of these minerals by Eastern-bloc countries added to the saliency of the view expressed by President Reagan in

1981 when he remarked: 'Can we abandon a country that has stood by us in every war we have fought, a country that is strategically essential to the free world in its production of minerals that we must all have?' (Bowman, 1985, p.132). The policy reasoning that flows out of these types of observations is obvious. The West needed South Africa, or at least needed to ensure a steady supply of these materials. The South Africans knew this, and played up to it. Government control of these para-statal industries was such that prices, availability and quantities were constantly monitored to ensure that South Africa retained its reputation as a cheap and reliable provider.

(c) Political: anti-communism

The third argument employed related to South Africa's anti-communist credentials and the pro-Soviet inclinations of the principal black liberation organisation, the African National Congress. Even though the ANC's alliance with the South African Communist Party (SACP) did not formalise until nearly 20 years after the NP came to power and notwithstanding that the Soviet Union only began to take a serious interest in southern Africa after the Portugese coup in 1974 and the accession to power of Marxist/Leninist regimes in Angola and Mozambique, South Africa pursued this theme relentlessly. From the beginning in 1948 the Soviet Union occupied a central place in the demonology of white South Africa, and it did not take much effort to tie in the 'evil empire' with the revolutionary black liberation organisations - because from the late 1960s onwards that connection became a reality (Evans, 1996). A favourite Afrikaner expression was that the *swaart gevaar* equalled the *roii gevaar*: the 'black menace' is the 'red menace' - the image that they projected was that South Africa physically shared a border with the USSR and the West should wake up to this fact. Indeed, when a Russian soldier was captured by South African forces in Angola in 1981 'South African officials could scarcely conceal their glee' (Bowman, 1985 p.126) as this was incontrovertable evidence that the Russians were employing an encircling strategy in order to establish their hegemony in southern Africa. As with other arguments, the spectre of the Soviet Union and its surrogates, particularly Castro's Cuba, roaming around southern Africa, underlined the importance of keeping South Africa on-side in the Cold War. This virulent anti-communism served to defuse the tensions and criticisms associated with its racial politics. This Soviet/Cuba argument again provided a much needed rationale for maintaining western ties with South Africa.

All of these arguments were pulled together to demonstrate why the West should continue to tilt towards South Africa, despite a formal commitment to human rights and an abhorrence of apartheid. In terms of the big picture, that is, overall US global strategy, South Africa was on God's own side. Colloquially this was variant of a familiar refrain of American Cold War warriors regarding US relations with Latin American dictators: 'You might be a son-of-a-bitch, but you are *our* son-of-a-bitch'. From President Truman onwards, this sentiment, attributed to F. D. Roosevelt, formed the bottom line of US geopolitical *realpolitik* regarding the Monroe Doctrine and US influences in the Western Hemisphere.

Western Misperceptions

In this way the relentless logic of containment and the clouded thought and loose generalities about Soviet intentions it spawned in the West which played into the hands of military and political elites in Pretoria. And this was, as Bowman demonstrated, despite the fact that all of these three arguments could be challenged, that South Africa's indispensability to the West was by no means absolute or indeed proven (Bowman, 1985, p.133). There were a number of counter-arguments to negate the propaganda emanating from South Africa, including the following:

i) The Cape Route was not as strategically decisive for Western oil interests for example as the Straits of Hormuz in the Gulf. In any case, once the Americans acquired a 50 year lease on Diego Garcia in the Indian Ocean from the UK in 1966 and developed a naval and communications base there access to Simonstown was irrelevant.

ii) There was no reason why a black South African government should not sell minerals to the West. Others did. Angola, for example, had been a Marxist/Leninist state since 1975 yet continued (and continues) to supply the West with petroleum.

iii) The long term strategic interests of the West clearly dictated staying on the good side of black African nationalists. To co-operate with white South Africa was therefore extremely myopic and inimical to US global interests.

iv) Apart from the holocaust, opposition to apartheid in South Africa was the only moral absolute in world politics on which the dominant ideologies - North, South, East and West - could agree. To co-operate with the South African regime therefore meant bucking the new normative climate of international relations and sacrificing a possible leadership role in world politics.

v) Finally, and most pertinently, the Soviet Union had no vital interests in South Africa.

In the hierarchy of world affairs, Moscow had always ranked southern Africa fairly low down on the list, certainly below Europe, East Asia and the Middle East (Albright, 1978, p.38-9). Unlike these geo-strategic locations in the 'great game', southern Africa was always peripheral rather than core.

Throughout the Cold War period, and contrary to Western perceptions, Soviet policy in sub-Saharan Africa as a whole was decidedly low key, low-risk and low-cost. Although the Soviet-bloc presence in Angola and Mozambique after 1974-5 alarmed Washington, overall direct Soviet commitment to the region was limited. There was certainly no evidence, beyond that alleged by Pretoria, of a communist 'grand design' for control of southern Africa.

In fact the biggest Eastern bloc presence in Southern Africa throughout the Cold War period - 50,000 Cuban troops in Angola - was paid for not by the USSR, but by Angola from hard dollar currency earned from petroleum exports to the USA (Marcum, 1976, pp.407-25).

In other words the Soviet threat to southern Africa, in so far as it materialised, was in fact indirectly bankrolled by the USA itself. This is a classic example of the self-fulfilling prophecy in international relations and stemmed from the fact that while the Americans persisted in perceiving the world in terms of a checker-board, the Soviets were from the outset playing chess!

Pretoria's repeated charges that South Africa had been subjected to a 'Total Onslaught' orchestrated from Moscow, played back into Soviet hands. Using this argument, South Africa gave the Soviet bloc undeserved credit for virtually all opposition to apartheid. There is plenty of evidence to show, for example, that the ANC went cap in hand to Moscow in the early 1960s, because it literally had nowhere else to go for support (Thomas, 1995). Western governments persisted in perceiving it in terms of the black/red equation provided by Pretoria and were thus blinded to the notion that there were indeed other games (and other grand masters) in town.

In doing this, South Africa ensured some kind of Soviet presence in the region, and this in turn guaranteed a US preoccupation with the Cold War and globalist dimensions of issues which were essentially North/South and local. This self-fulfilling prophecy and circular feedback loop created a Cold War distraction that distorted Western perceptions of issues on the ground in South Africa. Instead of viewing them as North/South developmental issues, they were seen as primarily East/West confrontational ones. This reached its apogee during the Reagan administration and the onset of the Second Cold War.

Thus it was a series of US policy errors reinforced by the relentless propaganda from Pretoria that led to the Soviet and Cuban presence in Angola. As John Marcum put it: 'All disclaimers notwithstanding, the United States here fell into a double trap. In addition to its *de facto* alliance with South Africa, it also over-reacted to the harsh rhetoric and socialist advocacy of a Marxist-influenced liberation movement by identifying it as the enemy' (Marcum, 1978, p.420).

Throughout the Cold War, therefore, the US viewed South and southern Africa as a theatre in which their task was to contain the advances of the Soviet Union and its proxies and to bar access to the Soviet Union to what were declared to be vital mineral resources and strategic routes. These alarmist assumptions (fuelled assidiously by the apartheid state) were largely incorrect. Soviet policy in Africa was opportunist rather than part of a grand geopolitical design. Crucially, the Soviet-supported Cuban intervention in Angola occurred only after the American-backed South African invasion of Angola in 1975.[13] Moreover, Washington often exaggerated Moscow's interests in Africa. On some occasions, the Soviet Union turned its back on willing clients as it did with Mozambique when it rejected its application for membership of COMECON.

While the Soviet Union had its own agenda in Africa during the Cold War, consisting mainly of strategies of denial coupled with diplomatic opportunism, the evidence shows that its policies were largely driven by its Western adversaries. And they were aimed mainly at recognition of equal superpower status on the continent. That is why Soviet activity in southern Africa only really materialised during the détente period of the late 1970s. The South African myth that the Kremlin was cunningly plotting to lay its hands on the treasures of the Cape nonetheless received wide credibility and helped to sustain the repression of democracy in the name of containment and anti-communism.

The End of the Cold War and the End of Apartheid

Those who see the Cold War paradigm as an important explanatory framework for understanding the processes at work in South Africa not unnaturally argue that the opening of the Berlin wall and South Africa's political liberalisation in the 1989-90 period are inextricably linked. The argument is that the transformation of the international structure occasioned by the end of the Cold War set in train a series of regional transformations, of which the ending of apartheid in South Africa was one. (The others were a settlement of sorts in Angola and the independence of Namibia in 1990).

For the Cold War neo-realists, this was but a new twist to the domino theory; once the central supportive structure collapses all the connecting parts tumble as a matter of course. The argument is that the National Party was able to deal with the ANC in 1989 because the ANC had lost its superpower patron. It was therefore considerably weakened and would be much more amenable to deal with and extract concessions from. On the face of it this seems a fairly plausible analysis. De Klerk moved towards negotiations with the ANC at a time when the organisation had been robbed of its Cold War partner, and was therefore in a weak bargaining position. In this way, the government could control the process of change and the transition would then occur more or less on its own terms and at its own pace. Since the ANC had been handicapped by events in Eastern Europe, this was the time to hammer out a power-sharing agreement favourable to the whites.

The trouble with this way of looking at things is, as Adrian Guelke argues, that it fails to explain why the ANC had such a crushing victory in the transition to a post-apartheid South Africa. The central weakness of this Cold War framework is 'that it begs an obvious question: if the ANC entered negotiation from such a position of weakness, how then did it achieve such a position of dominance at the end?' (Guelke, 1995, p.91).

One response to this would be to discount the role of the external environment altogether and put the emphasis back on the role of indigenous domestic factors, that is, that the ANC's link with the Soviet Union was more or less incidental to the demise of apartheid. What was crucial to it was internal opposition to the apartheid regime, in particular the township riots which had spread with alarming frequency since the mid 1970s. On this view, what the ANC did was what it had been doing, albeit rather unsuccessfully, since its founding in 1912: opposing the white regime and harnessing support for majoritarian rule within the broad context of the decolonisation process. So, once the government had yielded on the issue of universal suffrage, then the game was up, regardless of external influences. The organisation that represented the interests of the masses was bound to emerge triumphant.

However a more plausible explanation for the demise of apartheid lies somewhere between these opposing and somewhat simplified views.[14] We cannot discount altogether the role of external forces in the decision to negotiate with the ANC since de Klerk himself made frequent references to it in his famous speech of 2 February 1990.[15] And he has insisted on a number of subsequent occasions that it was the events of 1989 in Eastern Europe that made the new political dispensation in South Africa possible. There is no reason to doubt this, at least in respect of the timing of events (Waldmeir, 1997, pp.108-47). But of course, the collapse of communism was only one of a number of factors in the equation, the others being the increased ungovernability of South Africa since the late 1970s and continuing economic stagnation exacerbated by sanctions in which the West by the mid 1980s was playing an increasingly important role (Barber, 1994).

The National Party had been negotiating with Nelson Mandela and exiled leaders of the ANC long before 1989, and in truth had nowhere else to go. The capacity of the South African government to extract concessions from the West over the Cold War issue had been wearing thin since Soweto placed apartheid on domestic agendas throughout the world in June 1976. By 1989 de Klerk was looking for a plausible way out. The end of the Cold War made it easier to embark on this major initiative. But, like Gorbachev in the Soviet Union, de Klerk miscalculated. Like Gorbachev, de Klerk wanted to reform South Africa's political system, not to replace it. However, reform quickly developed into a revolution driven from below rather than controlled from above. The decision to abandon power-sharing and to go for full participatory democracy in the 1993-4 period was by then a decision that involved no choices. The die had been cast; South Africa's continuing crisis of ungovernability meant that there was no turning back. The only other alternative was bloody civil war, which the whites eventually were bound to lose. With the exception of a few die-hard right wing Afrikaners, no significant sector of South Africa's beleaguered white population doubted this.

On this view the pace of events in South Africa from 1989 onwards stemmed from de Klerk's miscalculations. Like Gorbachev he thought that the South African polity could be repaired, but in fact in trying to repair it, he punctured it. And like a rip in a tyre, once the 350 years of pent up pressures began to escape, they rapidly increased the opening and tore apart the system. There are indeed many similarities between Gorbachev's 'miracle' and de Klerk's. The difference though is that Gorbachev's mistake confined him to the dustbin of history, whereas, perversely, de Klerk's mistake gained him the Nobel Peace Prize. Such is the fickleness of History.

Conclusion

In sum the Cold War did impact on South and southern Africa, but not quite in the way that neo-realism would have us believe or expect. It did not condition the conflict over apartheid and decolonisation. But it was an aggravating, distorting and ultimately a misleading and delaying factor in the settlement of the conflicts. Furthermore, there is clearly a connection between the end of the Cold War and the end of the apartheid state. In this sense it is not a coincidence like the deaths of Princess Diana and Mother Theresa. The connection between the two events is secondary and tactical, rather than primary and strategic.

In terms of the agent/structure debate the evidence of the impact of the Cold War on South Africa between 1948 and 1994 is at best inconclusive. Structural bipolarity certainly factored into both the unfolding of the crisis and into its resolution, but the local agents were by no means the passive receptors suggested by uncritical proponents of neo-realism.

Notes

1 This is, in effect, the essence of Waltz's controversial thesis in his influential *Theory of International Politics* (1979). Not only does the prevailing international structure of power relations affect behaviour and outcomes, none of the actors or units in the system are immune from its influences. In this chapter the terms neo- and structural realism are used synonymously.

2 The National Party was in office continuously from 1948 until 1992-3. Thereafter, South Africa was governed by the Transitional Executive Council (TEC) which was a power-sharing arrangement principally between the African National Congress (ANC) and the '*ancien regime*'. South Africa's first multiparty, non-racial democratic elections were held in April 1994. In May 1994, Nelson Mandela was inaugurated as state President and head of the Government of National Unity (GNU).

3 The phrase is from Josef Janning, 'A German Europe - A European Germany? On the debate over Germany's Foreign Policy.' *International Affairs*, Vol.72, No.1, January 1996, p.33.

4 This term refers to the process of social perception whereby individuals and groups 'construct' their reality in all its manifestations. The view that individuals and groups respond and react to situations as they perceive them and not as they actually are has led foreign policy analysis to speak of a 'psychological environment' in which policy is made. This approach is encapsulated in the phrase 'if people define situations as real, they are real in their consequences'. The argument here is that both the Soviet Union and the United States - but particularly the latter - adopted incomplete or erroneous 'definitions of the situation'.

5 The term is usually associated with game theory and is used to denote a policy of defending a particular good regardless of its intrinsic worth in terms of any objective assessment of interests. In the southern African context, even if it could be demonstrated that the region had no vital strategic value in terms of US or Soviet interests, it was nevertheless important to prevent it 'falling' to the other side. Looked at in this way, the history of the Cold War could be written, at least in part, in terms of a mutual attachment to 'strategies of denial' since this is a logical consequence of zero-sum perceptions of conflict

situations.

6 I. W. Zartman (1985), *Ripe for Resolution*, Introduction. See also his 'Negotiation and the South African Conflict,' *SIAS Review*, Winter-Spring 1991, pp.113-33.

7 The agent-structure problem is at the heart of the controversy in IR theory between conventional (neo-realist) and critical theorists. It is associated with the level-of-analysis problems and refers to the question of how best to conceptualise the relationship between state actors and the international system. See especially Alexander Wendt (1987) 'The Agent Structure Problem in International Relations', *International Organization* 41, pp.335-70.

8 South Africa's first Foreign Minister, Eric Louw (1955-64) remarked that Pretoria's overriding foreign policy goal was to act as a 'permanent link between Western nations on the one hand, and the population of Africa south of the Sahara on the other.' Quoted in J. E. Spence, 'South Africa, the World Powers and Southern Africa' in T. M. Callaghy, (1983 pp.107-127).

9 See Geldenhuys, (1984 , pp.107-138).

10 These three were regarded as South Africa's 'strong cards.' Other arguments were employed to reinforce this trinity, depending on the target constituency. For example, relating to the UK, South Africans would point out that there were over 800,000 British passport holders amongst its white population (c.5 million). Therefore the defence of South Africa should be viewed as an intrinsic part of Britain's overall security calculus. Regarding the USA, South Africa's role as regional superpower would be emphasised. Under the Nixon/Kissinger doctrine South Africa expressed its willingness to act as regional deputy sheriff to maintain the *status quo* in the region. This would allow the US government to pursue its globalist foreign policy interests without large-scale military involvement of the kind characterised by the Vietnam war. This was directly in line with Kissinger's infamous National Security Memorandum 39 when he spelt out his vision of South Africa's role in the US's Africa-policy. See El Khawa M. A. and Cohen B. (1976). Also 'Beyond Constructive Engagement: US Foreign Policy Toward Southern Africa into the 1990's,' Picard, L. A. and Groelsma R. (1989) in Keller E. J. and Picard L. A. , (1989 pp.221-248).

11 See especially van Rensburg, W. C. J. (1978) 'Africa and Western lifelines', *Strategic Review* vol.6, no.2 (Spring) pp.41-50 and Burrell M. (1975) 'Simonstown and the Cape Sea Route' *African Institute Bulletin*, Pretoria, vol.13, no.2, pp.62-65. For an excellent overall assessment of South Africa's strategic significance to the West, see Bowman L. (1985) pp.120-161.

12 Quoted in Bowman, L., (1985, p.138).

13 See Mayall, J. (1985) 'The Soviet Union, Zimbabwe and South Africa' in Aluko O, and Shaw T., *Southern Africa in the 1980's*, (1985).

14 For an interesting rejoinder to Guelke see Daniel J. (1996) 'A Response to Guelke: The Cold War Factor in South Africa's Transition.' *Journal of*

Contemporary African Studies, 14, pp.101-104. For further evidence of the timing of events and 'Why the Boers Gave it All Away' see Waldmeir P., (1997, pp. 108-142).

15 In Parliament on 2 February 1980, de Klerk stated that 'the events in the Soviet Union and Eastern Europe, to which I have referred already, weaken the capacity of the organisations which were previously supported strongly from those quarters Guelke (1996). For further evidence of the timing of events, and 'Why the Boers gave it all away', see Waldmeir P., (1997, pp.108-142).

7 The United States and India: The Challenge of Neutralism to Bipolarity

JACQUELINE DIX

'At the present moment in world history nearly every nation must choose between alternative ways of life...One way is based upon the will of the majority, and is distinguished by free institutions,...the second way of life is based upon the will of the minority forcibly imposed upon the majority. It relies upon terror and oppression...The free peoples of the world look to us for support in maintaining their freedoms. If we falter in our leadership, we may endanger the peace of the world - and we shall surely endanger the welfare of this nation.'
Harry S Truman, March 12, 1947

'This whole approach of the cold war and military alliances, if persisted in, would sometime or other lead to final catastrophe.'
Jawaharlal Nehru, March 29, 1957

'The Soviet Union underlies all the unrest that is going on. If they weren't engaged in this game of dominoes, there wouldn't be any hot spots in the world.'
Ronald Reagan, 1980

Bipolarity has dominated thinking about the Cold War from its beginnings. When US President Harry S. Truman declared in 1947 that the world was engaged in a battle between good and evil he created a paradigm of the superpower conflict that would last through eight presidencies. The Truman Doctrine, quoted in part above, captured the sense that world politics was divided into two camps, led by the United States on one side and the Soviet Union on the other. All states would have to choose between these two blocs. For Americans there was no alternative to making such a choice because of Soviet ambitions. They believed that the USSR was determined to create a unipolar world, run from Moscow. It was the United States' responsibility to lead the rest of the world against them. Nearly forty years later Ronald Reagan still called on the same paradigm when he described the Soviet Union as an 'evil empire' responsible for all conflict around the world. Amongst the public, commentators and historians this picture has remained central to portrayals of the Cold War.

This bipolar imagery oversimplified things and tended to dominate thinking in the making of foreign policy. Practitioners were aware of greater variety in world affairs, but the main emphasis was on the actions and reactions of the two superpowers. This was because of their immense capacity to inflict nuclear devastation and also because policy-makers and politicians were sometimes trapped within confines set by their own rhetoric of bipolarity. They used the image of an implacable superpower confrontation to raise public support and to beckon allies to the front line. Other states were peripheral in the course of events, especially countries from the Third World. Nevertheless, as Truman's speech suggested, they were expected to play their part in the Cold War, take sides and participate in the West's containment strategy.

The case study of the relationship of the USA and India highlights, in particular, how intricate international relations were. India's foreign policy directly contradicted the argument that the world was bipolar and in no small way forced the USA to adjust to that - certainly in practice, even if its rhetoric remained stubbornly within the bipolar imagery. India aimed to remain independent from both superpowers, and its ambition was to play an active role in world affairs, especially in the United Nations. This policy became known as neutralism and it was to have a pivotal place in world politics. The history of the United States and India during the Korean War captures many of the issues that flowed from the confluence of India's neutralism with the Cold War policies of the USA. From this relationship a number of questions arise: First, how did the United States respond to India's neutralist policy, in the light of general Cold War concerns? Second, what policies did the Truman administration develop in order to respond to neutralism? Third, how did the Korean War alter the US-Indian relationship and what roles did the Indian government play in that conflict? And finally, how does this case study affect our understanding of the role of bipolarity in the Cold War?

US Post-war Security Concerns

After the Second World War, the Truman administration looked to the United Nations organisation to provide the world with peace and security. The framers of the UN used two methods in pursuit of those goals. The first was Franklin D Roosevelt's 'realist' idea that the great powers, the five permanent members of the Security Council, should act as the world's 'policemen'. However, they would all have to act in unison or not at all, otherwise they might cause the very thing the UN was designed to prevent, global war. So, each was given the power of veto. This was a rather traditional approach. More radical, and somewhat of more interest for the subsequent development of Cold War bipolarity, was the second method - collective security. Adopting collective security meant that there was no place for neutral states within the United Nations. Collective security relies upon the deterrence of aggression through the threat that the aggressor will be met with overwhelming force provided by the international community if it attacks. War is regarded as preventable and immoral and aggression by a state is thus subject to automatic condemnation by other states. If nations are free to choose neutrality they jeopardise the deterrence function by allowing the possibility that the force used to punish aggression will not be overwhelming. In this international dispensation to choose to be neutral is a moral failing.[1]

As the United States had become involved in the Second World War its prewar ideas about neutrality altered. Having been a traditional defender of neutral rights, the United States respected the right of non-military involvement of European neutrals in the Second World War, but placed tremendous pressure on them to join the allied economic warfare campaign. As the war progressed US attitudes towards neutrality became less tolerant and when the time came for postwar planning it excluded the neutrals and none of them were invited to the inauguration of the United Nations. The new organisation had no place for neutrality. UN members are obliged, according to the Charter, to agree to provide troops when required, which neutrals would refuse to do, hence their failure to be admitted to the UN unless they abandon their neutrality. It rejected the traditional laws of war, of which neutral rights were a part, in favour of a system where blame was allocated and the morality of conflict became a central issue (Gabriel, 1988, pp.45-69). This attitude carried over into Cold War thinking.

Events in Europe damaged American policy-makers' faith in the new order of the United Nations. The five policemen could not act in unison. However, as we shall see, specific circumstances pertaining to the outbreak of the Korean War allowed the USA to use the language of collective security for Cold War containment purposes. Between 1946 and 1947 the Soviets imposed their control over Eastern Europe. The United States and Western European governments came to fear that the USSR would take control of the whole continent. The devastation of the Second World War had made Western Europe vulnerable to communist encroachment, and the Americans felt that they had to institute a twofold effort to counteract this and save the European democracies. This was containment. Truman reversed usual US peacetime policies with unprecedented involvement in European affairs. He sought both economic and military security for Western Europe; first, by the Truman

Doctrine, which mobilised US support, secondly through the Marshall Plan designed to strengthen and build up Europe's economy, and thirdly, by the North Atlantic Treaty Organisation to add military weight to Europe's economic security.

Containment in Europe succeeded. The Western European democracies were saved from communism by the economic and military power of the United States and their own resolute action. Nevertheless, the Truman administration did not think that communist ambitions had been checked. NSC 68, the policy review ordered by Truman in 1950 in response to both the fall of China to communism and the explosion of the first Soviet atom bomb, developed US thinking and concluded that the Soviets threatened them at every point around the world. The periphery had now become as vital as the European core.[2] American policy makers were sure that, unless the Soviets were stopped, they would not halt until they had achieved global supremacy. Washington believed that it had to prevent the USSR and its new acolyte, the People's Republic of China (PRC) from making any further gains, or else Americans would find their own long-term security at risk. The method that they chose to meet this threat was the militarisation and expansion of containment to a global level. It was this policy that would cause difficulties in America's relations with the world's largest and newest democracy, India.

US Interest in India

In August 1947, two months after Truman committed America to the defence of the free world, India became independent from the British Empire. This new nation was important to the US government for several reasons. First, India had great significance in the psychological battle for hearts and minds in Asia and around the world. It shared a common history with the United States as both nations had been British colonies and had absorbed similar interests and liberal democratic values. Many commentators on both sides predicted a close relationship between the world's largest democracy and the first Republic.[3] Therefore to lose India to communism would have been a dreadful blow to American credibility as the best example of good government as well as a world power. Such a loss could have raised serious doubts in the minds of political leaders in other countries about the ability of the United States to fulfil commitments made in the Truman Doctrine, the Marshall Plan and NATO.

Secondly, India had strategic significance. It bordered the PRC, where the Communists' victory in the civil war was a heavy blow to US policy in the region. China had traditionally been very important to American sensibilities, and the defeat of Chiang Kai-shek and the Nationalists caused great difficulties for President Truman. The US could not afford for the same to happen in India. The Indian subcontinent was an important staging post between the Middle East and Southeast Asia. It had been the centre of the build-up by American and British forces for a possible decisive campaign against Japan at the latter end of World War II, and could be used for a similar purpose again but this time against China. India was also a source of vital resources and manpower, with a well-established military infrastructure. American intelligence believed that in Soviet hands India could tip the balance decisively in any conflict.[4] In addition, Washington wanted India to be a regional leader, to counteract the influence of Communist China. For the United States, India's role was both psychological and strategic. It provided the best example to colonial Asia and imperial Europe of successful, democratic independence and had economic and military potential to aid smaller states. This would prevent the 'domino effect'. The Americans feared that if India fell to communism other neighbouring countries would follow. The United States saw the Cold War as a zero-sum game, where any gain for communism was a loss for them. India therefore had dual significance to the United States; as well as being important in its own right it would also help in the containment of communism in Asia as a whole (McMahon, 1994, pp.11-35).

Washington therefore had plenty of cause to be concerned about India's fate. Policy makers were convinced that events in Europe would be repeated elsewhere, and that only the power of the United States could halt the Soviet advance. The Truman Doctrine had committed America to the defence of the 'free world' in Europe but NSC 68 suggested that this promise had to be kept globally. The earlier division between core and peripheral regions was abandoned (Gaddis, 1982, pp.41-42). As the Cold War progressed the United States took an ever more active interest in India.

America's unease about security in Asia arose from its conviction that India alone was unable to defend itself effectively against communist ambitions. US officials had two main concerns which mirrored their thinking about European containment. They feared for India's internal stability and worried about the character of its foreign policy.

Internal Insecurity

India faced tremendous domestic difficulties after independence. Its economy was under-developed and under-resourced. Agriculture required major improvements to alleviate the continual threat of famine. India had great potential, but lacked capital to invest. There was a shortage of jobs and of industrial infrastructure. The US regarded such conditions as a breeding ground for communism. India could not deal with its economic problems alone and needed help. The United States government had proved that economic containment was effective in Europe, therefore it seemed only natural for the Truman administration to bolster India against communism in the same way, by providing aid to help economic development. At first sight this would suggest the possibility of a close relationship.

As well as these economic difficulties, India and Pakistan had suffered terrible communal violence following the partition of the sub-continent after independence in 1947. The mass migration of people and cross-border violence, particularly over Kashmir, worried US diplomats who were concerned that such social unrest could also foster communism. Their concern about India's security arising from its domestic difficulties was compounded by Prime Minister Nehru's views on the Cold War.

External Insecurity

The USA thought that high level strategic priorities in its global struggle against the Soviet Union should override other considerations; the Indian government disagreed. It had become clear that the good relationship both governments had hoped for was not going to materialise. The divergent views of the American and Indian governments about the nature of the Cold War and their differing priorities in policy decisions were at the heart of the problems between them. Before analysing US policy towards India we will look at the thinking behind India's neutralism and how this was put into practice.

Jawaharlal Nehru, as Foreign Secretary and Prime Minister, was the architect of India's foreign policy. He had been the foreign affairs spokesman for the Indian National Congress during the Raj and had developed his ideas about international politics throughout the campaign for independence.[5] In 1946 Nehru stated that India would 'avoid any involvement with any bloc' and maintain a policy of non-interference in foreign affairs.[6] With the development of the Cold War Nehru grew more convinced that India would be best served by remaining free from political alignment with either superpower. He believed that Indian partiality to either could lead to a loss of independence and sovereignty. But India's stance was not the same as Switzerland's and other traditional neutrals. Instead, Nehru sought a mediatory role for India which would improve India's standing in world affairs and thus bolster its security. He was resistant to the application of policy labels, but India's position became known as 'neutralist' or 'non-aligned'.[7] These terms have been subject to much analysis and academic scrutiny, not least since the founding of the Non-Aligned Movement in 1955, but Indian 'neutralism' was quite distinct. It defied simple definition and instead one needs to see it as a convenient shorthand for Nehru's complex policies.

Neutralism was rooted in idealist principles. Nehru sought an end to the Cold War, but not through the American version of containment or the final collapse of communism. Instead, he wanted to mediate a diplomatic resolution of the conflict between the two superpowers. This was based upon the assumption that the Soviets were not engaged in an attempt to expand communism around the world. Unlike the Americans, Nehru did not see a Moscow-led conspiracy for global domination. Rather, the Cold War was the result of a clash of interests and much misunderstanding between the USA and the USSR. The solution to this confusion of motives and actions lay in a negotiated settlement. This clashed head on with American perceptions of the Cold War and how to resolve it. Obviously, Nehru could not accomplish the goal of a negotiated settlement if India was aligned, or perceived as aligned, to either bloc. For him the Cold War was a battle between two sides both with legitimate claims and interests, not an ideological struggle between good and evil as portrayed by Truman. He also thought that each conflict should be judged in isolation, and not as a part of a larger struggle between the US and the USSR. Whilst Nehru was a committed democrat, he disapproved strongly of the militarism of both superpowers and their apparent willingness to embark upon further conflict.

This idealistic desire to see an end to the Cold War via diplomacy was nevertheless based upon sound practicalities, at least from the Indian perspective. First, India had domestic problems which required urgent attention. It could not afford to be party to any superpower dispute. It lacked the financial resources for a military engagement. What little money was available was needed for internal investment. India would have been devastated by war, either as the theatre of conflict or as a direct belligerent. Secondly, more urgent problems required attention, such as Kashmir. This alone absorbed India's military capabilities, but it should be noted from this that neutralism did not imply pacifism. Nehru was prepared to use force when he judged that it was necessary. Thirdly, the Prime Minister thought that it was vital for India's security to have stable, if not friendly relations with the Communist Chinese. This would not be possible if the PRC saw India as an American ally. Despite its large communist neighbour, India did not see the Cold War as a global problem in the early 1950s but if it continued then there was a risk that all of Asia would be drawn in. Fourthly, Nehru was determined to preserve India's hard won independence. To be non-aligned was to pursue an independent path in foreign policy that would protect India's sovereignty from external pressures whether American or Soviet. India's long-term security was dependent on the end of Cold War rivalries, at least in the form they took in the late 1940s and early 1950s.

US Views on India's Neutralism; 1947-50

Given the above outline of Nehru's reasoning about neutralism, one can see its potential to cause strong adverse reactions in the United States. There were fundamental differences between New Delhi and Washington on a number of levels: in respect to the character of the Cold War; the perception of dangers; policy priorities; and both how to construct US-Indian relations and what their substance should be.

The clearest demonstration of the clash between US and Indian views of the Cold War centred on the Truman Doctrine. The President declared that all countries had to make a choice about which way of life they supported: freedom or totalitarianism. But Nehru took the attitude that both the Soviets and Americans were equally responsible for Cold War rivalries. He did not therefore want to choose between them. It had been recognised by all branches of the US foreign policy establishment that Indian non-alignment could not be reconciled with the sentiments of the Truman Doctrine. To remain indifferent to India's neutralism was inconsistent with Truman's speech.[8] The challenge for the United States was how to respond to India's persistent resistance to alignment with the West.

Nehru's determination to see a negotiated resolution of East-West tensions and his belief that both sides were at fault also collided with US views. Containment actively rejected diplomacy in its approach to the Soviet Union. It was a pointless exercise because Stalin could not be trusted to keep to any agreement. Kennan had pointed out that the USSR was impervious to reason in his Long Telegram on Soviet conduct (Gaddis , 1982, p.49; Kennan, 1947, passim). In addition, the Americans did not want to taint themselves by compromising with the 'evil' of communism, nor give the Soviets the opportunity to exploit differences in the Western camp, for example over the rearmament of West Germany. For Nehru to attempt any diplomatic moves to bring the two superpowers together was anathema for most of America's senior policy makers.

The United States also felt that India was putting itself at risk in pursuing negotiation with the Soviet Union. It might be tempted by promises from Stalin into moves that could provide him with a propaganda victory. This fear grew out of the American view of the Cold War as a zero-sum game. If India succumbed to communism it would have been a serious loss to the West, a psychological blow to US prestige, and a falling domino that could have destabilised the rest of Asia.

Neutralism and bipolarity clashed head-on in the Truman Doctrine, but it was the United States, not India, that faced greater problems because of this. By characterising the superpower conflict as a fight between good and evil Truman had achieved his objective of mobilising the American public and Congress against the Soviet threat to Europe, but in the process he constrained his administration's policy options. Containment was very much dependent for its success on both Western unity and credibility in the USA as leader of the free world. Truman had, in part, staked American success on presenting the Soviet Union with a united opposition of free nations, led by the United States (Gaddis, 1982, passim; McMahon, 1994, passim; McMahon ,1991, pp.445-471). India's failure to align with the West thus challenged US policies, US leadership, and US containment policy. The Truman administration also faced pressure at home from Congressional Representatives and the American public. They had been persuaded by the rhetoric of their President, and wanted consistent action against anyone who opposed the United States. This included any state which would not align with the West. Congress typified popular views about India's neutralism with its refusal to agree to a wheat loan unless India aligned with the West. Even within the executive there were similar feelings. The State Department would not endorse neutrality by giving aid to India (Merrill, 1990, p.29). By portraying the world as bipolar, US policy makers found that they were in danger of creating a self-fulfilling prophecy and this created constraints upon the policies that they could implement and alienated the very countries the United States wished to befriend.

In addition to the discordant nature of the publicly expressed policy positions of India and the USA, the latter was also concerned that neutralism made India vulnerable to Soviet advances. Nehru did not think that the Cold War had overwhelmed Asia, which was another reason for believing that non-alignment was a viable policy. But policy makers in Washington thought that the Communist threat to India was more serious than Nehru recognised. They were certain that the Soviets had ambitions in Asia and that they were making progress. Intelligence reports suggested that 'as in every other area of the world, the United States was being drawn into competition with the Soviets for access to the region's favors and resources'.[9] Events at the time seemed to confirm that assessment. The United States believed the new Communist government in China had given the USSR a foothold in the region. Any remaining doubts in Washington about all this were completely dispelled by the invasion of South Korea from the North in 1950. The Korean War would be the real test case for US-Indian relations, but even before the war Indian foreign policy, in American eyes, was based upon a false assessment of the Soviet threat and was dangerous for India and Asia as a whole. Washington thought that India had to be made to recognise the threat and face it, before it inadvertently assisted the 'fall' of countries in Asia to communism. Coming on top of domestic, economic and social difficulties, its foreign policy stance caused great anxiety amongst American officials.

The Americans crafted their policy towards India carefully, but they did so with certain constraints. In declaring the world to be divided between good and evil Truman had left little room for manoeuvre. His bipolar rhetoric influenced reality. Also NSC 68 clarified US concern about a global communist threat which had to be met. Policy makers could not ignore India, because they believed that it was important and at risk. Yet because of its neutralism they could do little to help. Accommodation with India's stance was impossible given the overall principles that underpinned containment. The US found only one suitable solution to secure India as a stable country, and therefore help to safeguard the whole region, - to change India's attitudes about the Cold War and for India to switch from non-alignment to alignment with the West. But having decided upon their objective the Americans had to overcome several hurdles to achieve their goal.

There were two approaches that the Americans adopted to achieve their objective. One was an attempt to reproduce the success of the economic policies towards Europe with India, but this failed. Throughout the Truman and Eisenhower presidencies there was consistent concern about India's economy, but it was not until the Kennedy administration and the appointment of the prominent economist J. K. Galbraith as ambassador to India that there was any serious improvement in levels of help from the United States. The second method to draw India away from neutralism was a concerted effort on the part of the United States to educate the Indian government and people that neutralism was based on a mistaken understanding of the Cold War and that it was therefore dangerous for India, for Asia and for the rest of the world for India to remain non-aligned.

There were strong feelings about India's policy of neutralism amongst US officials and diplomats which were voiced in telegrams and letters between New Delhi and Washington. American diplomats set out to tell the Indian government repeatedly about the failings of non-alignment and the error of its ways. US ambassador in New Delhi, Henry F. Grady, informed Nehru that the question of alignment with the West 'could not be straddled and that India should get on the democratic side immediately.'[10] Loy W. Henderson, the Director of the Bureau of Near East, South Asian and African Affairs between 1947 and 1949, took an even harder line. He stressed the common values of India and America, and stridently declared that 'we do not endorse the Indian desire to maintain its position of overt neutrality.'[11] The embassy in New Delhi described India's policy of 'neutrality' as unrealistic, and the consulate in Bombay thought of it as a 'fallacy' and that the Americans should 'in a restrained but nonetheless positive way' point out to the Indians that they would be best off in an alignment with the West.[12] American thinking continually emphasised the importance of the alignment of India with the West with no mention of any toleration of neutralism.

A serious complication that arose for America's policy to persuade India to end its non-alignment was the calibre of Indian officials. The State Department described them as inexperienced, cautious, inordinately sensitive and suspicious.[13] The discrepancy between Nehru's public statements and his conversations with US diplomats, and messages from other Indian officials was a recurring problem. The US embassy in New Delhi had the same difficulties. They reported that Indian officials associated Americans with the worst aspects of Western imperialism: 'American policy should be predicated upon the basis that India considers the United States in the same light as the European countries who are oppressing colonial peoples...The Indian people are either ignorant of, or choose to ignore, American actions to encourage the colonial powers to give a greater degree of independence to their Asian subjects.'[14] US officials had to deal with 'the concentration of power in the hands of inexperienced leaders in these countries (which demanded of the US) ... the greatest wisdom and forbearance in dealing with them.'[15] The Indian government had also established relations with the USSR soon after independence and the Americans believed that this was because India hoped for Soviet aid, and criticised them for 'the volatility of Indian political sentiment and the Indian tendency to flirt with the USSR whenever it is piqued by our inability to shape US policy to Indian wishes'.[16] It should be noted though that such attitudes were not unique to relations with India. George McGhee, Henderson's successor at the Bureau for North East, South Asian and African Affairs from 1949 to 1951, commented in his autobiography, that his department felt that these new nations as a whole were 'not so sophisticated as those of the Western World' and that the Bureau felt that it was the 'protector' of these defenceless peoples (McGhee, 1983, p.xix). Indians and other officials from Third World countries might have been naive and wayward, but Americans were no less difficult to deal with as they swung wildly from bitter criticism to patronising defence of the new nations. Misunderstanding on both sides was the result.

There was, therefore, great antipathy amongst US diplomats towards India. It had few defenders in the early Cold War period. Howard Donovan, Counselor at the New Delhi embassy, reported that Nehru had described India's policy of non-alignment as 'a positive approach to the problems of the world'.[17] Donovan demanded: 'How could a policy of neutrality be a positive approach to the problems of the world? And how can India's association with the Commonwealth be continued and yet not align India with (those countries with which) the older members of the Commonwealth are aligned?'[18] This comment reflected the American conceptualisation of the Cold War as bipolar. There was an inability to separate membership of one Western alignment from another. He continued that India had developed a concept of positive neutrality as an attempt to mediate between the power blocs, but that 'those attempts had been so unsuccessful and so devoid of any solid basis that one was tempted to look further afield for the reason why intelligent Indian leaders did not concede that "positive neutrality", in this sense at least, was bankrupt.'[19] Donovan believed that Nehru had developed this policy to meet public demand that India should assert itself in the international field. This was a popular policy and he sarcastically noted that it did not matter that 'it was difficult, if not impossible, to explain logically how neutrality can be positive.'[20] The negative attitudes surrounding neutrality were also applied to neutralism. Confusion of the two terms was recurrent in US communications about India.

The Cold War concerns of the Truman administration constricted policy options towards India. Nehru was criticised for developing a policy that was based on domestic limitations, and yet Truman could not easily accommodate Indian neutralism because his administration's public statements of policy were also tailored to public opinion in the USA. US policy makers could not reconcile neutralism with US foreign policy and the Truman Doctrine. They believed that if India remained neutralist it would put itself and the region under greater threat and directly challenge the United States. Some had developed a personal antipathy towards India because of its foreign policy, and could not contemplate any accommodation with India's failure to condemn communism and align with the West. Whether or not US policies to draw India into the West's embrace would work remained to be seen.

In the meantime the threat to Asia became more immediate with the outbreak of the Korean War in June 1950. US convictions about a rigid bipolar zero-sum conflict with communism were now reinforced, but what it had not considered were the potentially positive aspects of neutralism in a hot war. It was ironic that these would be revealed by the first Asian conflict in the Cold War. In addition, the war highlighted the complexities that really existed in the rivalry between the superpowers and the degree to which the US had to compromise with Indian neutralism. This war saw a direct challenge to the bipolar paradigm.

The United States and India in the Korean War

As the Korean War progressed there were significant developments in US-Indian relations that highlighted their different views on the Cold War and resultant policies. The collision of neutralism and containment produced unexpected results as an examination of the initial outbreak of hostilities, the decision to cross the 38th parallel, and the resolution of the problems of the armistice agreement all demonstrate.[21]

On June 25 1950 Communist North Korea attacked South Korea. The United States had to respond to the Korean conflict for several reasons, but central was the conviction that it was a part of the Cold War. The attack by the North Koreans demonstrated to the Americans that NSC 68's thinking was correct: the invasion showed communist determination to exploit any weakness and expand its sphere of influence. US policy makers were convinced that Moscow had conspired in the invasion of South Korea. Containment underpinned the United States' response to the war. The Americans feared that the communists might succeed in doing to Asia what they had failed to do in Europe. The USA needed to demonstrate its resolve against the communist threat. They had to prove their credibility to their allies, to their enemies and to the American public. Truman had declared that the United States was the leader of the free world, and now he had to demonstrate this by defending South Korea from communism. The Truman administration determined to meet such aggression with force. It would be the first military test of containment.

The Korean War was also an opportunity for the United States to mobilise the United Nations to gather support and gain legitimacy with the sanction of international law and to invoke collective security on behalf of the West. It was a forum for them to lead the free world against totalitarianism. American officials were anxious to capitalise on the absence of the Soviet Union, which had boycotted the UN in protest at the US' refusal to admit the PRC to the UN as the rightful occupant of the Chinese seat. (The United States continued to refuse to recognise the PRC and had no official diplomatic relationship throughout the war). The absence of the Soviet Union enabled the US to use the rhetoric of collective security as the basis of the UN's peacekeeping role and to gain support for the campaign against communist North Korea. American policy makers and diplomats wanted help from its allies to fight the war, to supply much needed troops for the immediate emergency and to consolidate the West in its determination to fight for freedom. The United States sought to use the United Nations to achieve these containment goals against the communist attack in Korea. However, just as they had clashed with India over such policies before, so they would conflict again during the Korean campaign. Neutrality was incompatible with the principles of the UN and it was difficult to reconcile US calls for action under the auspices of collective security with neutralism, especially when the enemy was communist.

The Indian Prime Minister and his officials did not agree with American assumptions about the invasion of South Korea. Nehru was convinced that the Cold War had not engulfed Asia even with this attack, and believed that neither the North Koreans nor the new Chinese regime were under Stalin's direct control. However, the Indian government was sure that, unless actively prevented, the war could involve ever more countries, spread across Asia and eventually encompass the superpowers themselves. It was, therefore, essential to confine this war, in terms of time and geography. Just as the Truman administration feared the spread of communism in Asia so Nehru and his government were concerned that Asia would be dragged into a hot war, country by country, as the Cold War took greater hold through Asia.

The aim of the Americans was simple, to end the war in Korea. Once the USA and fellow UN forces seized the initiative after the Inchon landings in September 1950 the Americans became convinced that the ending of the war could be accomplished with the unconditional surrender of the North Koreans. Military force was the one means that they would use. India also wanted to end the war, but by diplomatic means. Nehru aimed to bring peace to a localised conflict through collective action in the UN, whilst the United States regarded the hostilities as part of the Cold War and wanted to use collective security to mobilise the UN in order to achieve a Western victory against communism.

First Days

Two episodes from the first weeks of hostilities illustrate the differences between both the American and Indian understanding of the Korean War and their reactions to it. The United States led the action in the United Nations and was clear about what the objectives should be. There was a rapid succession of resolutions, first to condemn the action of the North Koreans and then to call upon the UN to restore peace. Force was to be met with force.

India's views of the Korean War became clear in the early debates in the United Nations. India was a temporary member of the UN Security Council at that time and its candidature had been supported by the United States. On the American resolution to condemn North Korean aggression, Sir Benegal Rau, the Indian representative in the Security Council, had no qualms about voting in favour. But only two days later India approached the US with a suggestion to appoint a mediator to settle the dispute. This set the pattern for India's attitude to the conflict, which was consistent with its ideas about the Cold War as a whole. It was not pacifist, but thought that negotiation could accomplish many of the aims of the UN; namely to end the war and resolve the problems which had caused it.

But Rau also caused a minor diplomatic storm when he failed to vote at all on the resolution about the use of UN troops to repel the North Korean attack. He claimed that he had not received instructions from New Delhi. India's failure to vote at all was a concern to American officials. The United States wanted to keep the new democracy on side for a number of reasons. They were very anxious to maintain unity in the action against aggression. That was a requisite of both collective security and containment. India was important in preserving such a united front in the Security Council, but was also valuable because of its status as the leading nation in Asia. Washington was so concerned about the lack of Indian support on this issue that the State Department pressed Loy Henderson, Henry Grady's successor as Ambassador, to meet with Nehru and persuade him to back the resolution. Nehru's response was not what the Americans hoped for. He stated that while India was supportive of the action in Korea it would not compromise its non-aligned stance on Cold War issues. The Prime Minister was determined not to do anything that appeared to move India towards an alignment with the West.

Henderson was not happy with this and informed Nehru that India's failure to support the United States' line in the UN would harm collective action against aggressors. He declared; 'if (the Government of India)...should fail to support collective action in this instance (the) result, in my opinion, would be (a) serious setback to (the) UN and to the whole principle of collective security. India, as (the) most powerful and influential free country of Asia, could not ... fail to give at least its moral support to collective action against aggression in Asia without making (the) principles of (the) UN meaningless so far as Asia was concerned.'[22] One could not get a clearer statement of the concerns of the Americans. The repeated calls for unity had restricted the Truman administration's ability to tolerate dissent. India did record a vote in support of the use of troops, but that did not mean that it had changed its position on the Cold War.

This diplomatic squabble demonstrated Indian determination to remain neutralist. Apart from the delay in supporting the use of force, Nehru promptly and consistently supported American initiatives in the UN in the early days of the Korean crisis, but he refused to be railroaded and resented US pressure to vote in favour of the UN resolution covering the use of military force (Berkes, and Bedi, 1958, p.106; McMahon, 1994, p.82). India would not uncritically follow America's lead on Korea or align itself with the West in the Cold War. This puzzled the Americans somewhat, but India saw no blatant contradiction in its behaviour, just as it saw nothing unusual in being a member of the British Commonwealth but not a Cold War ally of the West. The Americans thought that the Korean War would bring home to India the reality of the Cold War as they saw it, whereas Nehru saw no reason to depart from neutralism. He continued to seek diplomatic solutions to both cold and hot war problems, even though he recognised the need for, and supported, the use of troops for the immediate crisis in Korea.

The second episode of difficulties arose from an Indian initiative to find a diplomatic settlement to the war. This involved more substantive differences than the confusion over voting for the use of UN troops. In mid-July of 1950 Nehru sent messages to both Stalin and US Secretary of State Acheson with a proposal to end the conflict. It was one of many appeals that Indian diplomats made to both sides. Nehru suggested that the Soviets should resume their seat on the Security Council, and the People's Republic of China to replace the Nationalists in the UN. This would open the way for a great power conference to settle the issue of Korea. The plan was logical according to Nehru's reading of the superpower conflict and of India's purpose in international society.

Washington resisted this suggestion for a number of reasons. First, Truman believed that allowing the PRC to take the Chinese UN seat would be perceived as a reward for aggression, particularly by the US China lobby which was already highly critical of the administration's policies. Secondly, the Americans asserted that there was 'only one solution to the problem of Korea, and that is for the North Koreans to withdraw from the ROK (Republic of Korea) ... (or) to be driven out by the combined forces of loyal members of the UN.'[23] There was no question of using negotiation to deal with such aggression. This was after all a containment campaign. Lastly, the United States was anxious to avoid internationalising the conflict in a way that might lead to Western concessions, and therefore insisted that it was not to be made an issue for settlement by conference.

There was a certain irony in this. The US saw the Korean War in bipolar, Cold War terms, involving all the major powers, but despite the obvious dangers, it resisted any resolution of the war through means other than force against North Korea because the US and its allies were making great advances on the battlefield and there was little point to negotiation when military victory was in sight. In any case the Truman administration had made great use of the rhetoric of collective security, which called for complete defeat of the aggressor, not negotiation. Also, anti-communist rhetoric used in making the case for containment and virulent hatred of communism in the USA ruled out diplomacy and compromise. In Washington's opinion Moscow was responsible for the Korean War and could not be trusted. In addition, the Korean conflict was a test of American resolve and credibility. To succeed militarily was the best proof of these qualities.

Crossing the Line

By September 1950 the United States and its UN allies had achieved its main objective in the war of removing the North Koreans from South Korea. This was as far as the original UN resolution allowed them to go. But the USA expanded its aims. Because of such rapid military success Truman and Acheson saw an opportunity to do more than free South Korea. They resurrected a UN resolution from 1947 that sought 'an independent, unified Korean Government' and pressed for an additional resolution to allow the United Nations troops to cross the border on the 38th parallel and liberate North Korea (Acheson, 1969, p.448).

India would not support this. Sir Girja Bajpai, India's Foreign Minister, voiced the concerns of the Indian government that crossing the 38th parallel would not further the cause of peace.[24] Such action was contrary to the limited scope and objectives of the original UN resolution. There was a great risk that crossing the 38th parallel would expand the conflict into a broader crisis. Indian diplomats had been in close contact with the Chinese government, and India had a good idea of what their reaction would be. The United States was concerned about India's efforts with the PRC because it weakened Western unity in the war. In an attempt to persuade the Indian government to support the US, Ambassador Henderson again stressed the importance of unity amongst UN members because it had broad implications beyond the Korean conflict: these included the possibility of a return to the power of force in international relations rather than any code of international morality.[25] He was unsuccessful. The problem began to take shape in a late night meeting on 3 October 1950.

Chou En-lai, the Chinese foreign minister, warned K. M. Pannikar, the Indian ambassador in Peking, that the PRC would intervene in the Korean War if UN troops advanced above the 38th parallel. This was exactly the response that Nehru had feared and which threatened to widen the conflict. Pannikar reported the warning from Chou En-lai to New Delhi from where it was passed on to other governments; it met a variety of responses.[26] The Indian government took the threat seriously, as did the British and others with troop commitments (Dockrill, 1986, p.463). The majority of US officials, on the other hand, believed that it was a bluff, and that the Chinese were playing a game of nerves with the Indian government. Pannikar's reputation of being unreliable and volatile did not help. This was an occasion on which Nehru had difficulty in being taken seriously because some of his officials acted incompetently in their conduct of foreign affairs. In the end, the opinion of the Americans held sway and they managed to drum up a majority to push the resolution through the UN. But as UN troops crossed the 38th parallel, Chinese forces were mobilised. In November 1950 they engaged in the fight.

These developments did nothing to help US-Indian relations. The US had failed to take heed of Indian warnings, and now the conflict had spread.

The Indian government had been concerned to limit the scope of the war from its very beginning, and now saw their worst fears realised. From October a deep rift divided the two democracies. Not only had Indian diplomats been ignored, but they also felt that the US was compounding its errors by getting the UN to condemn China for aggression. They had warned the Americans of the action that the Chinese might take and felt that such condemnation would only increase friction. This diplomatic confrontation with America caused India to draw back from the United Nations: it lost heart and temporarily stepped away from attempts to mediate a solution to the conflict (Berkes, and Bedi, 1958, pp.132-33).

On the surface it seemed that the US and Indian policies were completely at loggerheads, but in actual fact it began to dawn on the USA that Indian neutralism could have some benefits for the West, at least behind the scenes. It could be a go-between: a means for the US to communicate with the PRC. India's neutralist position and its status as an Asian power independent from Western allegiance, as well as its open and friendly manner towards Peking, meant that the Chinese treated India as a diplomatic equal. No other non-communist state received the same courtesy. The warning given to Pannikar about the use of Chinese troops gave the Indian diplomatic service credibility as a channel of communication between Washington and Peking. The British, at least, were keen to exploit this in order to bring an end to the war. This was the first sign to the Truman administration that it was an error to dismiss neutralism completely, because it enabled India to perform a unique and valuable regional and global diplomatic role. To force India into alignment with the West would have pointlessly damaged its relations with the PRC and excluded an avenue which later helped to find a resolution to the Korean War. The US could rely on India as a fellow liberal democracy; the Chinese could rely on India as a fellow Asian and non-aligned state. Efforts at resolving the stalemate in Korea would demonstrate how useful this neutralist Asian nation could be.

Ending the War

Following the advance of UN troops into North Korea the fortunes of war changed. Engagement with Chinese forces first halted the UN advance and then the Communists forced the allies back south of the 38th parallel. By the summer of 1951 a stalemate line just north of Seoul along the old border between the two countries was established (MacDonald, 1986, p.214). On 23 June the Soviets had issued a statement calling for a cease-fire which opened the door for formal armistice negotiations between the UN command and the North Koreans. These took place in Panmunjong on the stalemate line with the military commanders of both sides. But India did not fade into the background as the two belligerents talked face to face. Nehru and his officials played a key part in finding a settlement and implementing its provisions.

There were many issues to be settled in the talks, which were complicated by the number of parties directly and indirectly involved: the Americans and their allies; the Chinese; the North Koreans; the Soviets; various neutrals; and militarily uninvolved members of the UN General Assembly. There were also several locations for the talks; Korea, the United Nations and bilateral talks at various venues. However, after months of negotiation only one item remained on the agenda that prevented agreement on an armistice: the issue of the disposition of prisoners of war (POWs). India had a central role in solving this problem.

The UN held 100,000 troops from North Korea and China, whilst the Communists held 6,000 UN prisoners and 28,000 soldiers and civilians from South Korea. International law laid down how prisoners should be treated. The Geneva Convention of 1949 stipulated that POWs were to be repatriated to their respective countries, regardless of their own wishes. It was a poignant irony that the United States had originally supported this to stop the Soviets using Germans POWs as forced labour after the Second World War. Now the United States was not prepared to accept blanket repatriation (Kaufman, 1986, pp.237-240). Truman and Acheson introduced the principle of 'non-forcible repatriation' to the negotiations, to allow Communist troops held by the UN to remain in the 'free world' rather than return to totalitarian 'enslavement'. They thought that 'the forcible repatriation of anti-Communists was politically impossible and ideologically repugnant' (MacDonald, 1986, p.134). The US military also did not want the Communists to be strengthened by the return of so many trained men in case the talks broke down and full scale hostilities were resumed.

There was much debate between the military commanders of the United States and North Korea at the negotiations in Panmunjong, but to little effect. By the middle of 1952 talks had broken down completely. The United States would not give way on the issue of non-forcible repatriation and could not get any agreement from the North Koreans. Behind the scenes India took an active interest in finding a settlement. Throughout the Korean War Nehru, Rau and Sir Girja Bajpai, India's Foreign Secretary, had made repeated efforts to resolve the conflict through negotiation.[27] This mirrored Indian views about the Cold War and the nature of the conflict between the USA and the Soviets. The Prime Minister appealed personally to Chou En-lai about the prisoners of war suggesting that a neutral nation should take responsibility for them. There had been much controversy about indoctrination and propaganda methods used by each side and the idea of involving a neutral in the repatriation issue was a good step towards solving the problem.

The autumn of 1952 saw several major figures at the UN assembly's new home in New York to debate the POW problem. As well as Secretary of State Dean Acheson, also present were the British Foreign Secretary, Anthony Eden, his Minister of State, Selwyn Lloyd and the Canadian President of thc General Assembly, Lester Pearson. They would become very involved in Indian efforts to find an armistice agreement. The Americans were faced with a complex situation. There were not only the Russians, Chinese and Koreans to consider, but also various opinions amongst American allies and of course India, with its neutralist ideas. Acheson had come to New York with his own proposal to present to the General Assembly. In a four hour speech he called for a resolution requesting the Chinese and North Koreans to agree to an armistice based upon 'voluntary repatriation' of POWs. The US tactic was to use a firm resolution backed by a large majority to take to the negotiating table in Panmunjon (Berkes, and Bedi, 1958, p.134).

India's pivotal role in finding an armistice agreement centred on a POW resolution sponsored by what Acheson described as the 'Menon cabal'. The story of Menon's proposal highlights the complexities of India's relations with the USA and the Cold War in general. At first the USA rejected Menon's proposal because they thought it was too weak and gave too much away. Then, when the Americans saw their Western allies come out in favour of it they reluctantly came round to supporting it. When the Soviets denounced it as an attempt to prolong the war the USA publicly praised the statesmanship of Menon's plan. The stark irony of all this exposes the oversimplistic categories with which the USA tried to conceptualise the Cold War.

The Menon Cabal was named after Krishna Menon, one of India's representatives in the UN General assembly, and included Eden, Lloyd and Pearson. Menon's proposal created great difficulties for US diplomacy, but it proved to be a major first step towards an armistice agreement.[28] Menon's aim was to combine the demands of the United States concerning non-forcible repatriation with the Communist Chinese insistence on the provisions of the Geneva Convention. He achieved this by suggesting that the POWs be turned over to the supervision of a civilian commission made up of neutral nations. India had been talking to the PRC about this proposal, which persuaded some of America's prominent allies that it had a chance of success (MacDonald, 1986, pp.170-172). It was a vague proposal by design because Menon thought its flexibility would facilitate an agreement. Despite the lack of clarity, its possibilities prompted interest and involvement. India's unique position for mediation was recognised by the British and Canadians: they remembered the crossing of the 38th parallel and China's warnings. But, when Selwyn Lloyd told Acheson of the Indian proposal, the Secretary of State had strong objections. It was so vague as to mean different things to each side, and as such it was 'very dangerous'.[29]

There were several problems with this proposal from the American point of view. First, in an attempt to ensure Chinese support Menon had not specifically mentioned non-forcible repatriation. This issue was one that the United States would not give way on. To return Communists troops to the Chinese and North Koreans would have been totally unacceptable. Second, there was no timetable for repatriation. Once the prisoners were turned over to the proposed commission, they could face indefinite incarceration and therefore would be likely to choose to go home rather than remain in the camps. Second, Acheson was also unhappy with the proposed member states of the commission: Sweden, Switzerland, Poland and Czechoslovakia. He was concerned that the latter two would be partial to the Communist Korean forces rather than neutral. Third, they wanted a more clear-cut finish with no opportunity for the communists to squeeze further gains. The lack of detail that Menon thought of as an asset meant that the Americans would not support it.

But the US delegates could not persuade Britain and Canada to alter their allegiance to the 'cabal'. Pearson, Eden and Lloyd worked with Menon to redraft the proposal and to try to meet American concerns. A timetable for repatriation was introduced, with the provision that unrepatriated POWs would be turned over to the political conference of great powers in Geneva that would follow the armistice. It was therefore clear that no prisoner would be forced to return home. A chairperson was introduced to prevent bias, with India as the most likely candidate.

The Menon resolution gained ground in the General Assembly while support for the US resolution slipped away. At a meeting of UN members on the 17 November US delegates realised the opposition they faced. Their resolution was supported by Turkey and Colombia; India was backed by Britain, Canada, Australia and France.[30] Four of America's strongest allies had rejected its resolution in favour of the proposal of neutralist India. Acheson had to accept the inevitable. There were still problems with the Indian proposal from the American point of view, but the US had to accept that it was the one that the UN would most likely adopt. Eden approached Acheson after the meeting to ask if the United States was still 'unalterably opposed' to Menon's efforts.[31] Acheson replied that he had never opposed the Indian's work nor would he now, a stark contrast to his earlier comments to Lloyd. What he did not mention was that there was still a possibility that the Americans would reintroduce their proposal at a later date.

But the efforts of the 'Menon Cabal' looked like being fruitless when, at the end of November, the Soviet UN delegate spoke out against the Indian resolution and criticised Nehru's government for introducing such a device to perpetuate the war.[32] Acheson found himself praising Menon's statesmanship and declaring that the resolution showed the common purpose of the UN on the issue of non-forcible repatriation.[33] But Menon was disheartened by the Soviet reaction and began to talk about withdrawing his proposal. This would have allowed the Americans to reintroduce their resolution, but they knew it lacked support and resurrecting it would have highlighted the disunity amongst their UN allies without achieving any movement towards an armistice. Instead, Acheson instructed the US ambassador to India, Chester Bowles, to pass on a message to Nehru 'congratulating him for the statesmanlike role which India ... played in the UN in rallying free world opinion behind moral principle' and that such a historic contribution should not be jeopardised by the divisive tactics of the Communists.[34] Soon Bowles was able to reassure his colleagues at the UN that India was prepared to continue with its proposal. Nehru knew that the Soviets' speech made it likely that the PRC would reject India's ideas, but he would not be tempted away from neutralism. He continued to make criticisms of US policy and declared that he would sooner move forward with the Menon proposal, even if it were doomed to failure, than see the return of the 'bad and aggressive ... resolution' that the Americans had originally introduced. He was as firmly committed to neutralism as he had been when the US had demanded Indian support after Rau's failure to cast a vote in June 1950.

On 3 December 1952, the Menon proposal was adopted by an overwhelming majority of the UN General Assembly. This was a significant diplomatic victory for India's neutralist stance and something of a moral victory. Unfortunately it was rejected by the communists. However, six months later when the armistice agreement was signed the final settlement bore a strong resemblance to Menon's ideas. India became chairman of the Neutral Nations Repatriation Commission, and sole provider of troops to police the camps in Korea. The United States had doubts about the inclusion of India fearing that they would be 'more neutral' towards the Chinese communists. But they agreed to India's role because they did not want to damage their bilateral relationship.[35] Having dismissed neutralism as dangerous for India and Asia, the United States ended the Korean War with India's help.

Conclusion

Neutralism challenged bipolarity. Its existence revealed that the bipolar paradigm was only one facet of international relations during the Cold War. An analysis of US-Indian relations shows that the Cold War conflict cannot be understood only as a collision of two blocs. The United States failed to persuade India to align, which demonstrated that another position was possible in world politics. And India was not alone. There were many newly independent nations in the Third World that did not wholeheartedly embrace either Western liberal democracy or Russo-Chinese communism. But this should not suggest that the Cold War was irrelevant to India. The hostility between the US and the USSR endangered world peace, and produced pressures for India to take sides. Nehru thought that both these factors threatened Indian independence and thus found it necessary to state repeatedly that India was going to remain non-aligned and try to mediate between the two.

For their part American policy makers were not blind to the intricacies of world politics but difficulties arose from the need to square policy with rhetoric. The Truman Doctrine was one focus of such problems. Truman had spoken of a bipolar world where all free nations, under US leadership, would act together against totalitarianism. Unfortunately for the Truman administration this very powerful image prevented it from pursuing certain policy avenues. It was inconsistent with the Truman Doctrine for the US to openly tolerate non-alignment. There was also a worry that the Indians would create their own 'domino effect' with other nations falling behind them into non-alignment. This proved to be the case, with the eventual formation of the Non-Aligned Movement in 1955. Given the reading of India's own vulnerabilities because of neutralism the US feared that whole regions would also become unstable. American concern was increased by their certainty that the Soviets had designs on India. Yet the US found itself in a 'catch-22' situation in attempting to deal with the problem of India's non-alignment. Aid was the best tool to bolster Indian security and to draw it towards the West, but Congress would not vote funds for a state that would not condemn the Soviet Union. So US dollars were in short supply and India turned elsewhere for economic help, namely to the USSR. This only heightened criticism of India in the US and pushed India closer to the Communists. While the American government was aware of Cold War complexities, their bipolar imagery threatened to become a self-fulfilling prophecy to the United States' detriment as its policies damaged relations with the very countries it wanted to have as allies.

Neutralism challenged bipolarity by its very existence, but India also actively involved itself in world affairs. The Korean War demonstrated that neutralism could be an integral part of a conflict between the superpowers. The war also highlighted the clash between containment and India's foreign policy. The US wanted to use the UN for its own Cold War ends in the Korean conflict. In contrast, India supported collective action in this instance but did not align with America in the Cold War generally. Nehru demonstrated early on, when he would not be bullied by the Americans into voting, that support for UN action by India did not mean alignment with the West. It was ironic that, having regarded neutralism as a dangerous fallacy, the Truman administration found India very useful in bringing the Korean War to an end. Once the two sides had reached a stalemate India, as a third party, came to the fore. Its support for collective action had not damaged its standing as a neutralist and it was able to intercede with both parties. India was a channel of communication between the United States and the PRC, and also talked with each side to find common ground for a settlement on the POW issue. This valuable role resulted in the strong support of Western allies for Menon's resolution on POWs. The US had to back down from its own position in favour of India. Americans even praised Menon in response to the Soviets' denunciation of his work. Further still, India became the executor of the agreement as the chairman of the Neutral Nations Repatriation Commission and the sole provider of troops to police the POW camps. If India had been aligned with the West it could not have performed this role. The final end of the Korean War was due to a complexity of factors including Eisenhower's threat to use atomic weapons and the death of Stalin, but the final agreement on an armistice owed much to Indian diplomacy.

Bipolarity fails to capture the complexity of either postwar international relations or the Cold War. The bipolar Cold War paradigm with its heavy neo-realist emphasis on security and structure does not account for the role India played at the highest level of international politics in the early 1950s. India stubbornly refused to accept the kind of alignment the United States and the logic of power politics dictated. Examining the US response to Indian neutralism makes clear the limits of the bipolar paradigm but it also reveals the centrality of the Cold War in the minds of all policy makers. Neutralism was not an attempt to remain isolated from world politics. The resolution of the Korean War through India as a channel of communication and an executor of the armistice agreement shows that third parties were important, even vital, in restoring and keeping the peace in the early Cold War. India performed roles that both fell outside the international arena demarcated by Cold War concerns and impacted upon them. In a very real sense it was both a part of, yet also detached from, the Cold War, but definitely not a creature of it.

Notes

1 For a detailed discussion of collective security theory see Inis Claude, (1971), (4th edition), also; A.Butfoy, (1993); A de Conde (ed.), (1957); C.A. Kupchan, (1995); J. Larus, (1965); H.J. Morgenthau, (1967); R.N. Stromberg, (1963) and (1956).

2 Gaddis, (1982, p.91).

3 For an account of this see Phillips, Talbot and S.L. Poplai, (1958, pp.2-13).

4 Harry S. Truman Library (HST Lib), Papers of Harry S. Truman (PHST), Presidential Secretary's Files (PSF)-Intelligence Files, Box 260, Situation Reports, Central Intelligence Agency SR-21, 'India-Pakistan' 16th September 1948.

5 For accounts of Indian foreign policy before independence see K.J. Clymer, (1990). For Cold War Indian foreign policy see R.N. Berkes, and M.S. Bedi, (1958); M.Brecher, (1959); P.C. Chakravati, (1963); P.J. Eldridge, (1965); D. N. Mallik, (1967); A.P. Rana, (1969); E. Reid, (1981); and Iqbal Singh, (1992).

6 *Foreign Relations of the United States* (Hereafter FRUS), 1947, III, pp 160-161, Telegram from Ambassador Grady, New Delhi, to the Secretary of State, July 9, 1947. For published statements by the Prime Minister see S.Gopal, (1985).

7 For general accounts of neutralism and non-alignment see; S.N. Anabtawi, (1965); C.V.D. Crabb, (1965); P. Lyon, (1960); P. Lyon, (1963); L.W. Martin, (1962).

8 National Archives (Hereafter NA), Record Group 59 (RG 59), Department of State 711.45/8-2448, Telegram from Charles O. Thompson, American Consulate General Bombay, to the Secretary of State, August 24 1948, "Comments Regarding Policy Statement on India" pp 3-4.

9 HST Lib., PHST, PSF-Meetings, Box 206, State-Army-Navy-Air force Coordinating Committee, SANACC 360/14, 19 April 1949, "Appraisal of US National Interests in South Asia" p.409. Also published in FRUS, 1949, VI, pp.8-31.

10 NA, RG 59, Department of State 845.00/12-2647, Memorandum of Conversation, "Discussion of Problems of Mutual Interest to Participants", those attending Ambassadors Grady (India), Alling (Pakistan), and Huddle (Burma), as well as officials from the Offices of North East Asian and South East Asian affairs, December 26, 1947.

11 NA, RG 59, Department of State 711.45/4-248, Memorandum for information from Assistant Secretary of the Bureau for North East and South Asian affairs, regarding the visit of Sir Girja Bajpai, to Robert Lovett, Secretary of Defense, April 2, 1948.

12 NA, RG 59, Department of State 711.45/8-248, Telegram from Howard Donovan, *Chargé d'Affaires* ad interim, New Delhi, "Comments on Department's Policy Statement on India", p.5: National Archives, RG 59, Department of State 711.45/8-2448, From Charles O. Thompson, American Consulate General Bombay, August 24 1948, "Comments Regarding Policy Statement on India" p.4.

13 NA, RG 59, Department of State "Policy of United States Towards India" statement, undated, p.7.

14 *Ibid*, p.11.

15 HST Lib., PHST, PSF-Meetings, Box 206, State-Army-Navy-Air Force Coordinating Committee, SANACC 360/14, 19 April 1949, "Appraisal of US National Interests in South Asia", p.409. Also published in FRUS, 1949, VI, United States GPO, Washington, pp.8-31.

16 NA, RG 59, Department of State "Policy of United States Towards India" statement, undated, p.7.

17 NA, RG 59, Department of State 845.00/4-2349, Howard Donovan, Counselor of Embassy, Telegram to the Secretary of State Re: "Prime Minister's Message to the People of India on his Departure for London", April 23rd 1949.

18 *Ibid*, p.2.

19 *Idem*.

20 *Idem*.

21 The following are focused upon the foreign policy of the Korean War rather than its military history; Rosemary Foot, 1985; Peter Lowe, 1986; Callum A MacDonald, 1986; W.W. Stueck, 1995; Bruce Kaufman, 1986; Bruce Cumings, (1983). For a detailed account of the armistice negotiations see Rosemary Foot, (1990).

22 FRUS, 1950;7, p.236, Telegram from the ambassador to New Delhi, Loy W. Henderson, to the Secretary of State, Dean Acheson, June 29,1950.

23 FRUS, 1950, 7, p.406, Henderson to Acheson, July 16, 1950.

24 FRUS, 1950, 7, p.743, Henderson to Acheson, September 20, 1950.

25 FRUS, 1950, 7, p.872, Henderson to Acheson, October 4, 1950.

26 FRUS, 1950, 7, p.839, the *Chargé* in the United Kingdom (Holmes) to Acheson, October 3, 1950.

27 For accounts of these attempts see Foot, (1985); MacDonald, (1986); Kaufman, (1986); Stueck, (1995) and Berkes and Bedi (1958).

28 In addition to sources already mentioned see also Dean Acheson, (1969), and Roger Bullen, (1984).

29 FRUS, 1952-54, 15, p.567, Memorandum of conversation by the Secretary of State in New York, Dean Acheson, with Selwyn Lloyd, Minister of State, October 29, 1952.

30 See *ibid*, p.647, editorial note.

31 FRUS, 1952-54, 15, p.659, Acheson to State, November 19, 1952.

32 FRUS, 1952-54, 15, p.684, Acheson to Truman, November 26 1952.

33 FRUS, 1952-54, 15, p.677, Acheson to State, November 24, 1952.

34 FRUS, 1952-54, 15, p.699, Acheson to State, November 28, 1952.

35 FRUS, 1952-54, 15, pp.979-984, Meeting of the Joint Chiefs of Staff, May 8, 1953.

Section 3: Beyond the Paradigms

8 The Cross and the Bear: The Vatican's Cold War Diplomacy in East Central Europe

DAVID RYALL

We Communists feel pretty sure we can triumph over Capitalism. But Rome will prove a harder nut to crack. If Rome did not exist, we would be able to deal with all the various brands of Christianity; they would all capitulate before us. Without Rome, religion would die. But Rome sends out in the service of her religion propagandists of every nationality. They are more effective than guns or armies. The result of the struggle, my friend, is uncertain. What is certain is that it will be long.
Soviet Foreign Minister Chicherin to Fr D'Herbigny SJ, 1925 (Quoted in Rhodes, 1992, p.1)

Introduction[1]

The confrontation between Catholicism and Soviet power remains an under-explored aspect of the Cold War. This chapter attempts to remedy that omission by analysing the Vatican's diplomatic initiative - its version of *Ostpolitik* - by which it attempted to secure the Church's survival in East Central Europe. The Vatican's *Ostpolitik* resembled its secular West German namesake, not least in its capacity to generate fierce controversy.[2] Dialogue replaced confrontation, and diplomacy propaganda, in a conscious attempt by the Vatican to prevent the Church suffering the kind of near extinction it had experienced under communist regimes in the Soviet Union and Albania. Catholicism represented a major social and cultural force in East Central Europe, above all in Poland, the region's pivotal state, where it was not only overwhelmingly the largest church, but also a crucial factor in the creation and preservation of Polish nationalism. Church-state relations therefore were a major concern of the post-1945 'Peoples Republics'; a concern which was not simply confined to domestic politics but which also embraced the international sphere because of the Church's cosmopolitan nature. From the Vatican's perspective the struggle of local churches to survive under communism represented its greatest challenge. The severe repression which Catholics, and all Christians, endured was a deliberate attempt to remove the Church's institutional, moral, and cultural influence which threatened to undermine the new regimes' attempts at social engineering.

This chapter will examine the Vatican's relationship with the three East Central European regimes - Poland, Czechoslovakia, and Hungary - in order to assess how the Church responded to Soviet hegemony; moreover it will try and place this version of *Ostpolitik* within the wider context of the Cold War and the changing strategies by which the Vatican attempted to protect its own interests. By combining both the regional and global levels of the Vatican's diplomacy we can piece together a neglected part of modern international history. That neglect has a long history[3], but the story of East Central European Catholicism can give us important insights not only into those three particular states but also into how the Vatican, as a micro state (in spatial and material terms), can exercise an influence disproportionate to its size. Instead of the usual emphasis on economic and military capacity, which are considered as defining fungibility, the Vatican's strength has resided in the allegiance of Catholics and in the realm of symbolic or 'expressive' power (Hanson, 1987, p.5). By looking at the way the Church used values, beliefs, and culture to protect its institutions we can perhaps gain a more nuanced and subtle sense of world politics during the Cold War. Studying Catholic international relations then allows us to recover something of a hidden history of resistance and struggle which the Holy See waged against both East and West[4], as well as expanding our understanding of the nature of power.

Although clearly there was prolonged antagonism between the Church and Moscow there were also attempts at rapprochement which tend to be overlooked. Similarly, although long identified as a member of the Western world, the Vatican's relationship with Washington was much more problematic than is normally supposed. For example, John XXIII and Paul VI both explicitly re-positioned the Church away from its previous allegiance to the United States, determined as they were to emphasise the dehumanising effects of unfettered capitalism on Catholic 'territories' such as Latin America, something which the Soviets were quick to recognise and exploit. We need to eschew the traditional analysis which saw the Vatican slavishly following the US line, or opposing every Soviet initiative, in favour of a model more sensitive to historical fact. This would see the Vatican as an independent actor with its own goals which were distinct from those of both

West and East; foremost amongst these were the protection of the Church's institutions, and the right of Catholics to receive the Sacraments. The Vatican's policies, such as *Ostpolitik*, were designed to achieve these objectives without necessarily aligning the Church with one or other bloc. Indeed, given the Holy See's juridically neutral status and its universal proselytising mission, Rome had no choice but to attempt to maintain relations with every state whatever its ideology. Although superficially the Vatican appeared to reflect wider geopolitical patterns of confrontation and *détente*, there was in fact a highly distinctive internal dynamic pushing the Church forward. This motor was the second Vatican Council which initiated a fundamental change in the Catholic perception of the world, moving it away from the North (and superpower relations) towards the developing South.

That process underwent a clear evolution during the reign of Pius XII, John XXIII, Paul VI, and finally, John Paul II. Each put a unique stamp on the Vatican's diplomacy, and each needs to be examined in turn. This will be done by developing both thematic and historical perspectives in order to give a comprehensive account of the way in which the Church dealt with its most serious crisis - the challenge of communist state power. Its response will be analysed at the bilateral, multilateral, and cultural levels. The overtly political level of state-to-state relations has been described in much of the existing literature but what is lacking is an analysis which takes into account the multilateral dimension such as the Conference on Security and Co-operation in Europe (CSCE), and above all, the philosophical and cultural struggle for legitimation in which the Church and Communist Bloc governments were involved. Yet it was precisely at the most fundamental level, that of values, where the battle between the two ideologies was fiercest. Both Catholicism and Communism were, in very different ways, totalising systems of belief which aimed to influence all aspects of life. They were thus, by definition, in tension with each other. In order to understand the Vatican's *Ostpolitik* we need first to place it within the context of Catholic-Communist relations before then going on to explore the repression which the new regimes directed toward the Church during the 1940s and 1950s. This repression effectively forced the Church to abandon hopes of a *modus vivendi* with the Marxist states. Instead, the Vatican desperately attempted to develop a *modus non moriendi* in order to avoid complete physical extinction (Weigel, 1992, p.88).

After first examining the internal bilateral level of church-state relations in the three Catholic communities, we will then analyse the way in which the Vatican, at the international and multilateral level, influenced events. Central to this is the changing way in which the Holy See saw its place in the world. No longer was the Church content to play out a form of

'Catholic Containment' in which it erected a bulwark of anathemas and excommunications against a hostile Soviet Bloc. This had been standard practice during the reign of Pius XII and was reflected in the United States by the fiercely anticommunist Cardinal Francis Spellman of New York. After Pius XII's death, the Church under John XXIII embarked upon a more constructive diplomacy, one far more in keeping with its traditions of engagement and dialogue. Rather than the singular identification with Washington which the Pius/Spellman axis had insisted upon (Weigel, 1992, p.66), a more neutral position was adopted which gave the curia's diplomats greater flexibility in their efforts to save what could be saved of the Church in East Central Europe. That change was motivated not only by internal events such as the second Vatican Council (1962-65), but also by an evolving Cold War context which placed greater emphasis on peaceful coexistence and *détente*. This easing of tensions allowed the Church to exploit its expressive power, a hand which John Paul II was to play with great deftness in his dealings with the Polish state. This chapter also allows us to see that not every actor during the Cold War saw international relations solely in terms of an East/West conflict. For the Vatican at least, the axis of world politics shifted increasingly towards the developing South and its economic and political struggle with the North.

Catholicism and Communism; an Ideological History

Despite the almost universal hostility which Communist regimes have directed against the Church, both Marx and Engels showed a subtle appreciation for religion which has often been overlooked. Marx saw religion, as part of the superstructure, as inevitably dying away; therefore it was not necessary to attack it directly. Communism's secularisation thesis argued that when the alienating effects of capitalism disappeared the need for consolation, i.e. religion, would also disappear. In this way, the recognition of faith as providing the 'heart of a heartless world' provides an important counter balance to accusations that Communist state power would inevitably result in violent repression of other belief systems such as Christianity. Attempts at dialogue between Christians and Marxists which occurred in Western Europe and Latin America tend to support this view. However, there remained within Marxist theory enough to nurture the type of systematic onslaught against religion, and especially Catholicism, which characterised Eastern Bloc church-state relations (Dunn, 1977, pp.18-21).

The history of Catholicism in Russia is especially instructive since it illustrates the permanent hostility with which Russian regimes have always viewed the Catholic Church. With the one exception, a brief respite under Kerensky's Provisional government, Catholicism was regarded as a foreign body, alien to the Orthodox traditions upon which Kievan Rus had been founded (Dunn, 1977, ch.1). What remains striking about official policy toward Catholicism was the continuity which it demonstrated, irrespective of the ideology of the regime. At the bilateral level of church-state behaviour there was often a pattern, which can sometimes be overlooked, in which pre-communist and communist regimes struggled with the Catholic Church over the perennial problem of Erastianism, i.e. state control of the Church. In many respects, post-1945 church - state relations in the Soviet Bloc assumed characteristics which would have been recognised in many different eras, for example over the insistence of Bloc governments that they approve or even appoint bishops. What did distinguish the postwar struggle was the absolute insistence of the Communists that they should enjoy complete dominance over every aspect of life. Bolshevism maintained and intensified that traditional hostility, reserving a special venom for Catholics because of their transnational loyalty to Rome. It was that allegiance to an extra territorial body which most antagonised communist regimes. They correctly recognised that Catholicism represented an obstacle to the totalitarian project upon which they had embarked. By physically trying to exterminate the Church, Lenin and his East European counterparts deformed orthodox Marxist thought by pre-empting the historically inevitable decline of religion. They did so, not out of a disregard for ideological orthodoxy, but rather because they realised that the Church acted as a focus of opposition (political, cultural, and moral) which had deep social and historical roots. Such was the strength of the latter that the post-1945 regimes felt that they had to eradicate them in order to effect their plans for social transformation.

The Church and the New Regimes

The Church's policy on the imposition of pro-Soviet regimes in eastern Europe was, (after initial attempts at conciliation had failed) to oppose the system which the Yalta Conference agreements of 1945 had legitimised. This was pursued doggedly by Pius XII on several grounds, not least his own deep seated personal antipathy towards Communism. However, Pius' fierce rhetoric appeared to be an inadequate riposte as repression mounted throughout the 1950s. The new regimes followed the Soviet model and alternated between co-option and oppression in order to break resistance and enforce allegiance to the state's goals.

At first there was a period of calm as the Soviets realised the mass support which Catholicism enjoyed in the region. That support came from the active wartime resistance which most Catholic hierarchies gave against Nazism (Dunn, 1977, p.122). Opposition to the Nazis differed from country to country, with Poland and Slovakia being at the opposite ends of the spectrum. In Poland the Church cemented its place at the heart of the nation through its vigorous resistance. For example, the aristocratic Cardinal Sapieha of Krakow acted as a powerful reminder of pre-war freedom, and as a symbol of hope for the future. Primates, in the mould of Sapieha, had long played a central role in Polish life, even to the extent of acting as *inter-rex* (Acting King) during an interregnum (Davies, 1984, p.337). Sapieha and others provided a continuity with Poland's history which was vital to the preservation of national identity in the midst of the country's tragic experience between 1939 and 1945. Poland suffered unequalled damage during the war (Bideleux & Jeffries, 1997, p.521), and the Church remained the only functioning institution able to provide welfare and reconstruction on a national scale; for example, the hierarchy mobilised resources to feed and clothe tens of thousands of refugees who had fled into the 'recovered territories' which Poland had received from Germany as part of Yalta. That aid was not only material, but also cultural, as the Church attempted, successfully, to integrate diverse groups into a common set of national values based around the identification of Catholicism with Polishness (Chrypinski, 1984, p.123-5). In Hungary too the hierarchy proved itself to be 'one of the main institutions offering both moral and political contravention to Nazism.' (Dunn, 1977, p.127).

In contrast to Poland, the wartime Slovakian Church had a more ambiguous record, with many Catholics sympathising with Fascism. Slovakian nationalism, fascism and Catholicism found an uneasy expression in the Slovak Republic led by a priest, Monsignor Joseph Tiso (Reban, 1990, p.143). Slovakian nationalism had always had a strong Catholic influence (for example, the Slovak National Party was founded in 1905 by Fr Andrej Hlinka), but the new Republic initiated a much more sinister form of 'clerico-fasciscm'.[5] Tiso's regime was deplorable but it distorted the overall historical record of the Church during the war. Tiso's isolated clerico-fascism was used by Moscow and its protégés as if it were the norm for Catholic behaviour when, in fact, it represented a highly distinctive form of nationalism specific to Slovakia. Even within the Slovakian Church support for Tiso was not unanimous as the opposition of Bishop Karol Kmetko to the regime showed (Sugar, 1971, p.52). Whilst the Croatian Ustasa also received some clerical sanction the general Eastern European pattern was one in which the Church opposed Nazi hegemony, especially in Poland, the principal Catholic state.[6] The Church's wartime record therefore represented an ideological barrier which the new regimes had to overcome. Even where, as in Slovakia, there had been a strong pro-Fascist element within the hierarchy, nevertheless the Church still retained some popular credibility because of its role in shaping national identities (Dunn, 1977, pp.117-18). However despite the residual (and mutual) suspicion between Catholics and communists there was a shared recognition that the ravaged societies of East Central Europe needed reconstruction above all else. Even as staunch an opponent of communism as the writer Czeslaw Milosz acknowledged that 'the Party was the only power that could guarantee peace, reconstruct the country, [and] enable the people to earn their daily bread' (quoted in Bideleux & Jeffries, 1997, p.526). In order to achieve the rebuilding of society radical social and economic measures were clearly needed. What was intolerable from the Catholic perspective was the attempt to undermine the Church's freedom of action in the religious, and especially sacramental, realm.

The Church had traditionally maintained a binary division between the respective rights of the Church and the state, with each enjoying primacy in their own spheres. Rome was, however, determined that its rights should prevail over those of secular authority in the event of a clash. In the case of the new regimes that clash occurred over the Church's provision of education and social services. Both of these areas were traditionally liable to upset the state's relationship with the religious authorities; for example the Nazis infringements of their own Concordat with the Vatican, belatedly alerted the Church to the Party's contempt for Christianity, and its desire to eradicate religion as an organised social force. A postwar example of the same phenomenon occurred in South Africa where the hierarchy's previously compliant attitude to the state hardened considerably after the National Party government introduced the Bantu Education Act. This effectively removed official subsidies to Catholic mission schools, thereby, at a stroke, undermining the bishops' entire strategy of evangelisation (Ryall, 1998, ch.3). We cannot hope to understand the experience of East Central European Catholicism unless we appreciate the continuities with general norms of Catholic political behaviour which informed the hierarchies' response to their particular situations. Indeed what is striking about post-1945 Church-state relations are the continuities with the past. Communism introduced a novel ideological element but the outlines of struggle between civil and religious authority were long established. For example, the pre-war Czechoslovak Republic, with its folk memories of Jan Hus and his opposition to Rome in the 15th Century, had an often tense relationship with the Church. It was a similar story in Poland where the Pilsudski government had a strongly anti-clerical temper (Dunn, 1977, p.163, Davies, 1984, p.342). So, far from there being a historically harmonious relationship between secular and religious authorities, there was often a long tradition of animosity. This gave the Church extensive experience in dealing with hostile politicians through a range of strategies, such as the Polish hierarchy's identification of nationalism with Catholicism. This served to inhibit criticism, even during Marshall Pilsudski's period of office. By the time communism was imposed on Eastern and Central Europe the Church had accumulated a reservoir of practical experience in coping with political hostility; however, the scale and ferocity of the new regimes' onslaught was unprecedented.

We can identify a pattern which Poland, Czechoslovakia, and Hungary all endured from the 1940s until the election of John XXIII in 1958, characterised as it was by a mounting curve of oppression and increasing and coercive attempts at co-option. There was also an important element of strong leadership on the Church's side with outstanding primates in each state resisting these differing forms of pressure, and in turn being persecuted as symbols of Catholic resistance to communism.

i) Bilateral Relations

The Iron Fist in an Iron Glove: East Central European Stalinism and the Church

The Catholic Church had a brief honeymoon with the new ruling parties because its war record provided it with a unique prestige which the new regimes were hesitant to challenge: in Hungary, for example, a Christian Democratic party was tolerated, two Catholic newspapers were published, and the Church was allowed to conduct its sacramental life unhindered (Dunn, 1977, p.127). The breathing space only lasted for as long as it took the workers' governments to become firmly established. Once in possession of the state the Polish, Czechoslovakian, and Hungarian Parties all began a systematic campaign against the Church and religion in general. It was however the increasingly frigid Cold War which dictated the pace of repression. With the promulgation of the Truman Doctrine and the creation of NATO the Soviets increasingly felt themselves to be under threat from a United States with a reinvigorated sense of purpose and urgency. In this context the Church was seen as an obstacle in the attempt to 'Stalinise' East Central Europe and was regarded as a US fifth column after its determined and successful efforts to stop the Communist Party in the 1948 Italian election. This combination of a pro-active and anti-communist USA and Vatican made the Soviets determined to crack down on potentially subversive elements such as the Church (Dunn, 1977, pp.144-45). In effect, geopolitical fear and traditional Catholic-communist antipathy had combined to usher in a period of fierce repression of the Church during the 1950s.

Central to that onslaught was the attempt to supplant the Church's traditional cultural role in national life. In Poland the Church had succeeded in conflating national identity with Catholicism to the extent that it 'was instrumental in inspiring Polish literature and art...and the entire national ethos' (Chrypinski, 1984, p.127). In order to neutralise the influence of the Polish Church the authorities undertook a series of measures, beginning with a propaganda offensive designed to paint the Church as reactionary, fascist, and corrupting. Attempts were made to woo the young away from Catholic influence with a compulsory *Komsomol* type youth organisation the *Zwiajek Mlodziezy Polskiej* (Union of Polish Youth); this was reinforced by attempts to suppress prayer and religious education in schools (Dunn, 1977, p.146). During 1950 all Church property was confiscated by the regime of President Bierut (Davies, 1984, p.6). Not content with this the regime censored the intellectually vigorous Catholic press, closed the Church's hospitals and clinics, and imprisoned hundreds of priests and members of religious orders (Dunn, 1977, p.146, pp.150-51). More subtle tactics were also employed to try and drive a wedge between the clergy and the people. Foremost amongst these was the co-option of amenable priests and laity into officially sanctioned organisations such as PAX which were severely critical of Rome. Divide and rule was a classic Communist strategy which many other regimes, such as the Chinese with their Chinese Catholic Patriotic Association, used to good effect (Leung, 1992). In Poland the tactic was less successful because of the deeply entrenched nature of Polish Catholicism. Nonetheless it represented yet another assault upon the foundations of the Church which the hierarchy found itself facing at a time when it was trying to overcome the wartime ravages of the Nazis. This was something which the Polish primate Cardinal Wyszynski recognised:

> We were so badly mauled at the end of the war as to be barely able to survive. Many priests survived imprisonment by the Nazis only to return to prison in Poland. We had to take this into account...In view of the situation in Poland the bishops saw it as their duty so to lead the Church as to spare it further losses. (Michel, 1991, p.29).

Wyszinski himself suffered at the hands of the regime because to both the people and the regime, the primate symbolised the Polish Church. In order to strike at the Church's leader and most visible figure, the government arrested the Cardinal in 1953 and imprisoned him until 1956 (Michel, 1991, p.28). Acutely conscious of the historical importance of his office Wyszinski refused to compromise on his basic position that the Church should be free to conduct its essential mission unhindered. By so doing he managed to confirm the popular perception of the Church as the only credible moral and institutional opponent of communism.

In Hungary too a similar pattern of violent repression, co-option, and heroic archepiscopal witness emerged. As in Poland Catholicism had left a profound mark on Hungarian culture and public life. Bishops had traditionally been *ex officio* members of parliament's upper chamber and the archbishop of Esztergom, as primate, had been considered the kingdom's second highest dignitary after the monarch (Laszlo, 1990, p.157). The initial focus of church-state tension arose over education where the primate, Cardinal Mindszenty, resolutely opposed official attempts to nationalise the Church's extensive schools' system. Such determined resistance led to the mass imprisonment of over six hundred clergy, nuns and religious brothers (Dunn, 1977, p.155, p.159). In many respects the history of the Church can best be told through the life of Mindszenty because of his iconic status for Hungarian Catholics. Mindszenty showed an implacable hostility to the Rakosi regime's onslaught against the Church, insisting that:

> I wish to be the conscience of my people. In my vocation as a guardian, I knock at the door of your souls. In opposition to the errors now appearing, I declare to my people and my nation the eternal truths. I wish to revive the sacred heritage of our people, without which the individual may perhaps live, but not the nation as a whole (Michel, 1991, p.29).

The policy of giving no quarter to a regime determined to destroy the Church saw Mindszenty detained and tortured before finally being sentenced after a show trial to life imprisonment.[7] Punishment meted out to leading figures such as Mindszenty and Archbishop Jozsef Grosz, president of the bishops' conference (Laszlo, 1990, p.159), sapped the will of a community already reeling from the blows of the war and Soviet occupation. Mindszenty's arrest 'substantially weakened' the Church's resistance, and allowed the Rakosi regime to instigate fierce repression and attack the Church's independence. The principal measure was a State Office for Church Affairs which supervised religious affairs (Dunn, 1977, pp.161-62). In a gesture which indicated both his popularity and the importance of the Church, Mindszenty was freed by troops supporting the 1956 Hungarian uprising. Once in Budapest he made a national broadcast in support of the revolution and was later forced to seek asylum in the US embassy after the Soviet invasion (Mindszenty, 1974, pp.210-11). Because the granite figure of Mindszenty acted as such a central symbol of Hungarian Catholicism, his internal exile robbed the Church of leadership at a crucial time. This afforded the Kadar government an opportunity to consolidate the state's hold which had been temporarily loosened under the more liberal regime of Imre Nagy.

In Czechoslovakia the Church enjoyed less cohesion because of the enduring tension between Czechs and Slovaks, something which the regime was quick to recognise and exploit. Indeed co-option was the enduring tactic used by the government to undermine a Church which, on pre-war figures, enjoyed the support of nearly 75 percent of the population (Reban, 1990, p.143). The record of the Tiso regime offered fertile grounds for the kind of divide and rule tactics successfully used elsewhere. In this case the Party intended to eliminate the Vatican's influence, co-opt the lower clergy, and reduce the bishops' hierarchy simply to an organ of the state, all of which aimed to create a regime-controlled national church (Reban, 1990, p.146). Czechoslovakia, like Poland and Hungary, possessed an outstanding ecclesiastic in Cardinal Josef Beran who attempted to retain the Church's unity whilst also being realistic about the possibilities available to Catholics in a Marxist-Leninist state. Beran, mindful of the weaknesses of the Church, played his hand in a fashion more resembling that of Cardinal Wyszinski than the obdurate Joszef Mindszenty. Despite Beran's best efforts the Czechoslovak Church found itself under the same pressures as its Hungarian and Polish counterparts, so that by 1951 Beran had been interned, Catholic schools closed, and two thousand priests out of a total of seven thousand had been imprisoned or expelled (Dunn, 1977, p.166, p.169).

Throughout Soviet Europe similar pressures were applied by the Party in order to obtain Catholic compliance with the new Socialist norms. An official instruction from the Czechoslovak party to its cadres in 1949 can serve as a strategic template which dictated what the Church had to countenance throughout the Stalinist era. Party members were urged:

1. To separate the bishops and the priests by the suppression of the *Acta Curiae*; to weaken the religious spirit of the priests by the prohibition of all meetings, retreats, clerical congresses, etc.
2. To separate the priests from the laity who might help them.
3. To limit religious activity to the inside of the Church buildings and to control it even there.
4. To liquidate whatever remained of Church property and thus to deprive the clergy of all economic independence (Dunn, 1977, p.165).

The Post Stalin Era

The period until around the late 1950s can be regarded as the bleakest episode of the Soviet experience for the East Central European Church. However, as the new regimes exerted a monopoly of physical control after the Hungarian revolution, and as the Church's sphere of influence narrowed, repression finally began to ease. Having established boundaries the state maintained close vigilance but reduced the level of overt violence, in the form of imprisonment, torture, and banishment, which had characterised the immediate post-war period. The carte-blanche given to the Soviets over Eastern Europe at the Yalta conference, and the sense of triumphalism which characterised the early revolutionary period, had not however eradicated the Church.[8] What sustained the Church throughout the communist era was the influence of the universal church in the form of the Vatican and an immense reserve of "cultural capital" which the Church could draw upon. Despite the easing of official repression Catholics remained second class citizens. For example, even the most politically docile believers regularly suffered from the denial of employment and educational opportunities. That, combined with an incessant barrage of official anti-religious propaganda, ensured that keeping the faith involved at least a constant series of disabilities and discrimination. Throughout the 1960s and 1970s the Hungarian and Czechoslovakian governments maintained a tight control on all aspects of religious life. They remained determined to ensure that religious sentiment should not act as a rallying point for a resurgence of national and anti-Soviet feeling. The reception afforded to Cardinal Mindszenty on his return to Budapest during the 1956 Revolution indicated the ideological danger which even a wounded Church presented to the Party.[9]

Acutely conscious of the resilience of faith the Warsaw, Prague, and Budapest regimes all ensured that religious observance remained within the pale through a complex set of safeguards. A network of dedicated ministries and bureaucracies, informers and policemen, and all the other instruments of a totalitarian state were deployed to restrain and channel an ancient, and still vital force. In Czechoslovakia and Hungary the Party's control was overwhelmingly effective as the savage post revolutionary purges after 1956 and 1968 ensured dissent was reduced to a few brave and isolated voices. For the Czechoslovakian Church the state proved to be an effective and tenacious enemy. Even after the ravages of Klement Gottwald's Stalinism had faded the Party was still determined to exert control over the Church by insisting on the right to control episcopal appointments. This, allied with the existing restrictions with which the government controlled all activities other than the giving of sacraments, meant the Church was bound hand and foot (Reban, 1990, p.147). The post 1968 regime of Husak made a special point of cracking down on the Catholic heartland of Slovakia. Even so, some 70 percent of the population there retained their faith in spite of attempts to create a pro-regime priesthood through the *Pacem in Terris* organisation (Reban, 1990, p.151). As the Slovakian example demonstrates, many believers kept the faith despite sustained official hostility. One of the major factors involved in this was the inspired leadership of Cardinal Frantisek Tomasek who retained links with Rome and refused to compromise on the principle of a government veto over the appointment of bishops. Because of Tomasek's stand eight out of thirteen dioceses had no bishop. In addition to this the Cardinal fought to retain the unity of the hierarchy in the face of a cabal of pro-regime bishops determined to assert the supremacy of the state (Reban, 1990, pp.152-53). Tomasek regarded the Church's situation in Czechoslovakia as being the worst in the Soviet Bloc because the government funded so much Catholic activity thereby robbing the Church of both financial autonomy and the will to acquire it, something which in turn eroded morale.[10] However despite Husak's 'normalisation' campaign, which succeeded in drastically restricting the Church's activities, the regime failed in its larger objectives of establishing a national church or eradicating Catholic culture (Reban, 1990, p.154).

In Hungary the fierce antagonism of the Rakosi regime had set the tone for successive governments; each, through the State Office of Church Affairs and a tame priests' organisation *Opus Pacis*, set out to undermine any real episcopal independence (Laszlo, 1990, pp.158-59, p.161). The Kadar government, perhaps confident it had neutralised the Church, eventually showed a willingness to begin a limited dialogue with the Vatican. This resulted in the 'Partial Agreement' of 1964 negotiated by Mgr Agostino Casaroli which paved the way for the appointment of bishops to vacant Sees and the participation of Hungarian bishops at the second Vatican Council (Laszlo, 1990, p.161). Mindszenty objected fiercely to the Agreement, arguing that the negotiations brought 'only advantages to the Communists and grave disadvantages to Hungarian Catholicism' (Mindszenty, 1974, p.226). The ultimately successful pressure put upon Mindszenty by the Vatican to leave the US embassy and go into exile might be seen as evidence of a *quid pro quo* for the regime's signing of the Agreement, certainly Mindszenty himself thought so (Mindszenty, 1974, p.235). An indication of the improved atmosphere between Rome and Budapest came in 1977 when Mindszenty's successor, Cardinal Lekai, led the Hungarian bishops on their '*ad limina*' visit to Rome, the first such delegation to be allowed during Communist rule. In the same year Kadar and his wife were received by Paul VI at a personal audience in a symbolic act of church - state rapprochement (Laszlo, 1990, p.172). From the Party's perspective it was necessary to ease pressure upon Catholics because of a belated recognition of the parlous state of Hungarian society; rather than creating a New Man, decades of communism had simply eroded many of the most basic civic qualities, leading to rampant corruption. The Party recognised that the social cohesion which Catholicism provided through its moral teaching was an important factor in holding Hungarian society together (Laszlo, 1990, p.164, Michel, 1991). Despite the Church's usefulness to the regime the benefits which the hierarchy had secured in return were debatable. Catholics were effectively condemned to second class status, and the hierarchy was split by the actions of Lekai, who, by clamping down on Catholic dissent in the form of the Base Community movement, appeared to be following the regime's wishes rather too closely (Laszlo, 1990, p.172).

The unique strength and size of the Polish Church frustrated the efforts of the Communist Party to eradicate it. Church-state relations were also eased by the resolution of the long running tension between West Germany and Poland over the Oder-Neisse border, in which the Vatican had played a part (Konczakowski, 1976). Despite the resources available to it, such as the Bloc's only Catholic university in Lublin (KUL), the Church still found itself under considerable pressure, in what was the Warsaw Pact's key state. Vincent Chrypinski regards the state's attitude as one of constant suspicion and hostility ameliorated by the occasional conciliatory gesture (Chrypinski, 1990, p.121). After the release of Cardinal Wyszinski in 1956 the conflict took on the appearance of a bureaucratic struggle on the part of the regime as it obstructed the hierarchy's attempts to build much needed churches. Although overt violence was only rarely directed at the institutional Church, for example the murder of Fr Jerzy Popieluszko in October 1984, the government did not hesitate to use it against lay Catholics, especially during the 1980s. A crucial difference between the Polish Church and its Czechoslovakian and Hungarian counterparts was that the Gierek, Kania, and Jaruzelski regimes all failed to deliver anything resembling prosperity. As a result of the widespread popular dissatisfaction with the economy the Polish Church became an even stronger opposition force. In contrast, Kadar and Husak had at least satisfied some basic material longings, which in turn made the penalties attached to active Church membership even higher (Garton Ash, 1991, p.361). The combination of dire poverty and powerful Catholic institutions and traditions allowed the Polish Church to play a crucial role in the Soviet Bloc's greatest single challenge - the Solidarity movement. However, it was the support given by the papacy, during the martial law period, which helped Solidarity to survive, and it is that multi-lateral level we now need to examine.

ii) Multi-Lateral level

The Role of the Vatican: Despite the catalogue of confiscations, imprisonments and deaths which the Church suffered in East Central Europe both Catholicism as a faith and its institutions survived the depredations of Stalinism. Indeed repression appeared to strengthen the Polish Church. In Norman Davies' words 'Common distress created the sense of a common purpose' (Davies, 1984, p.341). Whilst in Hungary and Czechoslovakia the Church was undoubtedly compromised by the degree of official control exercised over it, crucially both remained functioning communities in communion with Rome. Two factors lay behind this: the influence of the Vatican and the accumulated cultural capital which allowed the Church to draw upon deep reserves of loyalty. Often that support was not necessarily based on a conventional religious belief, but rather, as in Poland, on a recognition that the Church was a more authentic representative of basic rights and values than the state (Garton Ash, 1991, p.23, Michnik, 1985, p.327). It is inconceivable that Catholicism could have survived the particular ravages of the 1950s, let alone the next thirty years of official hostility, without the part played by that tradition of popular support and the role of the Universal Church.

During the 1950s curial diplomacy took an initially confrontational stance; a Catholic form of Containment which mirrored that of the Truman Doctrine. Although both Rome and the regimes adopted a confrontational stance that was by no means the whole story. Indeed, the Vatican was willing to reach diplomatic agreement if it thought that the Church would benefit. Although there was often fierce resentment from the national hierarchies, in particular from Mindsenzty, to curial interference, there was also an awareness that the carrot of recognition from Rome offered a certain, if limited, degree of leverage on otherwise implacably hostile opponents. The fate suffered by less hierarchically structured faiths which lacked a strong external voice, such as Pentecostal or Baptist, lend weight to the view that without Rome the Catholic situation would have been even worse. Despite the controversy surrounding Pius XII's wartime role the Vatican retained a moral authority which carried international influence. This 'expressive' power even during the 1950s meant that however much the Soviets might want to they could not entirely ignore the Church's influence in key states such as West Germany. That influence was to be given a distinctive structure during the papacy of Paul VI and his much vaunted *Ostpolitik* which attempted to map out a non-aligned role for the Church and to emphasise the Church's willingness to coexist and conduct a dialogue with all people of good will.[11] Although by the 1960s classic concordat style diplomacy had achieved as much as it could, it did nonetheless enable a channel of communication to be maintained as well as giving a crucial psychological boost to the beleaguered Catholic communities. Given the extremity of the situation in which the Church found itself, that represented an achievement. We need to beware of using conventional ideas to measure the success and failure of the Vatican's diplomacy in East Central Europe. Rather, anything more than the simple physical survival of Catholics represented a triumph. With no material resources to speak of, the bishops and curial diplomats were forced to rely on more intangible resources.

Several interlinked factors were behind the Vatican's more conciliatory approach to the Bloc governments. First and most crucial was the impact of the second Vatican Council on the way in which the Church perceived the world. Before Vatican II, suspicion and sometimes hostility had characterised many official Catholic attitudes towards contemporary ideologies such as socialism, liberalism, and nationalism. This hostility caused by the French Revolution, and fanned during the 19th century by an aggressive secularism, gave the Church and especially the papacy an insular and defensive mentality. Pius XII represented the culmination of this Church militant tradition. His successor John XXIII realised that radical change, albeit within the bounds of tradition, was needed if Catholicism was to continue as a vibrant force. John saw that a church which was growing faster in Africa and Latin America than elsewhere needed to engage in contemporary concerns, especially in relation to economic underdevelopment. Peace was clearly a major concern, with the Cuban Missile Crisis adding a fresh urgency to longstanding concerns about nuclear weapons; central to this new thinking about international affairs was a profound change in the way the Church perceived human rights. Rather than being concerned primarily with safeguarding the right of religious observance the Church became increasingly concerned, in the wake of the Holocaust, with the protection of the individual.[12] Allied to this was a belief that co-operation with people of good will, whatever their ideology, was the best way to achieve a just and peaceful world order.[13] This theological shift allowed the Church to free itself from an exclusive identification with the US which Pius XII had engineered to protect the Church against Stalin. Instead the Vatican saw its international role as one in which its juridically neutral status allowed it to reach out across the Cold War divide. Theology and hard political calculation came together as the Vatican offered its good offices across a range of Cold War issues such as the Vietnam War.[14] Moscow looked on these developments favourably, realising that there was a convergence of interest between Soviet notions of peaceful co-existence and the Vatican's desire for a more justly ordered international society. The relative lack of success which Pius XII's hard line had produced in East Central Europe made a different approach essential.[15] The new tack was aided immeasurably by the personalities of John XXIII and Paul VI who were far more open and willing to engage in dialogue with different political and religious traditions. Paul had also been identified with a more conciliatory line during his time as a curial diplomat during Pius' reign, an approach he institutionalised in the form of *Ostpolitik.*

From the Soviet perspective the Church's new emphasis on peace and economic justice fitted in usefully with Khrushchev's 'peaceful co-existence' (Crockatt, 1996, p.125, pp.222-23). It was also obvious by the 1960s that despite fierce repression the Church still survived as an influential actor in East Central Europe; given this reality Moscow could no longer ignore the possibilities which co-operation with the Church, rather than conflict, offered. Indeed a more conciliatory approach offered Moscow the opportunity to try and sow some discord between Rome and the national hierarchies; this was a tactic worth trying given the disagreements over authority and autonomy which had plagued relations between Rome and Cardinals Wyszinski and Mindszenty. A final factor in making the Soviets amenable to a *détente* with Rome was the change which had occurred in Moscow's own diplomacy. For decades Soviet policy towards the Church had been based on the Leninist premise that the progress of the Revolution required the destruction of organised religion. Soviet diplomacy had mirrored that attitude by displaying a hostile contempt towards the Vatican. Indeed, long after Moscow had assumed all the duties and obligations of a member of international society the policy of ostracising the Vatican had continued. Given the changed attitude towards a *détente* with communism, which the Church began displaying with John's election, it made clear sense to treat the Vatican as a normal state. That did not however mean that basic philosophical differences had ended, but rather that both sides saw practical advantages in talking with the other.

Ostpolitik, in classic Vatican style, was a long term policy. As its principal architect, Cardinal Casaroli, argued, *Ostpolitik* 'is designed for the long run, and there is no alternative to it' (Stehle, 1981, p.7). Hans Stehle sees *Ostpolitik* as having four main elements. First that it eschewed 'classical concordatory policy' in which Church support for secular authority was often explicit, in favour of a clear separation of church and state. Second, incremental, partial solutions offered more chance of success than comprehensive settlements, which were in any case much harder to negotiate. Third, in order for the Vatican to secure the right to worship, and other liberties, a stable international environment was imperative. It therefore became necessary for Rome to play a part in the broader process of East-West *détente*, hence the interest in arms control, CSCE, and a New International Economic Order. Finally, relations with Moscow assumed priority above those of its satellites, since only by reassuring the Soviets that the Church accepted Yalta and all it implied could bilateral relations be improved with

East Central European states (Stehle, 1981, pp.390-91). The first tangible signs of the new approach were seen in the Hungarian Partial Agreement of 1964, and the symbolically important meeting a year later of Paul VI and the Soviet foreign minister Andrei Gromyko (Weigel, 1992, p.74). Other significant events came with visits which key players such as Casaroli and Cardinal Koenig of Vienna paid behind the Iron Curtain to establish informal links. These became formalised in a set of agreements such as those concluded with Yugoslavia in 1964 and Czechoslovakia in 1977. There were also a number of high profile papal audiences with Bloc leaders such as Soviet head of state Podgorny, Rumanian leader Ceausescu, and Bulgarian premier Zhivkov, all of which would have been unthinkable before the advent of papal *détente*.[16]

An indication of the importance of the policy lay in the fact that John Paul II continued the basic outlines despite the intense criticism which papal *détente* had received. Critics accused the Curia of appeasing dictatorships by maintaining diplomatic relations and betraying a venerated history of martyrdom in favour of compromise, ironically mirroring in many respects the charges of selling out levelled at the Carter administration by some right wing critics.[17] John Paul II added a distinctive element to Ostpolitik because of the intense personal experience he had gained as a Polish bishop. Unlike the apparently more combative Wyszinski, Karol Wojtyla, the future pontiff, had maintained a lower profile but nevertheless still played a crucial role in negotiations with the state.[18] His clear support for Solidarity proved to be of crucial importance once the organisation had been banned during the state of emergency in December 1981. John Paul provided a symbol of hope and inspiration during a dark period and his unrivalled charisma meant that world wide attention was focused on basic questions of human dignity at a time when martial law in Poland, and 'Kadarisation' in Hungary were undermining individual liberties in different ways. John Paul's more assertive aproach also involved a much broader and disinterested critique of injustice - wherever it was perpetuated, so that the Pope criticised human rights abuses in Latin America, South Korea, and the Philippines, where the Church played an important role in the "People Power" revolution which overthrew the Marcos regime (Weigel, 1992, p.95). The Vatican strongly supported the CSCE process, and its advocacy of "Basket Three" of the final agreement served to emphasise the Church's opposition to communism and its belief that peaceful, incremental change offered a humane way of changing the system (Wiegel, 1992, p.26-30). Arguably the CSCE process also acted as a crucial catalyst for the overthrow of communism, as groups such as Charter 77 provided a rallying point for opposition and a training ground for a new leadership. Ultimately the Church's role in the collapse of the Soviet empire was very much secondary to the economic sclerosis which paralysed much of the Soviet bloc. However Catholicism as an institution and as a moral/cultural force did have a significant part to play in the events of 1989. Institutionally the Church acted, above all in Poland, as a competing source of legitimacy which the Yalta system could never undermine. In the moral and cultural realm the Church was able to offer an alternative value system which preached the importance of conscience and autonomy against the sterile ideology of official materialism.[19]

Conclusion

In conclusion we can see that careful diplomacy by the Vatican helped to retain a crucial institutional framework in East Central Europe, which in turn meant that the Church's sacramental life could continue even if crucial elements of its work, such as education, were drastically curtailed. The Vatican's diplomatic support rested on a bedrock of popular loyalty and was itself a product of the Church's central role in national life and its war record. That allowed the Polish, Czechoslovak, and Hungarian hierarchies to retain a form of organised worship until the communist storm blew itself out. Also vital to the Church's survival was the strong, dynamic and consistent leadership exercised throughout the period by a line of outstanding prelates such as Wyszinzski, Beran, Mindsenty, Wojtyla, and Tomasek. Ultimately, however, what preserved the Church in East Central Europe was a diplomatic strategy which simultaneously recognised the present power of the Soviet empire, while also affirming a long tradition of constructive and bounded opposition. Both the Vatican and the national hierarchies were always careful to stress their respect for legitimate authority and abhorrence of disorder. They also always maintained that repressing religion ran counter both to agreed human rights, and ignored the part the Christian faith had played in the traditions and histories of East Central Europe. A decision to step away from the rhetoric of the Cold War in the early 1960s was to pay rich dividends as the Church embraced and reshaped *détente* to recreate itself as a neutral and mediating element between East and West. In doing so it opened up for itself crucial room for diplomatic initiatives such as *Ostpolitik*; Casoroli and Popes Paul and John Paul II then used this space to trade the currency of diplomatic recognition and status in return for tangible improvements in the lives of Catholics. Such leverage as the Church possessed was based upon its moral force and this precious and limited currency was, in general, wisely spent.

Ultimately what makes the Church's role significant during the Cold War was that it, first, provided a space in which opposition groups could find some limited protection; second, it acted as a repository of certain threatened values such as personal freedom and artistic and moral autonomy; third, it preserved a sense of national identity, especially in Poland. Finally, whilst always focused upon the fate of Christians in communist states, especially with John Paul II, it also delivered fundamental attacks upon the nature of liberal capitalism and the effects this had upon the international political economy, so, to a degree, breaking out of the dominant international mindset in which East-West relations overshadowed all else. Ultimately the Church's international relations had an eschatological foundation which precluded an exclusive focus on any one area. To this extent the Church stands as a perhaps unique example of a state and transnational actor which was truly non-aligned, not only from calculation but also from principle.

Notes

1 For an analysis of the structure of the Vatican's diplomacy see D. Ryall (1998, ch.3). For stylistic purposes the Church, Vatican, Holy See, and Rome are used as synonyms in this chapter. For the precise meaning of each term see above thesis.

2 For an analysis of East-West *détente*, including the Church's role, see R. Davey (1992).

3 See the criticism of this tendency in William Wallace (1996, p.315).

4 Opposition to the West showed itself mainly in the economic realm with Paul VI and John Paul II in particular urging a radical re-ordering of the international political economy and especially third world debt.

5 For details of Hlinka's influence see A. Polonsky (1975, p.117).

6 For a different interpretation see Bideleux & Jeffries (1997, pp.492-4).

7 For his own account see Jozsef Cardinal Mindszenty, *Memoirs,* (1974). Mindszenty was however a deeply controversial figure who was regarded by many as being too inflexible in his dealings with the state during the Cold War. Since his death his status in contemporary Hungary appears to be high as the campaign to canonise him perhaps indicates.

8 For a critical analysis of Yalta and its impact upon European geopolitics see Weigel, (1992, pp.96-7).

9 See Mindszenty (1974, Ch.VII) for a graphic account of the Revolution.

10 (Reban, 1990, pp.152-53). See Michel, (1991, ch.2) for a sophisticated and nuanced sociological analysis of Czechoslovak society.

11 For a magisterial account of papal diplomacy see H. Stehle, (1981).

12 For an example of that concern see: *Pontifical Council for Justice and Peace* (1990). The Council is the organ charged with the promotion of human rights

work.

13 See the 'Pastoral Constitution on the Church in the Modern World' (*Gaudium et Spes)* as a profound expression of this (Flannery, 1992).

14 For an interesting discussion of Vatican policy see Kent & Pollard, (1994).

15 Although even a more conciliatory approach might well have failed given the brutal nature of the immediate post war regimes.

16 For a useful chronology of Ostpolitik see Stehle, (1981, pp.453-7).

17 For an indiction of how vehement the debate became see appendices in Stehle, (1981).

18 The most accessible general biography of John Paul remains T. Szulc, (1995). The best specialist treatment is Williams (1981).

19 For trenchant analysis of the moral poverty of communism see Havel, (1991).

9 Learning from the Cold War Nuclear Confrontation

PAUL ROGERS

Introduction

Since the ending of the Cold War in the early 1990s, two broad views of the confrontation have emerged. One contends that the Cold War ended in victory for the NATO alliance, with the Soviet bloc collapsing first into the Commonwealth of Independent States and a number of independent East European countries, and subsequently into an even looser alliance, with the Russian Federation itself under threat of decline if not disintegration. This analysis sees the nuclear confrontation as an essential part of the process, with stable nuclear deterrence providing a security context within which the much greater free market economic success of western liberal democracies could ultimately lead to the downfall of a rigid centrally planned economic system. Central to this was the manner in which the Eastern bloc was forced into crippling defence budgets in a desperate attempt to maintain military parity with NATO.

An alternative view acknowledges the role of excessive defence commitments in hastening the collapse of the Soviet bloc, but is critical of the Cold War era as being both massively wasteful of human and material resources and also a highly dangerous period with great potential for disaster. It is pointed out that when Cold War military spending peaked in the late 1980s, it made up rather more than 80 percent of world military expenditure of around $1,000 billion per annum (at 1998 prices). Not only is this held to be a wasteful diversion of state spending away from pressing national and international human needs, but it also required an immense commitment of scientific and technical capabilities which might otherwise have been available to civil use.

A further development of this view is that the 45 years of the Cold War produced a military/technological momentum which has given rise to numerous advanced military developments which are proliferating across the world in the post-Cold War era. These include biological and chemical weapons, ballistic and cruise missiles and conventional weapons of mass destruction such as fuel-air explosives, cluster weapons and other area-impact munitions.

The Cold War critique also places emphasis on the dangers of the nuclear confrontation, arguing that nuclear deterrence was far from stable, that there were nuclear accidents and near-disastrous crises and that the much-vaunted notion of stable nuclear deterrence was, to an extent, a myth.

In recent years, support for this view has come from some unlikely sources, in particular from a number of former senior military officers and security advisers such as one-time US Secretary of Defense Robert McNamara and the retired head of US Strategic Command, General Lee Butler. Such people are becoming strong advocates of proposals to move rapidly towards further reductions in numbers of nuclear weapons, with some raising the possibility of a nuclear-free world. They argue that the ending of the Cold War does not in any sense rule out the risk of nuclear confrontation, an argument given weight by an event occurring not during a period of peak tension at the height of the Cold War but several years after the East-West confrontation had begun to decay.

Early on the morning of 25 January, 1995, a Norwegian-US research team launched a large four-stage Black Brant XII rocket as part of a long-term programme to observe the Northern Lights. The rocket was launched from an island off the North Coast of Norway, an area which had been a very sensitive part of the Cold War, given that it could have been a launch zone for US submarine-launched ballistic missiles aimed at targets in the former Soviet Union (Blair, Feiveson and Hippel, 1997).

To avoid false alarms, such experiments were notified in advance to the relevant Russian authorities, and the Norwegian Foreign Ministry had sent a letter to them reporting an impending launch of a research rocket in late January or early February depending on weather conditions. Probably as a result of the chaotic state of the Russian bureaucracy at the time, this message had not been received by Russian radar crews. Moreover, the Black Brant XII rocket was much larger than previous experiments and its four stages resembled the multiple stages of a US submarine-launched Trident missile.

The Trident D5 missile carries six substantial thermonuclear warheads and, to the radar operators, it was not possible to dismiss the idea that it might be part of a surprise attack on Russia. Within minutes, the alert had reached the highest levels in Russia and, possibly for the first time, Yeltsin's "nuclear briefcase" was activated. It would have been possible for a Trident missile launched from off the Norwegian coast to have delivered its warheads over Moscow within twenty minutes, giving President Yeltsin very little time to decide whether to launch a retaliatory strike. In the event, the early warning system was able to detect, within those twenty minutes, that the Black Brant rocket was not heading for Russian territory, and the alert status was reduced (Hoffman, 1998).

Part of the explanation for this sudden and dangerous alert lay with an event in 1987 when a young German, Mathias Rust, flew a light aircraft right across Russia to Moscow and landed in Red Square. Rust's ability to evade detection by Soviet air defences had had a profound effect on the system, making operatives highly sensitive to the need to avoid being caught out. Thus, at several levels up the ladder of command, officers decided to play safe and pass on the alert rather than check in detail before doing so.

When they first detected the Black Brant rocket, the radar operators could be blamed for causing a false alarm if they passed on details of the launch, but they were concerned that the rocket could just have been part of a missile attack and passed on responsibility to a higher level. The general on duty adopted a similar stance, not least because the "missile" could have been equipped with an electromagnetic pulse warhead designed to explode high over Moscow and disrupt the Russia command and control system as a prelude to a more general attack (Hoffman, 1998).

Once the warning of the rocket's trajectory had been passed on to the Russian command and control system, Kazbek, predetermined procedures came into operation, ending with alerts in the three nuclear briefcases held by the Russia President, Defence Minister and Chief of Staff. With the command and control system now operating in combat mode, the trajectory of the rocket was monitored as Yeltsin and his colleagues conferred. Only when it was concluded that the rocket was not a threat was the alert terminated, the whole episode lasting just a few minutes.

The January 1995 incident happened after the Cold War and at a time of relatively low East/West tensions, yet it prompted an immediate high-level alert. Evidence from a number of sources now indicates that there were several false alarms during the Cold War, coupled with numerous nuclear accidents. Together, they indicate a degree of danger during many of the Cold War years which turns out to be fully supportive of the much-derided warnings of anti-nuclear campaigners, so often dismissed as scare-mongering at the time.

This chapter examines some of the developing evidence of these dangers and suggests some lessons which arise from this experience. To put this in perspective, though, a brief examination of the general history of Cold War nuclear weapons developments and a more detailed discussion of their potential use is appropriate, not least because this wider context also has a relevance to the future.

Origins and Development of Cold War Strategic Nuclear Arsenals

Nuclear weapons were originally developed as a result of the collaborative Manhattan Project in the United States, with the first atomic device tested on 16 July 1945 and atom bombs dropped on Hiroshima and Nagasaki on 6 and 9 August of that year. The Manhattan Project embraced an immediate production capability as well as being a research and development project - had Japan not surrendered in August 1945, as many as ten more atom bombs could have been produced within six months.

Following the end of the war, the United States Congress passed the McMahon Energy Act in 1946, one of its provisions being the ending of involvement in the nuclear project of states such as Britain, a factor which encouraged Britain's Atlee government to initiate its own nuclear programme. Within the United States, progress was rapid and an arsenal of some 50 free-fall atom bombs was available by 1948, these being deliverable first by World War II vintage planes such as the B29, but then by the first of the new intercontinental bombers, the B36.[1]

The Soviet nuclear programme was initiated by the mid-1940s and made rapid progress, leading to the first atomic test in 1949. Both states moved rapidly into the field of fusion or thermonuclear weapons, with the United States testing a device in 1952, followed a year later by the Soviet Union. Britain tested its fission bomb in the same year, and a fusion bomb in 1957. France started a nuclear programme in the early 1950s, testing its first device in 1960, and China followed suit in 1964. Israel's nuclear programme probably delivered useable nuclear weapons by the very early 1970s, India tested a device in 1974, and South African and Pakistani efforts came rather later.

By the mid-1950s, the United States and the Soviet Union were engaged in a full-scale nuclear arms race comprising very powerful nuclear weapons delivered initially by bombers. Concerns over their vulnerability to air defences resulted in intensive programmes to develop ballistic missile nuclear delivery systems, initially with medium and intermediate range missiles based in Europe (and an attempted Soviet basing in Cuba which resulted in the 1962 missile crisis).

The next stage was the development of 15,000-mile range intercontinental ballistic missiles (ICBMs); the first test was conducted by the Soviet Union in 1957 and the United States was the first to deploy them three years later. These ICBMs were based on land, were liquid-fuelled and were slow to prepare for launching, making them vulnerable to surprise attack. If a missile took several hours to prepare for launching, but had a flight-time of less than thirty minutes, there was a vulnerability which led on readily to the "use them or lose them" outlook.

More immediately, other solutions to this problem of missile vulnerability were sought. One was to develop ICBMs with storable solid fuels which could be kept at more or less instant readiness for launch. A second was to place them in heavily protected underground silos which could survive almost anything short of a direct nuclear strike, and the third was to develop submarine-launched ballistic missiles (SLBMs) which could be fired from large nuclear-powered submarines when submerged and which were, at least in theory, impossible to detect and destroy.

Both the United States and the Soviet Union went on to develop so-called "triads" of strategic nuclear forces based on ICBMs, SLBMs and heavy bombers. Overall, though, the Soviet Union placed most emphasis on ICBMs and least emphasis on bombers, whereas the United States developed a more balanced set of forces.

During the late 1950s, both superpowers developed extremely powerful weapons, with the largest of the missile warheads and free-fall bombs having destructive yields of 10 to 25 megatons, a megaton being equivalent to 1,000,000 tons of conventional high explosive such as TNT. Used against cities, these would be utterly devastating - a 25 megaton warhead detonated at an altitude of 100,000 feet would cause near total devastation over an area of 500 square miles and would cause serious fires up to 25 miles from the point of detonation. Many of the early devices were tested in the atmosphere at ground level and the resultant controversies over the effects of radioactive fall-out were early prompts for anti-nuclear campaigning in a number of countries.

By the late 1960s, production lines for several types of strategic nuclear weapon were operating intensively in the United States and the Soviet Union, and strategic nuclear arsenals were numbered in the thousands. There was a belief in the need to have very large forces to ensure the survival of some part of a nuclear arsenal in time of war, but the extent of the forces amounted to a remarkable degree of "overkill". Given that the destruction of a handful of major cities and centres of industrial production could devastate the economies of either the United States or the Soviet Union, there was already a developing air of unreality, but this was to be carried to extremes with two new strategic developments under way by the early 1970s (Polmar, 1982).

The first was the development of multiple warheads on each missile, a number of smaller warheads giving a wider "spread" over a larger target and ensuring greater destructive capability. These multiple re-entry vehicles (MRVs) were then superseded by multiple independently-targetable re-entry vehicles (MIRVs) in which each warhead could be directed at a different target. The US Poseidon SLBM was an example of a MIRVed missile - carrying 10 warheads (14 over a reduced range), it could direct them at targets spread over an area of well over 20,000 square miles (Rogers, 1988).

This MIRVing of missiles coincided with the second round of the Strategic Arms Limitation Treaty (SALT) negotiations from 1972 to 1979. At the very time when these talks aimed to curb increases in numbers of missiles, the two negotiating superpowers were rapidly increasing the number of warheads on each missile, negating the very basis of the talks. Thus, over the seven years of the talks, the United States increased its strategic warhead numbers from 5,700 to 9,000 and the Soviet increase was from 2,100 to 5,000.

In parallel with this MIRVing was a remarkable increase in warhead accuracy. Early missiles were able to develop large single warheads to within one to two miles of their target, but major improvements in guidance made it theoretically possible for warheads to be accurate enough to destroy missiles in hardened underground silos. By 1980 the United States had a missile, the Minuteman III, which had an accuracy of 600 feet CEP (circular error probable - a 50 percent chance of a warhead landing within this distance of the target).

Highly accurate missiles carrying multiple warheads could theoretically "disarm" an opponent's land-based missiles while leaving the attacker with many missiles in reserve. Developments in antisubmarine warfare and air defences also suggested that other legs of the strategic triad might have some vulnerability, and the notion of a "disarming first strike" acquired impetus, leading to the development of hair-trigger responses such as launch-on-warning. In such a scenario, a proportion of a state's nuclear arsenal could be launched in a pre-programmed sequence when warning of an incoming missile attack had been received but before the missiles hit their targets. A variant was launch-under-attack, in which retaliation would be delayed until the first detonations of an incoming salvo of missiles, but both strategies had worrying aspects because of the possible effects of false alarms.

By the early 1980s, the United States had over 10,000 strategic nuclear warheads and the Soviet Union about 8,700, and missile and bomber programmes then in progress indicated that the two states would have well over 30,000 strategic warheads by the early 1990s. In the eventuality, the peak was reached in the late 1980s, and improving relations, the ending of the Cold War, and the negotiation of the Strategic Arms Reduction Treaties (START) began to have an effect, not just on total warhead numbers but also on the most destabilising strategic weapons - the accurate multi-warhead missiles.

In terms, then, of numbers of weapons and sheer destructive power, the Cold War was characterised at the strategic nuclear level by an extraordinary degree of overkill, which would have been absurd if the policy objective for each state was primarily to be able to cause massive retaliatory damage to the opponent. In the public mind, this was the function of nuclear weapons - to provide an ultimate deterrent against nuclear attack. Thus, with both states able to cause such damage, the existence of mutually assured destruction (MAD) was the underpinning of nuclear stability. In reality, though, this was rarely, if ever, the actual nuclear targeting policy of either the United States or the Soviet Union.

The Strategic Nuclear Postures of the Superpowers

If the public perception of nuclear weapons has been to see them as ultimate deterrents, then the declaratory nuclear weapons postures of the United States and the Soviet Union systematically endorsed this perception. The difficulty was that declaratory policies and actual deployment policies were never the same. Furthermore, governments tended to promote the idea of mutually assured destruction in the public mind. This contrasted with military thinking, as demonstrated powerfully by an exchange between Senator Tower and General Jones, then Chairman of the US Joint Chiefs of Staff, at a Senate Hearing in 1979:

> **Senator Tower**: General Jones, what is your opinion of the theory of mutual assured destruction?
> **General Jones**: I think it is a very dangerous strategy. It is not the strategy that we are implementing today within the military but it is a dangerous strategy...
> **Senator Tower**: Your professional military judgement is that it is a dangerous strategy and it is not one which we should follow?
> **General Jones**: I do not subscribe to the idea that we ever had it as our basic strategy. I have been involved with strategic forces since the early 1950s. We have always targeted military targets. There has been a lot of discussion...about different strategies. We followed orders, but basically, the strategy stayed the same in the implementation of targeting.

> **Senator Tower**: Unfortunately I am not sure that your opinion was always shared by your civilian superiors.
> **General Jones**: I agree that there have been some, including some in government, who have felt that all we require is a mutual assured destruction capability. I am separating that from our targeting instructions in the field ...[2]

There is now ample evidence from the literature on nuclear targeting that both the Soviet Union and the United States targeted their opponent's nuclear forces. General Jones simply did not accept that the basic US strategy had ever been to achieve stability by threatening only retaliation against Soviet cities as in the popular misconception of nuclear strategy being based on assured destruction.

If mutually assured destruction was not the deployment policy for strategic nuclear forces, then what was the extent of the potential for pre-emptive surprise attack? Even as far back as the 1950s, there is evidence that US nuclear planners recognised the advantages to be gained from first strikes with nuclear weapons in time of crisis. A briefing from the Head of Strategic Air Command (SAC) at the time, General Curtis le May, illustrates this:

> **Q**: How do SAC's plans fit with the stated national policy that the US will never strike the first blow?
>
> **A**: I have heard this thought stated many times and it sounds very fine. However, it is not in keeping with United States history...I want to make it clear that I am not advocating a preventive war; however, I believe that if the US is pushed in a corner far enough we would not hesitate to strike first ... (Rosenberg, 1982)

From the late 1950s, the United States produced a series of integrated strategic nuclear targeting plans, designed to bring together the targeting undertaken by the ICBM, SLBM and bomber forces. These were (and are) known as the Single Integrated Operational Plans (SIOPs), and, with the rapid expansion of the strategic nuclear arsenals, reached their peak in the early 1980s.

By 1982, Desmond Ball could write of SIOP-5:

> As a result of these developments, the US Target plans for strategic nuclear war are now extremely comprehensive. The current version of SIOP-5

includes more than 40,000 potential target installations, as compared to about 25,000 in 1974 ... (Ball, 1983).

SIOP-5 had targets in four broad categories.

1. Soviet Nuclear Forces included ICBM and intermediate-range missiles and their launch facilities and command centres, nuclear weapons storage sites, airfields with nuclear-capable aircraft and ballistic missile submarine bases. There were approximately 2,000 targets in this category.

2. Conventional Military Forces included barracks, supply depots, and conventional air fields and comprised 20,000 targets.

3. The Military and Political Leadership included command bunkers, key communications and intelligence facilities, and represented 3,000 targets.

4. Economic and Industrial Targets comprised war-supporting industries such as munitions and arms factories, transport and energy facilities, and industries contributing to economic recovery including coal, steel, non-ferrous metals and cement. This economic and industrial base included 15,000 targets (Ball, 1983).

Furthermore, nuclear targeting plans such as SIOP-5 involved a number of levels of nuclear war-fighting, ranging from limited use of strategic nuclear weapons for specified actions, through to all-out nuclear war - a central nuclear exchange. Thus, SIOP-5 included:

1. Major Attack Options (MAO) involved substantial use of strategic nuclear forces against a wide range of Soviet assets.

2. Selective Attack Options (SAO) included the targeting of Soviet facilities adjacent to allied states, one example being destruction of Soviet military facilities such as air fields and army bases close to Iran, which, in the 1970s, had been an ally of the west. Another selective option, in the event of a war involving China against the Soviet Union, would have been destroying Soviet military forces close to China, an option known colloquially as "kicking the back door in".

3. Limited Nuclear Options (LNO) embraced the selective destruction of fixed enemy military or industrial targets, envisaging an attack which fell short of general destruction but might induce a negotiated end to the nuclear war-fighting short of a central nuclear exchange.

4. Regional Nuclear Options (RNO) could involve the destruction of leading elements of an attacking force, an aspect of strategic nuclear targeting relating closely to the use of tactical nuclear weapons (discussed later in this chapter).

According to Ball, within each of these groups of options, there was a wide range of further plans, including "withholds" - targets not attacked - such as population centres and national command and control systems. Decisions to avoid destroying centres of population ran in the face of the declaratory policy of MAD, and avoiding destruction of command and control systems made it more possible to envisage a nuclear war being controlled, with a negotiated end to the conflict. It is thus clear that SIOP-5 and the deployment policy which it embraced, was firmly based on the idea that nuclear wars could be fought without assured destruction - that victory was possible.

Furthermore, the idea of first strike was certainly embraced, not least in relation to potential Soviet action. As Ball comments, 'Special categories of targets have also been delineated for pre-emptive attacks against the Soviet Union and for launch-on-warning (LOW) or launch-under-attack (LUA) scenarios in the event of unequivocal warning of Soviet attack' (Ball, 1983).

By the early 1980s, another element was intruding into nuclear strategy, the Strategic Defence Initiative (SDI - popularly called "Star Wars") and its Soviet equivalent. SDI made superficial sense in that it appeared to suggest that a state could be protected from incoming ballistic missiles, but expert opinion was, from the start, dubious that any missile defence system could be so effective as to provide full protection from thousands of warheads. The more troubling aspect of SDI was the idea that it might be employed in conjunction with highly accurate MIRVed missiles. While an SDI system could not protect against an all-out missile attack, it might offer significant protection against a residual nuclear attack coming from a state which had lost the great majority of its nuclear forces to a disarming first strike.

By the mid-1980s, ballistic missile defence programmes, taken in conjunction with improved missile accuracy, were causing real concern to analysts of nuclear crisis management. Moreover they came in parallel with developments in tactical nuclear policy, especially in Central Europe where the NATO/Warsaw Pact confrontation was most obvious.

The Development of Tactical Nuclear Weapons

Although the early nuclear weapons were essentially strategic - intended for use against the core assets of an opposing state, the development of nuclear weapons intended for tactical use within particular war zones was an early feature of the East-West nuclear confrontation. By the late 1950s, both the United States and the Soviet Union were developing relatively low-yield free-fall bombs as well as early forms of nuclear-capable artillery. Over the next 25 years, a remarkable array of tactical nuclear weapons was developed and deployed, covering almost every type of military posture.

As well as free-fall bombs, short-range artillery missiles were developed along with nuclear-tipped anti-aircraft missiles and several types of nuclear artillery and mortars. Nuclear land mines, known as atomic demolition munitions, were developed which could be emplaced to destroy major bridges or tunnels or even block mountain passes. At sea, submarines were equipped with nuclear-tipped torpedoes, surface ships carried anti-submarine nuclear depth-bombs which could be delivered by missile or helicopter, and aircraft carriers could fly off strike aircraft carrying several kinds of nuclear bomb. There were even air-to-air missiles such as the US Genie, which were nuclear-armed.

By the 1980s, there were around 20,000 tactical nuclear weapons deployed by the United States and the Soviet Union, based in more than 15 countries and on warships and submarines throughout the world (Rogers, 1988). In the great majority of cases, the presumption was that if such weapons were used, they would not necessarily involve an escalation to a central nuclear exchange. In other words, nuclear war-fighting could be controlled. In the most tense region of the Cold War confrontation, both alliances had policies of the first use of nuclear weapons in response to conventional attack. While the policies of the former Soviet Union are not yet fully clear, those of NATO have been analysed by a number of writers.

The NATO Nuclear Posture of Flexible Response

In the 1950s, prior to the Soviet Union's having developed a large arsenal of nuclear weapons, NATO's nuclear posture was based on a military document, MC14/2, colloquially termed the "trip-wire" posture. Any Soviet attack against NATO would be met with a massive nuclear retaliation, including US strategic nuclear forces, and this assumed that the US could destroy the Soviet Union's nuclear forces and its wider military potential without suffering unacceptable damage itself.

By the early 1960s, the Soviet Union was developing many classes of tactical and strategic nuclear weapons, making it less vulnerable to a US nuclear attack. In such circumstances, MC14/2 became far less acceptable to western military planners who consequently sought to develop a more flexible nuclear posture for NATO. This became known as flexible response and involved the ability to respond to Soviet military actions with a wide range of military forces, but also with the provision that nuclear weapons could be used first in such a way as to force the Soviet Union to halt any aggression and withdraw.[3]

The new flexible response doctrine was progressively accepted by NATO member states in 1967 and 1968 and was codified in MC14/3 entitled *Overall Strategic Concept for the Defence of the NATO Area* and dated 16 January 1968. It was a posture with one particular advantage for the United States in that it might avoid nuclear weapons being used against its own territory. A US Army colonel expressed this rather candidly a few months after "flexible response" became accepted NATO strategy when he wrote that it '... recognizes the need for a capability to cope with situations short of general nuclear war and undertakes to maintain a forward posture designed to keep such situations as far away from the United States as possible' (Beinke, 1968, p.48).

Flexible response remained in operation for close to 25 years, including the period of maximum Cold War tension in the early 1980s. Operational plans for nuclear use were (and are) developed by the Nuclear Activities Branch of the Supreme Headquarters, Allied Powers in Europe (SHAPE) near Mons in Belgium, operating in conjunction with the US Joint Strategic Target Planning Staff responsible for the SIOP strategic nuclear posture.

By the early 1970s, flexible response was well established under the Nuclear Operations Plan which embraced two levels of the use of tactical nuclear weapons against Soviet forces, selective options and general response. Selective options involved a variety of plans, many of them assuming first use of nuclear weapons against Warsaw Pact conventional forces. At the smallest level, these could include up to five small air-burst nuclear detonations intended as warning shots to demonstrate NATO's intent.

At a higher level of use were the so-called pre-packaged options involving up to 100 nuclear weapons, the US Army Field Manual at the time defining a package thus, '...a group of nuclear weapons of specific yields for use in a specific area and within a limited time to support a specific tactical goal ... Each package must contain nuclear weapons sufficient to alter the tactical situation decisively and to accomplish the mission'.[4]

The belief was that such a first use of nuclear weapons would be enough to "win" a war with the Warsaw Pact but the possibility remained that this would fail, and a more general nuclear exchange would result. This was termed a general nuclear response, in which NATO nuclear forces in Europe would be used on a massive scale along with US strategic forces.

Thus, by the end of the 1970s, NATO had developed a flexible response strategy which involved detailed planning for the selective first-use of nuclear weapons in the belief that a limited nuclear war could be won. This was followed, in the early 1980s, by two further developments which made the strategy even more risky.

Since the formulation of MC14/3, the West Germans had been unhappy at the prospect of short-range nuclear weapons being used, since this would involve huge civilian casualties among their own people. They therefore argued within NATO nuclear planning circles that first use should involve the immediate selective targeting of places within the Soviet Union. This required highly accurate ballistic missiles with a very short flight time yet with a range sufficient to hit key targets such as command centres within the Soviet Union. The terminally-guided Pershing 2 ballistic missile was the first to have this capability and was deployed in West Germany from late-1983. It was one of a new generation of theatre nuclear forces (TNF) which included US ground-launched cruise missiles and Soviet SS-20 missiles, but it caused considerable concern in the Soviet Union which did not have a similarly accurate missile (Rogers, 1988).

The second development was a move to an "early first use" policy, outlined by the NATO supreme commander, General Bernard Rogers, who said that his orders were:

> Before you lose the cohesiveness of the alliance - that is, before you are subject to (conventional Soviet military) penetration on a fairly broad scale - you *will* request, not you may, but you *will* request the use of nuclear weapons ... (emphasis in the original).[5]

By the early 1980s, the essence of NATO nuclear planning policy was that nuclear weapons could be used selectively to win a limited nuclear war, they were available for use very early in a conflict, before NATO was losing a conventional war and they could be used immediately against key targets in Soviet territory.

The basis of NATO's first use policy was the perceived conventional superiority of the Soviet Union and its Warsaw Pact allies, although when the Cold War ended it became apparent that the competence, efficiency and technical capabilities of Warsaw Pact forces were highly questionable. At the time, though, the political context of, and commitment to, this policy were neatly summarised by the British government:

> The fundamental objective of maintaining the capability for selective sub-strategic use of theatre weapons is political - to demonstrate in advance that NATO has the capability and will to use nuclear weapons in a deliberate, politically controlled way with the objective of restoring deterrence by inducing the aggressor to make the decision to terminate his aggression and withdraw. The role of TNF is not to compensate for any imbalance in conventional forces. The achievement of conventional parity could have very positive consequences for the Alliance's strategy of deterrence. But it would not, of itself, obviate the need for theatre nuclear forces.[6]

US strategic nuclear policy, together with NATO nuclear policy, were both mirrored by the policies of the Soviet Union. Although the United States tended to maintain a technical lead, especially in such crucial areas as missile accuracy, the Soviet Union established a massive nuclear weapons industry, producing numbers of nuclear warheads which, as became clear after the end of the Cold War, even exceeded the apparently inflated western intelligence estimates of the Cold War years. Moreover, Soviet strategic weapons were often much more powerful than their US counterparts, somewhat compensating for US technical superiority.

Overall, there was a dynamic of two superpowers entrenched in a nuclear arms race where the first use of nuclear weapons was considered a rational part of military planning and where strategic nuclear developments were so destabilising that tactics such as launch-on-warning were considered necessary developments. Overall, there was a belief that a nuclear war could be fought and won.

Anti-nuclear campaigners, and a few conflict analysts, questioned such policies at the time, but they were roundly criticised as pro-Soviet defeatists, even when they pointed to the risks of nuclear accidents and crisis mismanagement. Since the ending of the Cold War, however, their views have begun to resonate with those of some senior retired military and even a few former nuclear planners who are now able to recognise the extent of the dangers faced during the Cold War, dangers exemplified both by the experience of actual nuclear accidents and also of crises which now appear to have been far more dangerous than acknowledged in public at the time.

Nuclear Accidents

During the Cold War years there were more than forty accidents involving nuclear weapons or military nuclear reactors, some of which resulted in radioactive contamination and others in the loss of nuclear weapons.[7] In addition, the United States, the Soviet Union and Britain all experienced major problems with their nuclear weapons industries. In Britain, for example, a serious fire occurred at the Windscale plant which produced plutonium for Britain's nuclear weapons programme. During routine maintenance at the Windscale Number One plutonium reactor, the reactor pile caught fire and burned for three days, releasing radioactive iodine and polonium into the atmosphere. Close to half a million gallons of milk from dairy farms in the area were withdrawn from consumption and poured into local rivers and the Irish Sea.

One of the early accidents involving nuclear weapons happened on 10 March, 1956, when a B-47 medium-range bomber on a flight overseas, probably to a US base in Europe, failed to rendezvous with a tanker aircraft over the Mediterranean. The plane was carrying two nuclear capsules, probably containing plutonium, and neither the plane, its crew or weapons were found.

Four months later, another B-47 crashed into a nuclear weapons storage igloo at RAF Lakenheath in Suffolk, killing the four crew members. Although the plane was unarmed, the major fire which followed enveloped the store which contained three B6 nuclear bombs. The high-explosive elements of the bombs did not explode although the bombs were burnt and damaged.

On 5 February, 1958, yet another B-47 was in collision with an F-86 Sabre interceptor over Georgia and had to jettison its nuclear bomb before landing safely. The bomb, which is believed to have landed in the Atlantic, was never recovered. Nine months later, a B-47 caught fire on taking off from Dyess Air Force Base in Texas and crashed shortly afterwards, killing one of the crew. The high explosive element of the nuclear bomb on board detonated, leaving a crater 35 feet across and 6 feet deep. "Nuclear materials were recovered near the crash site" according to official records, but the nature and extent of radioactive contamination was not made known.

During the 1960s, the United States maintained a substantial force of B-52 strategic nuclear bombers, and these experienced a number of accidents, three of which were particularly serious. On 24 January, a B-52 on airborne alert and carrying two nuclear weapons experienced catastrophic failure of the starboard wing and broke up in mid-air. One weapon fell free and broke up on impact with the ground. Part of the weapon containing uranium was never found, even though the waterlogged farmland in the vicinity was excavated to a depth of 50 feet.

In 1966, within four days, there were two major accidents, one in Spain and the other in Greenland, both involving B-52 aircraft carrying four nuclear weapons. On 17 January, seven out of eleven crew died when a B-52 and a KC-135 tanker aircraft collided over Palomares in Spain. One of the four nuclear weapons was recovered soon afterwards on land and a second was recovered from the sea after a 15-week search. The high explosive components of the other two nuclear weapons detonated, leading to substantial radioactive contamination. The subsequent decontamination operation involved the removal of 1,400 tons of soil and vegetation to a safe storage site in Texas.

Then, on 21 January, one crewman died when another B-52 crashed, this time while seven miles out on approach to Thule Air Force Base in Greenland. All four nuclear weapons on board were destroyed in the fire which followed. The resultant decontamination operation involved the removal of over 1.5 million gallons of ice, water and snow to a safe storage site in the United States.

Much more recently, on 24 June 1995, a B-52 practising for an air show at Fairchild Air Force Base near Spokane, Washington, crashed within 50 feet of a nuclear weapons storage bunker. Witnesses reported that the pilot appeared to throw the plane into a turn to avoid striking the weapons storage area. The pilot and the three other crew members were killed in the crash.[8]

The United States also experienced problems with tactical nuclear weapons. In one incident, on 5 December 1965, a US Navy A-4 Skyhawk strike aircraft loaded with one nuclear weapon rolled off the elevator of an aircraft carrier at an undisclosed location in the Pacific. Neither the pilot, the plane nor the nuclear weapon were recovered.

Both the United States and the Soviet Union suffered a series of nuclear-submarine accidents during the Cold War years. On 10 January 1970, the Italian cruise liner *Angelina Lauro* reported a collision with an unidentified object off Naples. Shortly afterwards, a Soviet *Foxtrot*-class submarine was observed with 25 feet of the bow section missing. The boat was subsequently repaired at a Soviet anchorage off the North African coast. This class of submarine was routinely equipped with a 15-kiloton yield nuclear-tipped torpedo and some may have sunk with the bow section.

Three months later, in April 1970, a much more serious incident occurred involving a Soviet *November*-class twin-reactor submarine when a reactor fire resulted in the loss of the submarine about 170 miles south-west of Land's End. This class of boat was also known to carry tactical nuclear weapons. Any western attempts at salvage were hindered by a Soviet naval vessel which took up station over the wreck for many months. Nearly three years later, there was a nuclear weapon accident on a nuclear-powered submarine off the North American coast, which resulted in the leak of radioactive material from a nuclear-tipped torpedo. Most of the crew were affected by radiation sickness and several died.

There were several serious incidents involving submarine bases. In 1966, a radiation leak is reported to have occurred in a nuclear-powered submarine near Polyarny, close to the Northern Sea fleet submarine base. According to some reports, members of the repair team may have died of radiation sickness. Early in 1970, another incident took place when a very large explosion wrecked part of the Gorki submarine yards leading to radioactive contamination of the Volga River and its Black Sea estuary.

The Soviet Union also experienced problems with nuclear-powered surface ships. At some time in the late 1960s or early 1970s, the large 17,000 ton icebreaker, *Lenin*, is reported to have suffered a catastrophic reactor melt-down killing up to 30 people and injuring many more.

During the 1980s, the Soviet Union experienced a series of submarine accidents, the most serious being the loss of a *Yankee*-class ballistic missile submarine in the Atlantic in October 1986. The 8,000-ton submarine carried 16 SS-N-6 ballistic missiles, each probably equipped with two 500 kiloton nuclear warheads rather than the earlier 1 megaton single warheads which the first version of the missile carried (Preston, 1986). The submarine experienced a fire and explosion of the propellant of one of the missiles, killing three crew and blasting a hole through the side of the submarine's hull. The fire was eventually extinguished, two days after the explosion, and an attempt was made to take the submarine in tow. This failed, and the boat was lost with all its 32 nuclear warheads still on board.

Among the most serious of the US submarine accidents was the loss of the *USS Scorpion* with all her crew, 450 miles south-west of the Azores on 21 May 1968. This followed an accident believed to have been caused by the explosion of an accidentally armed non-nuclear torpedo. The *Scorpion* is known also to have been armed with nuclear-tipped anti-submarine weapons, probably the UUM-44A SUBROC weapon which carried the W55 warhead with a 1-5 kiloton yield.

Perhaps the most remarkable nuclear weapon accident of the Cold War years took place on 19 September 1980, and involved a Titan II intercontinental ballistic missile. This was one of the earlier large US ICBMs, was liquid-fuelled and carried a massive 9-megaton W53 thermonuclear warhead in a Mark 6 re-entry vehicle. During routine maintenance of the missile, a mechanic dropped a wrench down the silo which hit the side of the missile and ruptured a fuel tank. Release of the propellant lead to a large explosion several hours later which killed two men. The force of the explosion ejected the re-entry vehicle with its nuclear warhead from the silo and threw it 200 feet. Although not reported in the press at the time, it was later confirmed that there had been contamination of the site.

A near-farcical event took place four years later, at a Minuteman III ICBM silo at Warren Air Force Base near Cheyenne, Wyoming, when a computer system appeared to indicate that the missile was about to launch itself. Air force officials promptly parked an armoured car on top of the silo door, so that the missile would be irreparably damaged if it started to launch. Officials later insisted that there was no risk of an accidental launch but could not explain why it was thought necessary to take this unusual precaution.[9]

Although many of the nuclear accidents took place in locations far from immediate zones of tension, there were exceptions. One example, which did not specifically involve a nuclear weapon, is salient for other reasons. On 25 May 1982, an RAF Phantom interceptor in North Germany accidentally fired a Sidewinder air-to-air missile which locked on to an RAF nuclear-capable Jaguar strike aircraft which was within range. The missile severely damaged the aircraft which then crashed, although the pilot ejected safely. That such an accident could happen caused grave concern, the more so as it took place at a time of considerable tension. At the time, the UK was involved in a bitter war with Argentina over the control of the Falkland/Malvinas islands, a major crisis was developing between Israel, Lebanon and Syria, and East-West tensions were high because of the impending deployment of cruise and Pershing missiles in western Europe.

The Experience of Cold War Crises

None of the numerous accidents with nuclear weapons during the Cold War caused the detonation of a nuclear weapon, and protagonists of nuclear strategy cite this as an indication of the extent of the safety measures in place. At the same time, it is likely that a number of the known incidents, and possibly some incidents which are still classified, may have been more dangerous than has so far become apparent. There are indications of this in the writings of some analysts who had access to classified material during the period. One of the leading strategists of the time, Fred Ikle, suggested this in a recent piece concerning the potential dangers of future nuclear proliferation.

> ...despite the several accidents and mistakes that could have sparked a large-scale nuclear war (and whose horrid details are still largely shrouded in secrecy), the superpowers always stopped just short of the abyss. At each of these fateful moments, the world escaped nuclear holocaust - seemingly by accident (Ikle, 1996).

During the Cold War, there were several crises, the seriousness of which is now clear. The details of some remain very limited, including aspects of the Korean War and of the Sino-American confrontation over the offshore islands of Quemoy and Matsu in 1954-55. Others have become more clear, and three deserve particular attention, the Cuba Missile Crisis of 1962, aspects of the Yom Kippur/Ramadan War of 1973 and the NATO *Able Archer* incident in 1983.

In the summer and early autumn of 1962, the Soviet Union began to deploy medium-range ballistic missiles to Cuba, capable of reaching a wide range of targets in the United States. Part of the motive was to counter the US ability to hit Soviet targets with Thor and Jupiter missiles based in western Europe and Turkey. When the United States became aware of the Soviet move in October, 1962, it considered it to be a grave threat to US security, and a naval quarantine was ordered to prevent further Soviet shipments to Cuba.

As the crisis deepened, the US began to organise for a possible air assault against Cuba followed by an invasion which would involve 180,000 troops. US intelligence reported that there were only 10,000 Soviet troops in Cuba and that they did not have tactical nuclear weapons. In both respects, the assessments were wrong - the Soviet Union had 43,000 troops on the island, alongside more than 250,000 Cuban troops. Furthermore, the Soviet Union already had 90 tactical nuclear warheads in Cuba, and as the crisis reached its peak, warheads were moved from storage sites to positions close to their delivery systems in anticipation of an invasion.

The US Secretary of Defense at the time, Robert McNamara, has recently reviewed these events:

> Clearly, there was a high risk that, in the face of a US attack - which many in the US government, military and civilian alike, were prepared to recommend to President Kennedy - the Soviet forces in Cuba would have decided to use their nuclear weapons rather than lose them. We need not speculate about what would have happened in that event. We can predict the results with certainty. Although a US invasion force would not have been

> equipped with tactical nuclear warheads - the President and I had specifically prohibited that - no one should believe that had American troops been attacked with such weapons, the US would have refrained from a nuclear response. And where would it have ended? In utter disaster, not just for the Soviet Union, Cuba and the United States but for all nations across the globe that would have suffered from the fall-out of the nuclear exchange (McNamara, 1996).

One of the most worrying aspects of the Cuban Missile Crisis concerns the behaviour of some sectors of the US military at the time. As the crisis developed, Strategic Air Command secretly placed nuclear warheads on nine of the ten test ICBMs being held at Vandenberg Air Force Base in California, and then launched the tenth (unarmed) missile on a scheduled test flight. This apparently took no account of the likely effect on Soviet intelligence if it had become aware of the arming of the other missiles (Sagan in Sagan and Waltz, 1995).

At one point in the crisis, the North American Air Defense Command system received data indicating that a missile had been launched from Cuba and was about to hit the city of Tampa in Florida. In reality, a test tape, simulating an attack, had been fed into the computer system (Sagan in Sagan and Waltz, 1995). Perhaps the most remarkable event occurred at Malstrom Air Force Base in Montana at the height of the crisis, when officers broke the safety rules and succeeded in jury-rigging their Minuteman missiles so that they could launch them themselves without having to receive orders in the usual way (Sagan in Sagan and Waltz, 1995).

Eleven years after the Cuban Missile Crisis, the Yom Kippur / Ramadan war between Israel and Egypt and Syria was an occasion when both tactical and strategic nuclear forces could have become involved. By 1973, Israel had a small number of Jericho ramp-launched surface-to-surface missiles fitted with 20 kiloton nuclear warheads. Early in the conflict, when Israel was very hard pressed by the Egyptian attack through the Bar Lev line across the Suez Canal and the Syrian attack across the Golan heights, there was huge concern that Israel's own territory might be occupied by Arab forces.

In three days of urgent activity, Jericho missile warheads were prepared for possible use at the Dimona nuclear weapons plant near Beersheba. The United States learnt of this, obtaining confirmation by a reconnaissance flight of an SR-71 Blackbird spy-plane. There is also some evidence that the Soviet Union was prepared to provide Egypt with a balancing force of nuclear warheads for its Scud missiles - a freighter with such warheads aboard is reported to have left the Nikolaev Naval Base at Odessa on the Black Sea (Kennedy *et al,* 1987).

In the event, Israel succeeded in holding the Egyptian and Syrian advances by means of conventional defences, and within two weeks of the start of the conflict was threatening the Egyptian Third Army with defeat. In these circumstances there were US fears that the Soviet Union would intervene in the conflict, precipitating a major regional war. As part of its response, the United States moved its nuclear forces to an unusually high state of alert around the world, from DefCon 5 (Defence Condition Five, normal peace-time operations) to DefCon 3. In doing so, the US neglected to inform its allies for several hours, including states such as Britain, which was a host to US nuclear forces (Jackson, 1986). Again, further escalation was avoided, not least as Washington put pressure on Israel to accept a cease-fire short of a potentially unstable victory against Egypt.

A more recent, and in many ways the most remarkable, crisis of the Cold War happened in Europe in the autumn of 1983 and did not enter the public domain until several years later (Rogers and Dando, 1992). From 1979 through to 1983, East/West relations deteriorated markedly. In part, this was in response to the Soviet invasion of Afghanistan, but it also related to the election of the hawkish Reagan and Thatcher governments in Washington and London, and the development of a range of new nuclear weapons systems including the US Trident and cruise missiles and the Soviet SS-20 and SS-24 missiles.

According to the Soviet defector, Oleg Gordievsky, the ageing Soviet leadership expected the incoming US President, Ronald Reagan, to emulate his Republican predecessor, Richard Nixon, and tone down his Cold War rhetoric once in office. In the event, the reverse happened as the US nuclear modernisation programme accelerated, bringing in more accurate ballistic missiles and discussions of countervailing (war-winning) strategies.

One Soviet response, code-named RYAN, was to require operatives in western countries to watch out for possible preparations for war, a process started in November 1981 and still in progress two years later as the Soviet Union experienced a leadership crisis with the illness of President Andropov. Soviet concerns peaked with the development of the US Strategic Defence Initiative and the deployment of the highly accurate Pershing 2 missile in Germany in late 1983, and they were not eased by the vigorous western anti-Soviet rhetoric, most notably Reagan's "evil empire" speech.

Early in November 1983, NATO commenced a set of highly secret exercises to test the release plans for nuclear warheads, *Able Archer* being the first such exercise to follow deployment of the Pershing 2 system.

Warsaw Pact surveillance systems monitored this process and NATO systems, in turn, monitored Warsaw Pact activity. According to one account, it quickly became apparent that NATO was listening in to a gathering crisis:

> Instead of the normal monitoring to be expected from across the Iron Curtain, a sharp increase was registered in both volume and urgency of the Eastern Bloc traffic. The incredible seemed to be happening, namely that the Warsaw Pact suspected it might really be facing nuclear attack at any moment (Brook-Shepard, 1988).

Documents released from Warsaw Pact military committees in East Germany confirm this view, 'On November 9, KGB stations in Europe were warned that American bases had been put on alert. The KGB suspected that a NATO exercise, Able Archer 83, could be a full-scale nuclear assault' (Brook-Shepard, 1988). As NATO officials became aware of the unexpected effect of *Able Archer*, significant changes were made to such exercises and the whole process of testing nuclear tactics was modified to avoid any such mis-interpretations happening again.

Lessons from the Cold War

A study of the Cold War nuclear confrontation leads to three broad conclusions. The first is that a clear distinction has to be drawn between the declaratory nuclear policies of, for example, the United States, and the actual targeting plans. The common perception that nuclear weapons were ultimate deterrents, solely for retaliatory use as a last resort, was a common but persistent myth. Much of the East/West strategic nuclear arms race was concerned with attempting to acquire a technical edge sufficient to be able to target the military forces of the opponent, especially the nuclear forces. This necessarily embraced issues of first use and damage limitation, a process which also incorporated ballistic missile defence programmes such as SDI. In particular, the existence of destabilising first strike strategic weapons greatly increased the risk of instability at a time of crisis, when the "use them or lose them" mentality would become especially salient.

The concept of strategic nuclear war-fighting was paralleled by similar attitudes concerning tactical nuclear weapons. Both the Warsaw Pact and NATO maintained policies of the first use of tactical nuclear weapons, with NATO particularly concerned to develop appropriate weapons and posture during a period of intense East/West tension in the early 1980s.

During much of the Cold War, proponents of nuclear strategy were at pains to point out that there were numerous safeguards built into nuclear systems and that crisis management, too, was robust and stable. Here again, practical experience suggests otherwise. Information on nuclear accidents and crisis instability is far from complete, but there is ample evidence to suggest that there were numerous nuclear accidents, many of them serious, and that there were crises which came very close to the nuclear brink.

The dangers of the Cold War nuclear arms race have recently been put with unusual candour and forcefulness by retired US Air Force General Lee Butler (Butler, 1998, p.102). General Butler was the former Head of US Strategic Command, responsible for the control of all of the US strategic nuclear forces, but now argues for rapid moves towards further massive disarmament of nuclear forces. Commenting on the role of deterrence with nuclear weapons, he argues:

> Appropriated from the lexicon of conventional warfare, this simple prescription for adequate military preparedness became in the nuclear age a formula for unmitigated catastrophe. It suspended rational thinking about the ultimate aim of national security: to ensure survival of the nation.

Butler argues that nuclear deterrence failed as a guide to setting rational limits to nuclear forces as an arms race developed with each side determined to develop survivable nuclear forces, which were simply perceived by the other side as intended for use in a disarming first strike. This, in turn resulted in further weapons developments:

> I participated in the elaboration of [missile] basing schemes that bordered on the comical and force levels that in retrospect defied reason. I was responsible for war plans with more than 12,000 targets, many to be struck with repeated nuclear blows, some to the point of complete absurdity.

Butler is one of a number of former senior military who now regard the Cold War period as one of particular danger and instability and who now support moves towards a nuclear-free world. If lessons are to be learnt from the Cold War nuclear arms race, then one of the most important is that the Cold War was not "won" or "lost" but that we survived more by luck than judgement.

Notes

1 For a general account of the development of strategic nuclear arsenals, see Polmar (1982).
2 Hearings on the *Military Implications of the Treaty on the Limitations of Strategic Offensive Arms and Protocol Thereto (SALT II Treaty)*, Committee on Armed Services, United States Senate, 95th Congress, 1st Session, 1979.
3 A useful source on NATO nuclear planning is, Charles, (1987).
4 *Operations: FM 100-5*, US Dept. of the Army, 1982.
5 Interview with General Bernard Rogers, *International Defense Review*, February 1986.
6 *Third Report of the Select Committee on Foreign Affairs*, House of Commons, London, 1987-88, p.35.
7 Unless otherwise stated, details of nuclear weapons accidents draw on three sources. (i) Gaines, (1981), pp 40-45, (ii) Gregory and Edwards, (1988), (iii) Breemer, (1986), pp.309-312.
8 "US Jet Crash Close to Nuclear Weapons Area", *Reuters News Reports*, (RN01W.042695.466) Wednesday, April 26, 1995.
9 "Vehicle Parked on Silo After Launch Signal", *Washington Post*, 29 October 1987, p 7.

10 Soviet and Russian Perspectives on the Cold War

ROBERT BIDELEUX

This chapter endeavours to explain Soviet/Russian perceptions of the Cold War, emphasising its interwar origins, the role of internal socio-economic imperatives and, in more recent decades, the importance of East-West *détente* in bringing the Cold War and communist rule to an end. My stance is broadly 'revisionist'. Until the late 1980s, the aims and motivations attributed to Soviet leaders were to a large extent based on conjecture, circumstantial evidence and mischievous propaganda. However, especially since the era of *glasnost* (openness, 1985-91), a steadily growing body of memoirs, documents and reminiscences has become available from the Soviet/Russian side. The new evidence has not yet been properly digested, and there are still significant *lacunae*, yet accounts of the Cold War need no longer be as speculative, one-sided or partisan as in the past.

Considered as an ideological war between Marxist-Leninist Communism and various liberal and not-so-liberal forms of capitalism, and as a 'battle for hearts and minds' which was waged as much *within* as *between* capitalist and communist states, the Cold War really began during the Russian Civil War of 1918-21. It was the aftermath of the Bolshevik Revolution of October 1917, rather than the events of 1945 to 1950, which precipitated the division of the world into ideologically opposed armed camps and spawned the Cold War vocabulary that survived until the 1990s. The notion of the Cold War as something that began in the late 1940s might have appealed to the new generations who were clawing their way up the Soviet hierarchy, but for seasoned 'Old Bolsheviks' it was merely a media catchphrase for something that had been going on since 1918. 'Molotov, just like Stalin, never recognised the Cold War as a new stage in international relations'. Their thinking remained tied to Leninist postulates, classic 'balance of power' and 'territorial security' concepts, and the demarcation of 'spheres of influence' (Zubok and Pleshakov, 1996, pp.37, 73 and 89).

After the defeat of Germany and Japan in 1945, admittedly, the Cold War occupied centre stage to a greater extent than before. Seen through

Soviet eyes, however, the years between 1945 and 1950 *did not* represent a major departure from patterns established during the interwar period, but merely a resumption of the ideological antagonism between 'the two camps' which had started in 1918 and only temporarily abated during the Grand Alliance against the Axis Powers (1941-45). The lethal nuclear threat posed by America's acquisition and use of atomic bombs changed the nature of the Cold War rather less than one might have expected. Nevertheless, the dropping of atomic bombs on Hiroshima and Nagasaki in August 1945, combined with the realisation that the Americans were in a position to do the same to Moscow and Leningrad, helped to re-ignite Soviet insecurity and paranoia (Zubok & Pleshakov, 1996, pp.7, 27-34, 40-43). If the decades following 1945 involved short bursts of seemingly implacable East-West confrontation as well as longer periods of 'peaceful co-existence' and *détente,* representing the pursuit of ideological and systemic competition 'by other means', then the same was true of the decades from 1918 to 1941. Form and focus may have changed from time to time, but the intensity of the ideological and systemic competition was often just as great during periods of 'peaceful co-existence' as it was during periods of more overtly aggressive confrontation. It was during a period of 'peaceful co-existence' between East and West that Nikita Khrushchev famously declared: 'We will bury you!'.

Many Western Cold Warriors have assumed that the Soviet Union was implacably 'daggers drawn' towards the capitalist world from beginning to end. Against such simplistic characterisations of the 'evil empire', which mainly found favour with the American right, it can be argued that Soviet conceptualisations of the relationship between the USSR and the capitalist 'camp' were always *deeply ambivalent*, even under Stalin. Strident insistence on the 'impossibility' of a durable stabilisation of, and peaceful co-existence with, capitalism alternated with a more sober and pragmatic recognition of the 'necessity' of peaceful co-existence with a capitalist world system which seemed set to survive for the foreseeable future. Successive reorientations were determined as much by changing economic and geopolitical considerations and contexts as by shifting ideological imperatives. Just as Tsarist Russia had vacillated between periods of accommodation and periods of confrontation with other parts of Europe, and between periods of outward-looking Westernism and periods of introverted Slavophilism and 'Eurasianism', so did the Soviet Union.

The Bolshevik Revolution and the Origins of the Cold War

The Bolsheviks had 'prematurely' seized power in 'backward' Russia in

October 1917 on the rashly optimistic assumption that their own *coup d'état* would almost immediately precipitate socialist revolutions in Poland, Germany and France. These more industrialised countries were to supply part of the financial and technical wherewithal for 'the construction of socialism' in underdeveloped Russia, according to Engels in his 1875 article on 'Social Relations in Russia' and his Preface to the 1882 Russian edition of *The Communist Manifesto*. Bolshevik foreign policy was thus initially subordinated to the goal of fomenting revolution elsewhere in Europe, particularly in the Germanic 'motherland' of Marxism (Bideleux, 1987, pp.11, 23-27, 104-05). By the early 1920s, however, it was becoming clear to the Bolshevik leadership that Europe's 'revolutionary wave' was subsiding, that Soviet Russia would have to depend largely on its own efforts and resources, and that the Soviet regime would therefore have to work out some sort of *modus vivendi* with the other major European states as well as with the peasantry and private entrepreneurs within the Soviet Union. This opened the way for a conciliatory 'New Economic Policy' (1921-27), the 'fence-mending' Treaty of Rapallo with Germany (1922), the gradual 'normalisation' of Soviet economic and diplomatic relations with most Western states thereafter, and significant inflows of Western capital, technology, engineers and managerial personnel into Soviet Russia (1924-28). Trotsky warned the 1922 Congress of the Communist International (Comintern) that 'we shall have to engage in large-scale transitional operations through the market over many years' and that 'market relations have a logic of their own, whatever goals we may have in restoring them', but he also emphasised that this would help to ensure that 'available resources are directed where they are most needed - into branches producing goods for personal or productive consumption by workers and peasants ... Only after gaining success in agriculture and light industry can real impetus be given to engineering, metallurgy, coal, oil' (Bideleux, 1987, pp.105-06).

In 1926 Trotsky presented the classic arguments in favour of 'peaceful co-existence' between the Soviet Union and the West. He pointed out that, since the factory industries of pre-revolutionary Russia had found it necessary to import almost two-thirds of their plant and equipment, 'it will hardly be economically advantageous for us to produce more than two-fifths or at most one-half of our own machinery'. Any headstrong attempt to adjust 'in one leap to the production of new machinery' would cause potentially devastating economic distortions and disequilibria. There were ways in which such constraints could be minimised: 'Every foreign product that can fill a gap in our economic system - raw material, intermediate goods and consumer goods - can under certain conditions accelerate our reconstruction.' Moreover, 'the dialectics of history involve capitalism assuming temporarily the role of creditor to socialism ... Our present order rests not only on the struggle of socialism against capitalism, but also, within limits, on co-operation between socialism and capitalism'. Of course, 'loans, concessions and greater dependence on exports and imports involve dangers'. However, 'there is a greater, opposite danger. It consists of delaying our economic progress'. Besides, 'the more diverse our international economic relations, the harder it will be for our enemies to disrupt them' (Trotsky, 1926, Chs. 8-12).

Trotsky was thus a thoroughgoing *internationalist*, a true Marxist, not an advocate of introverted economic nationalism and protectionism masquerading as socialism. In 1928 he reaffirmed that 'By introducing the New Economic Policy ... we created a certain place for capitalist relations in our country, and for a prolonged period ahead we must recognise them as inevitable' (Trotsky, 1928, p.31). Trotsky did not cease to give political encouragement to revolutionary socialist movements, yet he simultaneously advocated economic moderation and peaceful co-operation with the capitalist states during the 'construction of socialism' in Soviet Russia. Contrary to the impression given by most Western accounts of the great debate on socialist development which took place in the Soviet Union during the 1920s, this was also broadly the position of the chief economist of the so-called Left Opposition, Evgeny Preobrazhensky, as well as such well-known Bolshevik moderates as the finance minister Grigori Sokolnikov, the central banker Lev Shanin, the planner Vladimir Bazarov and the trade minister Leonid Krasin (see Bideleux, 1987, pp.83-114).

In its initial formulations, even Stalin's doctrine of 'socialism in one country' was essentially a holding operation rather than a harbinger of autarky, xenophobia and domestic coercion. In his *Foundations of Leninism* (1924), Stalin maintained that for the Soviet regime 'the whole point is to retain power, consolidate it, make it invincible', until such time as the 'proletarian revolution' is victorious in other countries. In December 1925 Stalin assured the Fourteenth Congress of the Communist Party of the Soviet Union (CPSU) that 'a certain temporary equilibrium of forces has been established between our country ... and the countries of the capitalist world, an equilibrium which has determined the present period of "peaceful co-existence" ... What we at one time regarded as a brief respite after the war has become a whole period of respite.' (Stalin, 1954, pp.267-68). Later in the same report Stalin contended that, as a result of the Bolshevik Revolution: 'The world split into two camps: the camp of imperialism and the camp of anti-imperialism'. But Stalin's 'two camp doctrine' was not meant to imply that the Soviet Union would be perpetually at war with a stable and monolithic capitalist bloc united against it. In the capitalist camp, 'there is no unity of interests and no solidarity'. On the contrary, 'what reigns there is a conflict of interests, disintegration, a struggle between victors and vanquished, a struggle among the victors themselves, a struggle among all the imperialist countries for colonies, for profits', as a result of which 'stabilisation in that camp cannot be lasting' (Stalin, 1954, pp.288-89). However, while Trotsky was arguing that Soviet Russia needed greater access to Western products, capital, technology, managerial expertise and markets, Stalin emphasised the extent to which the ailing economies of capitalist Europe needed to regain access to the Soviet Union's natural resources and large market (Stalin, 1954, pp.294-96).

Nevertheless, while Trotsky, Preobrazhensky, Shanin, Sokolnikov, Bazarov and Krasin rejected economic nationalism in favour of full exploitation of the potential gains from *foreign* trade, investment, loans, technology and managerial expertise, Stalin declared that 'we must exert all efforts to make our country an economically self-reliant, independent country based on the home market; a country that will serve as a centre of attraction for all the other countries that little by little drop out of capitalism and enter the channel of socialist economy. That line demands the utmost expansion of our industry' (Stalin, 1955a, p.306). Stalin's immediate, overriding priorities were to develop large-scale heavy industries, especially fuels and metallurgy (Stalin, 1955a, pp.323-24). From 1926 onward, as he consolidated his power, Soviet industrial investment went mainly into heavy industry, and the resultant disproportions, strains and shortages propelled the USSR down a path of lopsided and coercive industrialisation (Bideleux, 1987, pp.100, 118, 124-27). Yet the horrific human and economic implications of this economic strategy were not to become fully apparent until the 1930s.

Soviet Championship of 'Collective Security'

Notwithstanding the war scare of 1927 and the 1928 show-trial of a group of foreign engineers alleged to be 'saboteurs' and 'spies', the successive published 'variants' of the First Five-Year Plan (1928-32) actually envisaged that the USSR would remain a market economy with a preponderance of smallholder agriculture. All this was premised upon a continuance of high levels of East-West trade and substantial American, German and British involvement in the modernisation and expansion of important branches of the economy, including the oil, chemical, engineering, mining and timber industries. The Soviet Union could not afford to seek confrontation with the major capitalist states at that critical juncture. In 1935 the Soviet foreign minister Maxim Litvinov emerged as a leading proponent of 'collective security', and the Soviet Union signed treaties of mutual assistance with

France and Czechoslovakia. Hitler's remilitarisation of the Rhineland in March 1936 and the Nazi annexation of Austria in March 1938 prompted Litvinov to step up Soviet offers of participation in collective security arrangements to 'contain' Nazi expansionism.

During the 1920s and 1930s the USSR was also keen to establish closer relations with the USA. In Bolshevik eyes, the USA was a 'new' society (like the USSR), in contrast to decadent western and central Europe. Many Bolsheviks, from Lenin downwards, were mesmerised by American technology, industrial organisation and 'scientific management' (the cult of Taylorism), and they especially sought US business partners, methods and machinery. On 6 December 1921 the Soviet state newspaper *Izvestiya* declared that 'the US is the principal force in the world ... all possible means will have to be employed somehow or other to come to an understanding with the US' (quoted in Kennedy-Pipe, 1995, p.23). The First Five-Year Plan heavily relied on importing and copying American technology (Sutton 1968-72). Soviet courtship of the USA intensified during the 1930s, in response to Japan's occupation of Manchuria in 1931 and fears of further Japanese expansionism. The establishment of diplomatic relations between the US and the USSR in November 1933 was directed more against Japanese than Nazi militarism. In 1938 Litvinov sought a formal military pact with the USA, but he was rebuffed by the Americans (Kennedy-Pipe, 1995, pp.24-26).

It has been argued that it was the collapse in the world market prices of the Soviet Union's staple exports of oil, grain, timber and minerals, combined with the widespread adoption of protectionism and 'anti-dumping' measures in Europe, America and Asia, which forced the USSR to become more 'closed' and autarkic, even though this substantially raised the costs of Soviet industrialisation and agricultural mechanisation programmes (Dohan, 1976). However, since self-reliance was also one of Stalin's most frequently stated goals from 1925 onward, it is not plausible to blame this movement towards autarky solely on adverse world market conditions. Yet the 1930s Depression could not but affect the course of the internal development of the Soviet Union and Soviet perceptions of the capitalist world. In his report to the January 1934 Congress of the CPSU, Stalin gloated that the 'crisis of capitalism' was now in its fifth year, 'devastating the economy of the capitalist countries year after year'. Furthermore, 'the industrial crisis has become interwoven with the agrarian crisis which has affected all the agrarian and semi-agrarian countries', while 'the monopolist cartels which dominate industry strive to maintain high commodity prices, a circumstance which ... hinders the absorption of commodity stocks'. Consequently, the 'intensified struggle' for markets was promoting 'extreme *nationalism* in economic policy', straining international relations and sowing the seeds of 'military conflicts' and 'a new redivision of the world ... in favour of the stronger states'. The triumph of fascism in Germany in 1933 testified that the bourgeoisie was 'no longer able to rule by the old methods of parliamentarianism and bourgeois democracy' and could 'no longer ... find a way out of the present situation on the basis of a peaceful foreign policy'. It had to resort to 'terrorist methods of rule' and 'a policy of war' (Stalin, 1955a, pp.288-92, 297-300).

The Seminal Role of the Comintern Pronouncements on Fascism

The deepening global 'crisis of capitalism' after 1929 contributed to the proliferation and 'hardening' of fascist movements and regimes during the 1930s. It is worth examining the (1930s) Soviet/Comintern pronouncements on fascism at this point, because they not only furnished the main Marxist rationalisation of the eventual Communist take-overs in east-central and south-eastern Europe during the late 1940s (much as Lenin's *Imperialism: The Highest Stage of Capitalism* and associated writings provided a rationale for the Bolshevik seizure of power in Russia in 1917), but also paved the way for the Soviet conception of the 'imperialist camp' which came to prevail during the late 1940s, conventionally regarded as the high point of the Cold War.

In December 1933, in response to Hitler's rapid consolidation of Nazi rule and his government's expeditious moves to reactivate the German economy and rearm the Reich, the Comintern warned that: 'The bourgeoisie want to postpone the doom of capitalism by a criminal imperialist war and a counter-revolutionary campaign against the land of victorious socialism'. The deepening world crisis and the approaching war were seen as posing mortal threats to the very survival of the Soviet Union and Europe's Communist Parties, while also strengthening their chances of finally overthrowing European capitalism. 'The great task of the international proletariat is to turn this crisis of the capitalist world into the victory of the proletarian revolution ... The great historical task of international communism is to mobilise the broad masses against war even before war has begun, and thereby hasten the doom of capitalism.' (Degras, 1965, pp.299-303).

The communists' contempt for Western liberalism and social democracy sprang partly from a belief that *the only two forces which really counted in interwar Europe were communism and fascism*, which were now pitted against one another in readiness for the final showdown. Most communists then believed that the Western liberal democracies were a spent force, that European liberalism and social democracy were mere masks for the monopolistic and imperialistic 'finance capital' which had superseded nineteenth-century liberal capitalism, and that Europe's liberals and social democrats were therefore inherently 'soft' on fascism, which they were more inclined to *appease* than to resist. *Both Hitler and the communists believed that, in the approaching 'battle of the Titans', the defeated side would lose everything*: a fascist victory would lead to the extinction of not only communism but European humanist civilisation; a communist victory would hasten the downfall of European capitalism and permit a massive extension of communist rule. Therefore, whatever the costs, it came to be seen as the sacred duty of all communists to do whatever was necessary to ensure the survival of 'the socialist fatherland', without which *all* would be lost.

These Comintern *Theses* propounded a broad and far from monolithic conception of fascism, and they stipulated that 'fascist dictatorship is not an inevitable stage of the dictatorship of the bourgeoisie in all countries'. Fascism was seen *not* as a new 'highest stage of capitalism' towards which all 'advanced' capitalist states must inevitably evolve, but rather as the 'most reactionary' and 'most chauvinistic' form of capitalist regime, examples of which were also (not surprisingly) to be found among the fiercely nationalistic and less developed capitalist states of east-central, south-eastern and southern Europe (Degras, 1965, pp.296-97).

The Comintern saw increased support for communism as the *natural* popular reaction to the proliferation and 'hardening' of fascist regimes amid the profound and possibly terminal 'crisis of capitalism' during the 1930s. If the Communist Parties played their cards right, they could turn the situation to their own advantage, but they did not expect Europe simply to fall into their laps. The August 1935 Comintern Congress warned 'against dangerous illusions about an automatic collapse of the fascist dictatorship', emphasised that 'only the united revolutionary struggle of the working class at the head of all toilers will bring about the overthrow of the fascist dictatorship', and approved a significant change of attitude towards Europe's social democratic parties (Degras, 1965, pp.355, 360). The German Communist Party's earlier refusal to co-operate with the German Socialist Party had fatally divided the German left. The result was that the Nazis gained power in 1933, despite having won only 33 percent of the vote in the November 1932 Reichstag elections (less than the 37 percent combined share of the communists and the socialists). A chastened Comintern now promoted broad anti-fascist coalitions known as '*Popular Fronts*'. Social democrats were no longer to be denounced as 'social fascists', but were to be treated as *comrades-in-arms in the struggle against fascism* (Degras, 1965, pp.368-9).

The August 1935 Comintern Congress also passed a *Resolution on the Danger of a New World War*, warning that the 'frantic arming of fascist

Germany' had given rise to 'a new intensified race for armaments throughout the capitalist world ... The countries which have gone farthest in preparing for war (Germany, Japan, Italy, Poland) have already placed their national economy [sic] on a war footing'. The fear was expressed that these war-mongering 'fascist governments' would endeavour to reconcile their rivalries 'at the expense of the Soviet Union. The danger of the outbreak of a new imperialist war daily threatens humanity' (Degras, 1965, pp.373-4). The same *Resolution* affirmed that, if such a war were to start, the communists would strive to transform 'the imperialist war into a civil war against the fascist instigators of war ... for the overthrow of capitalism' (Degras, 1965, pp.377-8). This rebuts claims that, as a result of the Comintern's Popular Front policy, the USSR renounced its former goal of formenting international revolution.

The Anglo-French 'betrayal' of Czechoslovakia to 'the fascist camp' at Munich in September 1938 handed Europe's communist parties a golden opportunity to put themselves forward as the only 'reliable' champions of 'collective security', and as the 'true defenders' of European nations against the fascist menace and 'bourgeois liberal' duplicity. In November 1938 the Comintern claimed that, in reaffirming its readiness to defend Czechoslovakia against Germany (if France would do likewise), 'the Soviet government ... showed how agreements should be kept and collective security defended ... The Munich agreement was not only a blow at Czechoslovakia. It is a conspiracy against the small nations which Britain and France are betraying to the fascist plunderers'. Czechoslovakia could have been saved, since Germany was not yet fully rearmed and 'Czechoslovakia possessed an excellent army and was protected by a first class system of fortresses. The British and French fleets were in a position to blockade Germany. Action by the Soviet Union would have given rise to a powerful wave of the anti-fascist movement in defence of the just cause of the peoples. Faced by such forces, German fascism would have had no alternative but to retreat. But the British bourgeoisie who dragged France in the wake of their policy did not want to permit this political defeat of the fascist gendarme of Europe. Britain and France did everything possible to compel Czechoslovakia to capitulate' (Degras, 1965, p.430). Perforce, 'the task of the working class now is to head the liberation struggle of the enslaved nations and the defence of the peoples threatened by foreign domination. The nation is not the gang of fascists, reactionary financiers and industrial magnates who rob and betray the people. The nation is the many millions of workers, peasants and working people generally - the people that is devoted to its country, cherishes its liberty, and defends its independence ... The working class is the backbone of the nation, the bulwark of its liberty, dignity and independence' (Degras, 1965, p.432).

The Comintern was now eagerly extolling patriotism, not least because Stalin had revived Great Russia nationalism within the Soviet Union in anticipation of fascist incursions into his own domains. The new 'patriotic appeal' of communism was exploited to greatest advantage in 1940s Czechoslovakia, Yugoslavia, Albania, Greece, Italy, France, China and Vietnam.

From the Soviet viewpoint, Western 'appeasement' of Nazi Germany and the subsequent fight-to-the-finish between communism and fascism portended a menacing deterioration in relations between the USSR and the capitalist camp, notwithstanding the necessity of Soviet co-operation with Britain and the US against 'fascism' between 1941 and 1945. In his report to the March 1939 Congress Stalin wryly remarked that 'one might think that the districts of Czechoslovakia were yielded to Germany as the price of an undertaking to launch a war on the Soviet Union' (Stalin, 1955b, p.368). Therefore, the Nazi-Soviet Pact of August 1939 was partly 'justified' in communist eyes as (indispensably) buying time for the further industrialisation, rearmament and military reorganisation of the Soviet Union, while keeping its powder dry for an eventual showdown with the fascist powers. In the words of a distinguished Soviet military historian and biographer of Stalin, 'the Non-Aggression Pact appears extremely tarnished, and morally an alliance with the Western democracies would have been immeasurably preferable. But neither Britain nor France was ready for such an alliance. From the point of view of state interest the Soviet Union had no other acceptable choice. A refusal to take any step would hardly have stopped Germany. In any case, Britain and France had both signed similar pacts with Germany in 1938 and were conducting secret talks with Hitler in the summer of 1939 with the aim of creating an anti-Soviet bloc.' (Volkogonov, 1996, pp.356-57).

The Great Patriotic War

The Soviet Union did in fact bear the main burden of the land war against Nazi Germany. From June 1941 to June 1944, in one influential account, Hitler deployed '80 or 90 percent of his land forces against Russia ... According to German military sources, Hitler guarded the Atlantic coast with 59 second rate divisions, while 260 of his divisions, including the best, fought on the Russian front' (Deutscher, 1966, pp.485-86). Likewise, in his analytical study of the Second World War, Clive Ponting claims that from mid-1941 to mid-1944 'the Soviet union never fought less than 90 percent of the German army, and even after the Normandy landings the western Allies fought only about a third of the Wehrmacht. The British and Americans were content with a situation in which the very high casualties that would be necessary to defeat the Germans would be borne by the Soviets ... At no time were the British and the Americans prepared to adapt their own strategy to meet Soviet requirements.' They were unable or unwilling to create a second front in Europe to take some of the burden off the Soviet Union in 1942, 'and the Mediterranean strategy adopted in 1943 did nothing to relieve the pressure on the Soviets' (Ponting, 1995, pp.96-97). Although the Western Allies delivered vital supplies of aircraft, tanks, lorries and jeeps from 1941 to 1944, the deliveries of Western tanks and aircraft never exceeded 10 percent of Soviet output and 'dropped to 3 percent after late 1942' (Ponting, 1995, p.128). This is often portrayed as magnanimous Western aid to the USSR in its fight against the Nazis, but in reality the West was supplying it with meagre assistance to fight Germany in a form of warfare that only a regime such as Stalin's could have sustained for any length of time. (Stalin had already sacrificed millions of Soviet lives during the 1930s, although just how many millions is still hotly disputed.) The Western democracies would not have had the stomach to bear casualties on the scale entailed by land warfare against the main German armed forces at the peak of their strength and efficiency in 1941-43, nor the level of casualties involved in the capture of German-held cities on the eastern front during 1944. Out of about 20 million combat deaths during the Second World War, less than 600,000 were incurred by Britain and the USA combined, 2.3 million were incurred by Germany, and roughly 13 million were borne by the Soviet Union (p.203).

Victory over Germany gave the Soviet regime a new lease of life, a broader base of popular support, new cadres and a fresh crop of heroes and heroines. Between 1941 and 1945 the Communist Party of the Soviet Union (CPSU) recruited 8.4 million new members, 80 percent of whom were from the armed forces. Thus two-thirds of the post-1945 CPSU had joined during the Great Patriotic War, which played much the same legitimising and 'charismatising' role for post-war Soviet leaders as participation in the Russian Revolutions and the Civil War of 1918-21 had done for their predecessors. For forty-five years, thousands of books, war memorials and military bookshops sustained strong public awareness of the stupendous Soviet war effort. Yet the triumphalism of Stalin's final years can easily obscure the fact that, unlike the USA, the war-ravaged USSR became a 'superpower' largely by default. Germany had been occupied by the Allies and dismembered, France took nearly fifteen years to recover from the humiliating defeat of 1940, Japan was occupied by the United States and the achievement of victory had sapped Britain's economic and military strength. The 'superpower' role was a far greater strain on the USSR than on the USA. The US economy had grown by about 50 percent during the War, whereas

Soviet national income was about 20 percent smaller in 1945 than in 1940. In 1950 Soviet national income was merely 31 percent of that of the USA, and Soviet industrial output was less than 30 percent of that of the USA, even on official Soviet calculations (USSR, 1977, p.95). Therefore, in its struggle for military parity with the USA, the USSR had to devote a vastly greater proportion of its much lower per capita output to military purposes. The physically and emotionally drained Soviet peoples were in no mood to take on this labour of Sisyphus, which the Soviet regime inflicted upon them willy-nilly. At the start of the Second World War, moreover, Stalin had been quite out of his depth, which compounded the strain. 'He came to strategic wisdom only through blood-spattered trial and error' (Volkogonov, 1991, p.452). By 1945 the sixty-five-year-old leader was exhausted (Volkogonov, 1991, p.497). He was physically 'at the point of collapse ... A statesman in his condition generally either retires or delegates responsibility for world affairs to trusted subordinates', yet 'Stalin did neither' (Zubok & Pleshakov, 1996, p.26).

In such a context, the presumption of many Western Cold Warriors that a victorious USSR was now bent on world domination by escalating the Cold War and displacing the USA from Europe remains highly implausible. Indeed, three decades of hostile capitalist encirclement had induced a defensive 'bunker' mentality. 'There is little evidence that before the Marshall Plan Stalin had any master plan for immediate expansion. He had to digest what he had already gained during the war' (Zubok & Pleshakov 1996, p.130). The Red Army was reduced from 11.3 million men in May 1945 to 2.9 million in 1948 (Kennedy-Pipe 1995: 85). Moreover, with France temporarily out of action and Britain at breaking point, both Stalin and Molotov looked to the US for indispensable assistance in keeping the Germanic peoples prostrate and divided. Stalin 'wanted a US presence in Europe, but at the same time he wanted to deny it influence in what he considered to be his part of Europe' (Kennedy-Pipe, 1995, p.67). 'Every Soviet proposal for post-war Europe, and specifically the plans for Germany and Austria, envisaged a US or British military presence' (Kennedy-Pipe, 1995, p.44). Stalin even 'tried to persuade his Western Allies to arrive in Austria at the same time as the Red Army', so as to establish tripartite control (Kennedy-Pipe, 1995, p.56). Having suffered so much in the struggle against Greater Germany (including Austria), the foremost Soviet fear was that Germanic power might revive as speedily as it did after the First World War. At Tehran in 1943 Stalin asserted that German hegemonism would rear its ugly head again within twenty years unless the Germanic peoples were dealt with very harshly, for he did not believe that the Germans could change their 'national character', and he 'foresaw the German question as requiring long-term political and military co-operation between East and West' (Kennedy-Pipe, 1995, p.42). At a meeting with Yugoslav leaders in Moscow in April 1945, Stalin reaffirmed his belief that German power 'will recover, and very quickly. It is a highly developed country with an extremely skilled and numerous working class and technical intelligentsia. Give them twelve to fifteen years and they'll be on their feet again.' (Djilas, 1963, pp.90-91).

Stalin's Post-War Perceptions and Objectives

Stalin's immediate aim was not world domination, let alone world revolution, but the more limited one of creating a protective glacis of buffer states bound to the Soviet Union by treaties and ties of military, economic and ideological dependence. He regarded the territories 'liberated' by the Red Army as rightly belonging to a new Soviet 'sphere of influence', just as he recognised countries occupied by the Western Allies as belonging to *their* 'spheres of influence'. If the United States and Britain expected a free hand to foster pro-Western regimes in Italy, Japan, Greece, Libya, Egypt, Iraq, Iran, the Philippines and Japan, without direct Soviet 'intrusion' into *their* spheres, why did they presume to dictate the terms on which central and eastern European states were to be governed once they had been 'liberated' by the Red Army? Stalin informed the Yugoslav leadership in April 1945: 'whoever occupies a territory also imposes on it his own social system. Everyone imposes his own system as far as his army has the power to do so. It cannot be otherwise.' (Djilas, 1963, p.90). Similarly, he told a Yugoslav delegation which visited Moscow early in 1948: 'The West will make Western Germany their own, and we shall turn Eastern Germany into our own state.' (Djilas, 1963, p.119). The Soviet occupation forces 'Bolshevised' eastern Germany, 'not because there was a plan to do so, but because that was the only way they knew how to organise society' (Naimark, 1995, p.467).

Recent 'revisionist' literature based on hitherto unpublished memoirs and documents dealing with the 1940s and early 1950s has tended to confirm that the Soviet leadership truly believed that the co-operation with the Western powers which had begun during the Second World War was set to continue for several years after the war (Zubok & Pleshakov, 1996, pp.27-34). In view of the enormous loss of life, physical devastation and sheer exhaustion incurred by the Soviet Union and the immense debt of gratitude that the West owed to the Soviet peoples for their paramount role in defeating Hitler, it was widely believed that the West would help to rebuild the USSR's shattered economy and society and that it had incurred an unassailable moral obligation to do so. This made the dropping of American atomic bombs on

Hiroshima and Nagasaki in August 1945 all the more shocking in Soviet eyes. These awesome acts, undertaken without prior consultation with America's Soviet ally, were seen as being directed as much against the USSR as against Japan and as a demonstration of the fate that would befall the Soviet Union if it tried to reap the spoils of its hard-won victory over Germany - thereby enabling the West to renege on its debts to the 'heroic Soviet peoples' and on the 'spheres of influence' agreed at Yalta (Zubok and Pleshakov, 1996, p.41). According to Yuli Khariton, one of the 'fathers' of the first Soviet atomic bomb, 'The Soviet government interpreted Hiroshima as atomic blackmail against the USSR' (Zubok and Peshakov, 1996, p.42). Some Western academics have concurred that those bombs were indeed dropped more in order to intimidate the Soviet Union than to shorten the war and save lives (Alperovitz, 1995).

Nevertheless, the initial Soviet preparations for postwar reconstruction continued to be premised on the previously anticipated provision of Western (especially American) assistance at least for a few years after the end of the war, and for a time Stalin continued to negotiate with Western governments and restrain communist revolutionary movements outside the Soviet 'spheres of influence' explicitly recognised by his erstwhile Western allies in Moscow, Yalta and Potsdam in 1944-45. The death of Roosevelt in April 1945, Churchill's loss of office in July 1945 and the use of atomic bombs against Hiroshima and Nagasaki in August 1945 *severely strained but did not break* the relationship between Stalin and his Western allies. Stalin and Molotov still sought large-scale Western assistance for Soviet reconstruction and expected the West to respect the Soviet Union's freely acknowledged 'legitimate interests' in Eastern Europe. Conversely, they accepted that Britain and the United States were similarly entitled to do as they saw fit in their own 'spheres of influence', even if this involved some unwelcome 'dollar diplomacy' in Europe (Zubok & Pleshakov, 1996, p.105). They also initially welcomed the Marshall Plan (which took them by surprise) as a return to some sort of 'Lend-Lease aid' or as 'no-strings-attached assistance to the anti-Nazi allies' (including the Poles and the Czechs), with the result that Molotov participated in the preliminary discussions in Paris in June 1947 (Zubok and Pleshakov, 1996, p.104). Molotov still accepted that the US had useful roles to play in Germany in particular and in Europe more generally (Zubok and Pleshakov, 1996, p.101). Indeed, Soviet fear of any potential revival of Germanic might was so strong, and Soviet perceptions of the diminution in British and French power were so acute, that Soviet political and military leaders still looked to US assistance in the continued subjugation and containment of German power into the indefinite future. This also explains why Stalin eventually consented to 'French help in maintaining an effective stranglehold on Germany', having previously opposed French involvement on the grounds that France had discredited itself militarily, economically and politically (Kennedy-Pipe, 1995, pp.53-55).

The *decisive factor* in swinging the Soviet leaders against the Marshall Plan in July 1947 was not the implicit extension of US economic influence in Europe, nor even the invidious strings attached to receipt of Marshall Aid, but *the American determination to include Germany (along with other former 'enemy states') in the European Recovery Programme.* Influenced by the famous tract by J.M. Keynes on *The Economic Consequences of the Peace* in 1919, many British and American economists, politicians and publicists had considered the economic recovery of Germany to be essential to the economic recovery of Europe, and in their view it was absolutely vital to secure full German participation in the Marshall Plan. But in Soviet eyes this was a treacherous Western bid to restore Germany's economic (and hence military) power and turn the tables on their former ally, the USSR. The Marshall Plan came to be seen as 'a large-scale attempt by the United States to gain lasting and preeminent influence in Europe' and as 'a far-reaching design to revive German military-industrial potential and to direct it, as in the 1930s, against the Soviet Union.' (Zubok & Pleshakov, 1996, p.50).

These perceptions help to make proper sense of the infamous speech on 'the two camps' delivered by Andrei Zhdanov at the founding meeting of the new Communist Information Bureau (alias Cominform) in September 1947. This tirade against Western perfidy not only marked a *return* to the 'two camps' rhetoric of the interwar years, but expressed a plausible suspicion that Western capitalist 'imperialists' were again prepared to harness German might to another right-wing crusade to roll back Soviet influence in post-war Eastern Europe, just as they had hoped that the Munich agreement of September 1938 would have deflected Nazi expansionism eastwards against the USSR in 1939:

> The reactionary imperialist elements all over the world, notably in Britain, America and France, had reposed great hopes in Germany and Japan and chiefly in Hitler's Germany: firstly as in a force most capable of inflicting a blow on the Soviet Union ... secondly, as in a force capable of smashing the revolutionary labour and democratic movement in Germany herself and in all countries singled out for Nazi aggression and thereby strengthening capitalism generally. This was the chief reason for the prewar policy of "appeasement" and encouragement of fascist aggression, the so-called Munich policy ...
>
> Of all the capitalist powers, only one - the United States - emerged from the war not only unweakened but even considerably stronger economically and militarily ... But America's aspirations to world supremacy encounter an

> obstacle in the USSR, the stronghold of anti-imperialist and antifascist policy ... Accordingly, the new expansionist and reactionary policy of the United States envisages a struggle against the USSR ... and against the emancipationist, anti-imperialist forces in all countries ... The vague and deliberately guarded formulations of the "Marshall Plan" amount in essence to a scheme to create a bloc of states bound by obligations to the United States ... Moreover, the cornerstone of the "Marshall Plan" is the restoration of the industrial areas of Western Germany ... It is the design of the "Marshall Plan" ... to render aid in the first place, not to the impoverished victor countries, America's allies in the fight against Germany, but to the German capitalists, with the idea of bringing under American sway the major sources of coal and iron needed by Europe ... and of making the countries which are in need of coal and iron dependent on the restored economic might of Germany. (Zhdanov, 1947, pp.38-41)

These extracts highlight the very real sense of betrayal felt by the Soviet leadership and the deep resentment of the central role accorded to western Germany in the Marshall Plan, as well as the often neglected elements of continuity with the 1930s Comintern *Theses* on fascism and the 'appeasers'.

The Soviet Union was driven to adopt increasingly antagonistic postures towards the West. Some revisionist writings suggest that in such circumstances even a moderately nationalistic Russian regime would not have reacted very differently, so profound was the sense of shock and betrayal. Stalin's response to the Western decisions to offer Marshall Aid to Germany in 1947 and to launch a separate west German currency in 1948 was to blockade West Berlin in 1948-49. This was intended to challenge, not the US presence in Germany *per se*, but Western claims to West Berlin and to Western preeminence in Germany, whose defeat had been achieved largely by the USSR (Kennedy-Pipe, 1995, p.6). Yet this Soviet reaction merely reinforced US influence and leadership in the West. 'Stalin's actions in 1947-1948 were based upon the correct assumption that he was not risking war with the West. But he had miscalculated the effect of his preventive moves.' (Zubok & Pleshakov, 1996, pp.49-52).

Renewed Soviet insistence on the 'impossibility' of peaceful co-existence between the Soviet bloc and the capitalist states climaxed in the paranoia of Stalin's final years. At the same time, however, the establishment of communist China and the breaking of the Western monopoly on atomic weapons in 1949 seems to have persuaded Stalin that the Eurasian balance of power had shifted in the communist camp's favour and that it was now safe to risk a communist invasion of South Korea. The USA, having lost its Kuomintang ally, seemed to be making preparations to retreat from mainland

Asia (Zubok & Pleshakov, 1996, pp.62-63). Stalin realised that the communist offensive in Korea would violate the existing delimitations of 'spheres of influence' and that *in extremis* this could precipitate a Third World War. But he thought that it was safer to run such risks in 1950, while Germany and Japan were still subjugated by foreign occupation forces, than to wait until such time as the West would be strengthened by a Western-sponsored revival of the Axis states. Apropos East Asia, Stalin stated: 'If war is inevitable, let it happen now, and not in a few years, when Japanese militarism will be restored as a US ally, and when the United States and Japan will have a beach-head on the [Asian] continent ... in the form of Syngmans Rhee's Korea.' (Zubok and Pleshakov, 1996, pp.66-67). However, the scale of the American counter-offensive in Korea took Stalin by surprise; and it not only resulted in an unwanted escalation of the Korean War and the East-West arms race but also hastened the fulfilment of one of Stalin's worst nightmares, 'the rearmament of West Germany, with the help of some of Hitler's former generals' (Zubok and Pleshakov, 1996, pp.64-65).

The Return to 'Peaceful Co-existence'

Even before Stalin's death in March 1953, however, Georgi Malenkov was implicitly acknowledging the 'necessity' of peaceful co-existence between East and West. This rapidly resulted in a political 'thaw'. However, while consolidating his own power in the CPSU in 1954-55, Nikita Khrushchev denounced Malenkov's relatively pacific and pragmatic stance. Nevertheless, the exigencies of political and economic de-Stalinisation subsequently induced Khrushchev himself to advocate peaceful co-existence from 1956 until his fall from office in 1964. Ironically, the Cuba crisis of 1962 primarily arose from Khrushchev's endeavours to *reduce* Soviet reliance on massive conventional military forces and on an oversized and voracious military-industrial complex, to defend Soviet interests *more cheaply* by relying on nuclear missiles stationed on Cuba, and to achieve something more nearly approaching nuclear *parity* with the US, rather than from overtly aggressive intents. At the height of the crisis, Castro sent a secret telegram urging the Soviet Union to launch an all-out nuclear attack on the USA if US forces invaded Cuba. The reply sent by Khrushchev (published by both sides in 1990, along with Castro's request) indicates that he 'had no intention of ordering the use of nuclear weapons, regardless of what happened to Cuba' (Kramer, 1996/97, p.348). Unfortunately, the success of the US naval blockade of Cuba demonstrated the continued efficacy of 'conventional' naval power and made it harder for Soviet political leaders to resist the military's demands for the costly development of a massive Soviet navy with a more global 'reach'. This was a serious setback for Khrushchev's attempt to divert resources away from the military-industrial complex and into agriculture and consumer goods industries. It virtually undermined his economic programme.

In the main, however, the Khrushchev era was characterised by increased emphasis on economic, technological and geopolitical competition between 'the two systems' (the 'economics of overtaking and surpassing'), rather than by direct military confrontation. But the optimism of the 1960s was seriously deflated by a crackdown on student unrest and the radical-liberal intelligentsia in Poland in March 1968 and by the Warsaw Pact invasion of Czechoslovakia in August 1968. These acts of repression were accompanied by a barrage of virulently 'anti-Zionist' propaganda orchestrated by the Soviet regime. In the wake of the defeat of the Soviet Union's Arab allies in the Arab-Israeli War of June 1967, it was alleged that 'Zionist' Jews in Israel and in the Soviet bloc were acting as 'agents of American imperialism' in a three-pronged conspiracy to subvert communist rule in Eastern Europe, to deny the Palestinians an independent homeland and to provide pretexts for US interventions in the Middle East. Accordingly the Soviet media and other 'anti-Zionist' publications highlighted and wilfully exaggerated the important (but far from hegemonic) role played by a few Jewish intellectuals, dissidents and 'refuseniks' (Jews who had been refused permission to emigrate) in the Soviet and East European dissident and reform movements. Official 'anti-Zionism' rekindled a residual popular anti-semitism and anti-intellectualism within the Soviet bloc, thereby helping to alienate the radical-liberal intelligentsia from potential proletarian and peasant support. Indeed, 'anti-Zionism' was not just a diversionary tactic that damagingly isolated and vilified Jews, but also a means of isolating and discrediting the radical-liberal intelligentsia and dissidents in general, although Jews obviously bore the brunt of the persecution.

The Rise of *Détente*

Despite the widespread climate of repression, anti-Zionism, anti-intellectualism and demoralisation in the Soviet Union and Eastern Europe at the end of the 1960s, a more subdued and pragmatic optimism was rekindled in the early 1970s by the continuing reforms in Kadar's Hungary, by the initial two- or three-year 'honeymoon' periods of political relaxation following the accession of Eduard Gierek in Poland in December 1970 and of Erich Honecker in the GDR in May 1971 and, above all, by the process of

East-West *détente* initiated by Willy Brandt's *Ostpolitik* in 1969. West Germany's non-aggression treaties with the Soviet Union and Poland in 1970 and its state treaty with the GDR in 1972 paved the way for greatly increased East-West commerce, contacts, credit and technology transfers, as the West gradually followed Brandt's moral lead (described in Bideleux & Jeffries, 1998, p.563). The high-point of East-West *détente* was the 1975 Helsinki Final Act, which established the Conference on European Security and Co-operation (CSCE). The Soviet Union had long advocated the holding of a major international conference to foster international recognition of the GDR and a general endorsement of the territorial *status quo* in Europe, although in reality this was no longer under threat. That was what the USSR obtained at Helsinki in 1975. But the so-called third 'basket' of the Helsinki accords also committed all signatories to respect 'civil, economic, social, cultural and other rights and freedoms' (Stokes, 1993, p.24). These rights and freedoms were spelled out in detail, giving East European dissidents a legal basis on which to challenge their governments through Helsinki Watch Committees established to monitor East European compliance with the provisions of the Final Act. Thus, instead of endorsing the *status quo*, the Final Act became 'a charter for change. Instead of legitimising the Soviet sphere of influence, it legitimised Western intrusion into it. Instead of making frontiers immutable, it specifically affirmed the principle of peaceful change ... Instead of confining itself to interstate relations, it reinforced the principle that peace depends also on how states treat their people' (Davy, 1992, p.19).

At the time, Ronald Reagan appealed to all Americans to oppose the Helsinki Final Act. Another prominent right-wing Republican, Professor Richard Pipes, claimed that Helsinki 'legitimised Russia's conquests' in Eastern Europe (Davy, 1992, p.249), as did British right-wingers such as Margaret Thatcher. Pipes even declared that 'weariness and disillusionment with war and politics and, second, the pursuit of material wealth as a by-product of the social revolution have, between them, sapped the political will of [Western] Europe', while Leo Labedz warned that the 'pseudo-*détente* which led up to Helsinki will eventually lead to the Finlandisation of Western Europe as surely as Yalta resulted in the satellitisation of Eastern Europe.' (Davy, 1992, p.265). The opponents of *détente* were regarded as 'hawks' and its defenders were labelled 'doves'. But these labels were misleading, in that '*détente* was in many ways more threatening to Soviet interests than the confrontational policies advocated by the hawks.' (Davy, 1992, p.237). Ironically, the 'hawks' greatly underestimated the strength of the West, which they mistakenly saw as engaging in a process of 'moral disarmament', whereas the exact opposite was the case (Davy, 1992, p.257). Indeed, 'without the Final Act and the Western interest it aroused, opposition in

Eastern Europe would have been weaker, less coherent, easier to suppress' (p.251). In the longer term, by supporting the re-emergence of autonomous civil and political associations and activities and increased concern for the rule of law, Helsinki 'paved the way for a *smoother* transition to democracy when the [communist] regimes crumbled because it had fostered alternative structures and authorities to take their place' (Davy, 1992, p.263). Conversely, any return to East-West confrontation (as advocated by the 'hawks') would have provided pretexts for increased repression, a siege mentality, seclusion, austerity and a renewed domestic 'freeze' within the Soviet bloc.

But why did the Soviet leadership sign a treaty which was so profoundly against its real interests? Part of the explanation was that Brezhnev, having invested so much in the Helsinki initiative, had a large personal stake in securing an agreement and Western recognition of Europe's existing frontiers, while 'the nature of the Soviet system' made it difficult for anyone to tell him that he had blundered! Brezhnev also mistakenly believed that he could simply implement the bits he liked and 'bury the rest under a mound of verbiage' (Davy, 1992, p.19). In addition, 'Soviet officials had also acquired a very personal stake in the Helsinki process because it enhanced their own positions and gave them the opportunity of trips to the West', and 'East European regimes had developed a strong interest in the economic and political benefits of *détente*.' (Davy, 1992, p.21). During the 1970s East-West *détente* facilitated increased inflows of Western capital and technology into the still expanding East European economies. There was an uncontrolled proliferation of East-West joint-ventures, production licensing agreements and imported 'turnkey' installations, partly financed by recycled 'petrodollars'. The East European regimes eagerly accepted Western loans, investments, joint-ventures, industrial installations and 'technology transfers' as substitutes for more fundamental and more obviously hazardous reforms in their socio-economic systems.

The Beginning of the End

Nevertheless, increased reliance on Western capital, technology and firms had larger than anticipated *political and social repercussions*. Increased contact with Western tourists and businessmen, together with the proliferation of amenities catering to their needs, helped to diffuse Western values, consumerism and pop culture, especially among the young. The resultant Westernisation of East European attitudes, values, dress and leisure activities was, in the end, just as corrosive of communist influence on the minds of the young as any radical systemic reform. Moreover, through their clumsy attempts to curb the growing influence of rock concerts, Western pop music, blue jeans and consumerism, the ageing communist dictators made themselves seem increasingly old-fashioned, remote and ridiculous, especially in the eyes of the young.

Excessive reliance upon Western capital and technology transfers posed equally serious *economic hazards*. Production licensing agreements often incurred great expense for relatively little benefit for the East European economies (Stokes, 1993, p.19). Debt service payments rapidly became very burdensome and in the late 1970s began to exceed fresh inflows of Western capital. The latter quickly dried up as East European credit ratings fell. Some East European states even had difficulty in completing existing projects involving Western capital or equipment and in obtaining Western spare parts. This further impaired their capacity to increase exports on the scale anticipated or required. Indeed, the East European states found themselves under increasing pressure to expand their exports to the West to service their uncomfortably large hard-currency debts at the very moment when the doubling of OPEC oil prices in 1979, just a few years after the quadrupling of OPEC oil prices in 1973-74, plunged the West into deep economic recessions. This in turn depressed demand for, and raised trade barriers against, Western imports from Eastern Europe. Moreover, the 1979-82 world recession coincided with the nadir of the Brezhnev 'years of stagnation', during which Soviet economic growth sharply decelerated and crucial sectors such as oil, coal, iron and steel stopped growing altogether. The Soviet Union's inability to continue supplying ever-increasing quantities of fuel and raw materials to Eastern Europe on preferential terms reduced its willingness and capacity to absorb (in return) ever-increasing quantities of obsolete and/or poor quality East European industrial products. Eastern Europe was thus caught in a 'two-way squeeze' between a stagnating Soviet economy and a recession-stricken West. The crisis was compounded by the simultaneous start of the 'new Cold war', precipitated by a dramatic escalation of the nuclear arms race (1978-84), the Soviet invasion of Afghanistan (December 1979), the accession of Ronald Reagan to the US Presidency (1980-88) and the imposition of martial law in Poland (December 1981).

Ironically, the further escalations of the East-West arms race from 1963 to 1983 occurred not so much in order to wage war more lethally, as in order to avoid having to fight anything more than localised 'proxy wars', although this did not avert appalling cumulative loss of life in Indo-China, Angola, Mozambique, Ethiopia, Somalia, Afghanistan and elsewhere. Global war was to be avoided, but 'wars of liberation' were still permissible. Soviet leaders also acknowledged, rather more openly than their Western counterparts, that *détente* did not entail any diminution of East-West economic and ideological competition. As Leonid Brezhnev declared at the February 1976 Congress of the CPSU: '*Détente* does not in the slightest abolish, nor can it alter, the laws of class struggle ... We make no secret of the fact that we see *détente* as the way to create more favourable conditions for peaceful socialist and Communist construction ... As for the ultra-leftist assertions that peaceful co-existence is freezing the socio-political status quo, our answer is this: every revolution is above all the result of the given society's internal development.' (Davy, 1992, p.8). Moreover, recent 'revisionist' literature on Cuban intervention in African civil wars during the 1970s has shown that Fidel Castro's regime was not simply acting at Moscow's behest, but was motivated by radical Cuban interest and involvement in African liberation struggles dating back to the 1950s (Gleijeses, 1996/97, pp.5-21). Castro was at that time not so much a communist as a Third World anti-imperialist nationalist, who was ineptly driven into Moscow's arms by American knee-jerk 'anti-communism' (and by the US propensity to mistake any form of radicalism or anti-Americanism for 'communism').

Within Europe, however, the dangers inherent in East-West confrontation were too great to permit even 'proxy wars'. It was Leonid Brezhnev, *not* Mikhail Gorbachev, who first proclaimed that 'whatever may divide us, Europe is our common home. Common fate has linked us through centuries, it links us today too.' These portentious words were uttered by Brezhnev in Berlin in November 1981, in opposition to NATO deployment of cruise missiles in Western Europe and the attendant escalation of the arms race in Europe (Stokes, 1993, p.74). In 1987 Gorbachev declared that the USA was seeking 'to bleed the Soviet Union white economically, to prevent us from carrying out our plans of construction by dragging us ever deeper into the quagmire of the arms race.' (Gorbachev, 1988, p.219). The reckless expansion of nuclear arsenals 'is not our choice. It has been imposed upon us', because 'the United States is not ready to part with its hope of winning nuclear superiority' (Gorbachev, 1988, pp. 218, 239). Gorbachev believed that, like nuclear war, the nuclear arms race was 'unwinnable' (Gorbachev, 1988, p.138). At the Reykjavik summit in October 1986, he warned Reagan that 'our meeting could not produce one winner: we would both either win or lose' (Gorbachev, 1988, p.240). But on this point Gorbachev was mistaken. In the course of the 1980s, the Soviet system was forced to its knees, scuppering *perestroika* and confounding Khrushchev's earlier boasts.

Nevertheless, the Helsinki process was simultaneously contributing to a significant recrudescence of civil society and underlying pressures for 'a return to Europe', both in East-Central Europe and to a lesser extent within the Soviet Union. It fell to Gorbachev to recognise that the 'de-Sovietisation of Eastern Europe' had become a prerequisite for 'the Europeanisation of the Soviet Union' and the termination of the Cold War (Dawisha, 1990, p.198). He had the courage to take the Helsinki process to its logical conclusion. In 1987 he declared that 'Security can no longer be assured by military means', for 'the arms race is lowering the level of security, impairing it' (Gorbachev, 1988, p.141). The advent of nuclear weapons had made security indivisible. 'It is either equal security for all or none at all. Universal security in our time rests on the recognition of the right of every nation to choose its own path of social development, on the renunciation of interference in the domestic affairs of other states, on respect for others in combination with an objective self-critical view of one's own society. A nation may choose either capitalism or socialism. This is its sovereign right. Nations cannot and should not pattern their life either after the United States or the Soviet Union.' (Gorbachev, 1988, pp.142-43). These were the additional implications that Gorbachev discerned and acted upon in the Helsinki process and in the concept of 'the common European home'. In these respects he towered above his Soviet predecessors and his American counterpart, both morally and intellectually.

The Denouement

The Revolutions of 1989-91 were the result of a prolonged systemic crisis allied to Gorbachev's professed unwillingness to emulate his predecessors by employing force to keep Eastern Europe's communist leaders in power. As the ruling elites became increasingly divided as to how to react to the systemic crisis, civil society lost some of its former fear of the outwardly formidable security services and exposed the increasingly threadbare political legitimacy of communist rule. But the East European Revolutions might not have succeeded if Gorbachev had not unilaterally renounced old habits of Soviet military-political intervention in Eastern Europe's internal affairs. His programme of *perestroika* also provided a potent model and symbol of reform from above and liberalisation, which unleashed a ferment of ideas, debate and demands for democratisation. His announcement in 1988 that Soviet forces would be withdrawn from Afghanistan was widely perceived as a blow to Soviet military morale and prestige and as confirmation of a renunciation of military interference in the affairs of 'fraternal socialist states'. In addition, his marked reluctance to express approval of the Berlin Wall, let alone the Soviet invasions of Hungary in 1956 or Czechoslovakia in 1968, further reduced the security and legitimacy of the Honecker, Husak and Kadar regimes. Likewise, without his having to issue explicit disavowals or condemnations, the distaste with which Gorbachev regarded the hard-line rulers of the GDR, Czechoslovakia, Bulgaria and Romania became plainly visible to the millions of people who saw the official television coverage of his public meetings with and visits to East European communist leaders; and the spontaneous enthusiasm of the crowds that greeted Gorbachev during his visits to Eastern Europe sharply contrasted with their sullen indifference to their own rulers. Moreover, the absence of Soviet protests either against the opening of Hungary's border with Austria in May 1989 or against Hungary's decision to allow East German 'holiday-makers' to start escaping through that bolthole to the West in September 1989, combined with Gorbachev's refusal to sanction a military crackdown on mounting East German popular demands for freedom in October 1989, increased the pressure on the Honecker regime to allow East Germans freely to cross the Berlin Wall on 9 November 1989. This then imparted an unstoppable momentum to German unification and to popular challenges to brittle communist authority throughout Eastern Europe. Nevertheless, no one claims that Gorbachev had a master plan for the dismantling of communist rule in Eastern Europe. On the contrary, he hoped to ensure its survival by encouraging the deposition of hard-liners in favour of reformers in his own image. But the undermining of hard-liners unleashed forces which also dethroned the reform communists.

In the post-Cold War period, however, Russian politicians and publicists have been repeatedly forced to question the West's *bona fides*, since Western policies have seemingly sought to isolate and marginalise Russia even more than before and have forced the Russians to renounce the geopolitical gains that they had made as a result of their momentous victory in the Second World War, without offering them anything very substantial in return. Indeed, many Russians feel that their country has been cheated of the hardwon fruits of that victory, and that the West has reneged on its moral debt to Russia. The recurrent marginalisation and humiliation of Russia by the West since the collapse of Communist rule has starkly exposed the extent to which Western 'Cold Warriors' have been motivated, not just by 'lofty' ideals, but by prejudice, self-interest, imperialism and supremacism. The collapse of communist rule has not made Russia much more 'acceptable' to the West than it was under Gorbachev or even Khrushchev (indeed, perhaps less so!). Such perceptions have contributed to the resurgence of anti-Western feeling in Russia during the 1990s when, in the words of President Yeltsin (Kozyrev, 1995, p.4), the Cold War threatened to give way to 'Cold Peace'.

Conclusion

11 The Cold War in the Context of World History

CLIVE PONTING

For those of us born in the immediate aftermath of the Second World War the whole of our youth and most of our adult life seemed to bc dominated by the Cold War. World affairs, as presented by the media, were dominated by the struggle between the 'West' and the 'East' which symbolically stood for 'freedom and liberty' on the one hand and 'the evil empire' on the other. Events in any and every part of the globe were part of this overall struggle and were interpreted within this general context. Equally, if not more important, was the ever present threat of nuclear annihilation. Although the fear of surprise attack was not great, apart perhaps from the early 1980s, miscalculation in any crisis was always a danger. And the crises did occur frequently - Hungary in 1956, Berlin from 1959 to 1962, Cuba in 1962, the Arab-Israeli war of 1973, Afghanistan in 1979 and the deep hostility of the early Reagan years of 1981 to 1985. Through a mixture of caution and a rather greater amount of luck than leaders at the time or since have been prepared to admit, a nuclear war was avoided.

We are now almost ten years on from the end of the Cold War. It is therefore perhaps worth pausing to consider how far our perceptions of the events of the half century after the defeat of Germany and Japan have really changed. The aim of this paper is firstly to argue that in many ways our views have changed very little and that secondly this means that we are neglecting the wider and longer-term significance of events in the second half of the twentieth century. The reasons for this failure of analysis are, I would suggest, threefold. The first is partly inherent in the way the academic discipline of international relations has developed. It has always had a strong Anglo-American bias and has been increasingly dominated by American thinking. The result of this has been an obsession with international affairs post-1945, in part because this is the period in which the United States has been a dominant power. (It is perhaps only a slight exaggeration to say that for some American academics world affairs only begin with the emergence of the United States as a significant power.) The study of international relations also had to face the danger of too great an association with the policy-making elite. During the Cold War the development of security and strategic studies only emphasised this trend - some academics moved in and out of government and others seemed to gain an almost vicarious pleasure in being able to discuss the minutiae of weapons system performance, throw-weights and missile accuracy. For fifty years part of the international relations discipline became a discussion about how to fight and win the Cold War. Second, research efforts since the end of the Cold War have tended to reinforce this trend. The opening of United States, Soviet and British archives is to be welcomed as is the massive Cold War Research Project. But we need to remember that archives do not tell us the whole truth and over-reliance on them can seriously distort research conclusions. In the last resort official archives can really only tell us what governments were thinking. We knew before the archives were opened that policy-makers tended to see every development in terms of a conflict between two great power blocs and although we may now be better informed about the details of policy-making this mass of paper does not prove that this is the only way to analyse events in the world. The third problem is that much of international relations as a discipline is not just dominated by Anglo-American ideas but is also deeply western-centric and still influenced by older European/western views of the world.

Some of these ways of thinking can be seen in three recent works on the Cold War and modern history. In what will probably become one of the standard textbooks on the subject Richard Crockatt proclaims at the very beginning 'For fifty years relations between the United States and the Soviet Union were the deciding factor in international affairs.' (Crockatt, 1996, p.3). The argument of this paper is that such a proposition is not sustainable from the perspective of world history. Perhaps the most famous attempt to interpret the meaning of the Cold War came just as it was ending. In *The End of History* Francis Fukuyama argued that the whole of modern history should be seen as a conflict between liberal capitalism and communism (Fukuyama, 1992). That conflict was, of course, resolved in 1989-91 by the world-wide triumph of capitalism and the end of history. The underlying argument of this paper is that such a perspective on world history is much too western-centric. Both liberal capitalism and communism emerged from the mainstream of classical economics as it developed in late eighteenth and early nineteenth century Europe. From a global perspective their spread, and the conflict between them, can be seen as just one aspect of the much wider diffusion of European ideas in the world. It is also clear that the end of the Cold War did not mark the end of history - indeed it could be argued that the resolution of Fukuyama's conflict only made the tensions produced by global capitalism even more apparent.

One of the most brilliantly argued and influential accounts of twentieth century history is contained in Eric Hobsbawm's *Age of Extremes* (Hobsbawm, 1994). In it he argues for the so-called 'Short Twentieth Century' lasting from 'Sarajevo to Sarajevo' - 1914 until 1991. It is the contention of this paper that such an interpretation is too Eurocentric and that as an only partly reconstructed Marxist Hobsbawm gives far too much weight to the same conflict as Fukuyama. It might be argued that the outbreak of the First World War was an important moment in European history - although even in this area of the world 1917-18 probably marks a more important transition with the entry of the United States into the war and the collapse of the Russian, Austro-Hungarian, German and Ottoman empires. What is, however, clear is that for the majority of the world (Africa, Asia and Latin America) neither 1914 nor 1917-18 mark an important transition. For the countries in these parts of the world a much stronger case can be made for regarding the onset of the Great Depression in 1929-31 as marking the major transition from the world of the late nineteenth century. The collapse of commodity prices and the dislocation to world trade caused by the development of increasingly autarkic trading blocs produced a severe economic and social crisis and throughout Latin America a collapse of the political systems based on the wealth created by the export of primary products. Similarly although 1989-91 clearly marked a major change in Europe, especially in central and eastern Europe, it was not particularly important for the rest of the world. In this context the events of 1973-4 are of far greater global significance marking as they do the end of the brief 'golden age' of high growth that began in the early 1950s and the simultaneous collapse of the post-war international financial system and the era of cheap oil. This period marked the return to the economic conditions typical of the rest of the twentieth century - low growth and high unemployment - and increasing difficulties for the vulnerable economies of Asia, Africa and Latin America.

This paper argues two fundamental points. First, that the attempt to fit the events of world history in the half century or so after the Second World War onto the Procrustean bed of the Cold War inevitably produces serious distortion and tells us little about what was happening in the world and the major trends that were shaping world history. The second point follows on from the first - it is important to emphasise other trends of greater significance than the Cold War not just because they throw important light on the shape of the Cold War but because with the ending of that particular phase in international and strategic affairs they have become even more important in shaping the world. None of what follows is an attempt to argue that the Cold War was not important. It was a major international phenomenon and an important aspect of world affairs for half a century. It was also important because key policy makers in Washington, Moscow and the capitals of western Europe thought it was important and central to their decision taking. Because they believed they were engaged in a Cold War with intractable opponents and based their policies upon that perception, the study of the Cold War will always be an important part of the study of international history. However, in the longest perspective it will be seen as just one form of the world power balance. Using long historical frameworks can lead to many events seeming of little importance - who for example now sees much of fundamental significance in the Anglo-Dutch struggles of the seventeenth century? Nevertheless we should remember that at the time such events were of crucial importance.

The Cold War was obviously partly moulded by, and reflected longer-term trends and structures. For example, much of the development of the Cold War was shaped by earlier developments in science and technology and the combination of them that emerged in the period 1935-45. In particular, it was the development of four particular technologies that determined much of the strategic posture of the Cold War. First, the development and deployment of the long-range four-engined bomber in Britain and the United States between 1935 and 1942 combined with a long-established doctrine that such weapons could be used strategically against enemy citizens and cities. Second, jet engine technology as it emerged in Britain and Germany in the middle of the Second World War. Third, the development and use of rockets and pilotless bombs by Germany after the summer of 1944. Finally, the development by the United States of the atomic bomb with its unparalleled destructive power. The Cold War would not have taken the form that it did without these technologies. Indeed it is possible to argue that it might not have happened at all without all these earlier technical developments and the peculiar strategic position brought about by the war to defeat Germany. There was no common border of any significance between the United States and the USSR and no direct disputes between them of the sort that often lead to war. Despite their strong ideological confrontation the two powers did not and could not oppose each other until 1945. What was crucial was the growing ability to threaten each other with massive destruction even over the huge distances that separated them. This only became technologically possible after 1945 and then shaped much of the Cold War.

The obverse of this coin is that in many areas of the world the Cold War merely involved a new framework and language for long-established policies. The main example of this long-term trend came in Latin America where the 'threat' of 'Communism' after 1945 provided a new excuse for American intervention and for local elites to either suppress movements against the *status quo* or rely on that intervention. The United States had given itself the right to intervene on the continent in the Monroe Doctrine in the 1820s and reasserted that right in an even more extensive form under the Roosevelt Corollary in the first decade of the twentieth century. The United States intervened on a large scale in the first decades of the century in Haiti, Nicaragua, Cuba and elsewhere. It is difficult to argue that the interventions in Guatemala in 1954, the Dominican Republic in 1965, the overthrow of the Allende government in Chile in 1973, the anti-Sandinista campaign in Nicaragua, the support for the extreme right in El Salvador or the invasion of Grenada were linked to the Cold War or qualitatively different from earlier interventions before 1930. Similar interventions occurred after the Cold War as in Haiti in the mid-1990s. The one aspect that perhaps did change because of the Cold War was the opportunity it gave to the Castro government in Cuba to find outside support, resist American pressure and avoid the normal outcome for those who opposed the Americans in the region. It is perhaps this aspect, enshrined in the non-invasion pledge given by the United States after the missile crisis of 1962, rather than Castro's extremely lukewarm Marxism that explains the depths of the American hostility to, and obsession with, Cuba over the last three and a half decades.

In the following main part of the paper I want to argue that from the perspective of world history we should take a different view of the Cold War. In particular I would like to suggest that there was a series of historical trends that began long before the Cold War and which were of far greater long-term consequence. These trends were still in existence during the Cold War, indeed they helped shape many of its events, but concentrating on the Cold War as an explanatory phenomenon simply masks the fact of their existence and importance. These trends also help us to understand why the end of the Cold War in 1989-91 was of only limited significance. In particular I would like to concentrate on three particular themes - the structure of the world economy, the conflict within the 'Atlantic world' and the conflict between the 'Atlantic' and 'Pacific' worlds.

In his major works on the development of the world economy since the sixteenth century Immanuel Wallerstein has argued extremely persuasively that the best framework for analysing the world economy as it developed following the great expansion of European influence is to see it as divided into three very unequal parts - the core, semi-periphery and periphery (Wallerstein, 1974). This framework, which in many ways became more pronounced during the twentieth century, provides a valuable tool for analysing the structure and outcome of the Cold War. Despite the fundamental changes to Russian society and politics that followed the 1917 revolution and the Bolshevik victory in the civil war the new government of the Soviet Union found it very difficult to change Russia's economic position. Before the revolution Russia, despite being a large colonial power and a major factor in the European power balance, was a classic state of the semi-periphery. It had an economy overwhelmingly dominated by agriculture and a society primarily composed of illiterate peasants. It was, however, gradually shifting its agriculture into the norm for the semi-periphery - a high level of agricultural exports (especially wheat) to the industrialised countries. Russia had a rapidly growing industrial sector but overall its level of industrialisation was about the same as Britain in 1810 or France in 1860 (although, of course, it did have access to the most modern technology). The Russian economy was also characteristic of the semi-periphery in that it was highly dependent on foreign investment, especially from its ally France. All of the oil industry was foreign owned as were ninety per cent of the mines and half of the chemical industry.

By 1928, following the chaos of the revolution and recovery during the New Economic Policy period, the USSR was back to 1913 levels of output and industrialisation. The problem which the leadership faced, which was common to all states in the semi-periphery, was how to industrialise in the face of the dominant position of the core powers. Their difficult position was aggravated by the fact that for ideological and political reasons, both within the Soviet Union and the industrialised countries, reliance could not be placed on foreign investment to provide the necessary capital. The internal mobilisation of capital could only be achieved at a huge social cost but it did produce very high levels of growth during the 1930s. Even the most conservative western estimates accept that growth rates over the decade averaged at least eleven per cent a year. However, these figures are no higher than those achieved by Brazil in the 1960s and South Korea in the 1970s when they went through similar phases of rapid industrialisation. Like these two states the Soviet Union found that such high growth rates could not be sustained. What worsened the Soviet position were the huge losses of the Second World War - perhaps as much as a quarter of its pre-war population and about a third of its pre-war capital assets. The total cost of the war was equivalent to about ten years' GDP and even more if the huge population losses are taken into account.

After the Second World War the Soviet economy remained typical of a relatively advanced member of the semi-periphery. Growth rates slowed, the structural problems in the agricultural sector were never solved, the sclerotic state planning system was unable to adapt from developing heavy industry (at which it was quite successful) into providing a dynamic consumer goods sector and the pace of technological development was slower than in the core countries. The economy and the research and development effort remained badly skewed towards military sectors (even more so than in the core states) and the military-industrial complex was just as powerful as in the United States. Overall the result was that although by the late 1980s Soviet GDP per capita was about seven and a half times higher than in 1900 this performance was no better than many other states of the semi-periphery such as Portugal. The Cold War therefore was not a contest between equals. It was a contest between the most advanced of the core industrial states, supported by the other core powers, and a large state but one that was inextricably part of the semi-periphery.

In addition the Soviet Union was in a position of massive strategic inferiority. It faced many of the strategic problems and retained many of the military features of its Russian predecessor. Like Russia it maintained a large army which in theory was well-equipped but in practice was of dubious effectiveness as the campaign in Afghanistan in the 1980s demonstrated. Until the late 1950s it had no strategic bombing force and it was not until the late 1970s that it had even the semblance of an ocean-going navy. In addition, like Germany earlier in the century, it faced the threat of encirclement and had to plan on the possibility of a two-front war - by the 1970s it maintained more troops in the Far East deployed against China than it did in eastern Europe.

The comparison with the strategic situation of Germany before 1914 leads us to the second major theme - the conflict within the 'Atlantic world'. Twice during the twentieth century Britain and France had to rely on the United States in order to defeat Germany. The consequences of that dependence increased the pace of change within the Atlantic world and the replacement of British and French influence by American influence across the world. This trend was of far greater significance than the Cold War, although, like the Cold War, it did not lead to conflict between the rival powers. To see a major part of twentieth century history as a contest between Britain and France on the one hand and the United States on the other runs counter to the prevailing political, historical and popular ethos, particularly in Britain. From this perspective the obvious loss of power by Britain is overlaid by resonant political rhetoric about the 'special relationship' and the assumed identity of interests between the two powers. Similar assumptions dominate historical writing and continue what might be called a 'Churchillian' approach to the strategic balance within the Atlantic world.

If we go back to the late nineteenth century most politicians and many commentators accepted that the main long-term threat to Britain's dominant position as a *status quo* power came from the rising economic, financial and military strength of the United States. The British elite accepted that, in Joseph Chamberlain's phrase, 'the weary titan staggers under the too vast orb of its fate'. They concluded that Britain could not ultimately compete with the United States and therefore certain accommodations would have to made. The first signs of such an attitude were seen during the Venezuelan border dispute of 1895 and agreement to the American position on the building of the Panama canal. These developments were followed by the acceptance that a war with the United States could not be fought and the withdrawal of troops from Canada and ships from the West Indies. The decisions to reach agreements with France and Russia in order to protect a vulnerable empire and the drift into greater hostility to Germany only exacerbated this trend.

Equally important was growing American financial strength and the relatively weak position of sterling which was itself increased by the demands of financing the war with Germany. By late 1916 Britain was spending $80 million a week on arms orders in the United States and financing the purchases of its allies too. The assets available to finance this effort were rapidly dwindling. Reginald McKenna, the Chancellor of the Exchequer, warned his cabinet colleagues that: 'by next June, or earlier, the President of the American Republic will be in a position, if he wishes, to dictate his own terms to us.'[1] By the spring of 1917 the situation was desperate - Britain had enough reserves to fund the war for less than ten weeks. The Allies were saved from having to negotiate a compromise peace by American entry into the war in April. By the end of 1918 Britain had accumulated war debts of £1.3 billion which it was only able to repay at a very slow rate. New York also replaced London as the centre of world finance - a situation which was only reinforced after 1925 by the short-term cost and ultimate failure of the attempt to re-establish sterling at its pre-war rate against the dollar. In the aftermath of the war the British accepted that they would not be able to build a fleet larger than that of the United States, conceded naval superiority and also, at American insistence, scrapped their alliance with Japan thereby causing an unsolvable problem for imperial security in the Far East.

The renewal of war with Germany in 1939 caused an even quicker collapse of Britain's financial strength than in the First World War. In the summer of 1940 Britain traded naval and air bases in the western hemisphere for aged destroyers in another symbol of American superiority in the region. In August the cabinet were told that British spending in the United States at over £80 million a month would exhaust the remaining reserves before the end of the year. Once again the alternatives were peace with Germany or dependence on American help. As the draft message for Churchill to send to Roosevelt bluntly stated in early November 1940:

> It is only a question of weeks before the resources we have available with which to pay for our requirements and the munitions ordered from the United States are exhausted. Unless we can get financial assistance from the

> United States on the largest scale, it is obvious that our capacity to carry on the war on the current basis must abruptly come to an end.[2]

The British situation was resolved through the granting of free munitions and raw materials under the Lend-Lease legislation. However, even after US entry into the war the British economy was still subjected to strict American control so as to ensure dependence after the war was over. On 1 January 1943 the US government, without consulting the British, decided that: 'the United Kingdom's gold and dollar balances should not be permitted to be less than about $600 million nor above about $1 billion'.[3] The United States was able to largely achieve this aim by manipulating the goods available under Lend-Lease. The result was the British need for a large American loan at the end of the war, the consequent disastrous and short-lived attempt to allow sterling to be convertible, and continued British financial debility.

By 1945 the British (and French) were economically and financially weak and highly dependent on the United States. From the perspective of the previous thirty years (including the various American economic interventions in Europe in the 1920s over reparations) the creation of the Marshall Aid programme seems less of a Cold War measure and more one reflecting the growing US financial and economic predominance over western Europe. However, although Britain and France were not only financially but also strategically weak compared with the overwhelming power of the United States they did have one major asset - they still held a substantial position on the ground through their possession of extensive colonial empires. The emergence of the doctrine of 'containment' in the late 1940s was therefore highly ambivalent as far as the European powers were concerned. The vast expansion of American power to contain the Soviet Union was not made at the expense of that power - nowhere was it forced to retreat by the United States. Instead the expansion of American power took place at the expense of Britain and France and the subsidiary European powers such as the Netherlands. The first half of the Cold War should therefore be seen less as a duel between American and Soviet power (the Soviets had almost no influence outside of eastern Europe) but rather as the culmination of an historical process that had begun in the early twentieth century - the replacement of British and French power by that of the United States. This redistribution of power within the Atlantic world lasted from 1945 until the 1960s and the majority of the crises of the early Cold War involved this process rather than a confrontation between the United States and the Soviet Union.

It is possible to trace this power struggle in three areas - the Middle

East, the Far East and the Mediterranean. In the first two areas the process had begun before 1945 and intensified afterwards. In the Middle East the clash of interests began in the 1920s over oil. In the San Remo treaty of 1922 Britain and France awarded themselves a monopoly of oil concessions within the territory of the former Ottoman empire. However, it proved impossible to sustain this position following the discovery of the huge oil reserves in Iraq, the determination of the large American oil companies to secure a substantial part of that oil and the threat from Exxon, which controlled half of the British market, to cut off oil supplies. In 1928 the 'Red Line' agreement secured a monopoly position for the various consortia of British, American, French and Dutch companies but allowed American companies into the area for the first time on any major scale. By the 1930s the British were beginning to lose much of their influence to the Americans in what had once been their client state of Saudi Arabia as the Aramco consortium secured the oil concessions. During the war the British used their power to remove direct French control from Syria and Lebanon but after 1945 they found their own remaining influence being replaced by the Americans.

In 1948 after the British handed back their mandate in Palestine the United States became the main patron of the new state of Israel. The Iranian crisis of 1951-3 saw the British achieve few of their objectives in resisting the pressure from Iranian nationalism and after the restoration of the Shah the United States became the main external supporter of the new regime. In the early 1950s the United States refused to support the British idea of creating a Middle East Defence Organisation so as to secure their position in Egypt. The debacle at Suez merely hastened the process of replacing British by American influence - a situation that was symbolised by the announcement of the Eisenhower Doctrine giving the United States the right to intervene in the region. By the 1960s there was hardly any French influence in the region and the British were confined to the marginal states of the Gulf and after the final withdrawal in the early 1970s even that residual influence was largely lost.

Since the late nineteenth century the United States had taken a greater interest in the affairs of the Far East than any other part of the world apart from Latin America. The difference of interests between them and the other 'western' powers was apparent throughout the early twentieth century and during the Second World War there was almost continual disagreement between Britain and the United States over the future of the region. By 1942 the United States was offering advice on the future constitutional status of India, by 1943 its role as the patron of the nationalist Chinese was secure and in the last years of the war Roosevelt often mused about China regaining Hong Kong at the end of the war and the French having only a 'mandate' over their colony of Indochina. The Americans treated the Pacific theatre as their own private war and the British, who were unable to deploy any significant power in the area, were almost entirely excluded. This regime was continued during the nominally Allied but in practice American occupation of Japan after 1945. The most symbolic moment came in 1950 when, with the ANZUS treaty, the United States took over the historic British role of protecting Australia and New Zealand. In 1954-55 it took over from the French in trying to maintain South Vietnam as an independent state.

In the Mediterranean there had been little American influence before the Second World War and during the war the British, who had deployed much of their limited military power in the area, were determined to keep their influence predominant over the Americans. Yet within two years of the end of the war they had to admit defeat and hand over their historic influence in Greece and Turkey to the Americans. The deployment by the Americans of the Sixth Fleet into the Mediterranean, an area that had been dominated by British and French seapower for centuries, was the final confirmation of yet another decline in power. In Europe itself the Americans took over effective control of NATO forces by ensuring that they always held the post of SACEUR and even forced the British to accept a subordinate position in the Atlantic, the very centre of British seapower, through their determination to hold the post of SACLANT.

The result of all these changes in the two decades or so after 1945 was that under the guise of 'containment' and resistance to an often ill-defined 'communism' the United States had secured a huge extension of its power. What it also meant was the replacement of British and French influence and the major extension of American power into the various security complexes that emerged around the world as the European empires came to an end.

The end of the European empires was a fundamental aspect of the third major historical trend - the changing balance between the 'Atlantic' and 'Pacific' worlds. At the beginning of the twentieth century the long expansion of western influence in the world was reaching a climax. No area of the world could exclude itself from the increasing impact of the global economy dominated by the core states of western Europe and North America. Latin America was politically independent but economically dependent, China and the Ottoman empire were large states but it seemed unlikely that their nominal independence would survive much longer. Japan was the only example of a strong state able to absorb western influence whilst maintaining its own traditions and limited area of influence. In many ways it was therefore surprising that the twentieth century was marked by the revival of Asia and the decline of European influence. Some of the first signs were in fact evident early in the century with the nationalist 'Boxer' movement in China in 1900, Japanese victory over Russia in the war of 1904-5 and the emergence of nationalist movements in India, the Philippines and Indonesia.

The two key events came in the 1940s. Between 1940 and 1942 the Japanese effectively destroyed the European empires in the Far East. The Japanese government could not decide whether to attack the almost undefended empires when they were at their weakest in 1940 (they restricted themselves to taking over northern Indochina from the Vichy government). However, under growing American economic and political pressure in 1941, they eventually decided to attack. Between December 1941 and the middle of 1942 the Japanese conquered the Philippines, the Dutch East Indies, Hong Kong, Malaya, Singapore and Burma and their troops were on the frontiers of India and their bombers were attacking northern Australia. This was a blow to the prestige of the European powers from which they were never to recover. Although Japan was eventually defeated none of the European colonies had been fully reoccupied before the surrender in August 1945 and everywhere nationalist movements were in a strong position. In the immediate aftermath of the war the European powers (and the United States too in the Philippines) found that it was impossible to re-establish effective colonial rule. By 1950 the Philippines, Indonesia, India, Burma and Ceylon were independent, the French were fighting desperately to maintain some control over Indochina and the British faced a widespread revolt in Malaya.

The second key event of the 1940s was the reunification of China and the establishment of a strong government there. This was the culmination of a number of trends since the late nineteenth century and although it took place under the Communists led by Mao Tse-tung it is unclear how much Marxism Mao understood. (The idea that the peasants could be the class to lead the proletarian revolution was the direct antithesis of Marx's doctrine.) What Mao did understand was the dynamics of peasant revolt and guerrilla war in the societies of the periphery. Although to the Cold War politicians of Washington China was 'lost' (as if the Americans ever controlled it) the real significance of the Communist triumph was much wider than merely an ideological battle in the Cold War. For over a century China had been in political and economic decline and its revival under the new government was the start of a long process of a return to the more normal pattern in world history in which China was a major state and, for long periods of time, the most advanced economically and technologically in the world.

These two fundamental trends were reinforced after 1950 by two further developments. The first was the phenomenal economic growth of

Japan. In 1955 four out of ten workers were still in agriculture, it made less than 2 percent of the world's industrial output and it was the largest single borrower from the World Bank which remained deeply pessimistic about its future prospects. Between 1955 and 1973 Japan achieved steady GDP growth of ten per cent a year and industrial output rose at fourteen per cent a year. This was the fastest sustained growth ever achieved by a major economy. By 1968 Japan had the second largest GNP in the non-Communist world and its position as a major core industrialised state was symbolically ratified by its admission to OECD in 1964. The impact of its long-term growth and technological adaptation can be judged from the fact that in 1960 it made just 165,000 cars. By 1980 its output of vehicles was greater than that of the United States and by the 1990s it was making over nine million cars a year, over half of which were exported. In other industries too the Japanese were equally successful in destroying those of their competitors in the core states from motor-cycles to shipbuilding, cameras, television and consumer electronics. The Japanese came to dominate the East and South-east Asian regions and by the last quarter of the century had established the 'Greater East Asia Co-Prosperity Scheme' that they had been unable to achieve through the use of force in the early 1940s. Overall the Japanese economy was the most successful of the twentieth century - GDP grew fourteenfold, which was three times as much as in the United States and five times the level in Britain. This major increase in Japanese power and influence within the world economy as part of a revival of Asia was reinforced by the success of the 'follow-on' economies of South Korea, Taiwan and the trading economies of Hong Kong and Singapore in the last quarter of the twentieth century. Although these economies faltered in 1997-8 this was no more than a blip in their growth and increasing influence in producing their own transnational corporations and even overtaking Japan in some industrial sectors such as shipbuilding and televisions. Increasingly the United States too was turning towards a Pacific rather than an Atlantic focus. California became the largest state in the union and by the late twentieth century the Pacific area took a far greater proportion of American trade than the Atlantic area.

In strategic terms this major economic revival in Asia was matched by the limitations of 'Atlantic' influence. The United States found that it was unable to both replace Britain, France and the Netherlands as the dominant powers in the area and maintain their spheres of influence. Northern Indochina was lost by France by 1954 but for the next twenty years the United States fought an unavailing battle on a massive scale to stop the reunification of the country under a communist government. In Burma, Indonesia before 1965 and to a large extent in India nationalism and neutralism (symbolised by the Bandung conference of non-aligned states in 1955) were the prevailing trends. Although control was maintained over South Korea the part of the ex-Japanese colony in the north of the country fell under communist rule and American (and western) influence was also excluded from China for decades. Similar problems occurred elsewhere. The overthrow of the Shah in Iran in 1979 was followed by the installation of strongly anti-American and anti-western government as had also been the case in Libya a decade earlier.

In the light of these wider historical trends it is now possible to assess the world-wide importance of the Cold War and, in particular, why its end in 1989-91 was of only limited significance. The end of the Cold War did not, of course, change the structure of the world economy which had determined so many of the major historical trends of the twentieth century. What it clearly did do was reduce the ability of some states, not just the ex-communist states of central and eastern Europe but others such as Vietnam and Cuba, to stand outside of the prevailing system. To that extent the end of the Cold War did mark the 'end of history' but the wider reality, which could only be ignored by the most starry-eyed proponents of liberal capitalism, was that the prevailing thrust of the world economy was continuing to create acute problems. Many developments in the later part of the twentieth century were showing that highly specific and limited definitions of national security, of which the Cold War was a primary example, were becoming increasingly irrelevant. Many of these wider problems stemmed from developments in the world economy.

Over the course of the twentieth century world industrial output rose an unprecedented thirty-three-fold and world population quadrupled. The impact of both trends on the environment in terms of the increasing consumption of resources and growing pollution, particularly in the gases causing global warming, became increasingly acute during the period of the Cold War and were major international problems by the time it ended. These problems were compounded by the gross inequality in the distribution of the world's wealth. Over the course of the twentieth century the distribution of wealth in the world became more unequal with the core countries becoming relatively wealthier and the overwhelming majority of the world's population living in acute poverty. By the end of the century the richest 20 percent of the world's population in the core states controlled 80 percent of the world's wealth and the poorest eighty per cent the remaining 20 percent - indeed the poorest twenty per cent received less than two per cent. These were acute problems, which had become worse during the Cold War, and which seemed to be insoluble in both absolute as well as relative terms.

The end of the Cold War could not change Russia's position as a member of the economic semi-periphery, a position it had occupied throughout the century. Indeed to some extent Russia's position worsened after 1991 - life expectancy fell dramatically. It was largely reliant on foreign capital for the development of its resources and increasingly dependent on the export of these products, in particular natural gas from the huge Siberian fields, for its economic survival. Other former states of the Soviet Union continued to demonstrate the signs of their semi-peripheral status. The rush by the major oil companies and core states to obtain rights to own and develop the huge oil fields of Azerbaijan and the Caspian area bore uncanny parallels to the Russian oil industry around Baku in the early twentieth century which was entirely foreign-owned.

At the same time the economic shift towards the Pacific was increasing, despite the difficulties experienced in 1997-8. The most important development in this area was linked to the other major trend in the region - the revival of China as a great power. The economic reforms of the late 1970s and early 1980s in agriculture were followed by liberalisation of trade and industry, the opening of special economic zones for foreign investment in the south of the country and in 1997 the announcement of a mass privatisation campaign. The Chinese leadership was clearly adopting the same policy as the Soviet leadership in the 1920s under the NEP - economic liberalisation combined with strict political control. The growth rates in the Chinese economy in the late twentieth century were such that it is almost certain that by the first decade of the next century China will be the largest economy in the world.

In all of these areas the end of the Cold War made no appreciable difference to underlying historical trends. The one area where this did happen, perhaps surprisingly, was in Europe which had been the area of greatest stability during the Cold War. The events of 1989-93 brought about one of the largest-ever transformations in the European power structure and one which, from a long-term historical perspective, produced some rather unsettling features, including problems which it had been assumed had long been resolved.

The end of the Cold War resulted in the disintegration of nearly all of the Russian empire created since 1600 and of the Soviet zone of control in eastern Europe which had been created by the Second World War and reinforced by the Cold War. This left Russia weaker and further to the east than it had been at any time since the early eighteenth century. The new pattern of states in central and eastern Europe seemed to combine all the worst aspects of the Versailles settlement and the 'forgotten peace' of Brest-Litovsk of the spring of 1918 when Germany had been able to impose its long-term strategic aims on the region. The two 'mini-empires' created at

Versailles disintegrated. Czechoslovakia did so peacefully, Yugoslavia in acrimony, bloodshed and 'ethnic cleansing'. At the same time genuinely new states such as Ukraine and Belorussia were created which, despite their claims to an historic identity, had never really existed as states before. In addition other states with little independent history such as Estonia and Latvia were recreated. Poland was left, as an outcome of the Second World War, further to the west than it had ever been before and occupying areas that had been ethnically German for more than seven centuries. Perhaps even more important, the issue that had dominated Europe between 1870 and 1945, destabilised the existing power balance, helped speed the demise of Britain and France as world powers and which the Cold War seemed to have solved by *de facto* partition - an economically strong and united Germany in the heart of Europe - reappeared. It was a Germany that was within neither the historic boundaries of Prussia nor those of the German state of 1871 and 1918. The Cold War was a period of immense stability in Europe and the challenge facing the institutions largely created by the Cold War - NATO, the European Union and the OSCE - was whether they could create similar stability in a post-Cold War Europe that in places bore an uncanny resemblance to the worst features of the European security structure before 1945.

We are now almost ten years on from the end of the Cold War and it is becoming increasingly apparent that as a conceptual framework it has little to tell us about what was happening in the world in the second half of the twentieth century. All of the major trends within world history, of which I have only had space to outline a few - the development of the world economy, the conflict in the Atlantic world between the United States on the one hand and the European powers, in particular Britain and France, on the other, and the decline of Europe and the linked revival and rise of Asia, both economically and politically - were active throughout the period of the Cold War. They produced far greater changes and were of far greater significance than the Cold War. The attempt to fit all of these trends into a Cold War framework, as the United States and its linked elites in Europe tried to do at the time, especially in the 1950s and the early 1980s, is to seriously distort the events of world history. Even from a more limited strategic perspective it is possible to argue that the importance of the Cold War has been exaggerated. It is already clear that from a long-term perspective it will simply be seen as no more than one of the world strategic balances that occurred in the twentieth century. Its peculiar nature and its danger partly stemmed from earlier technological developments, in particular the development of nuclear weapons and the inability of politicians on both sides to control the expansion of their numbers far beyond the point where they had a strategic justification. Ultimately the Cold War was a sterile interlude of little, if any, longer term significance. The problems it created disappeared quickly and were replaced by others, economic, environmental, political and strategic that were older in origin and much more difficult to solve.

Notes

1 Burk, (1985 p.81).
2 PRO PREM 3/486/1 12.11.40.
3 Kolko, (1968, p.283).

Bibliography

Acheson, D. (1969), *Present at the Creation*, Norton, New York.

Adamson, D. (1990), *Defending the World*, St Martin's Press, New York.

Adler-Karlsson, G. (1968), *Western Economic Warfare, 1947-67: A Case Study in Foreign Economic Policy*, Almquist and Wiksell, Stockholm.

Allen, H.C. (1954), *Great Britain and the United States: A History of Anglo-American Relations (1783-1952)*, Odhams Press, London.

Alperovitz, G. (1965), *Atomic Diplomacy*, Simon and Schuster, New York.

Alperovitz, G. (1995), *The Decision to Use the Atomic Bomb*, Fontana, London.

Aluko, O. and Shaw, T. (eds), (1985), *Africa in the 1980s*, George Allen and Unwin, London.

Ambrose, S.E. (1971), *Rise to Globalism*, Allen Lane, London.

Anabtawi, S.N. (1965), 'Neutralists and Neutralism', *Journal of Politics*, vol.27, May, pp.351-61.

Anderson, I.H. (1981), *ARAMCO, The United States, and Saudi Arabia. A Study of the Dynamics of Foreign Oil Policy 1933-50*, Princeton University Press, Princeton.

Anderson, I.H. (1988). 'The American Oil Industry and the Fifty-Fifty Agreement of 1950', in W.R. Louis & J.A. Bill (eds), *Musaddiq, Iranian Nationalism and Oil*, Tauris, London.

Ashley, R. (1981), 'Political realism and human interests', *International Studies Quarterly*, vol.25, pp.204-36.

Ashley, R. (1984), 'The poverty of neorealism', *International Organisation*, vol.38, pp.225-286.

Ashley, R. (1988), 'Untying the sovereign state: a double reading of the anarchy problematique', *Millennium: Journal of International Studies*, vol.17, pp.227-262.

Ashley, R. (1989), 'Living on the border lines: man, post-structuralism and war', in J. Der Derrian, and M. Shapiro (eds), *International Intertextual Relations: The Boundaries of Knowledge and Practice in World Politics*, Lexington Books, Lexington.

Avineri, S. (1968), *Karl Marx on Colonialism and Modernisation*, Anchor Books and Doubleday, New York.

Baldwin, D. (ed), (1992), *Neorealism and Neoliberalism: The Contemporary Debate*, Columbia University Press, New York.

Baranovsky, V. (ed) (1997), *Russia and Europe: The Emerging Security Agenda*, Oxford University Press, Oxford.

Barber, J.W. and Barrat, J. (1990), *South Africa's Foreign Policy, 1945-1988*, Cambridge University Press, Cambridge.

Barnet, R.J. (1972), *The Roots of War*, Atheneum, New York.

Bartlett, C.J. (1992), *The Special Relationship: A Political History of Anglo-American Relations Since 1945*, Longman, London.

Baylis, J. (1984), *Anglo-American Defence Relations, 1939-84, The Special Relationship*, Macmillan, London.

Bell, C. (1964), *The Debatable Alliance: An Essay in Anglo-American Relations*, Oxford University Press, London.

Beloff, M. (1959), *The Great Powers*, George Allen and Unwin, London.

Beloff, M. (1986), 'John Bull and After. Anglo-American Relations', *Encounter*, vol.66, pp.62-63.

Benn S.I. and Mortimer, M.W. (eds), (1976), *Rationality and the Social Sciences*, Kegan Paul, London.

Berkes, R.N. and Bedi, M.S. (1958), *The Diplomacy of India: Indian foreign policy in the United Nations*, Stanford University Press, Stanford.

Beschloss, M. (1991), *Kennedy and Khrushchev: The Crisis Years,* Harper Collins, New York.

Bhaskar, R. (1989), *Reclaiming Reality*, Verso, London.

Bideleux, R. (1987), *Communism and Development*, Methuen, London, 1985, revised 1987.

Bideleux, R. and Jeffries, I. (1998), *A History of Eastern Europe: Crisis and Change*, Routledge, London.

Bissell, R.E. (Winter 1980), 'The West in concert: a very complex score', *Orbis*, vol.23, no.4, pp.825-843.

Blair, B.G., Feiveson, H.A. and Hippel, F.N. von, (1997), 'Taking Nuclear Weapons off Hair-Trigger Alert, *Scientific American*, pp.42-49.

Bloom, B. and Johns, R. (19 February 1986), 'The UK Saudi arms sale: a deal in a different dimension', *Financial Times*.

Bohman, J. (1991), *New Philosophy of Social Science*, Polity Press, Oxford.

Booth, K. (1991), 'Security in anarchy: Utopian Realism in theory and practice', *International Affairs*, vol.67, pp.527-545.

Booth, K. and Smith, S. (eds) (1995), *International Relations Theory Today*, Polity Press, Cambridge.

Borden, W.S. (1989), 'Defending Hegemony: American Foreign Economic Policy', in T.G. Patterson (ed) (1989), *Kennedy's Quest for Victory: American Foreign Policy 1961-63*, Oxford University Press, New York.

Brands, H.W. (1989), 'The Cairo-Teheran Connection in Anglo-American Rivalry in the Middle East, 1951-53', *The International History Review,* vol.11, pp.434-56.

Brecher, M. (1959), *Nehru, a Biography*, Oxford University Press, London.

Breemer, J.S. (May 1986), 'Soviet Submarine Accidents, Background and Chronology', *Navy International*, pp.309-312.

Brown, C. (1992), *International Relations Theory: New Normative Approaches*, Harvester Wheatsheaf, Hemel Hempstead.

Brown, S., Lynn-Jones, S. and Miller, S. (eds), (1995) *The Perils of Anarchy - Contemporary Realism and International Security*, M.I.T. Press, Cambridge, Mass.

Bull, H. (1969), 'International theory: the case for a classical approach', in K.Knorr and J.Rosenau (eds), *Contending Approaches to International Politics*, Princeton University Press, Princeton.

Bullen, R. (1984), 'Great Britain, the United States and the Indian Armistice Resolution on the Korean War: November 1952', *International Studies*, pp.27-44.

Bulloch, J. and Morris, H. (1991), *Saddam's war: the origins of the Kuwait conflict and the international response*, Faber and Faber Limited, London.

Burk, K. (1985), *Britain, America and the Sinews of War, 1914-1918*, Allen & Unwin, London.

Burnham, P. (1992), 'Re-evaluating the Washington Loan Agreement: A Revisionist View of the Limits of Power', *Review of International Studies*, vol.18, pp. 241-61.

Butfoy, A. (1993), 'Collective Security - theory, problems and reformulations', *Australian Journal of International Affairs*, vol.47, pp.1-14.

Buzan, B. (1991), *People, States, and Fear*, Simon and Schuster, Hemel Hempstead.

Buzan, B. (1987), *The International Politics of Deterrence*, Frances Pinter, London.

Buzan, B., Jones, C. and Little, R. (1993), *The Logic of Anarchy - Neorealism to Structural Realism*, Columbia University Press, New York.

Cairncross, F. (1991), *Costing the Earth*, Economist Books, London.

Callaghy, T.M. (1983), *South Africa in Southern Africa: the Intensifying Vortex of Violence*, Praeger, New York.

Calvocoressi, P. (1989), *World politics since 1945*, 5th edition, Longman, London.

Campbell, D. (1984), *The Unsinkable Aircraft Carrier: American Military Power in Britain*, Michael Joseph, London.

Carr, E.H. (1939), *The Twenty Years Crisis 1919-39*, Macmillan, London.

Carroll, F.M. (1989), 'Anglo-American Relations and the Origins of the Cold War: the New Perspective', *Canadian Journal of History*, vol.24, pp. 191-208.

'Carter's crises; Iran, Afghanistan and presidential politics', (5 May 1980), *The World Today*, vol.36.

Chakravati, P.C. (1963), 'India, nonalignment and US policy', *Current History*, vol.44, pp.129-34.

Chan, S. (1990), *Exporting Apartheid: Foreign Policies in Southern Africa, 1978-1988*, Macmillan, London.

Chan, S. (1996), *Towards a Multicultural Roshamon Paradigm in International Relations*, Tampere Research Institute, Tampere.

Charles, D. (1987), *Nuclear Planning in NATO*, Ballinger, Cambridge, Mass.

Chester, E.W. (1983), *United States Oil Policy and Diplomacy: A Twentieth Century Overview*, Greenwood Press, Westport.

Chrypinski V.C. (1984), 'Church and Nationality in Postwar Poland' in P. Ramet (ed), *Religion and Nationalism in Soviet and East European Politics*, North Carolina, Durham.

Churba, J. (Summer 1980), 'The eroding security balance in the Middle East', *Orbis*, vol.24, pp.353-361.

Clark, I. (1994), *Nuclear Diplomacy and the Special Relationship: Britain's Deterrent and America 1957-62*, Clarendon, Oxford.

Claude, I. (1971), *Swords into Plowshares: the problems and progress of international organisation*, 4th edition, Random House, New York.

Clymer, K.J. (1990), 'Jawaharlal Nehru and the United States: the Pre-independence Years', *Diplomatic History*, vol.14, pp.143-62.

Cobb, T.W. (Summer 1979), 'The Soviet energy dilemma', *Orbis*, vol.23, pp.353-385.

Conde, A. de (ed) (1957), *Isolation and Security*, Duke University Press, Durham, North Carolina.

Cordesman, A.H. (1984), *The Gulf and the search for strategic stability: Saudi Arabia, the military balance in the Gulf, and trends in the Arab-Israeli military balance*, Westview Press Inc, Boulder, Colorado.

Cordesman, A.H. (1987), *The Iran-Iraq war and Western security 1984-87: strategic implications and policy options*, Jane's Publishing Co. Ltd.

Costigliola, F. (1984), 'The Failed Design: De Gaulle and the Struggle for Europe', *Diplomatic History*, vol.8, pp.227-251.

Costigliola, F. (1994), 'Johnson, Germany and "the End of the Cold War"', in W.I. Cohen and N.B. Tucker (eds) (1994), *Lyndon Johnson Confronts the World: American Foreign Policy 1963-68*, Cambridge University Press, New York.

Cox, M. (1992). 'Western Intelligence, the Soviet Threat and NSC-68: A Reply to Beatrice Heuser', *Review of International Studies*, vol.18, pp.75-83.

Cox, M. (1994), 'Rethinking the End of the Cold War', *Review of International Studies*, vol.20, pp.187-201.

Cox, R. (1986), 'Social forces, states, and world orders; beyond international relations theory', in R.Keohane (ed), *Neorealism and Its Critics*, Columbia University Press, New York.

Crabb C.V.D. (1965), *The Elephants and the Grass: a study of non-alignment*, Praeger, New York.

Crockatt, R. (1995), *The Fifty Years War: the United States and the Soviet Union in World Politics, 1941-1991*, Routledge, London.

Cumings, B. (ed) (1983), *Child of Conflict: the Korean-American Relationship, 1943-1953*, University of Washington Press, Seattle.

Cumings, B. (1981 and 1990), *The Origins of the Korean War: 2 Volumes*, Princeton University Press, Princeton.

Danchev, A. (1998), *On Specialness: Essays in Anglo-American Relations*, Macmillan, Basingstoke.

Darby, P. (1973), *British Defence Policy East of Suez*, Oxford University Press, London.

Davidson, D. (1980), 'Actions, Reasons and Causes', in *Essays on Actions and Events*, Oxford University Press, Oxford.

Davies, N. (1984), *Heart of Europe*, Clarendon, Oxford.

Davy, R. (ed) (1992), *European Detente: A Reappraisal*, Sage/Royal Institute of International Affairs, London.

Dawisha, K. (1979), 'The Soviet Union and the Middle East: strategy at the crossroads?', *The World Today*, vol.35, pp.91-100.

Dawisha, A.I. (1980-81), 'Iraq: the West's opportunity', *Foreign Policy*, No.41, pp.135-153.

Dawisha, K. (1990), *Eastern Europe, Gorbachev and Reform*, 2nd edition, Cambridge University Press, Cambridge.

Degras, J. (ed) (1965), *The Communist International, 1919-1943, Documents*, vol.3, Oxford University Press, London.

Deighton, A. (1990), *The Impossible Peace: Britain, the Division of Germany and the Origins of the Cold War*, Clarendon, Oxford.

Della Cava, R. (1997), 'Religious Resource Networks: Roman Catholic Philanthropy in Central and East Europe' in S.H. Rudolph and J. Piscatori (eds), *Transanational Religion and Fading States*, Westview, Boulder.

Deng, F. and Zartman, I.W. (eds) (1991), *Conflict Resolution in Africa*, Brookings, Washington.

DeNovo, J.A. (1976-77), 'The Culbertson Economic Mission and Anglo-American Tensions in the Middle East, 1944-1945', *The Journal of American History*, vol.63, pp.913-36.

Deutscher, I. (1966), *Stalin: A Political Biography*, revised edition, Penguin, Harmondsworth.

Devereux, D. (1990), 'Britain and the Failure of Collective Defence in the Middle East, 1948-53', in A. Deighton (ed), *Britain and the First Cold War*, Macmillan, London, pp.237-52.

Djilas, M. (1963), *Conversations with Stalin*, Penguin, Harmondsworth.

Dobrynin, A. (1995), *In Confidence: Moscow's Ambassador to America's Six Cold War Presidents, 1962-1986*, Random House, New York.

Dobson, A.P. (1988), *The Politics of the Anglo-American Economic Special Relationship*, Wheatsheaf, Brighton.

Dobson, A.P. (1988a), 'The Kennedy Administration and Economic Warfare Against Communism', *International Affairs*, vol.64, pp.599-616.

Dobson, A.P. (1990), 'The Years of Transition: Anglo-American Relations 1961-67, *Review of International Studies*, vol.16, pp.239-258.

Dobson, A.P. (1995), *Anglo-American Relations in the Twentieth Century: Of Friendship, Conflict and the Rise and Decline of Superpowers*, Routledge, London.

Dobson, A.P. (1997), 'Informally Special: The Churchill-Truman Talks of January 1952 and the State of Anglo-American Relations', *Review of International Studies*, vol.23, pp. 27-47.

Dobson, A.P. (1998), 'The USA, Britain and the Question of Hegemony' in G. Lundestad (ed) (1998), *No End to Alliance: The United States and Western Europe: Past, Present and Future*, Macmillan, London.

Dobson, A.P. (Forthcoming), *The United States and Policies of Economic Warfare and Embargo: A Study in Economic Statecraft 1933-1990*, Routledge, London.

Dobson, A. (1990), *Green Political Thought*, Harper and Collins, London.

Dockrill, M.L. (1986), 'Anglo-American diplomacy and the Korean War, June 1950 - June 1951', *International Affairs*, vol.62, pp.459-476.

Dohan, M.R. (1976), 'The Economic Origins of Soviet Autarky, 1927/28-1934', in *Slavic Review*, vol.35.

Donaldson, P. (1986), *Worlds Apart: the development gap and what it means*, Pelican, Harmondsworth.

Dougherty, J. and Pfaltzgraff, R. (1971), *Contending Theories of International Relations*, Lippincott, Philadelphia.

Doyle, M. (1983), 'Kant, Liberal Legacies, and Foreign Affairs', *Philosophy and Public Affairs*, vol.12, pp.205-235.

*Dunn, D.J. (1977), *The Catholic Church and the Soviet Government 1939-1949*, New York.

Dunn, D.J. (1979), *Detente and Papal Communist Relations 1962-1978*, Westview, Boulder.

Dunn, D.J. (ed), (1987), *Religion and Nationalism in Eastern Europe & the Soviet Union*, Lynne Rienner, Boulder.

Dybvik, R.E. (25 August 1981), 'Backgrounder: the Reagan Administration's decision to sell air defense equipment to Saudi Arabia', in *International Communicational Agency*, Embassy of the United States.

Edgley, R. (1969), *Reason in Theory and in Practice*, Hutchinson University Press, London.

Edmonds, R. (1991), *The Big Three: Churchill, Roosevelt and Stalin in Peace and War*, Norton, New York.

Eldridge, P.J. (1965), 'India's non-alignment policy reviewed', *Australia Outlook*, vol.19, pp.146-57.

Elster, J. (1979), *Ulysses and the Sirens*, Cambridge University Press, Cambridge.

Engler, R. (1961), *The Politics of Oil: A Study of Private Power and Democratic Direction*, Macmillan, New York.

Evans, G. (1994), 'The International Community and the Transition to a New South Africa', *The Round Table*, pp.175-187.

Evans, G. (1996), 'South Africa in Remission: the Foreign Policy of an Altered State', *The Journal of Modern African Studies*, vol.32, pp.249-269.

Feis, H. (1957), *Churchill, Roosevelt, Stalin: the War they Fought and the Peace they Sought*, Princeton University Press, Princeton.

Fesharaki, F. (1976), *Development of the Iranian Oil Industry: International and Domestic Aspects*, Praeger, New York.

Finnegan, R.B. (1972), 'The field of international relations: the view from within', *Towson State Journal of International Affairs*, vol.7, pp.1-24.

Flannery, A. (2nd ed.) (1992), *Vatican Council II: The Conciliar and Post Conciliar Documents*, St Paul Books, Boston.

Foot, R. (1985), *The Wrong War*, Ithaca, Cornell University Press, New York.

Foot, R. (1990), *A substitute for victory*, Ithaca, Cornell University Press, New York.

Forland, T.E. (1991), 'Selling Firearms to the Indians: Eisenhower's Export Control Policy, 1953-54', *Diplomatic History*, vol.15, pp.221-244.

Forland, T.E. (1991), 'Cold Economic Warfare: the Creation and Prime of COCOM, 1948-1954', *PhD thesis*, University of Oslo.

Freedman, L. (1981), *The Evolution of Nuclear Strategy*, Macmillan, London.

Freedman, L. and Karsh, E. (1993), *The Gulf conflict 1990-1991, diplomacy and war in the new world order*, Faber and Faber Limited, London.

Fukuyama, F. (1992), *The End of History and the Last Man*, Hamish Hamilton, London.

Fungiello, P.J. (1988), *American-Soviet Trade in the Cold War*, University of North Carolina Press, Chapel Hill.

Gabriel, J.M. (1988), *The American Conception of Neutrality after 1941*, Macmillan, London.

Gaddis, J.L. (1982), *Strategies of Containment. A Critical Appraisal of Postwar American National Security Policy*, Oxford University Press, Oxford.

Gaddis, J.L (1983), 'The Emerging Post-Revisionist Thesis of the Cold War' and 'Replies', *Diplomatic History*, vol.7, pp.171-90 and following.

Gaddis, J.L. (1987), *The Long Peace: Inquiries into the History of the Cold War*, Oxford University Press, New York.

Gaddis, J.L. (1993), 'International Relations Theory and the End of the Cold War', *International Security*, vol.17, pp. 5-58.

Gaddis, J.L. (1992/3), 'International relations theory and the end of the Cold War', *International Security*, vol.17, pp.5-58.

Gaddis, J.L. (1997), *We Now Know: Rethinking Cold War History*, Clarendon Press, Oxford.

Gaines, M. (4 July 1981), 'Nuclear Weapons: How Safe?', *Flight International*, pp.40-45.

Gardner, L.C. (1970), *Architects of Illusion*, Quadrangle, Chicago.

Garton Ash, T. (1991), *The Polish Revolution*, Granta, London.

Geldenhuys, D. (1984), *The Diplomacy of Isolation: South African Foreign Policy Making*, Macmillan, Johannesburg.

George, J. (1988), 'The study of international relations', in R.Higgott (ed), *New Directions in International Relations? Australian Perspectives*, Australian National University, Canberra.

George, J. (1994), *Discourses of Global Politics: A Critical (Re)introduction to International Relations*, Lynne Rienner, Boulder, 1994.

Gilpin, R. (1981), *War and Change in World Politics*, Cambridge University Press, Cambridge.

Gleijeses, P. (1996/97), 'Havana's Policy in Africa, 1959-76: New Evidence from Cuban Archives', in *Cold War International History Project Bulletin*, Issues 8-9, Winter 1996/1997.

Goode, J.F. (1989), *The United States and Iran, 1946-51: The Diplomacy of Neglect*, Macmillan, London.

Gorbachev, M. (1988), *Perestroika: New Thinking for Our Country and the World*, Fontana, London. (Soviet edition, 1987).

Gregory, S. and Edwards, A. (1988), 'A Handbook of Nuclear Weapons Accidents', *Peace research Reports No.20*, University of Bradford.

Griffiths, M. (1995), *Realism, Idealism, and International Politics: A reinterpretation*, Routledge, London.

Gromyko, A. (1989), *Memories*, Hutchinson, London.

Grundy, K. (1990), 'The Demilitarisation of Southern Africa' in H.Gluckman (ed), *Toward Peace and Security in Southern Africa*, Gordon and Breech, New York.

Grundy, K. (1991), *South Africa: Domestic Crisis and Global Challenge*, Westview, Boulder.

Guehenno, J..M. (1995), *The End of the Nation State*, University of Minnesota Press, Minneapolis.

Guelke, A. (1986), 'The Impact of the End of the Cold War on the South African Transition', *Journal of Contemporary African Studies*, vol.14, pp.87-99.

Gwertzman, B. (13 October 1980), 'The US and Saudi Arms', *The International Herald Tribune*.

Hahn, P.L. (1987), 'Containment and Egyptian Nationalism: The Unsuccessful Effort to Establish the Middle East Command, 1951-53', *Diplomatic History*, XI, pp.23-40.

Hanson, E.O. (1987), *The Catholic Church in World Politics*, Princeton, Princeton University Press.

Harbeson, J.W. and Rothchild D. (eds), (1995), *Africa in World Politics: Post-Cold War Challenges*, Westview, Boulder.

Havel, V. (1991), *Open Letters*, Faber and Faber, London.

Herz, J. (1967), *International Politics in the Atomic Age*, Columbia University Press, New York.

Hess, G.R. (1974), 'The Iranian Crisis of 1945-1946 and the Cold War', *Political Science Quarterly*, vol.69, pp.117-46.

Heuser, B. (1991), 'NSC 68 and the Soviet Threat: A New Perspective on Western Threat Perception and Policy Making', *Review of International Studies*, vol.17, pp.17-40.

Hindness, B. (1988), *Choice, Rationality, and Social Theory*, Unwin, Hyman, London.

Hiro, D. (1985), *Iran under the Ayatollahs*, Routledge and Kegan Paul, London.

Hobsbawm, E. (1994), *Age of Extremes: The Short Twentieth Century 1914-1991*, Michael Joseph, London.

Hobson, J.A. 1902, (1968), *Imperialism, A Study*, Allen Unwin, London.

Hoffman, D. (1988), 'Doctrines of the Cold War Refuse to Die', *Washington Post*, 15 March.

Hoffmann, S. (1959), 'The Long Road to Theory', *World Politics*, vol.11.

Hoffmann, S. (1977), 'An American social science: international relations', *Daedalus*, vol.106, pp.41-59.

Hogan, M.J. (1987), *The Marshall Plan: America, Britain and the Reconstruction of Western Europe, 1947-1952*, Cambridge University Press, New York.

Hollis, M. and Smith, S. (1990), *Explaining and Understanding International Relations*, Clarendon Press, Oxford.

Holloway, D. (1994), *Stalin and the Bomb*, Yale University Press, New Haven.

Horowitz, D. (1965), *The Free World Colossus*, Hill and Wang, New York.

Hudson, D.J. (1977), 'Vandenberg Reconsidered: Senate Resolution 239 and American Foreign Policy', *Diplomatic History*, vol.1, pp.46-63.

Hurrell, A. and Kingsley, B. (1992), *The International Politics of the Environment*, Clarendon, Oxford.

Jackson, I. (1997), 'Co-operation and Constraint: Britain's Influence on American Economic Warfare Policy in COCOM, 1948-54', *PhD thesis*, The Queen's University of Belfast.

Jervis, R. (1976), *Perception and Misperception in International Politics*, Princeton University Press, Princeton, 1976.

Johnson, D. (ed), (1988), *South Africa: No Turning Back*, Macmillan, London.

Jones, R. and Willets, P. (eds), (1984), *Interdependence on Trial - Studies in the theory and reality of contemporary interdependence*, Pinter, London.

Kaiser, W. (1996), *Using Europe, Abusing the Europeans: Britain and European Integration, 1945-63*, Macmillan, Basingstoke.

Kanet, R., & Kozhemiakhin, A. (1997), *The Foreign Policy of the Russian Federation*, Macmillan, London.

Kaplan, M. (1957), *System and Process in International Politics*, John Wiley, New York.

Kaplan, M. (1961), 'Problems of theory building and theory confirmation', in Knorr, K. and Verba, S. (eds), *The International System*, Princeton University Press, Princeton.

Kaplan, M. (1964), *System and Process in International Politics*, John Wiley, New York.

Kaplan, M. (1969), 'The new great debate: traditionalism vs. science in international relations', in K.Knorr and J.Rosenau (eds), *Contending Approaches to International Politics*, Princeton University Press, Princeton.

Kaufman, B. (1986), *The Korean War: Challenge in crisis, credibility, and command*, Temple University Press, New York.

Keddie, N.R. (1992), 'The End of the Cold War and the Middle East', *Diplomatic History*, vol.16, pp.95-103.

Kegley, C. (ed), (1995), *Controversies in IR Theory - Realism and the Neoliberal Challenge*, St. Martin's Press, New York.

Keller, E.J. and Picard L.A. (1989), *South Africa in Southern Africa: Domestic Change and International Conflict*, Lynn Rienner, Boulder, pp.221-248.

Kemezis, P. (Winter 1980), 'The permanent crisis: changes in the world oil system', *Orbis*, vol.23, pp.761-784.

Kennan, G.F. 'X' (1947), 'The Sources of Soviet Conduct', *Foreign Affairs*, vol.25, pp.566-82.

Kennan, G.F. (1954), *Realities of American Foreign Policy*, Oxford University Press, Oxford.

Kennan, G.F. (1968), *Memoirs 1925-50*, Hutchinson, London.

Kennan, G.F. (1978), *The Cloud of Danger*, Hutchinson, London.

Kennan, G.F. (1984), *The Nuclear Delusion*, Hamish Hamilton, London.

Kennedy-Pipe, C. (1995), *Stalin's Cold War: Soviet Strategies in Europe, 1943-1956*, Manchester University Press, Manchester.

Kennedy-Pipe, C. (1997), *Russia and the World since 1917*, Arnold, London.

Kennedy, P. (1994), *Preparing for the Twenty-first Century*, Fontana, London.

Kent, J. (1993), *British Imperial Strategy and the Origins of the Cold War*, Leicester University Press, Leicester, London & New York.

Kent P.C. and Pollard J.F. (1994), *Papal Diplomacy in the Modern Age*, Praeger, London.

Keohane, R. (1984), *After Hegemony - Cooperation and Discord in the World Political Economy*, Princeton University Press, Princeton.

Keohane, R. (1986), 'Theory of world politics: structural realism and beyond', in R.Keohane (ed), *Neorealism and Its Critics*, Columbia University Press, New York.

Keohane, R. and Nye, J. (1989), *Power and Interdependence - World Politics in Transition*, 2nd ed., Little Brown, Boston.

Keohane, R. Nye, J. and Hoffman, S. (eds) (1993), *After the Cold War: International Institutions and State Strategies in Europe 1989-91*, Harvard University Press, Cambridge, Mass.

Khalilzad, Z. (1980), 'Afghanistan and the crisis in American foreign policy', *Survival*.

King, R. (Spring 1987), 'The Iran-Iraq war: the political implications', *Adelphi Paper 219*.

Kissinger, H.A. (1964), *A World Restored*, Universal Library, New York.

Kissinger, H.A. (1977), *American Foreign Policy*, W.W.Norton, New York.

Kissinger, H.A. (1979), *The White House Years*, Weidenfeld and Nicolson, London.

Kissinger, H.A. (1981), *For the Record*, Weidenfeld & Nicholson, London.

Kissinger, H.A. (1985), *Observations*, Weidenfeld & Nicholson & Michael Joseph, London.

Kissinger, H.A. (1994), *Diplomacy*, Simon and Schuster, London.

Kolko, G. and Kolko, J. (1972), *The Limits of Power: the World and United States Foreign Policy 1945-54*, Harper Row, New York.

Kolko, G. (1968), *The Politics of War: The World and the United States Foreign Policy; 1943-1945*, Randon House, New York.

Konczakowski, E.F. (1976), *Vatican Policy Towards The German-Polish Oder-Neisse Line: A Study of Foreign Policy Evolution, 1945-1972, Ph.D Thesis*, University of Pennsylvania.

Kozyrev, A. (1995), 'Partnership or Cold Peace?', *Foreign Policy*, No.99, pp. 3-14.

Kramer, M. (1996/97), 'Lessons of the Cuban Missile Crisis for Warsaw Pact Nuclear Operations' in *Cold War International History Project Bulletin*, Issues 8-9, Winter 1996/1997.

Krasner, S. (ed), (1983), *International Regimes*, Ithaca, Cornell University Press, New York.

Krasner, S. (1985), *Structural Conflict - The Third World Against Global Liberalism*, University of California Press, Berkeley.

Kratochwil, F. (1993), 'The embarrassment of changes: neo-realism as the science of realpolitik without politics', *Review of International Studies*, vol.19, pp.63-80.

Krock, A. (1968), *Memoirs: Sixty Years in the Firing Line*, Funk and Wagnolls, New York.

Kupchan, C.A. (1995), 'The Promise of Collective Security', *International Security*, vol.20, pp.52-61.

Lall. S. and Streeten, P. (1977), *Foreign Investment, Transnationalism and Developing Countries*, Macmillan, London.

Larres, K. (1995), 'Eisenhower and the First Forty Days after Stalin's Death: the Incompatibility of Detente and Political Warfare', *Diplomacy and Statecraft*, vol.6, pp.431-70.

Larus, J. (1965), *From Collective Security to Preventive Diplomacy*, John Wiley and Son, New York.

Laszlo, L. (1990), 'The Catholic Church in Hungary' in P. Ramet (ed), *Catholicism and Politics in Communist Countries*, London.

Layne, C. (1995), 'The unipolar illusion: why new great powers will rise', in S. Brown, S. Lynn-Jones and S. Miller (eds), *The Perils of Anarchy - Contemporary Realism and International Security*, M.I.T. Press, Mass.

Lebow, R.N. and Stein, J.G. (1994), *We All Lost the Cold War*, Princeton University Press, Princeton.

Lebow, R.N. and Risse-Kappan, T. (eds) (1995), *International Relations Theory and the End of the Cold War*, Columbia University Press, New York.

Lechuga, S. (1995), *In the Eye of the Storm: Castro, Krushchev, Kennedy and the Missile Crisis*, trans. M. Todd, Ocean Press, Melbourne.

Leffler, M.P. (1994), 'The Interpretive Wars over the Cold War', in G. Martel (ed) (1994), *American Foreign Relations Reconsidered 1890-1993*, Routledge, London.

Leffler, M.P. and Painter, D.S. (eds) (1994), *The Origins of the Cold War: An International History*, Routledge, London.

Leffler, M.P. (1992), *A Preponderance of Power. National Security, the Truman Administration, and the Cold War*, Stanford University Press, Stanford.

Lenin, V.I. 1917, (1966), *Imperialism, a Study*, Allen Unwin, London.

Leung, B. (1992), *Sino-Vatican Relations*, Cambridge University Press, Cambridge.

Levy, M. (1969), 'Does it matter if he's naked? Bawled the child', in K.Knorr and J.Rosenau (eds), *Contending Approaches to International Politics*, Princeton University Press, Princeton.

Lilenthal, A.M. (1957), *There Goes the Middle East*, Devin-Adair, New York.

Lincove, D.A. and Treadway, G.R. (1988), *The Anglo-American Special Relationship: An Annotated Bibliography of Scholarship 1945-1985*, London, Greenwood.

Linklater, A. (1995), 'Neorealism in theory and practice', in K. Booth and S. Smith (eds), *International Relations Theory Today*, Polity, Cambridge.

Lipton, P. (1991), *Inference to the Best Explanation*, Routledge, London.

Lissakers, K. (Fall 1981), 'Money and manipulation', *Foreign Policy*, No.44.

Little, R. and Smith, S. (1988), *Belief Systems and International Relations*, Basil Blackwell, Oxford.

Lloyd, C. (1992), *The Structures of History*, Blackwell, Oxford.

Loth, W. (1988), *The Division of the World 1941-1945*, St. Martin's Press, New York.

Lowe, P. (1986), *The Origins of the Korean War*, Longman, Harlow.

Lundestad, G. (1986), 'Empire by Invitation: the United States and Western Europe, 1945-1952', *Journal of Peace Research*, vol.23, pp.263-77.

Lundestad, G. (1997), *East, West, North, South: Major Developments in International Politics 1945-1996*, Scandinavian University Press, Oslo.

Lyon, P. (1960), 'Neutrality and the emergence of the concept of Neutralism', *Review of Politics*, vol.22, pp.255-68.

Lytle, M.H. (1987), *The Origins of the Iranian-American Alliance 1941-53*, Holmes and Maier, New York.

MacDonald, C.A. (1986), *Korea, the war before Vietnam*, Macmillan, Basingstoke.

Maddox, R.J. (1973), *The New Left and the Origins of the Cold War*, Princeton University Press, Princeton.

Madian, A.L. (Summer 1979), 'Oil is still too cheap', *Foreign Policy*, no.35.

Maier, C.S. (ed) (1996), *The Cold War in Europe: Era of a Divided Continent*, Wiener, Princeton.

Mallik, D.N. (1967), *The Development of non-alignment in India's foreign policy*, Chaitanya Publishing House, Allahabad.

Manderson-Jones, R.B. (1972), *The Special Relationship: Anglo-American Relations and the Western European Unity 1947-56*, Weidenfeld and Nicolson, London.

Marcum, J. (1976), 'Lessons of Angola', *Foreign Affairs*, vol.54, pp.407-425.

Marsh, D. and Stoker, G. (eds), (1995), *Theory and Methods in Political Science*, Macmillan, Basingstoke.

Martin, L.W. (1962), *Neutralism and Non-alignment: the United States in World Affairs*, Praeger, New York.

Mastanduno, M. (1992), *Economic Containment: COCOM and the Politics of East-West Trade*, Cornell University Press, Ithaca.

Mastny, V. (1979), *Russia's Road to the Cold War*, Columbia University Press, New York.

Maull, H.W. (Winter 1980), 'Western Europe: a fragmented response to a fragmenting order', *Orbis,* vol.23.

May, E.R. (ed) (1993), *American Cold War Strategy: Interpreting NSC 68*, Bedford Books, New York.

McCormick, T.J. (1989), *America's Half Century: United States Foreign Policy in the Cold War*, John Hopkins Press, Baltimore.

McCullough, C.B. (1984), *Justifying Historical Descriptions*, Cambridge University Press, Cambridge.

McFarland, S.L. (1980), 'A Peripheral View of the Origins of the Cold War: The Crises in Iran, 1941-47', *Diplomatic History*, vol.4, pp.333-52.

McGhee, G. (1983), *Envoy to the Middle World: adventures in diplomacy*, Harper & Row, New York.

McMahon, R. (1991), 'Credibility and World Power: Exploring the Psychological Dimension in Postwar American Diplomacy', *Diplomatic History*, vol.15, pp 455-471.

McMahon, R. (1994), *The Cold War on the Periphery: the United States, India, and Pakistan*, Columbia University Press, New York.

Mearsheimer, J. (1990), 'Back to the future: instability in Europe after the Cold War', *International Security*, vol.15, pp.4-57.

Mearsheimer, J. (1994-5), 'The false promise of international institutions', *International Security*, vol.19, pp.5-49.

Merrill, D. (1990), *Bread and the Ballot: the United States and India's economic development, 1947-63*, University of North Carolina Press, London.

Michel, P. (1991), *Politics and Religion in Eastern Europe*, Polity, Cambridge.

Michnik, A. (1985), *Letters From Prison and Other Essays*, Berkeley.

Milward, A.S. (1984), *The Reconstruction of Western Europe, 1945-51*, University of California Press, Berkeley.

Mindszenty, J. (1974), *Memoirs*, New York.

Molotov, V. (1949), *Problems of Foreign Policy: Speeches and Statements, April 1945-November 1948*, Foreign Languages Publishing House, Moscow.

Morgenthau, H. (1958), 'The state of political science', in *Dilemmas of Politics*, University of Chicago Press, Chicago.

Morgenthau, H. (1960), *Politics Among Nations - The Struggle for Power and Peace*, 3rd ed., Alfred. A. Knopf, New York.

Morgenthau, H. (1965), *Scientific Man Vs Power Politics*, University of Chicago Press, Chicago.

Morgenthau, H. (1970), *Truth and Power - Essays of a Decade 1960-70*, Pall Mall, London.

Mottahedeh, R.P. (Spring 1980), 'Iran's foreign devils', *Foreign Policy*, No.38, pp.19-34.

Murray, A.J.H. (1996), 'The Moral Politics of Hans Morgenthau', *Review of Politics*, vol.58, pp.81-107.

Murray, A.J.H. (1997), *Reconstructing Realism - between power politics and cosmopolitan ethics*, Keele University Press, Edinburgh.

Mylroie, L. and Miller, J. (1990), *Saddam Hussein and the crisis in the Gulf*, Times Books, New York.

Naimark, N. (1995), *The Russians in Germany: A History of the Soviet Zone of Occupation, 1945-49*, Harvard University Press, Cambridge Mass.

Neufeld, M. (1995), *The Restructuring of International Relations Theory*, Cambridge University Press, Cambridge.

Neuman, S.G. (ed) (1998), *International Relations: Theory and the Third World*, Macmillan, London.

Nicholson, M. (1996), *Causes and Consequences in International Politics*, Cambridge University Press, Cambridge.

Nye, J.P. (1997), *Understanding International Conflicts: An Introduction to Theory and History*, Longman, New York.

Oberdorfer, D. (1992), *The Turn: How the Cold War Came to an End: The United States and the Soviet Union, 1983-1990*, Cape, London.

Olson, W. (1972), 'The growth of a discipline', in B. Porter (ed), *The Aberystwyth Papers: International Politics 1919-1969*, Oxford University Press, London.

Outhwaite, W. (1987), *New Philosophies of Social Science*, St. Martin's Press, New York.

Painter, D.S. (1997), 'The Cold War', in B.W. Jentleson and T.G. Paterson (eds) (1997), *Encyclopedia of U.S. Foreign Relations 4 Vols*., Oxford University Press in association with the US Council on Foreign Relations, New York, vol.1.

Palmer, M.A. (1992), *Guardians of the Gulf: a history of America's expanding role in the Persian Gulf, 1833-1992*, The Free Press, New York.

Pfau, R. (1977), 'Containment in Iran, 1946: The Shift to an Active Policy', *Diplomatic History*, vol.1, pp.359-72.

Pimlott, J., and Badsey, S. (eds) (1992), *The Gulf War assessed*, Arms and Armour Press, London.

Polmar, N. (1992), *Strategic Nuclear Weapons: An Introduction*, Crane Russak, New York.

Polonsky, A. (1975), *The Little Dictators: The History of Eastern Europe since 1918*, Routledge, London.

Pontifical Council for Justice and Peace, (1988), The Holy See at the Service of Peace: Pope John Paul II addresses to the Diplomatic Corps, Vatican City.

Pontifical Council for Justice and Peace, (1990), Human Rights and the Church, Vatican City.

Ponting, C. (1994), *Churchill*, Sinclair-Stevenson, London.

Ponting, C. (1995), *Armageddon*, Random House, New York.

Porter, G. and Brown, J. (1991), *Global Environmental Politics*, Westview, Boulder, Colorado.

Putnam, H. (1981), *Reason, Truth and History*, Cambridge University Press, Cambridge.

Rana, A.P. (1969), 'The intellectual dimensions of India's non-alignments', *Journal of Asian Studies*, vol.28, pp.279-312.

Reid, E. (1981), *Envoy to Nehru*, Oxford University Press, New Delhi.

Reynolds, C. (1981), *Modes of Imperialism*, Martin Robertson, Brighton.

Reynolds, C. (1992), *The World of States*, Edward Elgar, Aldershot.

Reynolds, D. (1986), 'A Special Relationship? America, Britain and the International Order Since the Second World War, *International Affairs*, vol.62, pp.1-20.

Reynolds, D. (1988/89), 'Rethinking Anglo-American Relations', *International Affairs*, vol.65.

Reynolds, D. (ed) (1994), *The Origins of the Cold War in Europe: International Perspectives*, Yale University Press, New Haven.

Rhodes, A. (1992), *The Vatican in the Age of the Cold War*, Norwich.

Rittberger, V. (ed) (1995), *Regime Theory and International Relations*, Clarendon, Oxford.

Rosenau, J.N. (1971), *The Scientific Study of Foreign Policy*, Free Press, New York.

Rosenau, J. and Tromp, H. (eds), (1989), *Interdependence and Conflict in World Politics*, Avebury, Aldershot.

Rosenau, J. and Czempiel. E. (eds) (1992), *Governance without Government*, Cambridge University Press, Cambridge.

Rosenberg, J. (1990), 'What's the matter with realism', *Review of International Studies*, vol.16, pp.285-303.

Rouleau, E. (Fall 1980), 'Khomeini's Iran, *Foreign Affairs*, vol.59, pp.1-20.

Ruggie, J.C. (1986), 'Continuity and transformation in the world polity: towards a neorealist synthesis', in R. Keohane (ed), *Neorealism and Its Critics*, Columbia University Press, New York.

Ruggie, J.C. (ed), (1993), *Multilateralism Matters: The Theory and Praxis of an Institutional Form*, Columbia University Press, New York.

Ryall, D. (1998), *Caught Between God and Caesar: The Catholic Church in South Africa 1948-1990, (Ph.D Thesis),* University of Wales, Swansea.

Saivetz, C.R. (1989), *The Soviet Union and the Gulf in the 1980s*, Westview Press Inc., London.

Schofield, R. (1994), *Territorial foundations of the Gulf states*, UCL Press, London.

Scholte, J.A. (1993), 'From Power Politics to Social Change', *Review of International Studies*, vol.19, pp.3-31.

Shubin, V. (1994), 'Reflections on Relations Between the Soviet Union/Russian Federation and South Africa in the 1980s and 1990s', *Southern African Pespectives, no.37*, University of the Western Cape, Centre for Southern African Studies.

Simes, D.K. (Winter 1979-80), 'The anti-Soviet brigade', *Foreign Policy*, no.37.

Singer, J.D. (ed), (1965), *Human Behaviour and International Politics*, Rand NcNally, Chicago, Illinois.

Singer, J.D. (1966), 'The behavioural science approach to international relations: payoffs and prospect', *SAIS Review*, vol.10, pp.12-20.

Singer, J.D. (ed), (1968), *Quantitative International Politics: Insights and Evidence*, New York, Free Press.

Singh, I. (1992), *Between Two Fires*, Orient Longman, New Delhi.

Siracusa, J.M. (1978), *The American Diplomatic Revolution*, Open University Press, Milton Keynes.

Smith, M.J. (1986), *Realist Thought from Weber to Kissinger*, Louisiana State University Press, Baton Rouge.

Sorensen, T. (1965), *Kennedy*, Harper Row, New York.

Sorensen, V. (1989), 'Economic Recovery versus Containment: the Anglo-American Controversy Over East-West Trade, 1947-51', *Co-operation and Conflict*, vol.24, pp.69-97.

Spanier, J.W. (1972), *Games Nations Play*, Nelson, London.

Spaulding, R.M. (1993), 'A Gradual and Moderate Relaxation: Eisenhower and the Revision of American Export Control Policy, 1953-54', *Diplomatic History*, vol.17, pp.223-249.

Spence, J.E. (1984), *Change in South Africa*, Pinter, London.

Spero, J.E. (1990), *The Politics of International Economic Relations*, 4th edition, Routledge, London.

Stalin, J. (1954), *Works*, Vol 7, Foreign Languages Publishing House, Moscow.

Stalin, J. (1955a), *Works*, Vol 13, Foreign Languages Publishing House, Moscow.

Stalin, J. (1955b), *Works*, Vol 14, Foreign Languages Publishing House, Moscow.

Stern, J.P. (May 1980), 'Soviet energy prospects in the 1980s', *The World Today*, vol.36, no.5.

Stocking, G.W. (1971), *Middle East Oil: A Study in Political and Economic Controversy*, Allen Lane, London.

Stoff, M.B. (1980), *Oil, War, and American Security. The Search for a National Policy on Foreign Oil, 1941-47*, Yale University Press, New Haven and London.

Stokes, G. (ed) (1991), *From Stalinism to Pluralism: A Documentary History of Eastern Europe since 1945*, Oxford University Press, Oxford.

Stokes, G. (1993), *The Walls Came Tumbling Down*, Oxford University Press, Oxford.

Strange, S. (1970), International Economics and International Relations: A Case of Mutual Neglect', *International Affairs*, vol.46, pp.304-15.

Stromberg, R.N. (1963), *Collective Security and American Foreign Policy*, Praeger, New York.

Stueck, W.W. (1995), *The Korean War: an international history*, Princeton University Press, Princeton.

Sugar, P.F. (1971), *Native Fascism in the Successor States 1918-1945*, Santa Barbara.

Sutton, A. (1968-72), *Western Technology and Soviet Economic Development*, 3 vols, Stanford University Press, Stanford.

Szajkowski, B. (1983) *Next To God ... Poland: Politics and Religion in Contemporary Poland*, Frances Pinter, London.

Szulc, T. (1995), *Pope John Paul II*, New York, Scribner.

Talbot, P. and Poplai S.L. (1958), *India and America: a study of their relations*, Greenwood Press, Westport, Connecticut.

Thomas, S. (1995), *The Diplomacy of Liberation: the International Relations of the African National Congress of South Africa, 1960-1985*, Taurus, London.

Thucydides, (1959), The Peloponnesian Wars, University of Michigan Press, Ann Arbor.

Trachtenberg, M. (1985), 'White House Tapes and Minutes of the Cuban Missile Crisis', *International Security*, vol.10, pp.164-170.

Trotsky, L. (1926), *Toward Socialism or Capitalism?*, International Publishers, New York.

Trotsky, L. (1928), *The Real Situation in Russia*, New York, International Publishers.

Truman, H.S. (1955), *Memoirs, Vol.1: Year of Decision*, Hodder and Stoughton, London.

Vallier, I. (1971), 'The Roman Catholic Church: A Transnational Actor' in *International Organization*, vol.25, pp.479-502.

Vasquez, J.A. (1983), *The Power of Power Politics - a critique*, Francis Pinter, London.

Volkogonov, D. (1991), *Stalin: Triumph and Tragedy*, Weidenfeld & Nicholson, London.

Waever, O. (1996), 'The Rise and Fall of the Inter-Paradigm Debate' in S.Smaith, K.Booth, and M.Zalewski (eds), *International Theory: Positivism and Beyond*, Cambridge University Press, Cambridge, 1996.

Waldermeir, P. (1997), *Anatomy of a Miracle*, Penguin Books, Harmondsworth.

Walker, R.B.J (1993), *Inside/Outside - International Relations as Political Theory*, Cambridge University Press, Cambridge.

Wallace, W. (1996), 'Truth and power, monks and technocrats: theory and practice in international relations' in *Review of International Studies*, vol.22, pp.301-22.

Wallerstein, I. (1974), *The Modern World System (2 vols)*, Academic Press, New York.

Wallerstein, I. (1984), *The Politics of the World Economy in the States, the Movements, and the Civilisations*, Cambridge University Press, Cambridge.

Walsh, W.H. (1959), 'Colligatory Concepts in History', in P.Gardiner, (ed), *Theories of History*, The Free Press, New York.

Waltz, K. (1979), *Theory of International Politics*, Addison-Wesley, London.

Waltz, K. (1986), 'Reflections on Theory of International Politics: a response to my critics', in R.Keohane (ed), *Neorealism and Its Critics*, Columbia University Press, New York.

Waltz, K. (1993), 'The emerging structure of international politics', *International Security*, vol.18, pp.44-79.

Waltz, K. (1995), 'Realist thought and neorealist theory', in C.Kegley (ed), *Controversies in IR Theory - Realism and the Neoliberal Challenge*, St Martin's Press, New York.

Watt, D.C. (1984), *Succeeding John Bull: America in Britain's Place*, Cambridge University Press, Cambridge.

Weigel, G. (1992), *The Final Revolution*, Oxford University Press, Oxford.

Wendt, W. (1992), 'Anarchy is what states make of it: the social construction of power politics', *International Organisation*, vol.46, pp.391-425.

Wendt, W. (1994), 'Collective identity formation and the international state', *American Political Science Review*, vol.88, pp.384-396.

Whetten L.L. (October 1979), 'The lessons of Iran', *The World Today*, vol.35.

Williams, W.A. (1962), *The Tragedy of American Diplomacy*, Dell, New York.

Wilson, P. and Long, D. (1996), *Thinkers of the Twenty Years Crisis*, Oxford University Press, Oxford.

Yergin, D. (1977), *Shattered Peace: The Origins of the Cold War and the National Security State*, Houghton Mifflin Co., Boston.

Yergin, D. (March 1979), 'US energy policy: transition to what?', *The World Today*, vol.35, pp.81-89.

Yodfat, A.Y. (1983), *The Soviet Union and the Arabian Peninsula*, St. Martin's Press Inc., New York.

Young, J.W. (1996), 'Winston Churchill's Peacetime Administration and the Relaxation of East-West Trade Controls 1953-54', *Diplomacy and Statecraft*, vol.7, pp.125-140.

Zartman, I.W. (1985), *Ripe for Revolution*, Oxford University Press, New York.

Zartman, I.W. (1991), 'Negotiation and the South African Conflict', *SAIS Review*, vol. pp.113-133.

Zeiler, T.W. (1992), *American Trade and Power in the 1960s*, Columbia University Press, New York.

Zhdanov, A. (1947), 'The Two Camp Policy', reprinted in G. Stokes (ed) (1991).

Zubok, V. and Pleshakov, C. (1996), *Inside the Kremlin's Cold War: From Stalin to Khrushchev*, Harvard University Press, Cambridge Mass.

Index

Acheson, D. 75, 91, 95, 167-68, 170-73
Afghanistan 113, 120, 131, 246, 248
Al-Yamamah Contract 120
ANC 139-40, 143, 145, 147-48
Anglo-Iranian Oil Co. 89, 94, 101-2
Atlantic World
  conflict with Pacific World 263-66
Ayatollah Khomeini 123-27

Bajpai, G. 168, 170
Baruch Plan 7
Behaviouralism 30, 36-39
Beran, J. 191, 199
Berlin 6
Bhrezhnev, L. 10, 246-47
Botha, P.W. 139
Brandt, W. 10
Britain
  conflict with US 261-63
  East-West trade 80-85
  EEC 79
  Middle East 95
  military sales 122-23
  Polaris 78-79
  Special Relationship with US 74, 97
  US 93-97
Bush, G. 12

Carr, E.H. 27
Carter, J. 11
  Doctrine 114
CENTO 113
Churchill, W. 1, 75, 82-3
COCOM 80-4
Cold War Paradigms 1-3, 13-21, 25-41, 44-64, 69-73, 76, 85-86, 89-90, 102-4, 110-21, 131-32, 136-40, 146-49, 152-53, 173-75, 181-84, 189-200, 202-24, 226-27, 248-49, 253-68
Colligations 45, 60-62, 64
containment 7-9, 48, 103, 155, 159-60, 163, 195
C.S.C.E. 10, 183, 197-98, 244-45, 247-48
Cuba 8-9, 113, 143, 146, 247
  Missile Crisis 77, 205, 220-21
Czechoslovakia 182
  Catholicism 191

Détente, 10-11, 17, 197-98, 243-45
de Gaulle, C. 78
de Klerk, F.W. 137, 139, 147-48
Dependency Theory 18-19
Dulles, J.F. 8

Eden, A, 171-72
E.E.C. 10
Egypt, 127
Eisenhower, D. 8, 78, 161
  doctrine 262
En' Lai, C. 168, 170

France
  military sales 122-23

Galbraith, J.H. 161
GATT 4
Glasnost 12
Gorbachev, M. 12, 17, 139, 148, 247-49
Grady, H.F. 161, 166

Harriman, A. 74, 81

Healey, D. 119
hegemony 73, 85-86, 89-104
Helsinki Accords 10
  see also CSCE
Henderson, L. 98, 161-62, 166, 168
Hoffmann, S. 39
Hungary 182
  Catholicism 190-95, 198-99

ideology
IMF 4
India 156, 158
  external security 157-59
  internal security 156-57
  neutralism 159-63
Iran 7, 89-104
  revolution, 1979 113, 115, 123-26
  Tudeh Party 92
Iraq 117, 120, 128-29
Israel 10, 112, 122, 221
  nuclear weapons 205

John XXXIII 182-83, 196
John Paul II 183, 198, 200
Johnson, L. 77

Kaplan, M. 27, 30-31, 35-36
Kennan, G. 6, 27-29, 37
Kennedy, J.F. 9
Khrushchev, N. 8-9, 18, 197, 242
Kissinger, H.A. 28-29, 37, 112
Korean War 7, 153-54, 160, 163-75
  PoWs 170-75
Kurds 126
Kuwait 117

Macmillan, H. 78
Mandela 137, 148
Marshall Plan 7, 73, 155, 261
materialist explanations 58-60
McGhee, G. 96, 162
McNamara, R. 203, 220-21
Menon, K. 171-73, 175
Middle East 89-104, 110-32
Mindszenty, J. 190, 193-95, 197-99
Morgenthau, H. 34-35, 37-40
Mossadeq, 94, 98, 104

NATO 6, 11, 69, 78, 141-42, 202, 222-23, 247, 268
  Able Archer 222-23
  strategy 212-15
Nehru 152, 157-60, 162, 165-68, 170, 172-74
neo-liberalism 15, 16-17
neo-realism 15, 31-41, 49-55, 110, 136-37, 146-47
neutralism 152-75
  see non-alignment
non-alignment
  Non-Aligned Movement 157, 174
Norway
  missiles 203
NSC 68 7, 90-92, 104, 156, 161, 164
nuclear accidents 215-19
nuclear crises 219-23
Nuclear Partial Test Ban Treaty 9

OPEC 116, 118, 120, 246
Ostpolitik 10, 181-83, 195, 197, 244

Pacific World
  conflict with Atlantic World 263-66
Panmunjong Talks 169
Pannikar, K.M. 168-69
Paul VI 182-83, 193, 195-96
Peoples Republic of China 7, 11, 90, 155-56, 164, 167, 169-74
Perestroika 12
Persian Gulf 110-32
Pleven Plan 75
Pius XII 183, 185, 195-97
Poland 181-82
  Catholicism 186, 192, 194-95, 198-99

Rau, B 156-66, 170
Reagan, R. 11, 17, 152, 222, 244, 246

Doctrine 12
realism 26-29, 39-41
Reykjavik Summit 12, 139, 247
Roman Catholicism 181-200
communism 184-85
see Vatican
Roosevelt, F.D. 154

Saddam Hussain 127-129
Saudi Arabia 116-17, 119-21, 126, 129-30
SDI 11
Slovakia
Catholicism 186-87, 195, 198-99
Solidarity 194
South Africa
Catholicism 187
nuclear weapons 205
Western security 142
South African Congress Party 143
South African National Party 137, 139, 148
Soviet Union 152, 154, 158, 160, 169, 174, 258
Bolshevik Revolution 227-30
collective security 230-32
Fascism 232-35
nuclear weapons 205-208
perspectives on Cold War 226-49
Persian Gulf 112-15, 126, 130-31
Second World War 235-38
South Africa 138, 143, 144, 146
Vatican 181-82
Stalin 1, 82, 165, 231-32, 238-42
strategic nuclear weapons 205-11
structure of world economy
Cold War 257-61
Suez Crisis 9, 77, 262

tactical nuclear weapons 211-12
Thatcher, M. 12, 222
Third World 18, 162
Tomasek, F. 193, 199
Trident 203
Truman, H.S. 1, 75, 101, 152-53, 156, 160-61, 163, 169-70
Doctrine 6, 55, 104, 152, 156, 159, 174-75, 195

United Nations 154
General Assemby 172-73
Korea 165, 167-70
Security Council 166-67
United States
Britain 93-97
conflict with Britain 261-63
East-West trade 80-85
Iran 97-99
military sales 121-23
Mutual Defense Assistance Control Act, 1951 81, 98
Oil Mergers 99-102
Special Relationship 74, 97

Vasquez, J. 28
Vatican
Cold War 181-200
Vyshinsky, A. 1

Walensa, L. 11
Waltz, K. 27, 31-33, 36, 35-36
Wilson, H. 77
world history
Anglo-American conflict 261-63
Cold War in context 266-69
Pacific/Atlantic competition 263-66
world economy 257-61
Wyszinski, S 189-99

Yeltsin, B. 203-4, 249
Yom Kippur War 10, 221-22